THOMAS WENTWORTH
First Earl of Strafford

C.V. Wedgwood, one of the only two women to be made a member of the Order of Merit, began writing history when she was a child. Her first book was published in 1935 and she went on to specialise in the English, Scottish and European sixteenth centuries.

Also by C. V. Wedgwood

The Thirty Years War

Oliver Cromwell

William The Silent

Velvet Studies

Richelieu and the French Monarchy

English Literature in the Seventeenth Century

The Last of the Radicals

Montrose

Poetry and Politics under the Stuarts

The King's War

The King's Peace

Truth and Opinion

The Trial of Charles I

The Spoils of Time (Phoenix Press)

THOMAS WENTWORTH
First Earl of Strafford 1593–1641
A Revaluation

C.V. Wedgwood

PHOENIX PRESS

5 UPPER SAINT MARTIN'S LANE
LONDON
WC2H 9EA

A PHOENIX PRESS PAPERBACK

First published in Great Britain
by Jonathan Cape in 1961
This paperback edition published in 2000
by Phoenix Press,
a division of The Orion Publishing Group Ltd,
Orion House, 5 Upper St Martin's Lane,
London WC2H 9EA

Copyright © 1961 by C.V. Wedgwood

A CIP catalogue record for this book
is available from the British Library.

Printed and bound in Great Britain by
Clays Ltd, St Ives plc

ISBN 1 84212 081 6

CONTENTS

ILLUSTRATIONS

To A.H.P.

These initials appeared as the dedication
of my first book, *Strafford*, in 1935. They
stood for the name of my grandfather,
Albert Henry Pawson, whose love, wisdom
and knowledge had surrounded my childhood. Twenty-six years later I dedicate
this new version of the life of Strafford in
gratitude to his memory. I should have
offered him my first book whatever its
subject, but there was another reason
which made the dedication suitable; he
also, like Strafford, came from the West
Riding of Yorkshire.

INTRODUCTION

SINCE I WROTE the life of Strafford twenty-seven years ago much detailed research has been done on the early Stuart epoch, more especially on its economic aspects. Important new material has also become available. Shortly after the war the Strafford papers which had long been preserved by his descendants at Wentworth Woodhouse were generously deposited at the Sheffield Central Library by their owner Earl Fitzwilliam. I would like to thank the present Earl Fitzwilliam and his Trustees of the Wentworth Woodhouse Settled Estates for giving permission to quote from these documents. My thanks are also due to the Librarian and staff of the Sheffield Central Library for the kindness and efficiency which make working there so easy and so pleasant.

Two of Strafford's biographers, Lady Burghclere (1931) and Lord Birkenhead (1938), had had access to these papers while they were still at Woodhouse. Both of them quoted with discrimination from this unpublished material. But the documents which comprise the great mass of Strafford's private and public correspondence fill over forty boxes and volumes. It was thus impossible for any biographer to make full use of them while they still remained at Wentworth Woodhouse, without taking more advantage of the hospitality of their owner than could reasonably be asked.

The basis of all work on Strafford therefore remained until recently the selection made and published by Dr William Knowler as early as 1739. His two folio volumes will always be useful to students of the reign of King Charles I, but we can now see that the impression which they give of Strafford is a partial one.

To understand the impact of this new material, it is necessary briefly to recall earlier interpretations of Strafford. For the last three hundred years he has been seen, first and foremost, as a dramatic figure in the great struggle between King and Parliament. For Macaulay he was the 'lost Archangel, the Satan of the

Apostasy', the man who, after leading the House of Commons to resounding triumph against the Crown by the passing of the Petition of Right in 1628, deserted Parliament, became the ruthless agent of King Charles I during his absolute rule, and was overtaken by fate in 1641 when the King feebly sent him to his death.

Others have praised in him the devoted servant of the Crown who strove to implement a policy of which reverence for royal authority and justice to the poor were the two pillars. He was the great administrator who made Ireland prosperous and who, in the final catastrophe that overtook the government of King Charles, advised his master to propitiate the people by signing his death warrant.

The emphasis on Strafford's greatness as an administrator was in part the result of his own flattering elucidation of his policy as it appeared in his eloquent letters, published by Knowler. The same opinion was confirmed and strengthened at a later date when historians began in general to take a more sympathetic view of the personal rule of King Charles. As early as 1884, S. R. Gardiner accepted Strafford as the probable author of the King's well-intentioned social policy. In 1900 E. M. Leonard's *The Early Poor Law* deepened the impression of the benevolence of King Charles's government. In 1921 came R. R. Reid's *The King's Council in the North* which was on the whole favourable to Strafford as an able and benevolent administrator. Finally in 1923 Hugh O'Grady's lengthy, rambling, eccentric, and in some ways fanatical, *Strafford in Ireland* seemed to vindicate his Irish policy. Such testimony from an Irish hand was particularly welcome to English readers, who were gratified to find an English governor praised in these terms. In this way an image of Strafford was formed as the brain and hand of the authoritarian government which was at least in intention benevolent.

This was the view which I held, in common with Strafford's other biographers, in the thirties of this century. Twenty years later, when I consulted the Strafford papers at Sheffield for my book on the collapse of King Charles's personal rule, I began to modify these views, but at first only slightly. It was evident, for instance, that I had underestimated the wide range and the political significance of Strafford's financial interests and of his remarkable talent for accumulating wealth.

The King's Peace, the book on which I was engaged when I first worked on the Strafford manuscripts, covers only the last three and a half years of Strafford's career (1637 to 1641), and the letters dealing with that period contain less to disturb the favourable view of him which I had earlier formed than do those of the preceding five years. It was only when I began to study more closely the letters of the earlier sixteen thirties that I became fully aware of the need not only for revisions and additions to my earlier work, but for drastic reappraisal of Strafford.

William Knowler, on whose selection of the papers my original estimate had been based, had aimed at illustrating his political life and the essentials of his character. Strafford's energy, his ambition, his astonishing grasp of detail, his love of power, his deep affections, his practical and pragmatic turn of mind, and his guiding faith in the necessity of order and authority, are all well brought out. So also is his obsessive need for praise.

There is nothing wrong in the impression that is given, as far as it goes. But it is incomplete. Knowler left out, or played down, many details of Strafford's business transactions, and he published in general only the high-lights of his political and administrative correspondence. He left out many (though not all) of the letters which reveal Strafford's extraordinary disingenuousness and his unscrupulous treatment of his political opponents and business rivals. Very little of his unedifying relationship with Sir Arthur Ingram appears in Knowler. The ruthlessness of his onslaught on the Earl of Cork and the devious recklessness of the way in which he contrived the ruin of Mountnorris can only be appreciated through the perusal of the unpublished material.

As knowledge of Stuart finance and administration has increased, historians have reached a fuller understanding of the ineptitude, corruption and confusion which prevailed. Strafford pursued his ends, in public and in private, by the usual methods of his time. The correspondence, taken as a whole, reveals a much more complex and contradictory character than I had previously recognized. At his worst he now appeared as an unscrupulous man of powerful intelligence, limited inspiration and enormous energy. He cherished genuine delusions about himself, for he constantly represented himself as modest, forbearing and straightforward. He was none of these things, though it must be admitted, perhaps in his favour, that his capacity for deceiving himself was much greater than his capacity for deceiving other people. Moreover he had strong redeeming features — a compelling sense of duty to the King and the state, a vein of real generosity and genuine tenderness towards his family and his few close friends, and an ideal of government that was nobler by far than the means by which he tried to realize it.

In a recent clear and very perceptive estimate of him, in *Past and Present* (April 1961), Mr Terence Ranger has referred to his mixture of 'cunning, idealism and self-interest'. In my earlier version of his life I recognized chiefly his idealism. Being at that time still very young in the ways of the world I took him altogether too much at his own valuation. In the present version I have tried to deal more fairly with his failings. The result is I hope not merely better history but a more interesting and in some ways a more tragic portrait. If he had been a worse man, or if he had been a much better one, he might have escaped disaster. He brought ruin upon himself, and failed to avert it from his King, because the inextricable confusion of his motives increasingly hampered his judgment and clouded his vision.

This reappraisal of Strafford owes much to Mr J. P. Cooper's searching investigation of the sources of his wealth, published in the *Economic History Review* in 1958. I am also indebted to Mr H. F. Kearney's monograph *Strafford in Ireland* (Manchester University Press, 1959) and to Mr G. E. Aylmer's recent book *The King's Servants* (Routledge, 1961). I have to thank Dr Leslie Hotson for drawing my attention to a manuscript account of Strafford's trial in the British Museum which escaped the notice of all his earlier biographers.

Every chapter in the original version has been expanded and in some degree modified by the addition of new material. The chapter on the Parliament of 1628 and the whole of the middle section dealing with Strafford in the North and in Ireland have been entirely rewritten. The chapters on Ireland in particular embody substantial modifications of opinion.

I have retained the structure of the biography more or less as it was in the first version, though the present version is very much longer. I can say, without falling into Strafford's sin of self-praise, that the original structure was good. It was not my own work but a careful attempt to carry out the advice of Professor Sir John Neale who, after reading my first draft, showed me how to rearrange and rewrite it. I would like to record my gratitude to him for advice so constructive and so helpful that it served me not only for my first book but for many later ones.

London, August 1961

PART ONE

APRIL 1593 – DECEMBER 1628

All rising to great place is by a winding stair.
BACON

CHAPTER ONE

THOMAS WENTWORTH

> Power to do good is the true and lawful end of aspiring, for good thoughts, though God accept them, yet towards men are little better than good dreams, except they be put into act; and that cannot be without power and place, as the vantage and commanding ground.
>
> BACON

THE second son of William Wentworth of Wentworth Woodhouse and his wife, Anne, was born in London on Good Friday, April 13th, 1593, at a house in Chancery Lane. [1] Nine days later he was baptized at the Church of St Dunstan in the West by the name of Thomas. The father, a wealthy Yorkshire landowner, whose family had long been established in the West Riding, was lord of two manors and master of a yearly income of several thousand pounds. Something less than a nobleman, something greater than a country squire, he belonged to that rising aristocracy of wealth who counted themselves inferior to none. His wife was the daughter and heiress of Sir Robert Atkinson of Stowell in Gloucestershire; little is known of her forbears but their estate in the heart of the sheep-raising country suggests that their wealth had come from the wool trade. Besides the manor of Stowell, Sir Robert had a house in London and it was here that his daughter gave birth to her son. But it was on Sir William Wentworth's broad acres in the North, between his two principal manors of Gawthorp and Woodhouse among the hills of southern Yorkshire, that she brought up her young family.

Thomas was the third of twelve children, but the death of his elder brother in infancy, leaving him with only a sister older than himself, made him early his father's heir. Possibly the character of his numerous younger brothers and sisters encouraged in him an assertive and domineering spirit. William, the next in age, was of a docile nature, and the third son, John, was quiet and studious. Of the younger boys — Robert, Michael, Matthew and Philip — Matthew alone was later to prove something of a rebel, but he was too many years younger than Thomas ever in childhood to question his power. [2]

He grew up in a society and among neighbours from whom he must early have learnt the importance of authority effectively based on force. It was a harsh country inhabited by bold, resourceful, often unscrupulous people. Violence was common. When he was four years old his father, who had refused to fight a duel with Sir Thomas Reresby, was attacked by him at Rotherham Sessions. Though insulted and slapped in the face, Sir William Wentworth, with more regard for the public peace than his private honour, did not hit back. Reresby was prosecuted and fined £1,000 in the Star Chamber. [3] At another time his father's brother-in-law, Thomas Gargrave, was arrested for the murder of one of his servants. With desperate fortitude he refused to plead. A criminal who by this means obstructed the normal course of trial could save for his family his estate and goods which would be forfeit to the state if he were condemned. But refusal to plead was punished by *la peine forte et dure*, which meant death by degrees from starvation and the pressure of heavy weights, and very few endured it to the end, as Gargrave did. [4]

William Wentworth educated his son to a high sense of his position and pride in his family, which claimed descent from John of Gaunt. His own mother had been a Gascoigne, descended from the Lord Chief Justice who had, according to tradition, ordered the arrest of Henry V, in his wild youth, before he became King. More important, she brought to the Wentworth family an inheritance which doubled the size of their estates. A fine tomb on which effigies of the wealthy husband and the wealthier wife lie flat on their backs side by side in their stiff, stone finery was set up in the church of Wentworth by their grateful heir. William Wentworth, in his turn, continued to enlarge the property; in spite of litigation and vicissitudes, he also steadily enhanced his position in the county, being Sheriff in 1601. [5] His son was always to speak of him with affection and respect, but the indications which have survived suggest an ambitious, weak and credulous man. He seems to have set some store by a dream vision recorded in the family, a confused prophecy of future greatness. His instructions to his son, which have survived, indicate a deep, if conventional, Puritan piety and a most meticulous attention to detail which his son either inherited or acquired from him. He was evidently a methodical and probably a fussy man. [6]

The stronger character was evidently Thomas Wentworth's mother, Anne, described on her tombstone in Wentworth church as 'rightly religious, learned, very wise, modest, mild, merciful and bountiful to the poor': [7] the variants on the conventional terms of praise in this inscription suggest a devout, kind and serious woman from whom, perhaps, her son inherited the unexpected vein of contemplation in his otherwise active nature.

During Wentworth's childhood the reign of Queen Elizabeth drew to an end among gathering storms. The Spanish war dragged on, no longer tense and glorious as in the year of the Armada. There was no money to pay for it. Soldiers and sailors went in rags, the streets swarmed with discharged veterans and out-of-work journeymen, while on the highways sturdy vagabonds defied the savage Poor Law and the gallows, begging by day and stealing by night. The medieval revenues of the Crown could not bear the strain of a national war and new demands galled the people. The Commons made difficulties over subsidies and the Queen sold monopolies for ready money. These were hard years of circumvention, subterfuge and postponement. Yet these things were the necessary complement of great achievement. In forty years Queen Elizabeth had consolidated a national state, she had made England a great power and left a secure throne to her successor. With that inheritance she left also the new and urgent problems that her success had itself created: an empty treasury, an over-confident people, a critical Parliament, and an unfinished war.

When James VI of Scotland ascended the English throne in March 1603, Thomas Wentworth wanted a month to the completion of his tenth year: during the uneasy time that followed he grew to manhood. He had been educated at first under the care of the Dean of Ripon, Dr Higgins, who took a few pupils in his house at Well. Here he made two friendships which were to last his lifetime, one — very gratifying no doubt to his family — with Henry, Lord Clifford, eldest son to the Earl of Cumberland, and the other with a Yorkshire neighbour's son, Christopher Wandesford. [8] At fourteen he travelled southwards and spent the next four years between the Inner Temple and St John's College, Cambridge, where his tutor was Richard Senhouse, later Bishop of

Carlisle. (9) He was a grave young man though not over given to study, as he confessed in later life: 'Of all things I hated great volumes.' (10) But if he had little taste for ancient learning he took a deep interest in practical matters, and studied the law with attention. At the University and at the Inner Temple he was in the heart of English life where he could see and hear all that went on, listen to the arguments of lawyers and theologians, read the most recent books and commentaries, and discuss the political gossip of the day with his fellow students.

Sir Edward Coke, Lord Chief Justice, was during those years elevating the authority of the Common Law, claiming — on one notable occasion — that the Crown itself was under the Law. His rival, Francis Bacon, though he did not achieve his ambition of becoming Chancellor until 1617, supported with the subtlety and force of his remarkable mind the theory of a central and dominating sovereign power whence all law derived.

The King himself believed with absolute conviction in the holiness of his task, as one chosen by God to rule over men. He was conscientious, a good scholar, and — in his youth at least — astute in his political judgments. As he grew older his wits lost their sharpness, he came to be swayed by his unruly emotions, and he lost what little power he had ever had to conduct himself daily as befitted his high office. Falling off his horse — repeatedly, going to sleep at a Court masque, and hanging with uncouth adoration on the neck of his favourite Robert Carr, he was not a dignified, not even a respectable figure. The youthful gentry, growing up at the Universities and the Inns of Court, can have felt little personal reverence for anything they knew or heard of this unseemly monarch.

Wentworth deepened his knowledge and cultivated his essentially practical talents. He had a remarkable memory and the power of concentrated logical thought, but academic knowledge did not interest him and he early determined to turn his abilities to material ends. By listening to the pleading of great lawyers he learnt the power of words well used and determined to become a master of words. He had none of the natural smoothness which makes for persuasive eloquence, but he threw himself into his task with the more zeal and set himself to study the speeches of the greatest orators, classical and modern. Before reading the speech of a master he laboriously composed another of his own, then opened the book and carefully compared the two. [11] Spontaneousness was the last grace he gained, for that only came to him in later years with confidence and knowledge of his power. But the natural style was not valued at the time; what was expected, and what he learnt, was the fluent application of approved rhetorical devices and a facility for apt quotation from Cicero, Seneca, Lucan and the rest of the fashionable classics. Into this framework Wentworth came in time to insert the knotty, homely phrases more typical of his northern mind, and the stock rhetorical forms that he had learnt were enriched, as he gained more experience, with a vigorous growth of native metaphors drawn from the living world he knew — from hawking, hunting, tillage, from the crafts of the builder and the stonemason and the arts of painting and music. But his outstanding virtue was his ability to organize his thoughts, whether in exposition or in argument, with a lucid and compelling force.

Wentworth's father was proud and fond of his eldest son. He already valued his judgment and esteemed his character; he discussed his estate with him, consulted him about his will, and advised him on the generous portions to be made for his other children. [12] The young man was certainly precocious, grave, responsible and sober, preferring the society of his elders. But he had a violent and moody temper, suddenly provoked and difficult to control. Sloth and hesitation irritated him beyond endurance and his active, impatient character revealed itself in a forthright, domineering manner.

In appearance he was tall, spare and sallow, with muscular limbs and a cultivated dignity of manner. His thick dark hair and pale complexion emphasized the strength of his features. His expression in repose was grave, and was later to become forbidding, but when he spoke his features became animated and a frequent attractive smile transfigured his face. No one in the course of his life ever thought him handsome, though Queen Henrietta Maria, who was a good judge of such things, said that he had '*les plus belles mains du monde*'. [13]

When he was eighteen his father presented him at Court. In the year 1611 Whitehall was bustling with intrigue. While Court factions caballed for power, the good-natured Scottish lad, Robert Carr, held incontrovertible sway over the King's person, and the

23

beautiful Danish Queen encouraged indiscreet admirers and indulged in the lavish masques that bored her husband. The Prince of Wales, now seventeen years old, impatient of base motives and ungenerous deeds, frequently visited Sir Walter Raleigh in the Tower, and longed to bring back the old days of conquest and championship. His sister, Elizabeth, recently brought to London from the seclusion of a country house, was her brother's equal in high spirits and fluent wit, and added to these a pure, noble and lively beauty. The Prince and Princess were looked upon with rising hope: already it was said that the Prince had drawn his father away from his friendship with Spain, already there were negotiations to marry the Princess to the Elector Palatine, the leader of the German Calvinist princes, an alliance which should make England the champion of the Protestant cause in Europe.

Meanwhile the Crown was poor and the King dealt freely in honours for ready money. In 1611 the new rank of baronet was created, frankly for sale, although the numbers were to be limited. In June 1611 Wentworth's father bought a baronetcy from the King. [14] This established his position on the edge of the nobility and he followed it up by proposing his son for the hand of Lady Margaret Clifford, daughter of the Earl of Cumberland. The young man obediently wooed the bride of his father's choice and his sense of duty so far directed his taste that he appeared to the girl and her father as an earnest and affectionate suitor. The wedding took place at the Earl of Cumberland's seat at Londesborough on October 22nd, 1611. [15] In the winter the bridegroom was again with the Court at Royston and there received the accolade from the unsteady hand of the King. [16]

In spite of marriage and knighthood young Wentworth's education was incomplete, and shortly before Christmas he took leave of his wife and, promising to return before he was twenty-one, set out on a tour of France. A tutor had been chosen to go with him, a young clergyman, Charles Greenwood of University College, Oxford. He was not many years older than his pupil, a learned, tolerant, retiring young man. [17] In this pleasant company, and with a substantial train of servants, Wentworth travelled for fourteen months.

In Paris he was received with great hospitality by his old school friend, Henry, Lord Clifford, now his brother-in-law; they renewed the friendship formed in their boyhood and Wentworth wrote to his wife with high praise of her brother — a letter which gave great satisfaction to the Earl of Cumberland, whose ancient family and dwindling estate had need of the robust and rising Wentworths to strengthen their old stock. [18] For six months at Orléans, Wentworth studied French until he spoke it well. On the fly-leaves of the notebook in which he recorded his impressions (together with proverbs, idioms, anecdotes of French history and other useful information) he assiduously practised his handwriting, acquiring a clear, flowing, well-formed hand. He then spent rather more than three months making the tour of France usually followed by English visitors: down the Loire to Nantes, south to La Rochelle and Bordeaux, across by Toulouse and Carcassonne (where he thought the country 'doth much resemble Yorkshire'), thence to Narbonne, Montpellier, Avignon, Arles and Marseilles, then up the Rhône to Lyons. Here the deterioration of the weather (it was November) and his own indisposition caused him to abandon a project for going down the Rhine, and soon after, news of his father's illness made him return home.

During the tour he bought a large number of books. Some — contemporary plays for instance — were no doubt for the improvement of his French. He bought the fashionable novel *Astrée*, which may reflect his taste for pastoral romance; he certainly also bought Guarini's *Il Pastor Fido*, though this may have been simply for exercise in Italian. He bought a large number of Protestant and some Catholic works of rhetoric and controversy. At Saumur he had called on the veteran Huguenot statesman, Duplessis-Mornay, once the right hand of King Henri IV. He found him old, melancholy and blind, but thereafter bought all of his books that he could lay hands on, to the value of six pounds. [19] He also bought some books of devotion, among them *Le Jardin Sacré de l'Ame Solitaire* by Antoine de Nervèze, a work of contemplative devotion. In this little book he wrote the Latin phrase: '*Qui nimis notus omnibus ignotus moritur sibi*' — he who is too well known to all, dies without knowing himself. Was it a warning against the worldly ambition which he must have known to be working strongly within him? [20]

By the end of his journey Wentworth was fluent in French and had some Italian and Spanish. He had learnt a certain amount about French customs and European politics and had visited all the sights then thought necessary; these included a number of modern or modernized fortresses so that he had at least a rudimentary understanding of the art of contemporary fortification. His diary reveals his assiduity in learning facts and observing buildings, agriculture, and sometimes landscape. He had the attitude to foreigners which is fairly typical of a confident young stranger: on the whole he disliked what he did not understand, especially the superstitious worship, as he thought it, of the Roman Catholics. He was apt to write off the inhabitants, unless they were exceptionally welcoming, as 'dogged and ill-natured'. [21] But if his capacity for human understanding was, and was to remain, limited, he had acquired much useful knowledge of other kinds.

Early in 1613 he was back in a discontented England. In the previous November the Prince of Wales had died on the eve of his sister's marriage to the Protestant Elector Palatine. Although the wedding had been solemnized in the following February, its consequences in enhancing the position of England in Protestant Europe were not so immediately apparent as was the heavy cost of all the junketings that surrounded it.

In desperate straits for money, the King called Parliament in April 1614, and Wentworth, a week before he completed his twenty-first year, took his seat as one of the members for Yorkshire. The Addled Parliament, as it came to be called, was atrociously ill-managed by the King's friends and by those who opposed him. There was an almost complete lack of guidance and co-ordination both among the King's supporters and among the vocal critics of the government, so that Parliament foundered after a month of jangling cross-purposes. The total deadlock between a King who wanted money and a Parliament which wanted the initiative in shaping royal policy was now complete. After the Addled Parliament it was evident that one side must increase its power at the expense of the other: the even balance between the King and his 'Great Council', the balance on which the old idea of the constitution rested, could no longer be maintained. [22]

It is significant that this, the Parliament which marked the real breakdown of the old constitutional theory, should have been the first political experience of Wentworth, who was to try to solve the problem of government by strengthening the power of the

King and to be killed by the House of Commons for his attempt. At the time, his dutiful reports to his father dealt chiefly with the commercial matters discussed, especially with the complaint against monopolies and the alleged decline of West Country trade. That too is significant, for his understanding was always to be clearest and most powerful on such domestic questions. [23]

At Michaelmas, Sir William Wentworth died, leaving his eldest son master of an annual income of six thousand pounds and guardian of nine children not yet of age.

NOTES

[1] Knowler, II, p. 430.

[2] Ibid., I, pp. 1, 2, 484.

[3] Sir John Reresby, *Memoirs*, ed. Browning, p. xxxiv; Strafford MSS, XX, Nos. 73-4.

[4] Hist. MSS Commission, MSS at Hatfield, XI, p. 443.

[5] J. P. Cooper, 'The Fortune of Thomas Wentworth, Earl of Strafford', *Economic History Review*, Second Series, XI, p. 227.

[6] H.M.C., VI., App. I, p. 459; Strafford MSS, XL.

[7] Hunter, *South Yorkshire*, II, p. 213; a sheaf of tributes to her memory in Strafford MSS, XL, bear out the claims of her epitaph.

[8] Strafford MSS, XXXIV.

[9] Cambridge Matriculations, p. 715; Students of the Inner Temple, p. 182.

[10] Strafford MSS, VI, folio 30, Wentworth to Laud, 7th March 1633.

[11] Knowler, II, p. 435.

[12] Ibid., I, p. 484.

[13] Strafford MSS, XXXIV; Warwick, p. 112; Madame de Motteville, I, p. 196.

[14] Nichols, II, p. 424.

[15] Whitaker, *Craven*, p. 364.

[16] Nichols, II, p. 435.

[17] Knowler, II, p. 430; *Radcliffe Letters*, pp. 76, 80, 81.

[18] Whitaker, *Craven*, pp. 364-5.

[19] Strafford MSS, XXX; extracts from this most interesting personal notebook of Wentworth's French tour are given in Stoye, *The Grand Tour*, pp. 64-9.

[20] I have to thank Mr K. B. McFarlane of Magdalen College, Oxford, for lending me this book from Wentworth's library, now in his possession.

[21] Strafford MSS, XXI; letters from Thomas Wentworth to Sir William Wentworth, September 1612 to January 1613.

[22] See T. L. Moir, *The Addled Parliament of 1614*, Oxford, 1958.

[23] Strafford MSS, XXI; Thomas Wentworth to Sir William Wentworth, 15th April 1614; XXXIV; the same to the same, 25th April 1614.

CHAPTER TWO

SIR THOMAS WENTWORTH OF WENTWORTH WOODHOUSE

Have but a little patience, and the command and government of that part of the country will infallibly fall into your hands, with honour to yourself and contentment to others.

Wentworth to his nephew, Savile, 1633

WENTWORTH returned to Yorkshire with many cares on his shoulders. About the time of his father's death his eldest sister, Anne, was left a widow with two young children of whom he was the guardian. His own brothers and sisters were also his wards, and though the eldest of them was already a man and had an estate of his own, there were eight children still under twenty, and he might confidently expect to be a father himself long before the last of his brothers was launched into the world. The family estates and houses, besides those of his nephews, George and William Savile, would need his exact attention. The portions of his younger sisters, settled by his father at £2,000 apiece, would have in due course to be paid, and he fully intended to increase his own fortune and enlarge his estate by purchase as opportunity offered. [1] He was to learn about administration, land-management and finance in the care of his own large property. The desire to build up still further his wealth and influence was natural at the time in an ambitious and gifted man of his standing in society. But with his business acumen and personal ambition went also a strong sense of duty to his family, his dependents and his own good name.

His brothers and sisters dutifully submitted to his care: Matthew and Elizabeth alone, two of the younger ones, periodically leagued themselves against him, [2] causing an irritation which grew with years. The further responsibility of children was for the moment denied him as Lady Margaret remained childless. It was a disappointment to Wentworth's ambition, since he longed for a son to bear his name, but his strong affections found their outlet in the education of his brothers. As the years went by he considered making his second brother, William, his heir, but it was the youngest, George, born in 1609, who became in time dearest to him; sixteen years younger, George was for many years to fill the part of a son, and his almost filial devotion in later life was to be a source of strength and reassurance to his eldest brother.

For the management of his estates Wentworth evolved an efficient plan. As a master he was exacting, but swift to praise where praise was due and with a precise understanding of detail that commanded the respect of all who worked for him. Between him and his steward Richard Marris there existed that friendship which is possible between master and servant when each has a respect for the other's character. The family solicitor, Peter Man, was also his friend and adviser. To these two counsellors he added his old tutor Charles Greenwood, and some years later a neighbour, George Radcliffe, who had married a kinswoman of his. The conclave met three times a year to discuss the management and improvement of his estates; every March and September he made up his accounts, and no debts might remain longer outstanding.

In spite of his pride of position, his tastes were simple; he was happier discussing agricultural projects with Marris over a pipe of tobacco than dining abroad with his wealthy neighbours. He kept a good table, but ate sparingly himself, preferring raw fruit and simple country dishes; he drank by way of good-fellowship when he had company, but seldom more than a glass or two. It was a source of some distress to him that the otherwise admirable Marris was an inveterate and excessive drinker. Not to play the Puritan, Wentworth took part in an occasional game of cards at festal seasons, but his favourite recreations were out of doors; he loved hawking and hunting, or simply walking and riding over the countryside. During the whole of his life it was always to the woods and fields that he turned for rest and peace. [3]

In giving so much careful attention to his estates and income he had in view something more than the maintenance of his family's position in the county. He was often in London. This was partly in the interests of his Savile nephews, whose inheritance was involved in litigation. But it was also because, like other substantial landowners who had consolidated their local power, he was ambitious to extend his influence further. Only through the

Court would he be able to achieve the position that he coveted, and to have a voice not merely in the affairs of Yorkshire but in those of the nation. To be noticed, to gain some appointment if possible in the royal household, this was the best way by which an ambitious man could insert himself into a position of influence at the heart of affairs. Wentworth was to have a long and disheartening struggle before he achieved his end.

Both at Court and in Yorkshire his movements were watched by his neighbour Sir John Savile of Howley Park, a scheming veteran, whose ambitions at sixty were still as eager as Wentworth's at twenty-two. Savile was the head of an illegitimate branch of an ancient family. He had built up a great estate in the West Riding; he was patron of the growing town of Leeds with its thriving manufacture of wool, and a great number of the West Riding weavers worked to his orders. [4] In local politics he understood well how to make use of the zeal of his dependents.

Conscious of the reproach of bastardy in his family, Savile made a show of contempt for the Wentworths, who had now linked themselves by marriage to the legitimate branch. But his first relations with the young Sir Thomas Wentworth showed a deceptive friendliness. He had for some time held office as Custos Rotulorum, or Keeper of the Rolls in the West Riding, but 'his disorderly and passionate carriage of himself' — as Lord Chancellor Ellesmere described it — had caused him to be cited before the Star Chamber by a fellow Justice of the Peace whom he had threatened. To forestall his imminent dismissal, Sir John, in December 1615, hurriedly wrote to the Lord Chancellor tendering his resignation. [5]

What happened then is a little puzzling. Either Sir John or his son (who was in a plot with him) suggested Wentworth as a possible successor. So at least the Clerk of Peace told Wentworth in announcing his appointment to succeed to Savile's place. Wentworth, suspicious of what might lie behind this, sent his trusted friend Greenwood to sound Sir John. Nothing could be got out of him: he seemed perfectly good-humoured and sincere in putting forward Wentworth's name. [6] Since Wentworth, for his part, was pleased with the advancement, he could do no more than accept it in good faith.

Sir John Savile meanwhile went to Court to see what he could do to regain the influence he had lost. It was a critical time for those seeking advancement, as the King was in process of turning from an old favourite to a new. Robert Carr had fallen into the control of the Howard group through his marriage to the Earl of Suffolk's daughter; the opposing factions, profiting by the deterioration in his looks and manners, presented a new candidate for the King's affections, the dark, vivacious George Villiers, son of a Leicestershire squire. For several months the King wavered, then came the revelation that Carr's wife had been involved in the murder of Sir Thomas Overbury in the Tower; the favourite and his wife were arrested, tried, sentenced to death, and at length reprieved to lifelong imprisonment, while Villiers, now Earl of Buckingham, slipped into the empty place.

To this brash youth, old Sir John Savile was not ashamed to pay his addresses, and the good-natured, high-spirited boy gladly agreed to help him. It was easy at this time to gain the favour of Buckingham; the younger son of a Leicestershire squire, he had by common report been without the price of a bed at an inn or a suit of clothes suitable for frequenting the Court when he first came into the orbit of the King. Now suddenly he was rich, courted, a power in the land. He could 'open the sluice of honour' to whom he pleased, [7] and he asked for nothing better.

Savile convinced him quickly enough that all his troubles in the Star Chamber had arisen through the malice of his enemies and that, once he was restored to favour, Sir Thomas Wentworth would gladly stand down for him. Buckingham accordingly wrote easily to Wentworth asking him to withdraw from the post that he had held during Savile's temporary disgrace and promising rewards for this compliance later. Whether or not Savile had really counted on Wentworth's willingness to step in or out of office at his pleasure, Wentworth in his answer to Buckingham denied any such obligation and refused to give up his place, reiterating what he knew to be the real causes of Savile's withdrawal. This firm and explicit answer embarrassed Buckingham, who now saw that Savile had tricked him into making an unjustifiable request to a man of some importance in his county. He apologized courteously for 'doing the least indignity to a gentleman of your worth', and for the time being the matter dropped. [8]

Wentworth's smooth upward course in his own county continued, and two years after this incident with Savile he was appointed a member of the Council of the North, [9] the body to which, for the Government of the turbulent shires beyond the Humber, the King and his Council delegated their authority.

But Wentworth was not content. He was still angling for a position nearer to the centre of affairs. He was often in London, and was a familiar, but not a popular, figure at Court. His manners were against him. He was stiff and arrogant in society and showed a rather Puritan contempt for fashion by wearing his hair and beard as he liked best, not copying the favourite or the King. His pride, too, offended families older than his own, and his constant talk about his family tree was often boring and out of place. Gervase Holles has left an entertaining account of his father's exasperation at being persistently interrupted by Wentworth during a game of cards with unwanted information about their family connections. Once when he boasted that he could trace his descent back to John of Gaunt, Lord Powis was heard to remark, 'Damme, if ever he come to be King of England, I shall turn rebel.' [10] When there was rumour of honours for sale, and that was often enough at the Court of James I, Sir Thomas Wentworth was fairly sure to be among those who offered to buy, and twice at least he negotiated unsuccessfully for a peerage. [11]

His energy and strength of character must have been evident to all, but only those who penetrated his armour of pride and reserve found in him that love of justice and order which with his abilities and vigour might make him a great man. His friends were few but staunch. There was Lord Doncaster, one-time favourite, the fantastic spendthrift who had eloped with Lucy Percy, the accepted beauty of the Court; for all his follies, he was a shrewd observer and an able diplomat. There was the austere Archbishop Abbot, co-trustee with Wentworth for his Savile nephews, whose deeply Protestant piety was sympathetic to Wentworth's own simple and rigid faith. There was the suave, indolent, humorous knight Gervase Clifton, 'Gervase the Gentle' as he was called, and Lord Clifford, Wentworth's brother-in-law, who had married into the Cecil family and had some inner knowledge of the stirrings in that widespread group at Court. There was Sir George Calvert, one of the Secretaries of State, an active, practical man, busied with colonial schemes and teased with religious doubts, and the learned diplomat, Sir Henry Wotton. Less creditable but more useful was his friendship with the wealthy Sir Authur Ingram, whose advice alike in money matters and the shadier politics of the Court was at Wentworth's service. [12]

Meanwhile he watched all that passed about him, storing in his mind every detail ready for his after use. He saw the civil Buckingham, 'our English Alcibiades', concentrate all power little by little in his hands; he saw Prince Charles grow 'every day stronger and bettered in his stature', [13] yet never approaching what his brother had been: shy, thoughtful, and uncertain, where Henry had been active, quick and sure. He knew that Francis Bacon, now Chancellor, eloquently supported the majestic theory of the King's supreme authority over a state united in itself, an image of God's power on earth; he knew that Lord Chief Justice Coke defended the rights of the Common Law Courts against the prerogative of the Crown, and had declared to King James's face that the King was below the law. In the divided and impoverished Church his friend Archbishop Abbot strove for stability and simplicity and opposed the clergy who followed the new-fashioned symbolism in worship, fitting their Church to stand with Bacon's State, while sectarians and Catholics watched with satisfaction the rift in the English Church. He learnt from the diplomats, Lord Doncaster, Sir Henry Wotton and Sir George Calvert, that Spain though gravely weakened could draw unceasingly on the wealth of her American silver mines, that Holland was strong and growing, stretching out greedy hands for the trade of the world, that Germany was ready at any moment to fall asunder in religious war. Everywhere alongside poverty and discontent and greed and growth, was the same question: how best to govern in a rapidly changing world.

The essential function of government as Wentworth saw it was to give order and security to the people, as the father to his family, the landowner to his tenants. Such order could only be given by one coherent, sole, accepted and solvent power. As Wentworth contemplated the widening circle of his own life, his family, his household, his lands, his county, he grew naturally to accept the idea of paternal government as the best, and to see that paternal government could not be maintained, either by King or by landowner, without a substantial revenue.

For more than six years he learnt his lesson between Yorkshire and the Court before the uneasy politics of King James gave him an opportunity to speak. In 1619 Frederick, Elector Palatine, the husband of the English Princess Elizabeth, accepted the crown offered him by the rebel Protestants of Bohemia. At the same moment the deposed Catholic King, Ferdinand, head of the Austrian branch of the House of Habsburg, cousin and brother-in-law of the King of Spain, was elected Emperor. All attempts to mediate between him and his rebel subjects failed and the Elector Frederick, youthfully convinced of his mission as a Protestant leader and relying on the support of his father-in-law of England, found himself at open war with the Emperor. Many of the English, in the city of London above all, were for joyfully embracing the glorious opportunity of making themselves the champions of oppressed Protestants and renewing the old warfare with Spain; they even raised money to help the cause. But the King, appalled at the prospect of a European conflagration, clung to the idea of a negotiated settlement and believed he could achieve it with the help of Spain.

The Londoners insulted the Spanish ambassador in the streets and beat drums for Protestant volunteers outside his door. They cried out against the Papists and declared that they would save the Protestants of Bohemia; they drank healths to the gallant young Protestant King of Bohemia and his lovely Queen, their own admired Princess. But King James made no warlike move on behalf of his children.

On November 20th, 1620, before the writs went out for the Parliament which was to vote supplies for his help, the Elector Frederick, the 'Winter King' of Bohemia, was utterly defeated outside Prague at the Battle of the White Hill. He and his wife had fled for their lives long before Wentworth, on Christmas Day, was returned to Parliament as one of the knights of the shire for Yorkshire.

NOTES

[1] Knowler, I, p. 169; II, p. 430; for Wentworth's care of his fortune see J. P. Cooper, op. cit., pp. 228-31.

[2] Knowler, I, p. 484; numerous letters in the Strafford MSS, II, indicate Wentworth's care of his brothers.

[3] Knowler, II, p. 433.

[4] Reid, *King's Council in the North*, p. 395.

[5] Knowler, I, pp. 2-3.

6 Strafford MSS, XX, Greenwood to Wentworth, 26th December 1615 (incorrectly dated 1617).

7 Symonds d'Ewes, I, p. 166; Hacket, *Scrinia Reserata*, I, p. 39.

8 Knowler, I, pp. 2-4; *Fortescue Papers*, pp. 23-7; Strafford MSS, XXI, letter 11.

9 Reid, p. 498.

10 James Howell, *Familiar Letters*, London, 1903, II, p. 325.

11 Nichols, III, p. 550; *C.S.P.D.*, 1619-23, p. 262.

12 A useful biography, *Sir Arthur Ingram* (Oxford, 1961), by Mr Anthony Upton, came out while this book was in the press. It gives many interesting details of the use that Wentworth made of Ingram's friendship over a period of more than fifteen years.

13 Knowler, I, p. 5.

CHAPTER THREE

MEMBER OF PARLIAMENT

Shepherds of people had need know the calendars of tempests in state;
which are commonly greatest when things grow to equality; as natural
tempests are about the Equinoctia.

BACON

WENTWORTH's colleague as member for Yorkshire in the
Parliament of 1621 was the Secretary of State, Sir George
Calvert, a Yorkshireman by birth but long a stranger to
his county. It was essential for the King to have as many officials
as possible to act as his mouthpieces in Parliament, and Wentworth
had offered his best services to the Court in promising to secure
Calvert's return at the same time as his own. He had shown more
self-confidence than caution in making this proposal. Sir John
Savile, smarting with resentment from their previous quarrel,
determined to prevent the election of Calvert and perhaps of
Wentworth too, and so not only to humiliate his young rival in
Yorkshire but discredit him at Court. He first spread rumours
against Calvert as a non-resident and a creature of the Court 'so
closely and cunningly as if he had no part therein'. Wentworth
for his part enlisted the help of Sir Arthur Ingram, who was quite
as wily as Savile, in canvassing supporters and assembling a
mob to shout for him, He cared little for the authentic views
of 'those clowns' the electors. 'If the old knight should but endanger
[the election], faith, we might be reputed men of small power and
esteem in the country', he wrote some days before the poll. Meanwhile he urged the Sheriff to use stronger terms than usual in
summoning the freeholders to vote, and asked to know which
gentlemen refused their support. Sir John Savile detected in these
manoeuvres and irregularities a case strong enough to unseat his
overbearing rival. [1]

Parliament met on January 30th, 1621. The King rode down
in state with the Prince of Wales; contrary to his usual custom he
stretched out his hands to the people who pressed forward to see

him, saying 'God bless ye, God bless ye.' It was a grave time both for him and for his country. (2) To Parliament he spoke graciously but didactically, lecturing them on their duty to him and the commonwealth, showing them the disasters abroad, and asking for trust in his policy and for generous help. Francis Bacon then briefly exhorted the Commons to 'know themselves', and to 'carry themselves with all duty and reverence befitting towards his most excellent Majesty'. (3)

Of the five hundred members of the House of Commons, only a few had any clear or well-informed idea of the political situation, but many were concerned for the peril of Protestant Europe and perturbed by the decline of trade at home. The country was sinking fast into a deep economic depression, which was to aggravate the troubles of the King in getting subsidies and on which no suggested remedies were, for some years, to have any effect. The prevailing anxiety only irritated Parliament into blaming the nation's troubles on the mistaken policies of the Crown.

The Commons, even if they had had at this time any clear alternative policy to offer, had no power to enforce their will on the King. They had power only to prevent his actions, when they did not approve of them, by withholding supplies. For the most part they knew too little of the European situation to grasp the significance of the King's foreign policy. They were most unwilling to believe that their Princess and her husband could be helped in any way by diplomacy with Spain. They wanted denunciation of Spain and threats of intervention on the Protestant side, and this regardless of the expense that would be involved in implementing the threat, since they were averse to voting the very large sums which alone could have defrayed the costs of war.

Only a well organized and astutely led Court group in the House of Commons could have prevailed on them to support the Crown's policy and to vote the necessary grant of money in spite of the trade depression. Such a group, always active in the time of Queen Elizabeth, was present in the Parliament of 1621. Wentworth's colleague Calvert, as Secretary of State, was an important figure in it. But the skilful leadership and management which had existed twenty years ago was no longer there. The ability to shape and manipulate Parliamentary argument seemed now to be passing to the King's opponents: the King and his Council had lost the art of giving clear directives to their friends, and their spokesmen were no longer skilled in manoeuvring the day-to-day business of the House.

Little more than a week after the opening of Parliament, an inquiry was set on foot into the election of Calvert and Wentworth, on the grounds that the electors had been intimidated. The case was heard before the Committee of Privileges and later debated in the House: the possible unseating of a Secretary of State naturally aroused considerable interest, and certainly Wentworth's behaviour in securing his own and Calvert's election had been high-handed. He did not deny it; throughout he behaved with coolness as if to indicate that the House of Commons was wasting its time over a trifle. In the end he proved right, for it was ruled that the strong wording of the Sheriff's warrants, though out of order, could not be regarded as an act of intimidation on Wentworth's part. The election was confirmed, though the constables were reprimanded and Sir John Savile was heartily thanked for his zeal in the public welfare. [4]

Meanwhile Wentworth's colleague Calvert, as a principal spokesman of the Court, had put forward the King's demands for subsidies with only limited success. Unsatisfied of the royal intentions in Europe, the Commons made no more than a token vote of subsidies, withholding an adequate offering until their grievances should be remedied. Wentworth, still doing his duty to the Court, went to Yorkshire to expedite the raising of the money, and in a speech to the burgesses of Rotherham urged them to believe that only by their full co-operation with the King and the honest payment of the subsidy would they be able to secure and perpetuate in England a just and efficient government. [5]

Wentworth was right to recognize the fatal effect that a breach between King and Parliament would have on the state of the country, but his solution lay in the submission of Parliament to the King. Even so, and in spite of the services that he willingly rendered to the Court in the matter of subsidies, he followed his own judgment, and in this Parliament began very clearly to show his own resolute and practical turn of mind. Early in the proceedings he suggested a bill to repeal obsolete and useless laws which were, as he put it, a snare to the subject. Several times he intervened in the discussion of measures concerning the lot of the 'meaner sort' — on a bill which affected the fishermen of the York-shire coast, on another dealing with the cutlers of Hallamshire, and on more than one occasion on the regulation of the West Riding wool and cloth trades. [6]

In religion he supported the strong Protestant views of the majority. When a bill, supported by John Pym the member for Calne, was put forward 'for better keeping the Sabbath day', one Mr Sheppard, who disliked it, burst into an attack on Puritans as perturbers of the peace. 'Shall we make all these engines and barracados against Papists and not a mousetrap to catch a Puritan?' he asked. Wentworth was one of the foremost who rose in wrath aganst this speech, to defend honest Protestants and the good intentions of the bill. [7]

But Parliament's preliminary vote of money was not sub-stantiated, and now the Commons began to attack monopolies with which King James had tried to supply his wants. In the process they crushed two of the lesser financial vermin who surrounded the Court, before turning with sudden venom on Francis Bacon for his part in these doubtful matters. While this significant prose-cution was yet incomplete, another hare was started, and off went the pack in full cry after a bankrupt Roman Catholic lawyer who had sneered at the misfortunes of the defeated King and Queen of Bohemia. His offence was trivial but his religion encouraged the Commons to avenge on his person the reverses suffered by the Protestant Cause in Europe. They could not persuade their King to declare war on Popish Spain; they could not even get him to prohibit the sale of arms to the Spanish government; but they could show their true religious faith by the savage punishment of a single defenceless man. On this question Wentworth, following the Court line, behaved with restraint. When the King finally announced his intention of removing the matter from the juris-diction of the Commons he intervened in an angry debate to defend the legality of the royal action. [8]

King James had by this time decided to adjourn Parliament at Whitsuntide. In the resentful atmosphere caused by this message Wentworth delivered his first major speech. It was moderate and conciliatory. If the Commons, he argued, felt that the King had not done for them all that they desired, they must remember that they too had failed to do what the King had asked. In the present state of affairs he urged them not to 'depart with a mistaking between the King and his people'. Since their session was now limited, let them waste no time in complaint, but sit for longer hours and try at least to complete the legislation on which they had begun. 'Twelve good bills' which were before them could easily be passed before they broke up. [9]

Parliament met again in the autumn. By that time the state of Europe and the trade depression had both worsened. The fortunes of the Protestant Cause steadily declined, while indignation in England increased with every fresh rumour of the war; but the King would not stir from his Spanish policy. It was noised about that he intended to marry his son to the Infanta. Friendship with Wotton and Doncaster gave Wentworth first-hand knowledge of European affairs and he could see that Spain, involved in a Dutch war, would do much for English support; Philip III could surely be persuaded to use his influence with the Emperor towards making an accommodation in Germany and saving some of their hereditary land for the unfortunate daughter of King James and her husband. The popular alternative was that England should at once dispatch an army to the help of the defeated King of Bohemia. Here there was another difficulty: English trade rivalry with the Dutch was by now very bitter, but the Dutch were the only friends that the King of Bohemia had so far found in his exile, and he was hardly likely to abandon them for the hypothetical support of the English. Diplomacy being a stream of so many cross-currents it seemed better to Wentworth that Parliament should trust in the guidance of the King.

These considerations governed his actions when Parliament re-assembled on November 14th, 1621. Although the question of subsidies was by now urgent, the Commons prepared once again to criticize rather than to assist, and they were angered when James, with some asperity, requested them to find the means for relieving his daughter and her husband and to leave the method to him. A breach between the Commons and the Crown was again imminent, and in the interests of both Wentworth exerted his talents and his energies to prevent it. He was now beginning to be noticed as an active and eloquent young man who knew his own mind. On November 23rd, in a speech of some length, he urged the Commons to show greater confidence in the King and to avoid embarking on new grievances. Let them draw up those that they had already discussed in an orderly form. By trying to compass too many demands they would lose all and be 'like hinds that calve in the fields and forsake their calves'. Another version gives a more Biblical metaphor — 'we shall tread the olive and lose the oil.' [10]

The Commons were not in any mood for practical advice; a majority were set rather on the maintenance of their privileges, which they believed to be menaced by the constant interventions of the King. Three days later, in an angry debate on supply, Wentworth in vain tried to secure an adjournment until the passions of the moment had cooled. On November 27th he appealed once more for supply and unity. John Pym in his notes of the occasion set down drily that Sir Thomas Wentworth 'stated the business rather than argued it'. In effect, he urged the House to set forth their grievances with moderation. Let them first 'satisfy His Majesty with some competent sum' and then present their own views to him in the form of a 'humble request'. He now stated very clearly his belief that the security of the whole country depended on maintaining the strength of the Crown: 'the greatness and power of His Majesty is our prop and therefore ought to be dear to us.' The decision between peace and war must be left wholly 'in the King's hands'; it was for them, as subjects, to be willing to lay down 'our lives and fortunes when the King shall make a war'. But with this sense of obedience there must also go the sense of unity. 'The King and his people are to be considered jointly and not apart, for that is the end of our meeting.' [11]

But the time for such an appeal had gone by, or the Court spokesmen were not well organized enough to support it. The Commons continued to attack the King's grants of monopolies. These were hated and feared, partly because they represented an increasing source of income to the King which was not controlled by Parliament, but also because they were held responsible for the general trade depression which was a cause of genuine alarm to many members and of widespread distress in the country. The religious question seemed to many of equal urgency; the King's policy to Spain abroad and to Papists at home was too much of a piece. There was an inevitable attack in the Commons on the royal policy of granting exemptions from the penal laws to Roman

Catholics in return for cash payments. A remonstrance was proposed against this practice. It was coupled with a projected protest against the King's intention of marrying his son to a princess of Spain.

At this point King James sharply commanded the Commons to cease meddling with what did not concern them. His intervention was mistaken. It could only have quelled the Commons if he had had strong enough support from the Court spokesmen to bring the House under control. In the storm which the message aroused Wentworth once again stood out, not indeed as a supporter of the King's action, but as a conciliator. He spoke several times in the angry days of December which preceded the dissolution, suggesting at first a resolution or declaration defining the privileges of the Commons, but not in the form of a protest to the King. Later on he asked with a touch of impatience for 'an end of disputing our privileges'. [12] It was becoming evident from the tone of his interventions that he saw privilege as a means to an end, not as an end in itself. In so far as freedom of debate was helpful to better government he believed in it, but by the end of the 1621 Parliament he was already beginning to see that 'privilege', too persistently urged, became a block to all practical business. But his opinions were those of a minority. The Commons worded the resolution on their privileges in terms that could not but offend the King. James dissolved Parliament, sent for the Journals, and tore out the resolution with his own hand.

The first Parliament in which Wentworth had sat, the Addled Parliament of 1614, had seemed to reveal a deadlock between Crown and Commons. The second Parliament in which he had sat showed that the attempt of either party to break the deadlock — and both had tried — could only lead to some more drastic clash between them. Wentworth returned to Yorkshire in January 1622 despondent and irritated. Here he was disturbed to find that he had given offence to the Lord President of the North, Lord Scrope, who with unexpected rudeness refused to receive him when he called at his residence in York. [13] The cause of the quarrel does not appear, but it was probably connected with Wentworth's opposition to Savile, which was by now a matter of some consequence in the local politics of Yorkshire.

By the summer he was back in London, on business for his nephews, and in the heat of July he moved out to Stratford, hoping to recuperate in the country air from one of those nervous illnesses to which he seems always to have been subject. Here, early in August, his wife fell ill of a fever which ran its fatal course in less than a week. He was constantly with her, and every turn of her swift decline can be followed in the laboriously careful account of it which he wrote as a pious and private memorial to her. It is a typically Puritan document. Husband and wife faced death together; while she had strength she prayed, sometimes with him, sometimes alone; he knelt at her bedside or ceaselessly paced her room in silent prayer; he read the Bible to her; they repeated psalms together, and he was at her side when she took the last Sacrament. Later they prayed again in unison, until her failing voice sank into silence, a few minutes only before she died. [14]

They had been married for eleven years, and though her childlessness must have been a grief to him, he seems to have loved her with something more than that 'hallowed care and circumspection' which he defined as the duty owed by a husband to a wife. His letters to his brother-in-law in the next few weeks are those of a man suffering to the full the dark loneliness of bereavement.

It was Wentworth's misfortune that his too harsh and arrogant manner repelled friendship, for his letters nakedly reveal how much the trust, approbation and tenderness of his near relations and his true friends meant to him. His outward appearance gave the impression of strength, and his public conduct was never designed to propitiate or please, but he was at heart painfully sensitive to criticism and over-anxious for approval and applause. Lady Margaret, a 'most obedient and loving wife', had no doubt always been ready with consoling words of praise and respect whenever he needed them; there is no need to doubt his sincerity when he spoke of his 'unspeakable loss'. [15]

His wife's death, by deeply intensifying his personal need for a sympathetic audience and for the sustaining help of friendship, brought into being the two great friendships of his life, with George Radcliffe and Christopher Wandesford. To these two he was able to elucidate his political ideas, and when at last he achieved power they would become his devoted instruments in helping him to realize them. Radcliffe had married Wentworth's cousin Anne Trappes; he had also been a pupil of Charles Greenwood, Wentworth's tutor. Their acquaintance was therefore of long standing, but it was not until after Lady Margaret's death that they became deeply attached. Radcliffe was a pious man of simple tastes and manners, not exceptionally gifted, but businesslike and skilled in the law; he was indiscreet and rather meddling, irritable, didactic and intolerant, but he had the corresponding virtues of courage and thoroughness. Besides, he shared Wentworth's religious views, and at the crises of his life it was always to Radcliffe that Wentworth unburdened his heart. [16]

Christopher Wandesford, whom Wentworth had known since they were schoolboys together, was very different. He was retiring, almost self-effacing, tolerant, and even-tempered; he could bring himself to think or speak ill of no one. Like Radcliffe, he was a relatively poor man, and he had inherited an estate burdened with debt, so that he had not even Radcliffe's advantage of self-reliant independence. He was quietly observant, devout and a great thinker but with practical knowledge and experience of the law. He was idealist enough to hope that he would one day see a judicial code in England that would ensure justice to the poor in all circumstances. Wandesford had recently married the daughter of another Yorkshire gentleman, Alice Osborne, and Wentworth stood godfather to their eldest son. [17]

Two older friends were brought nearer to Wentworth by his wife's death. Her brother Lord Clifford was often at Woodhouse, where until recently one part of the building was called 'Clifford's lodging'. Sir Gervase Clifton, who had married one of Lady Margaret's sisters, also drew closer to him. Through him, on more than one occasion, Wentworth seems to have hinted at his continued desire for employment at Court, a desire which was still disappointed. It was rumoured that he was to be raised to the peerage — an honour which he had at one time been willing to buy — and that he was to be Comptroller of the Royal Household, but neither of these things happened. His few public employments in the last years of King James were not of a kind to fulfil his ambitions or stretch his capacities to the full. He was a member of the commission of inquiry into the causes of the decay of trade; a little later he was appointed, apparently on the recommendation of Lord Treasurer Middlesex, Receiver General for the Crown lands of Yorkshire. It seems possible that the attention of Middlesex was drawn to him by Sir Arthur Ingram, a business man of dubious honesty and enormous wealth who was very close to the Treasurer. Ingram, one of the ablest and most distrusted 'undertakers' of the day, had risen from very small beginnings in London, and had of later years acquired lands in Yorkshire and built the noble mansion of Temple Newsam. Wentworth, rather surprisingly in view of his pride in the antiquity of his family, was for some years in fairly close association with this unscrupulous upstart. It was probably from him that he learnt the ways in which money could be made out of revenue collecting and tax-farming as well as commercial and industrial projects. One of the results of this not very reputable connection may well have been his appointment to the receivership in Yorkshire. But he did not hold the place long. The office seems to have been worth about £340 a year, and before the end of his second year Wentworth passed it on to a successor whom he nominated. The nominee would of course, in the usual manner of the time, pay him for this valuable favour. The whole transaction looks as though he was in need of ready money. At about the same time he contemplated selling some of his by now very extensive lands, and he was certainly, within a year or two of Lady Margaret's death, in quest of an heiress for a second wife. [18]

Politically and financially his fortunes were, in the early 1620s, at their lowest ebb. He had not received those marks of favour from the Court to which he hoped his services in and out of Parliament had entitled him. His prolonged visits to London, partly on account of his Savile nephews, but also in pursuit of Court favour, had trenched into his fortune. The education of his brothers and the dowries of his sisters were other heavy calls on his estate at this time, while the general depression was probably affecting his rents. In Yorkshire, his feud with Savile was going badly. The wily old knight was on better terms with the Lord President of the North, Lord Scrope; he was also much more ingenious than Wentworth in currying favour at Court.

Looking beyond his personal interests and personal quarrels at the affairs of the nation, Wentworth can have seen little to cheer him. A licence to go abroad, granted to him at this time but never used, [19] seems to suggest some momentary project of abandoning his saddening country and his childless home. But Wentworth was too deeply rooted in his native land for the prospect of residence abroad ever deeply to have attracted him. The deadlock between

45

King and Parliament seemed now to be absolute, and this, for a man of Wentworth's keen, active and ambitious temperament, was bitterly frustrating. He was now thirty, childless after an eleven years' marriage, and scarcely at all on the road to high advancement in spite of season after season spent in calculated endeavour to gain respect in his own county and connections at Court. Though he was still a young man he was, by the standards of his time, at an age when something more should have been achieved as an earnest of future success. His impatient bitterness in later years, his angry and persistent belief that he was being thwarted, must have grown in him as a habit of mind during this overlong and tedious apprenticeship to power.

By far the greater number of his surviving letters date, naturally, from the time of his success, but the character, temperament and outlook which they reveal had already been formed in earlier life. Personal ambition, the desire for power and with it the desire for money without which power could never be secure, were driving forces in his conduct; but so also was the conviction that power should be used for good ends, and that abilities such as his were meant by God for the service of the common weal. The confusion of private with public ambition and of wordly calculation with an authentic desire to serve the state is not at any time uncommon; in the earlier seventeenth century this otherwise commonplace confusion of motives was often intensified by a profound belief in divine guidance. In Wentworth all three elements were strongly present, and his letters, quite apart from the direct information they convey, are documents of exceptional value to the student of the seventeenth-century mind. In page after page he elucidates his actions, explains or defends his policy, praises his own achievements and blames other men for their corruption, indolence and self-seeking. His confidence in his own judgment and his sense of mission are never for a moment in doubt; it is also clear that his conviction of God's guidance led him — as it has many others — into extraordinary self-deceptions. He was capable of condemning in others actions which he saw no objection to in himself, having the licence of the Almighty for whatever he saw fit to do.

The deeply Puritan element in Wentworth's character, which it is superficial to describe as hypocrisy, is often overlooked because his fate was to make him one of the great opponents of the Puritans.

It went far too deep for him to be able to alter it even when it stood in his way — as at this period it probably did — at Court.

His old colleague Calvert faithfully kept the King in mind of him and suggested him for deputy lieutenant of Yorkshire; James spoke kindly of him but did nothing. [20] While Wentworth remained in the shadows the political situation developed rapidly. The King persisted with the projected marriage between his son and the Infanta of Spain. The Prince and the Duke of Buckingham went to Madrid to urge the suit in person, but angered by their reception suddenly returned home declaring themselves heartily sick of the whole business. Buckingham even averred that the Spaniards had been fooling them from the first, and he, for his part, was for an instant declaration of war. Only by such decisive action could the English princess and her husband be restored to their lands; Spanish promises were worthless.

For once the favourite had popular opinion with him and the King was forced to yield. Parliament was called, and met on February 19th, 1624, in the hope of initiating a war which it was also determined to direct. Mansfeld, in the service of the King's dispossessed son-in-law, was coming to England to recruit, and busy secretaries were already drawing up lists of necessary expenditure for the maintenance of an expeditionary force to Europe.

In Yorkshire the decline of Wentworth's fortunes was clearly shown by his inability to secure his own return as one of the Knights of the Shire. He was reduced, instead, to appearing in Parliament in the less aristocratic character of burgess for the town of Pomfret. This Parliament was to be unlucky to him in other ways. The King's principal financial adviser, the Earl of Middlesex, who had, as Lord Treasurer, managed the royal income with uncanny skill, was soon a target of attack. He was strongly opposed to the war with Spain and although the King strove feebly to protect him, the Prince of Wales and the Duke of Buckingham, in the interests of their war policy, encouraged the Commons to hunt him down. The disgrace of Middlesex was achieved by reviving an obsolete form of prosecution known as 'impeachment'; this method, in the ensuing years, was to become habitual and familiar.

For Wentworth, the fall of Middlesex meant the disappearance of a powerful figure on the King's Council who had wished him well. Although he was not in sympathy with the war policy which had been forced upon the ageing King, Wentworth strove as usual to support the Court party in the House of Commons. If there was to be a war, Parliament must give the King some means of waging it, but the gentry of England still doubted James's good faith and it may be they were not wrong. On May 29th, having gained four subsidies, and that only at the expense of an act against monopolies, the King prorogued Parliament. A fortnight later Wentworth noted with dry amusement that while an alliance had been signed with the Dutch to help the exiled King of Bohemia, the Roman Catholic nobility were openly recruiting soldiers for the Spanish army. [21]

One thing was clear: the war would not be for King James to win or lose, but for his son. Prince Charles was twenty-four years old; he was small but of a graceful build, with light brown hair and glancing light grey eyes. With his large-browed, intellectual head and diffident manner, he seemed at first a pleasant young man. A closer view revealed that this diffidence was not altogether that of youth and inexperience; it might well have something to do with the cold, reserved and haughty temper that, by fits, veiled his grey eyes and set his lips in a hard line. At the time of his return from Spain he was the hero of the people, or at least of the Londoners, who now looked to him to be the figurehead and leader of the nation in a glorious aggressive war. He was always with Buckingham. Indeed the 'inwardness' which Wentworth noticed between Charles and Buckingham seemed to some even closer than it had been between Buckingham and the King. The King's death would make no difference to the real governor of the country. Meanwhile the two went about together, easing the last months of the old King's life by the joyful spectacle of cloudless unity between the two human beings whom he loved above all others. [22]

The spectacle was not so pleasing to Wentworth, who was not beloved of the all-powerful Buckingham. This was in part the doing of his old enemy Sir John Savile, now very much in favour at Court, but it was also the inevitable consequence of his own political views. He had been a useful Court spokesman in the House for as long as the King held to his policy of maintaining peace with Spain. But now that war was to be declared, he and all the advocates of Spanish friendship were out of favour.

In the summer and autumn of 1624, therefore, his comments on the political scene, and especially on the Spanish war, became bitterly ironic. When the Spanish ambassador withdrew he noted cynically 'the great joy and exultation of all the cobblers and zealous bigots of the town'. Later he wrote disparagingly of the newly recruited soldiers for this unwelcome war who spent their time 'entertaining the town with great feathers and buff jerkins'. [23] His contempt was well founded; the European expedition was a failure.

After ten years spent in trying to gain a foothold at Court, in the inner circle of power, Wentworth was now to be found in the company of those who were out of favour like himself, or critical, or in opposition. He went sometimes to the house of Archbishop Abbot, whose rigid and rather Puritan views — so like Wentworth's own — were notoriously at variance with those of the Prince of Wales. He saw much of the Earl of Clare and his family; Clare was a formidable landowner in Nottinghamshire who had bought a title some years earlier. Though he and his family had a fairly secure foothold in the Court circle of power, his ambition made him also impatient and critical.

Wentworth's association with the Clare family had other besides political causes. Since Lady Margaret's death he had been in quest of a second wife. He had unsuccessfully approached the families of three heiresses. These were Mary, daughter of the City magnate Sir William Craven, with a portion of £25,000; Lady Diana Cecil, daughter of the Earl of Exeter; and a widow, the Countess Dowager of Dorset, who was by birth Lady Anne Clifford, and a cousin of his first wife. He failed to win the first two because his previous childless marriage had caused rumours of his impotence. [24] The third negotiation seems hardly to have matured at all.

But in the autumn of 1624 he made suit for Lord Clare's daughter, Lady Arabella Holles. Her portion, which seems to have been £6,000, was handsome, if not to be compared with that of Mary Craven. But almost immediately Wentworth 'grew passionately in love with her', a development not at all surprising, for the young girl whose character and features have been preserved in a fragment of manuscript written by George Radcliffe, was indeed a nonpareil. She was at the time of the wooing not much above

C

sixteen, well-educated, speaking French, reading Italian and Spanish; graceful, gay, intelligent, with all the easy social gifts and with generosity and considerate kindness as well. Years later Radcliffe was to grow lyrical in his recollection of her sweet expression, her smile, her dimples (which her children inherited), her splendid eyes, the thick and lustrous hair which, when he once called upon her in the early morning, he saw loose, covering her like a veil. Beautiful, charming and gifted, she was also becomingly modest, 'apt to blush upon all occasions which always added a new beauty to her'. With this delectable young creature Wentworth spent his every free afternoon from the autumn of 1624 until the 24th of February 1625, when the marriage was solemnized and he entered upon the seven happiest years of his domestic life. [25]

Exactly a month later the old King died.

NOTES

[1] Knowler, I, pp. 8-10; *Commons Debates*, ed. Notestein, Relf and Simpson, II, p. 45; IV, pp. 23, 48-9; Strafford MSS, II, Nos. 52-62; Upton, *Sir Arthur Ingram*, pp. 153-4.

[2] D'Ewes, *Autobiography*, I, p. 170.

[3] *Commons Debates*, V, pp. 425-9. Wentworth's own account of the first month of this Parliament was printed by Notestein, Relf and Simpson (V, pp. 423-93) from the transcript in the Bodleian Library acquired by Sir Charles Firth from the papers of William Knowler. The original is in vol. XXXIV of the Strafford MSS.

[4] *Commons Debates*, II, p. 45; VI, pp. 161-2; *Commons Journals*, I, pp. 556-7, 570-1.

[5] Strafford MSS, XXI, No. 17.

[6] *Commons Debates*, III, p. 279; V, pp. 16, 455.

[7] Ibid., IV, p. 53; V, p. 467; *Commons Journals*, I, p. 521.

[8] *Commons Debates*, III, pp. 166-7; *Commons Journals*, I, pp. 598, 602, 608.

[9] *Commons Debates*, III, p. 350; IV, p. 392; VI, p. 178.

[10] Ibid., II, p. 441; III, p. 433-4; E. Nicholas, *Proceedings and Debates*, p. 197.

[11] *Commons Debates*, II, p. 435; III, pp. 463-4; IV, p. 443.

[12] Ibid., II, pp. 504, 525; VI, pp. 244, 239.

[13] Strafford MSS, XXI, No. 20.

[14] Ibid., No. 16; Knowler, II, p. 430.

[15] Strafford MSS, II, folios 89-92.

[16] Knowler, II, p. 35.

[17] Ibid., I, pp. 17-18.

[18] J. P. Cooper, pp. 230-1; Strafford MSS, II, folios 98-9; XII, No. 2; see also Upton, *Sir Arthur Ingram*, Chap. IX.

[19] Strafford MSS, XII, No. 3.

[20] *C.S.P.D.*, 1623-5, p. 7.

[21] Knowler, I, p. 20.

[22] For the popular hopes associated with Prince Charles at this time see the present writer's *Poetry and Politics*, Cambridge, 1959, pp. 25, 31-3; Knowler, I, p. 20.

[23] Knowler, I, pp. 21-2.

[24] J. P. Cooper, p. 230; Strafford MSS, XXXIV, No. 3.

[25] Loc. cit.; Knowler, II, p. 430.

CHAPTER FOUR

SHERIFF OF YORKSHIRE

It asketh a strong wit and a strong heart to know when to tell truth, and
to do it.

BACON

CHARLES I ascended the throne with a war newly declared
on Spain and an alliance newly made with France. His
bride, the sister of Louis XIII, was expected daily and
Buckingham had gone to fetch her.

The first act of the young King was to issue writs for a Parliament. Supported by his neighbour, Sir Thomas Fairfax, Wentworth contested the county with Sir John Savile. Both sides
assiduously courted support, and since Wentworth was on the
whole better respected by the established gentry, Savile fell back
on riot and roused the weavers of Leeds and Halifax in his favour.
On the day of the election Savile demanded a poll; while the
Sheriff's officers were making the necessary preparations he ingeniously spread a rumour among Wentworth's supporters that the
voting would last two or three days and when some of them began
to drift away he gathered his own voters and, strengthened by a
crowd of idlers, made a rush upon the booths. Cries of 'A Savile!
A Savile!' reverberated from the polling-place, and the Sheriff to
prevent a brawl put a stop to the voting, cleared the courtyard
and proclaimed the election of Wentworth and Fairfax. [1]

The Sheriff's high-handed action could be justified on the
grounds of common sense and necessity, but Sir John's party
suspected, with some reason, that Wentworth had forced his hand.
More would be heard of the Yorkshire election when Parliament
met.

The Commons assembled in the third week in June 1625. On a
petition presented by Savile, Wentworth's election was called in
question. Savile's case, that the poll had been stopped by the
Sheriff, was indeed a strong one, and Wentworth's contention that
Savile had brought in men who were not freeholders to join in the

voting seemed to need more support than his mere word. Time was asked to send for witnesses, and while this motion was before the House, Wentworth himself entered, a breach of the rules which he seems to have committed in ignorance rather than out of intentional defiance. Sir John Eliot, the member for Newport in Cornwall, was speaking. The brief report of the day's proceedings in the official journals gives no indication of any drama, but several years later, after Eliot had become the leader of the opposition to the Court and had quarrelled finally with Wentworth, he gave his account of the incident. In this he represented himself as denouncing, even at this early stage, Wentworth's haughty disregard of the rights and rules of Parliament. According to himself he drove him from the House with blistering words:

'Mr Speaker, the violation of our rights may be well excused by others when they suffer violation by ourselves. A greater dishonour and contempt this House has no time suffered than what does now affront it. Should I compare it, it could have no parallel but that Roman's against whom Cicero does inveigh. *In senatum venit*, he comes into the senate, but with a will to ruin it; for so I must interpret the intention of that act, that would destroy the privilege.... But did I say it was a member did it? I must retract that error in this place or be false to the opinion which I have; for either by the election which he pretends, or for this act of insolence, I cannot hold him worthy of that name, and so as a full determination of his case let us from hence expel him.' [2]

Wentworth's election was duly quashed, though how far as a result of Eliot's intervention it would be hard to say. He hastened back to Yorkshire, presented himself for re-election, and was returned without a single dissentient voice, a notable triumph against Savile. By August 8th he was back again in Parliament, now in session at Oxford to avoid the plague which was bad in London. [3]

War for the Protestants was still the cry and Eliot's group were insisting on the removal of Buckingham from office before they would grant adequate supplies. They had assumed too quickly that the King was a mild young man; irritated by criticism of the favourite, he had assumed an unexpected bullying tone and sent petulant messages that the Commons must grant supplies or adjourn. They in turn ardently defended their privileges while public business was delayed. This delaying of necessary business provoked Wentworth's disgust and he attempted to steer a middle course as he had done in 1624. 'Let us first do the business of the Commonwealth,' he argued, 'and afterwards for my part I will consent to do as much for the King as any other.' [4] Whatever his policy, he had no time to make it effective; on August 12th Charles dissolved Parliament, the fourth impotent assembly in which Wentworth had sat.

Strong in his knowledge of the Court, he realized that the Commons had made a strategic error in attacking Buckingham, whom the King would defend in all circumstances and at any cost. At the coronation the Duke had tried to help the King up the steps of the dais, but Charles, evading him, had slipped his hand underneath his friend's arm and said audibly, 'I have more need to help you than you have to help me.' [5] He would stand by the word he had given on the very steps of the throne.

The little Queen, a thin child of sixteen, with a pale complexion and prominent eyes, allowed her jealousy of the favourite to divide her from the King, a division which Buckingham did nothing to heal. Her vivacious charm, if not her youth and bewilderment, with no experience and almost no English, should have made her an object at least of protective pity to her husband, but she had begun by allowing her suite to act offensively to the English Protestants, and when they were removed from her, had further prejudiced herself by sulky resistance. Meanwhile Buckingham had scolded her, unbidden, in her private dressing-room for her ungracious manner towards his relations; the King, when she complained, took the favourite's part, indicated that she must learn to behave herself prettily to his friends, and forced her to accept both the mother and the wife of the Duke as her attendants. [6] It was rumoured that he no longer lived with her; if the marriage were childless the English Crown would pass to the eldest son of the King and Queen of Bohemia, for whose hand it was believed Buckingham had already proposed his infant daughter.

Buckingham alone was the source of advancement, and Wentworth, at the time of Parliament's dissolution, nourished a brief hope that he had regained the favourite's good-will. [7] He proved to be wrong, for his intervention in the culminating debates, slight as it had been, was interpreted as opposition to the Court; though he had expressed himself moderately enough, he had come down in favour of combining redress of grievances with the granting of supplies. Before a new Parliament met, the King and the favourite were equally anxious to prevent the election of as many as possible of those members who had argued that supply must be dependent on redress of grievances. Accordingly in the autumn of 1625 some of the more prominent Parliament men were, on Buckingham's suggestion, appointed sheriffs of their respective counties, an office which could not be combined with serving in Parliament, for the very sufficient reason that a sheriff was not supposed to return himself. The King, as he looked down the list which was intended to cripple the opposition in the next Parliament, did at least observe that Wentworth was 'an honest gentleman', a comment which his friends at Court took to mean that he had no personal animosity against him. [8]

Wentworth received the news of his appointment as sheriff philosophically. He could see some advantage for himself in staying for a time in his own county to counteract the influence of Sir John Savile, which had increased since the last election. [9] He did not doubt that he would so discharge his part in Yorkshire as to enhance his own reputation. It was not a time at which outer misfortune could wholly cast down his spirits, for his wife was pregnant, and the hope that he could build a great place in the land, not merely for himself but for a son of his own, had been reborn in him.

When Wandesford wrote to sympathize over his appointment, Wentworth answered at length, explaining his plans for the present and his hopes for the future. If he bowed to the King's pleasure, or rather his displeasure, it was yet possible that he might by his willing obedience recover his position in the royal favour. For the time being, he wrote:

> I will fold myself up in a cold, silent forbearance, apply myself cheerfully to the duties of my place ... for my rule which I will not transgress, is never to contend with the prerogative out of a Parliament nor yet to contest with a King, but when I am constrained thereunto, or else make shipwreck of my integrity and peace of conscience.

He did not doubt but that Charles, like King Ahasuerus in the book of Esther, would one night 'cause his chronicles to be read, wherein he shall find the faithfulness of Mardocheus, the treason of his Eunuchs, and then let Haman look to himself'. [10] By Haman, Wentworth seems to have meant Savile and his other enemies at Court. In any case he was staunch to his decision to bow to the King's will, and rejected the ingenious scheme of one of his fellow-victims that they should circumvent the royal intention by each conniving at the election of the other in a borough within his own jurisdiction. [11] Such an action could only have exasperated the King and Buckingham, whose favour Wentworth was still working hard to regain.

With unfounded confidence he believed himself to have done so by the spring of 1626; at least he felt himself strong enough to put forward a request to the King that he be appointed Lord President of the North. [12] A rumour had circulated that Lord Scrope, the President, was likely to withdraw. His favour to Roman Catholics had singled him out for attack in the House of Commons, and it was thought that the King wished him to resign, so that his replacement could be represented to the Commons as a conciliatory gesture. But Sir John Savile persuaded Buckingham to let Scrope retain the place, on condition that Savile became his Vice-President. This was the culmination of Savile's steady campaign to build up his personal power in Yorkshire. With the Lord President holding his office almost by the good-will of Savile, his own Vice-President, Wentworth, whose enmity with Savile was notorious, and who had lost Scrope's good-will by trying to succeed to his office, was placed in an embarrassing and perilous position. His ambition, and his humiliating failure to achieve it, were well known in his own county and at Court. [13] Savile's triumph as Vice-President was further enhanced by the success that he had soon after in obtaining from the King a charter for Leeds, the wool town whose trade he had stimulated and to which he owed much of his wealth. [14] Alike in the North and at Whitehall the future prospects of Sir Thomas Wentworth were clouded and insecure. He had two alternatives: he could either accept defeat or fight back by opposing Sir John Savile and making himself, more vigorously than heretofore, the leader of the still fairly substantial group of landed gentry in Yorkshire whose mainly agricultural concerns were opposed to the industrial interest of Savile and the West Riding clothiers. Wentworth was not the man to abandon a fight. The feud with Savile, Savile's triumph with Buckingham, and Wentworth's own dislike of the favourite's war policy, pushed him now, inevitably, into opposition to the Court.

Meanwhile the time of his wife's confinement was fast approaching, and on June 8th, 1626, between ten and eleven o'clock at night, to Wentworth's boundless joy, she was happily delivered of a son, who was baptized soon after by his grandfather's name, William. [15]

Scarcely a month later he felt the first heavy blow of the King's displeasure, prompted by Sir John Savile and his friends. He was dismissed from the post of Custos Rotulorum, in which he had succeeded Savile nine years earlier. The order for his dismissal was handed to him while he was presiding at a session, but he showed a spirit and dignity equal to this intentional public affront. He made no attempt to muffle the import of the note he had received. Rising to his feet he briefly dismissed the Court. 'My Lords and Gentlemen,' he said,

'I have here, even as I sit, received his Majesty's writ for putting me out of the Custoship I held in the Commission of the Peace, which shall by me be dutifully and cheerfully obeyed. Yet I could wish they who succeed me had forborne this time this service, a place, in sooth, ill-chosen, a stage ill prepared for venting such poor, vain, insulting humour. Nevertheless, since they will needs thus weakly breathe on me a seeming disgrace in the public face of the county, I shall crave leave to wipe it away as openly, as easily, seeing I desire not to overlive the opinion of an honest man amongst you, which in the course of the world we see others regard too little…. The world may well think I knew the way which would have kept my place. I confess it had been too dear a purchase, and so I leave it, not conscious of any fault in myself, nor yet guilty of the virtue in my successor that should occasion this removal.' [16]

With this sidelong reference to the intrigues of Savile, Wentworth left the court.

Meanwhile the Parliament of 1626 ran its course no more smoothly than its predecessor. Wentworth's father-in-law, Lord Clare, had predicted that it would only bring 'worse hobgoblins' than the last, and his opinion was justified. Sir John Eliot, who became its moving spirit, organized a frontal attack on the favourite. The old method of impeachment had been revived in 1624 to bring down the Lord Treasurer Middlesex; Buckingham and Prince Charles had then joyfully stimulated the Commons to apply this antiquated instrument, although the old King had warned them that they would live to regret it. Now, two years later, Sir John Eliot lifted the old, weighty, two-handed sword once again and aimed it at Buckingham. The attack was misconceived and the charge clumsily drawn. Parliament was dissolved with ill-feeling on both sides and no money voted. The King had to fall back on the dubious alternative of raising funds for government by imposing a compulsory loan on the gentry equivalent to what they would have paid in the subsidy.

It was probable that some, who had opposed him in Parliament, would carry their resistance further and refuse to pay. But Wentworth's decision not to pay came as a surprise to his friends, who had not expected him to go so far in opposition. This defiance of the King would destroy all chance of reconciliation with the Court, and put an end to his hope of public employment. The King, exasperated by opposition, was in no mood to brook defiance. 'His heart is so inflamed in this business', wrote Clifford, 'as he vows a perpetual remembrance, as well as present punishment.' [17]

Wentworth remained firm to his decision. His reasons are not easy to determine. He had only a few months before declared that he would not, except in a case of conscience and integrity, contest with the prerogative out of Parliament, but in refusing the loan this was precisely what he was doing. Was this the case of integrity and conscience which justified defying the Crown? Apparently it was. Driven by the Savile feud, he had made himself the spokesman of the Yorkshire landed gentry, the 'country' party, the group opposed to Savile, who lived on the revenues of their estates and not on the hope of grants and favours from the Court. He was therefore bound to take the view that the property of subjects could not be at the mercy of the needs and whims of the Crown. The

57

Forced Loan, unless resisted, could be the beginning of unparliamentary taxation and arbitrary levies, which would undermine the security of the gentry once for all. Apart from this argument, Wentworth disliked the war policy which made the tax necessary, and wholly distrusted the capacity of Buckingham to use the money efficiently. For the first time in his life, therefore, he joined the extreme opponents of the Court and would not be deflected by the anxious warnings of Calvert, Clifford and his other friends.

Besides the inevitable fall from Court favour that must be the consequence of his refusal, they also feared that he might be subjected to physical evils beyond his strength. The King was bound to make examples of some of the more prominent refusers. Wentworth's health was not good and imprisonment in London during the height of the summer and with plague about was not lightly to be risked for a point of conscience. He should think of his son and his young wife, who was again with child. His conviction was proof against dissuasion: Lord Clare with thirteen other peers had protested against the loan and his daughter could not but share the feelings of her husband and father. Calvert, who was leaving for America in May, wrote anxiously to Wentworth before he sailed:

> Your too much fortitude will draw upon you suddenly a misfortune which your heart may, perhaps, endure, but the rest of your body will ill suffer.... The conquering way sometimes is yielding; and so it is as I conceive in this particular of yours, wherein you shall both conquer your own passions, and vex your enemies who desire nothing more than your resistance. [18]

Wentworth took no notice and a month later he was sent for to answer for his conduct before the Privy Council. He repeated his refusal and was committed to the Marshalsea prison where his friend George Radcliffe was already in confinement for the same cause. [19] Almost at the same moment Savile crowned his upward progress at Court by attaining to the dignity of Comptroller of the Royal Household, [20] the office for which Wentworth had hoped in vain some years earlier.

Radcliffe, meanwhile, reassured his family in Yorkshire with the information that they had in the Marshalsea 'exceedingly good company, pleasant and sweet walks and every kind usage'. [21]

With the heat of the summer the prisoners petitioned to be removed from London and a group of them were sent to Dartford. Here Lady Arabella Wentworth hastened to join her husband, and here in October 1627 their daughter, Anne, was born. [22]

Meanwhile seventy-six of those who had refused the loan were imprisoned, and five who brought an action for relief on bail lost it. But the refusers, though they enjoyed the sympathy of many of their fellows, remained a minority. The loan brought in less than the subsidies would have done, had they been voted, but not so much less as to prevent Buckingham from preparing his naval expedition. As he gathered his forces at Portsmouth, the south coast became dangerous with unpaid, undisciplined sailors and soldiers. 'Since these wars our trading is dead', wrote Wentworth's brother-in-law Denzil Holles:

> land, sheep, cattle, nothing will yield money, not to speak of other petty inconveniences we have found by the soldiers ravishing men's wives and daughters (getting them with child otherways was fair play and counted a favour); killing and carrying away beefs and sheep off the ground, (stealing poultry was not worth speaking of), killing and robbing men upon the highway, nay in fairs and towns (for to meet a poor man coming from the market with a pair of new shoes or a basket of eggs or apples, and take them from him, was but sport and merriment) and a thousand such other pretty pranks.

The mismanaged expedition sailed for La Rochelle and ended in disaster. 'Since England was England,' wrote Holles, 'she received not so dishonourable a blow.' [23] He echoed only the indignation of those who were likely to form any future House of Commons.

Wentworth and his companions were released on December 27th, 1627, and he hurried back to Yorkshire to make ready for a new election. Writs for the third Parliament of Charles I were issued in March 1628. The political deadlock had only tightened since the beginning of the reign: Buckingham was still in power, and the Commons, after the catastrophe at Rochelle, were less likely than ever to come to terms.

The lesson was plain enough. Two years before Wentworth had declared that the State was 'neither able to overcome the exulcerated disease nor to endure a sharp, prevalent remedy'. [24] Without 'a sharp, prevalent remedy' government could not go on: the question was, to which organ of the State — King or Parliament — should the remedy be applied?

NOTES

[1] *Commons Journals*, I, p. 801; Knowler, I, p. 27.

[2] *Negotium Posterorum*, I, p. 102; *Commons Journals*, I, pp. 801, 803 ff.

[3] *Fairfax Correspondence*, I, p. 9; *Yorkshire County History*, III, p. 407; *Commons Journals*, p. 812.

[4] *Debates in the House of Commons in 1625*, ed. S. R. Gardiner, p. 113.

[5] D'Ewes, *Autobiography*, I, p. 293.

[6] Bassompierre, *Ambassade en Angleterre*, Cologne, 1668, p. 14; Birch, *Court and Times of Charles I*, pp. 134, 139.

[7] Knowler, I, pp. 34-5.

[8] Ibid., p. 21.

[9] Ibid., p. 32.

[10] Ibid., p. 33.

[11] Ibid., p. 31.

[12] *C.S.P.D.*, 1625-6, p. 228.

[13] Reid, pp. 391-402.

[14] Heaton, p. 222.

[15] Knowler, II, p. 430.

[16] Ibid., I, p. 36.

[17] Ibid., p. 38.

[18] Ibid., p. 39.

[19] *Radcliffe Letters*, p. 139.

[20] *Yorkshire County History*, III, p. 417.

[21] *Radcliffe Letters*, loc. cit.

[22] Knowler, II, p. 430: some personal letters in the Strafford MSS, vol. XXII, relating to the imprisonment of Wentworth are printed by Lady Burghclere, I, pp. 80-1.

[23] Knowler, I, pp. 41-2.

[24] Ibid., p. 32.

—◦❦ ❧❀⟨⟨❀❧ ❦◦—

CHAPTER FIVE

WENTWORTH LEADS THE COMMONS

This is the crisis of Parliaments: we shall know by this if Parliament live or die.
Sir Benjamin Rudyard in the House of Commons, March 1628

THE Parliament of 1626 had been dominated by the Cornish knight, Sir John Eliot. Once a supporter of Buckingham, he had been finally alienated by what he had seen of the mismanagement of the Cadiz venture in the previous year. He had attempted in the ensuing Parliament, with more fervour than discretion, to bring the favourite to a reckoning. The daring impeachment of Buckingham, for infringing the fundamental laws of the Kingdom, marked a further increase in the boldness of the Commons but was in itself unsuccessful. The abortive Parliament had been dissolved and Buckingham was still chief minister.

Wentworth was not the only man who knew, when he came to Westminster for the Parliament of 1628, that this meeting would be critical. If the deadlock between Crown and Commons could not be broken at this third assembly within four years, then the traditional means of governing England could hardly survive. He himself still saw Parliament in the old Elizabethan way. Whatever he felt about Buckingham, and his distrust of him was extreme, he regarded the first duty of Parliament as something other than the impeachment of individual ministers. The Commons had a right and a duty to report what was amiss in the parts of the kingdom they represented; they had a right and a duty to insist that grievances be inquired into and set at rest; they had a right and a duty to see that the just and ancient laws of the land were respected and maintained for the general good of the realm. In Wentworth's opinion the misdeeds of Buckingham were chiefly that he had encouraged the King to override the law by imposing the Forced Loan, by imprisoning his subjects without trial, and by exploiting the necessities of war to oppress his opponents. Troops had been billeted on those whom the King wished to punish, and their sons had been pressed for service abroad. The remedy to these abuses lay in a re-enactment of the laws protecting the subject, not in the removal of Buckingham.

Some preliminary discussions evidently took place between the principal opponents of the Court, among whom Wentworth was unequivocally accepted since his refusal to pay the loan. During these meetings there would seem to have been an agreement to abandon the attack on Buckingham, as a tactical error, at least until an attempt had been made to reach agreement with the King on other points. [1] There was of course no formal acceptance of any one man as leader of the party, but Wentworth, whose temperament inclined him rather to lead than to follow, was evidently determined to play a dominating part in a sane and well-planned campaign for the redress of grievances.

The King, who opened Parliament on March 17th, 1628, was as hostile as usual. In a cold and rather threatening speech he told his faithful Commons that, should they fail to vote him supplies, he would have to obtain them by 'those other means which God hath put into my hands'. [2]

After all that had happened in the last year it was not surprising that Sir Edward Coke almost immediately introduced a bill for protecting subjects against arbitrary imprisonment. Not until a few days later did the question of supplies come up, and Sir Francis Seymour opened the debate pugnaciously. 'If his Majesty shall be persuaded to take what he will, what need we to give?' he asked. Next came a member of the Court party, pleading for oblivion and conciliation, but Sir John Eliot rose to answer with quivering eloquence: single oppressions were nothing, he argued fiercely; it was the principle. 'Upon this dispute not alone our lands and goods are engaged, but all that we call ours. These rights, these privileges which made our fathers freemen, are in question.' After his vigorous attack on the royal policy Sir Benjamin Rudyard made a feeble appeal for trust and harmony. They had come to a crisis, he repeated, with pessimistic entreaty. 'Men and brethren, what shall we do? Is there no balm in Gilead?' [3] It was then that Wentworth rose.

'This debate carries a double aspect,' he began, 'towards the sovereign and the subject, though both be innocent, both are injured, and both to be cured.' He had the Commons under the spell of his calm, powerful voice, and with rising confidence, he continued:

'Surely, in the greatest humility I speak it, these illegal ways are punishments and marks of indignation. The raising of loans strengthened by commissions with unheard of instructions and oaths, the billeting of soldiers by the lieutenants and deputy lieutenants, have been as though they could have persuaded Christian princes, nay worlds, that the right of empire had been to take away by strong hand, and they have endeavoured as far as was possible for them to do it. This hath not been done by the King, under the pleasing shade of whose Crown I hope we shall ever gather the fruits of justice, but by Projectors, who have extended the Prerogative of the King beyond the just symmetry which makes a harmony of the whole. They have rent from us the light of our eyes, vitiated our wives and daughters before our eyes, brought the crown to greater want than ever it was by anticipating the revenue. And can the shepherd be thus smitten and the sheep not scattered? They have introduced a privy Council ravishing at once the spheres of all ancient government, imprisoning us without banks or bounds. They have taken from us all means of supplying the King, taking up the root of all propriety, which if it be not seasonably set again into the ground by his Majesty's own hands, we shall have instead of beauty, baldness.'

He had got the House behind him now, and went on confidently. 'To the making of all these whole I shall apply myself, and propound a remedy to all these diseases. By one and the same thing have King and people been hurt, and by the same must they be cured.' He began to outline his programme, asking the Commons to trust in the goodness of the King who would not refuse them. Four main subjects of complaint they had, that they were imprisoned without cause, pressed for service abroad, taxed without leave of Parliament, and oppressed by the billeting of soldiers in their houses. Of religion he spoke no word, and on the last of the four he hung longest, for he well knew that this was the most dangerous of their public grievances. He blamed the King for nothing, only the administration; and he offered the logical remedy — legislation which would strengthen 'our sober, vital liberties by re-enforcing of the ancient laws made by our ancestors.' [4]

He had calculated rightly. For the next weeks he was to be tacitly accepted as the architect of the Commons' policy. The 'country' party, and even Sir John Eliot himself, were ready on all important issues to follow his lead. But his success in breaking the bitter deadlock between King and Parliament would depend in the last resort on the King more than on the Commons, and the King, sustained by Buckingham, was as intransigent as ever. On March 25th the Secretary of State, Sir John Coke, speaking for the King, bluntly required that the granting of supply should precede the discussion of grievances. The request had no effect, and on April 2nd Wentworth in a well-considered speech strongly argued that discussion of supply should be postponed for two days more. 'Unless we be secured in our liberties we cannot give', he argued. 'I speak not this to make diversions but to the end that giving I may give cheerfully.'

The firmness of the Commons seemed to be working the desired effect. On April 3rd the King sent a conciliatory message on the subject of grievances, and on April 4th Wentworth was a moving spirit when the House in Committee voted five subsidies. These were however not to go further, 'not at least by my consent', Wentworth wrote to a friend, 'till we be in something a better readiness for the security of the subjects in their fundamental liberties.' Supply and redress of grievances 'shall go hand in hand as one joint and continued act'. [5]

This was Wentworth's serious hope, and he felt confident that it would be realized. But everything depended on the willingness of the King to meet their demands, and Charles, after momentary expressions of pleasure, in which Buckingham effusively joined, changed his tone when he realized that the confirmation of the subsidy vote was wholly dependent on the bill to guarantee the liberties of the subject. On April 12th he sent a peremptory message protesting against the long debates on the new bill, an 'unexpected stopping' of the vote on supply 'almost beyond example after so good beginning'. He was if anything angrier than if no subsidies had been promised, and he certainly had reason on his side when he pointed out that unless the subsidies materialized soon 'we shall not be able to put one ship to sea this year.' He gave no sign of favour to the proposed bill to secure the liberties of the subject, and two days later he made it clear in a personal speech to the Commons that he would pass no such bill: they could rest assured that he would respect the rights of his subjects, he said, without any further legislation on the question.

In these conditions the Commons continued for the next fortnight to debate their bill, neglecting the King's demand for supplies. They hoped by obstinacy equal to the King's to force him out of the position he had taken up. But on April 28th he once again sent a message reiterating his intention of respecting all existing laws, so that new legislation was in no way necessary.

The Commons continued to debate their bill and Wentworth, more than once, tried to put the intentions of the House into words that made clear the firmness of their purpose while indicating that the prerogative of the Crown was not in danger. 'All our hopes, all our desires are met in this bill,' he argued, but went on to say: 'it imports us therefore to look well about us and as in all things else, so principally in this, to carry ourselves evenly between Prince and people that so the stream of sovereignty and subjection may run still and smoothe together in the worn and wonted channels ... ' [6]

The King, in the face of the obstinate debates on the bill, changed his tactics and told them he would accept the bill but only if it re-enacted Magna Carta and the other relevant ancient statutes; he would not consider anything that contained additional explanatory matter. Most of the discussion in the Commons had been concerned with just such matter, which was indeed essential if what they considered the true modern bearing of the ancient statutes was to be enforced. The King's message made it clear beyond doubt that he had refused in advance their projected bill of rights. The House considered his statement in deep gloom until Sir Edward Coke put forward a new plan for circumventing it. This was to draft the bill in the form of a Petition of Right: that is, not as a piece of legislation but as a petition for the maintenance of the laws as elucidated by the present Parliament. The King's acceptance of it, if he could be made to accept it in this form, would bind him as effectively as an Act of Parliament. Wentworth supported Coke's plan, and the House of Lords was persuaded to agree.

D   65

The King now attempted to divide his opponents by addressing a letter to the Lords in which he undertook that there should be no more imprisonment without trial. Mollified by this, the Lords took exception to the Petition of Right when the Commons sent it up to them, on the grounds that it trenched too far on the royal prerogative. There was, for a moment, a danger that the Commons would accept this as final and weaken their case altogether by presenting the petition as theirs alone, instead of jointly from both Houses of Parliament. Wentworth in a firmly moderate speech prevented this. His words, as he recorded them for his friend George Radcliffe on the following day, were something of this nature:

'We have laid aside a bill here debated for securing unto subjects their just, fundamental, vital liberties: we are now fallen to a Petition of Right, lower than which we cannot go, with honour to the House, with faithfulness to the trusts for which we are accountable.

'Now unless the Lords co-operate with us herein, the sinew is cut in pieces that gives motion, the stamp taken off that must imprint value upon this action. Join with them, the benefit communicates itself to posterity, becomes a record; separate from them, our labours are as the grass upon the house top, of small continuance....

'There are therefore two expedients in this business, the one not to recede from our Petition, no, not in a tittle, either in the whole or in the parts; the other to win the conjuncture and concurrence of both Houses therein, for if we fail in either of those we destroy our own work.

'Our minds, our intentions are met; we desire no new thing for the subject; we intend not to diminish the just prerogative of the Crown; we lessen no power of his Majesty's to punish a criminal, we only desire to preserve, to secure the innocent ... surely the wisdom of both Houses is able to express their joint meaning in words, in manner, without disadvantage, either to King or people....

'Give me leave humbly to move you that we may close up this conference mannerly as towards their Lordships and to avoid in some measure their present voting of anything till we be upon nearer terms of agreement....

'So we now again profess our equal cares with their Lordships to preserve the sacred rights of the Crown without the least diminution.' [7]

He carried the House with him, though some, notably Sir John Eliot, were in two minds about it, feeling that to court the Lords in this way was to make the Commons appear to be no more than 'cyphers to nobility'. [8] There was some criticism too of a kind of duplicity — 'obliquity' was the word used — in Wentworth's handling of the matter; he was annoyed at this, not seeing any such tendency himself in his effort to avert a breach between the two Houses. [9] But the criticisms foreshadowed the end of his accepted leadership of the Commons, and his last achievement was this re-union of the two Houses, so that on May 26th the Petition of Right went forward from them both to the King.

The King at first attempted evasion; at this the frustrated indignation of his fiercer opponents in the Commons burst through the restraint of the last weeks. Buckingham, as the King's evil genius, was assailed, sidelong by Eliot, and a few days later, openly by Sir Edward Coke, who called him boldly 'the grievance of grievances'. To stem the attack and perhaps at last to gain his supplies, the King gave formal approval to the Petition on June 7th, but delay had cost him all the advantage he might have gained from an earlier agreement. The Commons, it is true, now at last voted the subsidies, but they also prepared a remonstrance attacking those elements of the royal policy that they did not like, and they showed signs of raking up the entire question of the royal revenues. Owing to quarrels with previous Parliaments the King had never had his ordinary revenue from the customs confirmed to him. Since his officers had naturally gone on collecting it, there were some in the Commons who wanted to declare the whole of this procedure illegal because the customs rates had never been legally voted. Faced by this new development, Charles, on June 26th, prorogued Parliament until the winter.

During the last three weeks of Parliament, Wentworth had been silent. His plan for a joint act for supply and redress of grievances which had seemed in theory hopeful, had failed owing to the intransigence of the extremists in Parliament and the delaying obstinacy of the King. By the end of the session it must have been evident to a man of his clear head and practical ability that the Elizabethan system of government by King and Parliament was no longer workable.

As the session drew to an end he received an overture from the Court. The Treasurer, Weston, approached him. [10] The move was not surprising, for in this last Parliament, Wentworth had undoubtedly given proof of energy, abilities and judgment of a kind that the King and his advisers would be unwilling to lose. It was not until they saw him in opposition that they took the full measure of the man whose efforts to serve the Crown had, for the past ten years, met chiefly with rebuffs. But there was an additional reason why Wentworth might be brought back into the service of the Court at this juncture, and why Weston was the chosen instrument.

Weston had always disliked the costly war with Spain, which was an interruption to trade and brought no compensating returns, but when Buckingham became the violent advocate of the Spanish war, Weston had not shared in the general disfavour which had fallen on others who, like Wentworth, were known to favour friendship with Spain. He was at once too useful to be dispensed with and too cautious to press his criticism of the favourite's policy. Now, with a French war also on hand, and with military and naval affairs going so badly, Buckingham was veering back towards the idea of friendship with Spain. By about midsummer of 1628 it was clear that negotiations would not long be delayed. [11]

This Spanish friendship as the basis of foreign and home policy was to be a dominant idea with Wentworth for the next twelve years. It therefore seems more than probable that it was fully discussed between him and Weston and that, as a result of this interview, offers were made to Wentworth which satisfied both his long frustrated ambition and his sincere desire to serve the Crown in the way he thought best. At any rate within a month of Parliament's prorogation Wentworth was at last raised to the peerage. A courtier, writing contemptuously of the batch of new creations, described him as 'a northern lad, Thomas Wentworth, baron of I know not where'. [12] He had taken the cumbrous title of Baron Wentworth of Wentworth Woodhouse, Newmarch and Oversley. He was not the only 'northern lad' to secure the purchasable but still coveted honour of a barony. His neighbour and rival, Sir John Savile, became Lord Savile of Pomfret at the same season. As far as the Yorkshire factions were concerned it would seem that Wentworth, after a period of defeat and eclipse, was once again in the field and ready to challenge his old antagonist on equal terms. Only time was to show that rather more than this had happened.

Among Wentworth's colleagues in the last Parliament the news of his elevation to a peerage and return to Court favour must have provoked reactions of surprise, bitterness or cynicism. But the settled and angry hatred of the 'grand apostate' did not develop until later, when his defeated, silenced or imprisoned colleagues saw him mounting to ever greater and more formidable power as the pillar of a sovereign authority that they hated and feared. In prison, Eliot would condemn him as a predatory place-seeker: 'His covetousness and ambition were both violent, as were his ways to serve them.' (13) Twelve years after Wentworth's return to Court favour he would find himself the object of an execration greater even than that aroused by Buckingham. Then, in 1640, when he faced charges of treason before an angry Parliament, apocryphal stories would be circulated about his 'apostasy' in 1628, and it would be said that John Pym, the ablest of all his colleagues in opposition, had told him 'You may leave us, but we shall never leave you while your head is on your shoulders.' (14) But there was no reason why John Pym should have said anything so extreme in 1628, though doubtless, like others of Wentworth's colleagues (among whom were his own brothers-in-law, John and Denzil Holles), (15) he felt resentment of a man who, after showing so much Parliamentary ability and doing so much to secure the passage of the Petition of Right, was content to throw in his lot once more with the courtiers.

A fairly commonplace shifting of opinion, a move away from and back to the Court, would not in a lesser man have caused much comment. The day of fixed party allegiances lay far in the future, and the whole structure of seventeenth-century politics, where so much depended on the veerings of royal policy and the opportunities of patronage, lent itself to such shifts and turns and tergiversations. What made Wentworth's change memorable and dramatic was what came after it. He had been, briefly, the tacitly acknowledged leader of the 'country' party, the principal pilot who steered the Petition of Right to success. He was to become the chief minister of King Charles during his absolute rule, and to be prosecuted to death by some of the same men whom he had led in the Commons in 1628. But at the time of the change no one could have foreseen this. He had a peerage; he was back in favour and might expect — at long last — that some important position would be conferred on him. But he was not yet even a member of the Privy Council, and his future, though brighter, was still doubtful.

Ever since the drama of his apostasy was exploited at his trial it has become one of the myths of English history. Macaulay, in unforgettable prose, sounded it forth like a trumpet call:

He was the first Englishman to whom a peerage was a sacrament of infamy, a baptism into the communion of corruption. As he was the earliest of that hateful list, so was he also by far the greatest; eloquent, sagacious, adventurous, intrepid, ready of invention, immutable of purpose, in every talent which exalts or destroys nations pre-eminent, the lost Archangel, the Satan of the Apostasy.

It is a prosaic drop from an Archangel of the Apostasy to the 'northern lad' who had become 'baron of I know not where'. But, though the truth was less dramatic, Wentworth's move from 'country' to 'Court' in the summer of 1628 was the last and critical change in his career, and it proved to be within a surprisingly short time the gateway to power. In his own mind, at any rate, there was no dire and difficult decision and no sense of betrayal. He had the strength and the weakness of an essentially practical man, and he judged events, men and theories by their usefulness to the immediate cause of efficient government and his own advancement.

He was, for instance, as strongly prejudiced against the Roman Catholic Church and all its works as any other Protestant English gentleman of his age and was in favour of rigid application of the penal laws: but he was against a war for the Protestant Cause in Europe and in favour of the Spanish friendship for England because this seemed to him to suit English commercial interests, and so to be best for the prosperity of the nation. In the same way, he valued the 'fundamental liberties' secured by the Petition of Right because they guaranteed the property rights of the King's subjects, and he regarded security of property as a basic factor in orderly and prosperous government. He did not, in his political judgments, follow theories at the expense of facts. His ideas were not petty ideas, for they were applied to the whole field of English politics, not simply to local and personal advantages; but they were practical ideas. His vision, though not lacking in grandeur, was essentially material: he believed in sound finance, sound economic policy, and even-handed justice which would inspire confidence and so create stability. These conditions, especially sound finance, could never be achieved while King and Parliament quarrelled not only over subsidies but over the basic revenues of the Crown. In so far as he gave a theoretical covering to his practical views, he followed the Elizabethan idea of a balanced constitution. The Sovereign governed, with advice from Parliament. At best, as in the high days of Elizabeth, there was harmony between the two. That this harmony was based on Parliament's ultimate submission to the Crown in any case of dispute he did not doubt; nor did he doubt that this was rightly so. 'His experience taught him that it was far safer that the King should increase in power, than that the people should gain advantage on the King', his friend George Radcliffe wrote of him. '*That* may turn to the prejudice of some particular sufferers, *this* draws with it the ruin of the whole.' [16] It was not in Wentworth's nature to inquire how and why the Elizabethan system was breaking down, or even to examine very closely the theoretical claims of Parliament against the Crown or of the Crown against Parliament. What he saw, quite simply, was that government by both was no longer working; that the Crown, though it might be hampered by the absence of Parliamentary support, was the undoubted central and supreme authority in government, and had at its disposal the central mechanism of power: a Privy Council, secretaries, ministers, an acknowledged authority to issue proclamations, to make treaties, and in case of national emergency to defend the realm. Parliament, without the Crown, had none of these things. It was therefore obvious to him that, until the correct harmony should be restored, the Crown *must* govern, since Parliament had neither the power nor the mechanism to do so.

Such was Wentworth's candid, practical, in some ways ingenuous, approach to the struggle between King and Parliament of which he was himself to be the first victim. In the foreground of his views on English government was of course his own unshaken belief that if he, Wentworth, could but exercise his skill, the King's service would be very much improved to the satisfaction of all honest men.

While he was yet uncertain what developments might follow the prorogation of Parliament, the situation was suddenly and drastically altered. On August 23rd, 1628, the Duke of Buckingham was murdered at Portsmouth. The King endured his agonizing loss with an unnatural calm, veiling his feelings even to his nearest friends, but the murder scarred his memory for life and he never forgave his people for the heartless rejoicing with which they celebrated the death of the man he had loved so dearly.

Wentworth was about the Court in the autumn. In December, less than five months after his barony, he was advanced to the rank of Viscount. The elevation was prelude to the public announcement that the King had appointed him Lord President of the North. Within two months of Buckingham's death Wentworth had attacked his old enemy and fellow peer Lord Savile, forwarding to the Council complaints which had been made against him for taking bribes. The complaints were well-founded and Savile, who no longer had Buckingham's powerful hand to keep him in office, was dismissed from his place as Vice-President. The aged and no less vulnerable Lord Scrope had been dependent on the good-will of Savile and the support of the Duke; he too was now removed. [17] Over the prostrate rivals whom he had discomfited, Wentworth marched on to advancement, marched on, as some thought, too relentlessly. His gentle and cautious friend, Wandesford, though pleased at his appointment, was dismayed at the immediacy with which he assumed his new functions. [18]

The national impact of his abandonment of the 'country' for the 'Court', of Parliament for the King, was not yet apparent. But his sudden leap to power in the North was bound to cause resentment with the followers of Savile, and some bewilderment among those of his own supporters who had sent him to Parliament in the spring of that same year as an opponent of the Court, a refuser of the Forced Loan, and a champion of the property rights of the gentry against the Crown. The zigzag career of the new Viscount Wentworth in the last nine months needed some explanation.

On December 30th, 1628, in the very month of Lord Scrope's removal, Wentworth made his opening speech as Lord President of the North. He did not precisely offer an explanation, though he indicated that there had been a very considerable change in his fortunes, if not in his outlook; he expressed his gratitude to the gentry of Yorkshire for their past support, and to the King for his present favour. Was there anything incompatible between these two? If so, Wentworth refused to admit it. What he uttered on this occasion was an eloquent tribute to the good judgment of his supporters in the North and to the benevolence of the King: followed by an impressive exposition of his political belief, and his sense of obligation both to King and people.

'I must set forth myself before you this day for the most obliged man in the world; an evident, a manifest truth. My testimonies are your own great trusts.... When I was as infection to others, you vouchsafed then again to take me into your bosoms. What confidence greater: Or what affection warmer? ...

'But cast the free bounties of my gracious Master into the other scale; there weigh me — within the space of one year, a bird, a wandering bird cast out of the nest, a prisoner, — planted here again in my own soil amongst the companions of my youth; my house honoured; myself entrusted with the rich dispensation of a sovereign goodness.... Can you show me so sudden, so strange variety in a private fortune? Tell me, was there ever such overmeasure? The like credit given to so weak a debtor? Baulked indeed before I begin, owing more to both King and people than I shall ever be able to repay to either. Yet, to the joint individual well-being of sovereignty and subjection do I here vow all my cares and diligences through the whole course of this my ministry. I confess I am not ignorant how some distempered minds have of late very far endeavoured to divide the considerations of the two, as if their ends were distinct, not the same — nay in opposition; a monstrous, a prodigious birth of a licentious conception, for so we should become all head or all members.... Princes

73

are to be indulgent nursing fathers to their people, their modest liberties, their sober rights ought to be precious in their eyes, the branches of their government be for shadow, for habitation, the comfort of life.... Subjects, on the other side, ought with solicitous eyes of jealousy, to watch over the prerogatives of a Crown. The authority of a King is the keystone which closeth up the arch of order and government which contains each part in due relation to the whole, and which once shaken, infirm'd all the frame falls together in a confused heap of foundation and battlement, of strength and beauty.... Verily these are those mutual intelligences of love and protection descending, of obedience and loyalty ascending, which should pass ... between a King and his people. Their faithful servants must look equally on both, weave, twist these two together in all their counsels; study, labour, to preserve each without diminishing or enlarging either, and by running in the worn, wonted channels, treading the ancient bounds, cut off early all disputes from betwixt them. For whatever he be which ravels forth into questions the right of a King and of a people, shall never be able to wrap them up again into the comeliness and order he found them.'

He spoke further of his own responsibilities to his master and the people, and adjured the gentlemen of Yorkshire to help him in his services both to them and to the King. 'This is my greatest ambition,' he said,

'above any earthly thing to serve his Majesty and you acceptably and fruitfully. I challenge your best help then, I require it of you; you will not as friends, you may not as Christians, you cannot as lovers of your country deny it me.'

He told them it was his desire to 'shelter the poor and innocent from the proud and insolent', and asked them 'to lay aside ... private respects, to join hands and hearts, that we may go on cheerfully as one man in the service of the public.' His own life, he assured them, was consecrated to that end.

'I do here offer myself an instrument for good in every man's hand, he that thus useth me most hath the most of my heart, even to the meanest man within the whole jurisdiction.' [19]

NOTES

[1] See Hulme, *Sir John Eliot*, pp. 184-5, for a discussion of the evidence for these meetings; also Gardiner, VI, p. 226. Wentworth, some years later in a letter to Laud, denied that he had ever taken part in such preliminary planning; but it is hard to believe this.

[2] *Lords Journals*, III, p. 687.

[3] Rushworth, *Historical Collections*, I, pp. 499 ff.

[4] The evidence on the debates in the 1628 Parliament is very confused. I have followed the reconstruction made, by comparison of the six manuscript diaries which have survived, by Professor Harold Hulme in the relative chapters of his life of Sir John Eliot. Gardiner appears to have been mistaken on a number of points, but it is by no means easy to assess the exact bearing of the debates from existing accounts.

[5] Strafford MSS, XXI, No. 47, Wentworth to Stanhope, 6th April 1628.

[6] This version of Wentworth's speech in Committee on May 2nd is in Strafford MSS, XXI, No. 48; the quotations from the King's speech are also from a version evidently used by Wentworth in this Parliament and now in Strafford MSS, XXV.

[7] Strafford MSS, XXI, No. 210.

[8] See Hulme, pp. 233-4.

[9] Wentworth's postscript to his speech in Strafford MSS, XXI, No. 210.

[10] Hacket, *Scrinia Reserata*, II, p. 82.

[11] Kearney, p. 28.

[12] H.M.C., IV, p. 90; *Fairfax Correspondence*, I, p. 128.

[13] Eliot, *Negotium Posterorum*, I, p. 104.

[14] Welwood, p. 47.

[15] Collins, *Historical Collections*, p. 95; correspondence with his Holles brothers-in-law ceases in the Strafford MSS after 1628.

[16] Knowler, II, p. 434.

[17] Reid, p. 403.

[18] Knowler, I, p. 49.

[19] A contemporary copy of this speech is in the Bodleian Library, Tanner MSS, LXXII, folios 300-3; it was printed in the *Academy*, June 1875.

PART TWO

JANUARY 1629–AUGUST 1639

I looked upon my lord of Strafford as a gentleman whose great abilities might make a monarch rather afraid than ashamed to employ him in the greatest affairs of State.

EIKON BASILIKE

—◦❧ ❧◦❧◦❧❧◦❧◦❧ ❧◦—

CHAPTER ONE

VISCOUNT WENTWORTH

From the prince, as from a perpetual well spring, cometh among the
people the flood of all that is good and evil.

SIR THOMAS MORE, *Utopia*

ENTWORTH took his seat in the House of Lords when
Parliament met for its second session on January 20th,
1629. [1] Few of his colleagues believed the meeting would
end more profitably than its predecessors. Although the murder of
Buckingham had removed the chief grievance of the Commons,
they were quick to find another, and now chiefly concerned
themselves with their fears and doubts about the King's attitude
to religion.

English Protestant gentry with a Puritan bias feared the
ritualism favoured by Bishop Laud because it seemed to them
Popish; they also associated it with an attitude of religious
reverence for the Divinely Appointed King which they thought
politically undesirable. Archbishop Abbot had been suspended
from his functions because he would not license for general
publication a sermon on this question which had greatly pleased
the King. [2] Laud was now admittedly the dominant power in
the Church, and the King had shown his indifference to criticism
from the Commons by elevating to the Bishopric of Chichester
Richard Montagu, whose writings had been the object of persistent
attack from Parliament.

Wentworth, whose own religious views were Puritan, had come
to feel that unity between Church and State was more important
than doctrine. He had said in his speech at York that there should
be 'a close conjunction with the reverend clergy, that they to us,
we to them, may as twins administer help to each other'. [3] He
was therefore entirely out of sympathy with Eliot and the other
leaders of the Commons who now refused to confirm the King's
traditional revenues by passing the bill for Tonnage and Poundage
until he modified his religious policy. The King peremptorily

ordered them to confine themselves to matters they understood; they defied him, and he sent down to the Speaker on March 2nd an order to prorogue the House. The Commons had suspected something, and when the Speaker attempted to rise and dismiss them Denzil Holles threw himself upon him, swearing 'by God's wounds' he should sit as long as the House pleased. A series of resolutions against the royal Church policy were tumultuously carried, and on the following day the King dissolved Parliament by proclamation.

Little good the violence of Holles and his friends had done to their cause. Charles arrested Sir John Eliot, Holles and some others. They showed neither regret nor shame. Eliot refused to answer for any of his alleged offences. 'Being but a private man, he would not trouble himself to remember what he had either spoken or done as a public man', he said; he was committed to the Tower, where three years later he died.

Holles was less haughty and desired 'he might rather be the subject of his Majesty's mercy than of his power.' 'You mean rather of his Majesty's mercy than of justice,' one of the Councillors reproved him. 'I say of his Majesty's power, my Lord,' answered Holles, and he followed Eliot to prison. [4] Later, he made a modified peace with the Crown. Others who had been arrested were treated leniently or allowed out on bail; but two, Benjamin Valentine and William Strode, remained prisoners for the next ten years. All told, it was an inauspicious beginning for the King's attempt to rule without Parliament.

During the summer of 1629 Wentworth seems to have been much in the North attending to his duties as Lord President. The old feud with Savile was not quite ended, and his defeated rival still from time to time made trouble for him. He opposed him over the complicated question of the drainage of Hatfield Chase. Cornelius Vermuyden, the famous Dutch engineer, had undertaken to reclaim the land of this marshy region, with the help of a number of 'adventurers' or shareholders. Their reward was to be the greater part of the drained land.

Vermuyden and his work people had not been prepared for the resistance they were to meet with among the inhabitants of the region who feared that their time-honoured rights to what had once been common land would be disregarded. The works, moreover, interfered with their immediate livelihood and filled the district with foreign workmen whom the inhabitants deeply resented, a resentment shared by some of the gentry; Vermuyden and his employees, afraid of the sullen hostility of the fenmen, took to going armed, and a brawl broke out in which one of the fenmen was killed. [5] As Savile was one of Vermuyden's supporters, his opponents appealed to Wentworth, who, even before he became Lord President, took up their cause and carried their complaints to Court. But Vermuyden had won the favour of the King for his drainage projects which were soon to be extended yet further. All Wentworth seems to have got for his pains was a public rebuke from Charles for interfering. [6] The Vermuyden party were mistaken if they thought this would deter Wentworth. He continued to support the fenmen against the intruders, and when a few months later, as Lord President, he was required to deal with further disturbances reported by Vermuyden, he answered that there had been no disturbance within his jurisdiction, implying that Vermuyden was a liar. [7] This was not the last that would be heard of Hatfield Chase; Wentworth would stick doggedly to the rights of the fenmen until King and Council came round to his side.

These developments lay in the future. In the summer of 1629 Wentworth was steadily rising in favour at Court. It was rumoured in London that he would replace Weston as Treasurer; this persistent whisper during the next years was based on Wentworth's known skill and interest in money matters, and it did not endear him to Weston. In August, Francis Cottington, the gay and talkative Chancellor of the Exchequer, told him that the King seemed to be wooing him almost as a mistress: 'you must be cherished and courted by none but himself.' [8] But Cottington was given to easy-tongued flattering exaggerations: he liked to laugh and to please. It was not until November 1629, fully eight months after the dissolution of Parliament, that Wentworth was at last appointed a member of the King's Council and so secured a foothold in the central government.

The King elevated him in gratitude for bringing to his notice a dangerous paper which was being irresponsibly circulated. This was nothing less than a scheme by which the King could bridle Parliament and hold his people in effective subjection by establishing

E

garrisons at key-points, to be manned by mercenary soldiers. With Parliament recently dissolved and several of its members in prison, the chances that such a plan would be taken for genuine and would stimulate bitter feelings against the King were not to be disregarded. Wentworth may have thought that it was being circulated by those who wished ill to the royal government. He must certainly have known that Lord Clare, his father-in-law, was one of those who had read the paper, and with his usual lack of personal forethought he had not considered the possible consequences to him of being implicated in the matter.

The incident turned out to be a mare's nest. The scheme had been put before King James I in 1614 by Sir Robert Dudley, then an exile in Florence. Dudley, who was prone to wild schemes, had lived abroad too long to have any coherent idea of English politics or possibilities; he had dashed off his crack-brained plea when he heard of King James's disagreement with the Parliament of that year. King James set it aside as absurd, and the document somehow found its way to the library of that indefatigable accumulator of manuscripts Sir Robert Cotton. Here, fifteen years later, a faithless secretary found it, and seeing its topical value, made and distributed a number of copies. At the investigation no one concerned appears to have had any deliberately ill intent, and proceedings against them were eventually stopped by the King in honour of the happy birth of his eldest son. [9] This did not wipe out the effects of the business. Lord Clare was never again restored to favour at Court and can hardly have failed to resent his son-in-law's part in his disgrace.

Wentworth had not yet achieved the pinnacle of his ambition, but he was well on the way to it. As Lord President of the North he exercised great power since he was the King's deputy in a third part of the Kingdom. But he was no more than a provincial magnate, the governor of a region, with no say in the central government. Once he was raised to the Council, he would have opportunities, if he could use them, of gaining the ear of the King and perhaps, in time, becoming one of the inner group of his personal advisers. In those early days, the difficulties which faced the King, governing now without the support and advice of Parliament, were not underestimated by Wentworth. But the opportunities seemed to him greater; indeed they probably seemed to him greater than they were. Frustration and disillusion were to come later. In those early years he seems to have seen, with luminous clarity, how the Crown could be made great and the Kingdom happy by the increasing, and increasingly efficient, exercise of the central authority. More clearly than the King, more clearly than most of his colleagues at the Council table, he saw what they ought to do and what, with energy and purpose, they could do for 'the joint individual well-being of sovereignty and subjection'.

His authoritarian nature and his past political experience made him agree with the King's decision to dispense with Parliament for a time, but unlike the King he saw the dangers ahead. He believed that the country had outgrown the taut rule of precedent and that only new cures would meet new diseases; for the next ten years the monarchy must assert its authority, and he staked his life that it would succeed. But it was time for action not theories, 'an age', he himself declared, 'wherein I wish with all my heart men knew less and practised more.' [10] The dissolution of Parliament could not in itself put an end to criticism of the Crown, nor could it be silenced by sending Sir John Eliot to the Tower. Wentworth despised the people's intelligence but he cared for their welfare; he believed in the power of the prerogative because of the disorders and delays he had seen in the last years. The sovereign alone could, by the just use of his power, break the deadlock which, since the Parliament of 1614, had crippled the government of England.

Wentworth has been called an Elizabethan, and certainly his belief in the authority of the sovereign owed something to the position which the Tudors had built up. But he was a practical man, alive to the problems of a situation that had never arisen under the Tudors. He had travelled in France and had been influenced, as many Englishmen were, by reading about the French religious wars and the disaster and anarchy that can ensue from a weak central authority. From his knowledge, no less than from his experience in Yorkshire and at Westminster, he had learnt to value highly the unity and security that are created by a strong central authority, a sovereign who can both answer for and command an obedient nation. '*Stare super vias antiquas*' was a frequent motto of his, but he used the ancient ways as channels for new experiments. The ancient ways were not static, they led somewhere. There was the whole question: could they lead to a new monarchy fit for a new age? To Wentworth's thinking, they could.

He did not share the prejudice of the King against Parliaments in general; he objected only to certain Parliaments in particular. He neither forgot that he had been a member of the Lower House nor rejected the views he had then held. It would have been better for everyone had King and Commons come to an agreement in 1628; this was a self-evident truth that to the hour of his death he never denied. [11] But the behaviour of the last Parliament had retarded this solution indefinitely; in the light of later history one may wonder if such an agreement would in any circumstances have been possible. Wentworth could not read the future. He saw the period of rule without Parliament as a transitional stage forced on the King by the action of the Commons, and he believed if the King handled his opportunities rightly he could establish himself in his people's affections by just government, until such time as the grievances of his first years were forgotten and a docile Parliament, reconciled to his rule, could be called again. 'Happy it were if we might see [a Parliament] in England', he once wrote,

> everything in his season; but in some cases, it is as necessary there be a time to forget, as in others to learn, and howbeit the peccant humour be not yet wholly purged forth, yet do I conceive it in the way, and that once rightly corrected and prepared, we may hope for a Parliament of a sound constitution indeed, but this must be a work of time ... and this time it becomes us all to pray for and wait for, and, when God sends it to make the right use of it. [12]

In his theory, Parliament formed an essential part of the State. The Crown should use it to discover the needs of the country. He distinguished between legitimate needs and unjust demands and he objected to the Parliaments in which he had sat on the grounds that they had sacrificed the one to the other. They had thrown away their opportunities of offering practical advice in a mistaken attempt to gain control of religious and foreign policy. In his speeches and letters Wentworth loved to contrast true liberty with mere licence, and he firmly believed that he could protect the former from the encroachments of the latter. He believed in a state built up broadly on the welfare of the majority. Active obstruction or the misuse of power and authority was the kind of conduct that he considered worthy of persecution, and he believed that punishment was to be used sparingly but should be inescapable and drastic when it was deserved. Furthermore he actively preferred that the victims should come from the higher ranks of society, partly because they had not the excuse of ignorance, and partly because punishment inflicted on 'men of quality' seemed to give positive proof that the Crown was no respecter of persons, but also, reasonably enough, because men of rank were precisely those on whom responsibility for government devolved, and their insubordination or abuse of office could and did undermine the authority of the sovereign in whose name they served. This peculiarity of Wentworth, his persistent attacks on men in the highest places, was to be a cause of recurring embarrassment to a King who would have preferred a quieter life, and a Court many of whose members were themselves vulnerable.

The crux of the political question was for Wentworth a matter of definition: where did liberty end and licence begin? He had his own ideas on the subject: liberty ended with reasoned and respectful argument, and licence began with obstructive protest. He failed to realize that other men's ideas on these matters might legitimately be different from his own.

The political question was theoretical only. The administrative question was the central problem which faced the royal government. The King had no Civil Service on which he could rely to carry out his will. The efficiency of the administration depended, at the centre, on the energy of the various officials in the relatively small and highly confused secretarial and revenue offices of the Crown; it depended at the perimeter on the co-operation of Justices of the Peace, of county, borough and parish officials. At the centre, the King's servants lived largely on fees and perquisites; in the countryside the Justices were not paid at all.

Wentworth seems to have believed that the gentry, whose task it was to carry out the King's decrees in the countryside, would be willing to co-operate when they were convinced of the good order and prosperity ensured them by the royal government. He never seems to have realized how many of them had become, during the last twenty years, resentful of the policies of the Crown and aware of the curbing power that they could exercise by simply doing nothing. He also failed to realize that neither at the centre of the government nor in its outworks were there enough men ready or able to put public duties before private ease and private interest. Their indolence astonished him. He was deeply shocked when his friend Sir Gervase Clifton wished to resign an official post which he held. 'When you think better of it,' he wrote, 'less inwards upon your own ease, more outward upon the duties we owe the public, I assure myself you will not desire it.' [13]

There were worse things than indolence. The sale of offices and the sale of reversions of offices hampered the choice and appointment of the right men in the right places. Greed for gain or greed for power led to the accumulation of posts in a single hand. The burden of work that fell on the central administration, such as it was, was already too heavy and was made heavier by the intrigues, the manoeuvring, the jockeying for position, which took up much of the time of officials. A constructive and thorough reorganization at the centre, ensuring to the King's servants salaries which would put them above the temptation of making money on the side, and eliminate the wasteful system of payment by fees and perquisites, would have done much to increase the efficiency and thus the strength of the central government. From time to time Wentworth had flashes of insight in this matter; in his correspondence he can be found condemning pluralism or advocating higher salaries, but he never seems to have contemplated or worked consistently towards any far-reaching changes. All he seems to have meant by the 'Thorough' reform which he held up as an ideal was a higher standard of loyalty, responsibility and hard work among those who served the Crown.

His failure to see the necessity for radical changes is the more remarkable because he had lived long enough in the jungle of West Riding local politics to know very well that every larger issue was subordinated to regional interests and to personal rivalries, and that local justice, administration and finance were all more or less at the mercy of the ingenious depredations of the unscrupulous and the carelessness of the lazy. The same weaknesses also beset the central administration. Moreover, though his career had shown, and was to show still more, that he could think and act on very much larger principles, he was not himself above furthering his own interests and indulging on occasion in some very dubious practices. He knew, inside and out, the weaknesses of the administration. Yet he continued to believe that improvement and achievement were possible.

He was not, of course, absolutely wrong: some improvements were possible and some were achieved. But it never seems to have occurred to him that, before the King could make his government effective and permanent, he needed servants dependent only on himself. Such a reform, such a centralization as was being quietly carried forward in France by Cardinal Richelieu, was never envisaged by Wentworth. His solution to problems of administration, time and time again in the next ten years, was to perform essential tasks himself, or to appoint one of his tried and trusted friends. At best there was heroic energy in this method; at worst there was encouragement to pluralism and favouritism; there was not even the beginning of a permanent solution. [14]

The King under whose control he had to work had a complex and difficult character that Wentworth never wholly understood. He was a man in whom religious and political doctrines counted far more than spontaneous human emotions. Delicate and backward as a child, small and unimpressive as a man, his disabilities had made him shy of contact with the world and he fulfilled the exacting public duties of his office only by subjecting himself to a rigorous discipline of self-control. He was slow in thought and speech but not stupid, although his lack of confidence in his own judgment could make him seem so. Like his father he was subject to unreasoning affections and dislikes, and although he never allowed them to dominate his policy as they had done his father's he allowed them to influence his decisions. Afraid of his own judgment he gave in easily to the persuasions of his friends and let himself be swayed always by those with whom he was in sympathetic contact at the actual moment.

Charles loved beauty in his surroundings and in his friends. Dearest of his attendants were the fair, soft-spoken Duke of Lennox with his gentle manners and the vivid, impetuous Hamilton. He liked to discourse gravely of learning and the fine arts, to move in a well-regulated, aesthetically satisfying world disturbed by no jarring interruption. In the cultured harmony of the circle that

Charles loved to collect about him, Wentworth could never be anything but an intruder. Certainly he was no worse educated than his fellows and could be as entertaining a talker in society as the best of them, but his manners were brisk and too often haughty, he had no outward charm, and he was far too masterful to please the King. Besides, Charles had a long memory for his enemies and there were incidents in Wentworth's past career that he taught himself to ignore but did not forget.

Wentworth's own feeling towards his master remains a mystery. He schooled himself to say nothing unguarded and Radcliffe averred that he had a deep personal attachment to him. It is not impossible that there was on Wentworth's side a certain half-sentimental tenderness towards the young King whom he had watched almost from boyhood, and the personal feeling was mingled with a symbolic reverence for his position. Whatever the extent of Wentworth's affection it was not reciprocated. Charles had a keen eye for his minister's faults; he knew him to be over-confident, impatient and proud and he did not spare to tell him so. The dregs of his old resentment remained always in the King's mind to inhibit his confidence in his best minister and most faithful servant.

There was as much to disquiet Wentworth as to cheer him in the situation both at Court and in the country in 1629. The judges and the lawyers almost unanimously declared themselves in favour of the King's decision temporarily to dispense with Parliament; and England at large had a healthy respect for legal opinion. But changes had taken place at Court since the death of Buckingham which did not seem likely to produce unity of interest in the royal counsels.

King Charles was easily governed by others, but he was no mere cipher and he chose himself to whom he would yield. To the general astonishment it was the Queen who slipped into the favourite's place. Already in 1629 her power was so much spoken of that Charles, always jealous lest any should think him weak, was heard to say to her sadly, 'I wish that we could always be together, and that you could accompany me to the Council; but what would these people say if a woman were to busy herself with matters of government?' [15]

The shy girl of 1625 had grown in four years into a gracious woman. She had learnt English prettily, and without losing her youthful freshness she had gained assurance. A few months after the murder of Buckingham it became known that she was at last with child; in the following year she was delivered of an infant son that died within the hour. Drawn together by a common grief, the King and Queen became inseparable, and on May 29th, 1630, she bore him a second and this time a healthy son. Charles might have taken note that among his Puritan subjects the rejoicings were hollow; they had counted on the barrenness of the Papist and had hoped the succession would pass to one of the many sons of the King's Protestant sister, the Queen of Bohemia. [16]

Henrietta Maria in character and outlook was not unlike the favourite she succeeded. Like Buckingham she alternately dazzled and consoled her lover, varying her determination with an exquisite playfulness. Like Buckingham she was compassionate and of boundless charity, with the same feckless good nature. It was with Henrietta Maria as with Buckingham, all good-nature, passion and impulse. Only she had behind her something more than Buckingham, a great tradition of government and a belief in the sanctity of Kingship and the greatness of her family. There would be none of Buckingham's puzzled mismanagement of power with this new favourite; she was a Bourbon and a Medici, a Navarrese and an Italian, with all the determination that Buckingham, of the easygoing midland stock, had lacked.

Nevertheless she did not govern the King as completely as her predecessor, for her religion always separated them and he made a sustained effort to think and rule for himself. Only her influence was paramount and she gathered about her a faction among the King's counsellors so that none of his advisers could afford to disregard her.

As a newcomer to the Council, Wentworth cannot at first have exercised very much influence. The King's most important advisers at this time were the Bishop of London, William Laud, the Treasurer Weston, and Sir Francis Cottington, the Chancellor of the Exchequer. Weston and Cottington were both advocates of the policy of friendship with Spain to which Wentworth himself adhered, and were therefore superficially friendly to him. But Weston was a jealous and difficult man who seems fairly early to have suspected Wentworth of wanting to succeed him, and they were on somewhat uneasy terms thereafter. Cottington was amiable and gay, and quickly won the approval of Wentworth's young wife, who was delighted by his apt sayings and shrewd wit. She persuaded her husband to cultivate his friendship, advice which he never regretted, for though Cottington was not always to be trusted, he remained, within the limits of his volatile nature and so far as it suited his own purposes, a friend to Wentworth throughout his career.

Arundel, the Earl Marshall, also at this time belonged to the group of Councillors who strongly supported peace and alliance with Spain, but his chief interests lay elsewhere, in the patronage of artists and in collecting antique marbles and other rarities. His tastes were not Wentworth's; they had little in common and within a few years were to quarrel irrevocably. A more friendly member of the Council was the Lord Keeper, Coventry, an amiable, conscientious and learned man, admiringly fond of the much younger Wentworth, to whose nephew, Sir William Savile, he married his daughter.

Among Wentworth's other friends at Court were two northerners, the Earl of Northumberland and the Earl of Newcastle. Northumberland was a man of considerable character and talent, but wary and careful of committing himself too far. Newcastle was a versatile cavalier, a dilettante of the arts, well-pleased with his own gifts. Both had wide territorial power in the North.

By far the most influential Councillor with the King was the Bishop of London. He was nearly twenty years older than Wentworth and there was no particular reason for sympathy between them, nor, for some months, did they discover how much they had in common. In June 1630 the Council passed sentence on a singularly troublesome Presbyterian minister, Alexander Leighton, who after leaving Scotland, working as a doctor in London and practising his ministry again in Utrecht till his congregation turned him out, had issued a furious attack on bishops called *Sion's Plea against Prelacy*. It was a ferocious but rather striking work, in which, while professing loyalty to the King, Leighton called the Queen a 'daughter of Heth' and used very injurious terms of Buckingham. He received a sentence of staggering severity from the Council, the first — and probably the worst — of the half-dozen such sentences which in the next ten years were to give the King's government its reputation for barbarity. He was to be pilloried, whipped, branded, and to lose his ears, before being consigned to prison for life.

Years later, when he had been released by Parliament and hailed as a martyr to their cause, he wrote an account of his sufferings in which he said that after sitting in judgment on him, the diabolical Wentworth had entered into an unholy compact with Bishop Laud: 'they struck a league, like moon and sun, to govern day and night, religion and state.' [17]

The statement is unlikely to reflect much more than a general impression that Laud and Wentworth began to work systematically together shortly after the Leighton judgment. Whether there was any connection between their growing amity and Leighton's case is at most doubtful. Both had been present at the sentence. Laud, as might be expected, had spoken at great length and with deep indignation against the accused. There is no evidence of what Wentworth said except Leighton's statement that he 'used many violent and virulent expressions'. He probably did: Leighton's book would be of a kind to arouse his anger, his contempt and his prejudice.

The case was however tried in June 1630, and not for another six months is there any entry in Laud's diary to imply close association with Wentworth. Then, on January 21st, 1631, occurs the entry 'The Lord Wentworth, Lord President of the North and I etc.... in my little chamber at London House.' [18] The cryptic entry probably stood for a conversation too long and too significant to summarize, if not precisely the sinister league that Alexander Leighton imagined. The two men must, in the long interview — sought, one imagines, by Wentworth in the first place — have laid the foundations of their mutual understanding. From this time on there was a deep and inspiring confidence between them. Laud had found in Wentworth the man whose zeal and energy would match in secular politics his own zeal and energy in the care of the Church. It was a friendship based on strong temperamental similarity, the impatient desire for action, the need to be for ever up and doing which they shared, and in which none of their colleagues were their equals.

William Laud came from stock very different from Wentworth. He was a Berkshire man, the son of a draper in Reading, where he had received a sound education at the Grammar School. At Oxford his insatiable thirst for learning had soon made him known;

he had been patronized by the Earl of Devonshire, whose marriage with Penelope Devereux the divorced wife of Lord Rich he had solemnized: the sin lay always heavy on his conscience. Buckingham had discovered him next, and through this patronage he had been raised to the see of St David's, then to Bath and Wells, lastly to London. King James had agreed to his elevation with a bad grace, and when approached on the subject had frankly admitted his reasons. 'The plain truth is,' he said, 'I keep Laud back from all places of rule and authority, because I find he hath a restless spirit, and cannot see when matters are well but loves to toss and change, and to bring things to a pitch of reformation floating in his own brain, which may endanger the steadfastness of that which is in good pass, God be praised.' [19]

King James was wiser than his son; his death removed the chief obstacle in Laud's path.

In person Laud was 'a little, low red-faced man'. His features were undistinguished but for the high forehead and piercing, alert eyes. Like Wentworth, he was a natural administrator, a highly practical man with unusual gifts for organization and confidence in his own powers of management. But with this he also had the persistence and accuracy of the scholar and a vision which enabled him to work for the future. He was one of the finest Hebrew scholars of his time, and as he rose in worldly power he financed the search for important manuscripts in the darkened realms of the Turk. It is to him and to his well-chosen emissary Edward Pocock that the Bodleian Library owes some of its most notable treasures.

With all his learning and power Laud remained at heart a very simple man: the draper's son from Reading with his homely wit, conventional reverence for the great, and ingenuous superstitions. He set down in his diary the silliest dreams as though they had some profound significance, and he laughed with his friends over remarkably childish jokes. In this too he had a temperamental affinity with Wentworth. In so far as either of these very earnest men can be said to have had a sense of humour, they had the same one. Their letters, as they grew to know each other well, are full of schoolboy nicknames for their fellow councillors and chuckling, laboured parentheses, a kind of epistolary digging of each other in the ribs.

Mutual respect between these two developed rapidly into a friendship in which their very considerable difference in age, rank and education was forgotten. 'I have wondered many times to observe', wrote Wentworth, 'how universally you and I agree in our judgments.' Their agreement in temperament, in methods and in motives made it possible for them to jest over the difference in their religious background, for Wentworth was deeply imbued with Calvinist Protestantism; he believed as the Puritans did in a strongly personal relationship with God, he had no great need for or belief in ritual, and his manuals of devotion were mostly those used by the French Calvinists. He seems even to have had some sympathy with the orderly organizations of the Calvinist churches abroad, which would indeed be very appealing to one so preoccupied as he was with the efficient regulation of all things. 'I see the errors of your breeding will stick by you', Laud once scolded him. 'Pastors and Elders and all will come in if I let you alone.... Good Lord! How ignorant you can be when you list.' [20]

William Laud regarded these particular manifestations of Calvinism as inimical to the English Church, and believed intensely in the value of universally practised rituals, ceremonies and forms of prayer to bring the common people together in an orderly form of worship that would give beauty and meaning to their lives. Wentworth must have been drawn to Laud's religious policy not so much because he felt himself in sympathy with its spiritual qualities as because he saw in it a powerful support for his ideas of order in the secular sphere. It was not because the Arminian clergy taught the value of ritual that Wentworth came to support them but because they preached obedience to the King. As for the ceremonial side of worship by which Laud set so much store, he was prepared to believe in its value though he never seems to have regarded it as more than an external decoration without inward significance. Ceremonies were to him 'things purely and simply indifferent'. He neither liked nor disliked them, but if higher authority imposed them he assumed that no intelligent Christian need have any reason to object. It throws some light on the character of these two men, who were to be coupled in power and later in execration, that there was between them a real difference of attitude on this question, and that it never disturbed their profound and mutual understanding. Ultimately Wentworth's deep-rooted Calvinism made him tractable and docile to the spiritual guide of his choice, and much as Laud may have disliked the word, Wentworth certainly looked upon him not only as a friend but also, respectfully, as his pastor.

The opening years of the personal rule of King Charles were remarkable for an intermittent but noticeable effort on the part of the central government to improve the administration of the laws dealing with poverty and distress, and to inaugurate by proclamation measures tending towards better hygiene and social welfare. A body of Commissioners was appointed to see that the provisions of the Poor Law were carried out. Another Commission was set up to inquire into ways of relieving debtors. Yet another was to work out a system by which able-bodied felons, condemned for crimes less heinous than murder, could be reprieved to do the King's service abroad, presumably in the navy or merchant shipping. A proclamation was issued against subdividing houses into tenements and running up ramshackle buildings in the suburbs of London, and this primarily hygienic measure to prevent the creation of slums was paralleled by plans, more ambitious than practical, for beautifying the city by restoring the crumbling fabric of St Paul's and, possibly, replacing the congested and old-fashioned London Bridge by a more splendid structure modelled on the Ponte Sant' Angelo in Rome. Finally there was the famous and unpopular order to the gentry to go home and look after their estates, their tenants and their country duties instead of wasting their rents by high living in London. [21]

Of all these measures, by far the most elaborate was the appointment of the Poor Law Commissioners in January 1631. They were a group of Privy Councillors, including Wentworth, evidently chosen so that they could cover between them, by the diffusion of their lands or influence, the entire country. Under their guidance, further orders were issued commanding Justices of the Peace to meet regularly once a month to make sure that parish officials were carrying out their duties. The Justices, in turn, were to report every quarter to the sheriffs of counties, who were to report to the judges on circuit. Through the judges, therefore, the central government would be kept informed of the relative efficiency and docility of the various regions. Justices could thus be checked for negligence if it occurred, and they in turn would keep a sharper eye on the negligence of parish officials.

Furthermore, the lords of manors were to make sure that the manorial courts met twice yearly, that each landlord relieved the poor or found work for the lazy among his own tenantry, and that they or their stewards saw to it that the time-honoured laws about the conditions and wages of labourers, about apprenticing children, about weights, measures, and the quality of bread and ale, were all enforced.

These measures of King Charles's Council brought no innovations, but they were a significant attempt on the part of the central government to see that the numerous measures, which from the Middle Ages to the time of Queen Elizabeth had been agreed on in Parliament, should be generally respected, instead of being left to chance and the good or ill will of Justices of the Peace, landowners and parish constables.

The laws were, by intention, benevolent. They aimed at securing a minimum of justice for the poor, reasonable security in their work, reasonable prices for their food, some training for their children; they aimed at protecting them from bad bread, watery beer, short weight, and other kinds of cheating or exploitation. They also aimed at keeping everyone, rich or poor, master or servant, in his or her fixed position in society. Evolved in a predominantly medieval society, they had tended to fall into disuse or to be deliberately disregarded, as the medieval pattern of life changed. The Elizabethan statute of apprentices and the Elizabethan Poor Law had been passed to deal with the great gaps and gashes made in the closely integrated medieval community by the upheavals of the sixteenth century — somehow to knit society together again on a basis of known mutual obligations, of the master's responsibility for his servants, the manor for its tenants and the parish for its members.

But little provision was really made for the rapid urban and commercial developments of the new age, for the unnerving fluctuations of prosperity and depression that were beginning to arise because of the expansion of overseas trade, the development of new industries and the repercussions of foreign wars or of the economic policies of expanding, rival nations.

Something can be said for the good will of the government of King Charles I, but its members had little idea beyond that of maintaining and re-enforcing regulations made to suit a different and much less fluid state of economic development. This is evident from their attitude to the problems created by chronic local depressions or by shifts in the demand for labour. So far from making it easy for the unemployed to move about in search of work, the whole tendency of the system was to maintain the ancient units intact and to keep towns, villages, manors and parishes as separate groups each looking after itself. The principal fear of the government was that too many of the poor might fall outside the system devised to control and protect them: they might drift away from their masters or their parishes, they might fail to learn a craft, or cease to practise it, or join, or even be born, into the increasing band of lawless, masterless wanderers, the 'rogues and vagabonds' who infested the roads or congregated in the slums of London.

They do not seem to have grasped that the rigidity of their laws often forced the unemployed craftsman who had taken to the roads in a genuine search for work to become a vagabond against his will. There were undoubtedly rogues and vagabonds who were by taste and temperament nothing else, but the increase in their number, which all governments for the last hundred years had feared, and had vainly tried to reduce, was partly caused by the ineptitude of the laws which they enforced.

In this respect the government of King Charles was no exception. There had been considerable depression in the cloth trade — a Commission had been set up by King James to inquire into it — and the unemployment resulting from it had caused the usual increase in vagabondage. But the Poor Law Commissioners of 1631 concluded their, on the whole, excellent instructions for local supervision and relief by a series of orders about vagabondage which were savagely at variance with the general benevolence of their suggestions. They condemned casual charity and went so far as to recommend the punishment of those who gave succour to unlicensed beggars or allowed wandering vagrants to take shelter or sleep in their barns. If such irresponsible encouragement ceased, they argued, the roads would soon be free of this riff-raff, who were attracted to the wandering life — they ineptly added — simply because it gave them freedom from moral restraint. Of any other causes for vagabondage, apart from mere human wickedness, they seemed serenely unaware. These provisions, together with the general encouragement to informers, who would be rewarded for reporting any breaches of the law, give an unpleasant twist to the basically benevolent plans of King Charles's Poor Law Commissioners. [22]

That they were unsuccessful in curbing casual charity or in reducing vagabondage goes almost without saying. In the more constructive part of their programme they seem to have been, at least in some regions and for a little time, rather more effective. The personal government of King Charles has sometimes been over-praised on this score. The measure of actual success is hard to gauge, though he and his Council deserve credit for a genuinely benevolent intention and for an attempt, within the framework of existing laws, to care for the general welfare of the people.

The King had a high sense of duty towards his people, but there was a political side to his social policy. It was an ancient rule of monarchical government to woo the support of one section of the population as a counterpoise to the hostility of another. Medieval monarchs had sustained the merchants and the cities as a counterpoise to the nobility; so now the King sustained (or attempted to sustain) the artisan and the craftsman, the 'meaner sort', against the richer and more established sections of the population who had shown themselves hostile to his power.

It is difficult to estimate Wentworth's part in this guiding policy of the King's personal rule. He was a member of most of the special commissions. His name was soon added to that for inquiry into excessive fees which had been set up in 1627. He was on the Commissions for the Poor Law, for the reprieve of able-bodied criminals, and for the restoration of St Paul's. But the commissioners nearly always included a large number of the King's Council, so that there is no reason to conclude from the presence of his name that he had been particularly forward in urging the adoption of the measures involved. There is little evidence at this date that he carried much weight in the Council to which he had so recently been elevated. Secretary Windebanke at a later time mentioned his nervous habit, during meetings, of scrawling faces on his notes — 'Vandyking' as he gaily called it — but of his influence and opinions at this time we have little direct knowledge. [23]

He was not, however, a man to sit silent. He certainly made himself felt on the Commission for fees, where in 1630 he was enunciating the principle that officials were responsible for the excesses of their subordinates — an obvious and salutary theory for preventing extortion at the lower levels of the public service. It can be said with certainty that he wholeheartedly approved of that policy of authoritarian benevolence which in the North, as Lord President, he put energetically into effect. His correspondence a year or two later when his reputation both as executant and councillor was more firmly established hammers relentlessly the theme of good government and justice for everyone, but especially for the small man, under the unquestioned authority of the Crown. It seems unlikely that so eloquent a man as Wentworth failed to express himself on points that greatly interested him, or that so forceful a man did not influence his colleagues. The most active phase of the Council's social policy certainly seems to coincide with his appearance at the board and it is very noticeable that the Council's interest in this aspect of the King's government flagged after Wentworth had gone to Ireland in 1633. [24]

The opening years of the King's personal rule were inauspicious. The harvest of 1630 was thin, and the Council had to make provision in the traditional manner for a possible emergency. The price of corn was fixed, export was prohibited, brewing was limited, and Justices of the Peace were instructed to search out and distribute corn which was held back, to prevent engrossing of corn by the rich, and, if necessary, to insist that the poor were satisfied with corn at a fixed price before other buyers were allowed to trade in the market. [25]

Wentworth was in London during the winter of 1630-1, where, owing to the size of the town, the corn shortage was acute. Large shipments from Ireland were expected but did not arrive until the spring was well advanced. In the North the trouble was less bad; the price of wheat in south-west Yorkshire did not rise noticeably between Christmas and Lady Day. There were, in many places, good stores which could be released; Lancashire had had a good harvest and was willing to supply the neighbouring regions if necessary. The grain chiefly consumed by the poorer folk in the North was oats, so that there might be, even in a bad year, no great shortage of the more expensive wheat.

In February 1631 Wentworth was writing to his steward Richard Marris to buy and ship wheat to London. It would be consistent with his repeated asseverations about justice for the poor if it could be shown that this plan was intended merely to supply the crying needs of London. But Wentworth gave no such motive; he merely informed Marris that the price in London was very high as the Irish shipments had not come, and that it would be excellent business to buy cheap in Yorkshire and sell dear in London. It is fair to assume that he knew that the shortage in Yorkshire was not acute, but this was hardly a justification for conduct which was in clear defiance of orders issued by the Privy Council of which he was himself a member. In effect he was instructing Marris to engross as much wheat as he could; we cannot know if he was irritated or gratified to hear from his steward that the Justices of the Peace were performing their duties so strictly that the wheat had to be bought through agents and 'with very great care and privacy'. By April, Marris reported 'a great murmuring and muttering amongst the people' against engrossers, and though Wentworth does not appear to have repeated his orders after getting this letter, a few more loads of wheat were nevertheless shipped to him in early May. By this time, however, wheat from Ireland had reached London, and the price had fallen. The dearth in the city was over; 'God be praised,' wrote Wentworth to his steward, 'gains there will be none.' [26]

The final comment reflects some confusion of mind. He praised God that famine was averted and that he could therefore make no profit out of it, but earlier he had urged Marris to make every effort to help him to profit out of it. Though he may have been genuinely concerned to bring provisions to London, as well as to make money out of doing so, the fact remains that he was disobeying the authority of the King's Council, an offence which in others called down the thunderbolt of his wrath.

This was not the only time in his life that Wentworth showed, in a very marked degree, his tendency to assume that he was exempt from laws and duties which he most intensely believed in for others. If this kind of conduct were consistent throughout his career it could be said that he was not merely self-deceived but frankly hypocritical. But he did not act consistently in this way; he merely had lapses, as though there were certain areas of conduct where his theories of integrity were simply not relevant.

Within a few months of this secretive transaction, which remained discreetly buried in his private correspondence, he was behaving with courage and self-sacrifice in pursuit of his duty, and setting an example to his neighbours and colleagues as meritorious as the other, had it been known, would have been deplorable.

The occasion was the plague which in the summer of 1631 followed hard upon the dearth. Again the Privy Council issued orders; all except necessary movements about the country were forbidden; Southwark and Stourbridge fairs were cancelled; buildings were taken over for temporary pest-houses and the families of the plague-stricken isolated. Towards the end of July the infection reached southern Yorkshire and Wentworth at once hastened to York to take all the necessary measures. 'These are not things to be jested withal,' he sternly told the Lord Mayor, and went on to indicate, what the quailing civic authorities must already have known, that the Lord President was not to be jested with either. He promised them he would keep a diligent watch on their proceedings, and any negligence of the orders for providing for the sick would be rigorously dealt with by the Council. 'Wilson, the chirurgeon,' had already been found wanting and should smart for it. [27]

The plague, inevitably, reached York, but as a result of Wentworth's supervision the death roll was kept down. The afflicted and those suspected of infection were removed to the emergency pest-houses, where they were 'well provided not only for the necessities of nature, but of all such drugs and other medecines as the Physitians advise'. Wentworth himself and his family remained in York, since, apart from the vigilance which he thought necessary to maintain the medical services, he feared that the inhabitants 'would fall into affrights and confusion if we should leave them'. He appears to have had very little faith in the capacity of the Mayor to handle the crisis. [28]

The decision to stay in York with his wife and his young family cannot have been an easy one to take. Lady Wentworth was in her fifth pregnancy and had been strongly advised against the wearisome journey to the North that summer, but had insisted on following her husband. [29] The three elder children were all well and growing old enough for their father to take great delight in them, especially in the elder girl, Nan. At four years old she already gave proof of having inherited her father's managing character, and complained that the workmen engaged on building a new wing for the Presidential house did not get on with their work unless she was bustling up and down among the planks and mortar keeping them up to the mark. [30] The fourth and youngest child, a sickly little boy, died that summer; he was buried quietly at night in York Minster, so that the mourning in the Presidential household could be concealed from the townsfolk. [31]

Once all measures had been taken and the epidemic seemed to be under control, Wentworth could enjoy some respite from his anxieties; the coming winter would no doubt put an end to the infection. George Radcliffe had joined the family party in the great house at York, and in the fine autumn days Wentworth could enjoy his company and that of his wife and children. One morning he came in from the garden to speak to his wife, who was resting indoors; she rose to meet him and was making to brush off an insect that had settled on his coat when the creature spread its wings and flew suddenly in her face. She started back, tripped and fell before he could come to her help. The sudden shock brought on a premature confinement, and towards midnight on October 4th it was evident that she would not rally. Wentworth was stunned; Radcliffe went to the children's rooms and brought the eldest in his arms to his mother's bedside. She had just strength enough to give him her blessing. Before morning she died. [32]

Wentworth's courage gave way under the shock, and for several days and nights Radcliffe dared not leave him alone. He let his suffering engulf him, unresisting. He tortured himself with the recollection of her merits and his unworthiness, pouring out brokenly hour after hour the heavy burden of his heart. To what end now the accumulation of riches, the achievement of power, the service of the commonwealth, or the honour of the sovereign? Yesterday he had been hopeful and triumphant, his brows crowned with glory; today by one act of God he was old and weary, 'without anything below to trust or look to'. While the citizens in the streets hushed their voices and mourned for their beloved lady, the Lord President sat hour after hour, behind the silent doors of his great house, alone with his sorrow and his friend. [33]

NOTES

[1] *Lords Journals*, II, p. 5.

[2] C. H. Firth, *Stuart Tracts*, London, 1903, pp. 309 ff.

[3] Bodleian Library, Tanner MSS, LXXII, folio 301.

4 Crew, *Proceedings and Debates in 1629*, pp. 161 ff.

5 *C.S.P.D.*, 1628-9, p. 262.

6 Hunter, *South Yorkshire*, I, pp. 160-1; *C.S.P.D.*, 1628-9, p. 392.

7 *C.S.P.D.*, 1629-31, p. 35.

8 Knowler, I, p. 51.

9 Rushworth, I, Appendix X; *Fortescue Papers*, p. 6; Birch II, p. 37; d'Ewes, *Autobiography*, II, pp. 39-42; *State Trials*, III, p. 396; Holles, *Memorials*, pp. 107-8.

10 *C.S.P.D.*, 1629-31, p. 78.

11 Rushworth, *Trial*, p. 759.

12 Knowler, I, p. 420.

13 H.M.C. *Various*, VII, p. 400.

14 The whole question of the Civil Service under King Charles has been investigated by Dr Aylmer, *The King's Servants*, where numerous references to Wentworth establish his somewhat ambivalent attitude.

15 Gardiner, VII, p. 106.

16 W. Sanderson, *Reign of Charles I*, pp. 141 ff.

17 Leighton, *Epitome*, 1644.

18 Laud, *Works*, III, p. 213.

19 *Scrinia Reserata*, I, p. 64.

20 Knowler, I, p. 254.

21 Rymer, XIX, pp. 177-81, 194-5, 272, 374-6, 406-8.

22 The text of the Poor Law Commission is in Rymer, XIX, pp. 231-5; the text of the orders was printed in London in 1632; most of it can be found in F. M. Eden, *State of the Poor*, London, 1797, pp. 156 ff; see also W. K. Jordan, *Philanthropy in England, 1480-1660*, London, 1959, pp. 133 ff.

23 Knowler, I, p. 161.

24 Gardiner saw Wentworth's influence in this policy and his opinion has been consistently followed with enhancement by later writers. In the first version of this biography I accepted Wentworth's domination without question. Mr H. F. Kearney in his *Strafford in Ireland* perhaps goes too far in the other direction. Wentworth, he points out, was not a particularly important member of the Council, largely dominated at this time by Weston, Cottington, Arundel and Laud. G. E. Aylmer, p. 129, gives his opinions on fees.

25 Rymer, XIX, pp. 169-70, 185, 195-8, 250-1.

26 The whole story with the relevant references is given in Cooper, op. cit., pp. 234-6; the state of supplies in Yorkshire can be deduced from the documents cited in J. J. Cartwright, *Chapters in the History of Yorkshire*, pp. 319-20; see also *C.S.P.D.*, 1631-3, p. 24. On February 15th Wentworth was present in the Council when disturbances among the poor of Rutlandshire were discussed and it was agreed that 'the best means to prevent all disorders' was to 'deal effectually in causing the market to be well supplied with corn and the poor to be served at reasonable prices'. Leonard, pp. 338-9.

27 Letter from Wentworth in the *York Corporation House Book*, quoted by Lady Burghclere, I, p. 142.

28 *C.S.P.D.*, 1630-1, pp. 150-1; the letter is given *in extenso* in Cartwright, pp. 248-51.

29 Collins, *Historical Collections*, p. 95; Strafford MSS, XXI, Lord Clare to Wentworth, 22nd August 1631.

30 Knowler, I, p. 55.

31 Register of St Olaves, York, p. 90; Strafford MSS, XXI, loc. cit.

32 Knowler, II, p. 430.

33 Ibid., I, p. 60; II, p. 435; *Fairfax Correspondence*, I, pp. 237-8.

CHAPTER TWO

LORD PRESIDENT OF THE NORTH

Go it as it shall please God with me, believe me, my Lord, I will be still Thorough and Thoroughout, one and the same.
Wentworth to Laud, August 1634

WENTWORTH had shaped for himself a career in which there was little time for private sorrow, yet for some weeks he was so far broken by his grief that his friends grew anxious. Calvert besought him gently to

> remove from those parts, where so many things represent themselves unto you as to make your wound bleed afresh; and let us have you here where the gracious welcome of your master, the conversation of your friends, and variety of businesses may divert your thoughts. [1]

His sorrows were deepened by the hostility of his dead wife's family. Arabella's mother was persuaded, apparently by an evil tongued servant, that Wentworth was responsible for her daughter's death, because he had made her travel to Yorkshire so late in her pregnancy and had then, in a moment of anger, struck her so that she fell. Whether or not the father and brothers of his wife believed the whole of this slander, they made Arabella's death an excuse for breaking off all friendship with him. [2]

The bitter conduct of the Holles family echoed the criticisms of Wentworth as a harsh and ruthless man which were the theme of political small-talk among the opponents of the King's government, and which were also beginning to reverberate round Whitehall. The reason for some, if not all, of these murmurs was no discredit to Wentworth. He had been too successful. He had not let 'business mould upon his hands' [3] and he had used his authority as Lord President of the North to its full extent and with little respect of persons.

The Council of the North had originally been set up to deal with local administration, to enforce the laws of the kingdom and to control the disorders, riots and acts of violence which in the North, with its history of family feuds and its tradition of turbulent and bullying magnates, were fairly frequent. [4] Of recent years it had fallen itself into the control of factions and individuals bent on securing their own interests, so that it had, at times, become the engine of the very evils it was supposed to check. The Scrope-Savile regime had been deplorable, and under weak Presidents the jurisdiction of the Council had been successfully challenged or evaded by delinquents who could afford the time, and the lawyer's fees, necessary to obtain a 'prohibition', an order transferring their case from the Council's Court at York to one of the Courts at Westminster.

'Prohibitions' was already, both north and south, one of the key-words in the constitutional cold war between the Crown and the common lawyers. Early in the reign of King James I there had been a vehement tussle between the Court of King's Bench and the Council of Wales and the Marches (a body which fulfilled on the Welsh border the same judicial functions as the Council of the North). It had been claimed by the defenders of the Common Law that cases could be removed into the King's Bench from the Council of Wales because the latter was merely a prerogative Court, the King's Bench a Common Law Court. Later the same crisis had arisen between the King's Bench and the Court of Chancery. With equal fervour and ultimately with success, it had been asserted by the defenders of the Crown, especially Francis Bacon, that Chancery and the Council of Wales could not be thus curtailed of their powers. The same struggle had not, however, been fought and won in the North, where 'prohibitions' for a generation past had limited the scope of the Council's action and lowered the respect in which it was held.

It was no intention of Wentworth's to extend the powers of the Council beyond what he believed to be their legitimate bounds, but he had the King's specific instruction to prevent 'prohibitions', so that the Council of the North ranked as of equal status with the Council of Wales and the Court of Chancery. Wentworth had made it clear in his opening speech as Lord President that this was the King's intention, which he would support with his full authority. He had also made it clear that the purpose of this firmness in re-establishing the shaken authority of the Council was simply to see that justice was done, without the expenses and delays which were habitually exploited by rich litigants to ruin their poorer opponents. 'May the tent of the Court be enlarged,' he said, 'the curtains drawn out, the stakes strengthened, yet no farther than shall be for a covering to the common tranquillity, a shelter to the poor and innocent from the rich and insolent.' [5]

His power and influence as a landowner put him above intimidation and he feared no one, either in the Council or outside it. 'He loved justice for justice itself', [6] wrote George Radcliffe, but this was not quite true; at times Wentworth seemed to love justice chiefly — if not only — when it humbled the mighty. As President of the North he saw before him a triple task: to enforce the salutary social measures initiated in the Privy Council, to protect the rights of the powerless against the powerful, and to uphold the authority of the prerogative, vested in the Council of the North, against the expanding claims of the Common Law.

He began by reducing the legal fees generally charged in the Court. 'What greater honour,' he asked, in his opening speech, 'than for a man by those abilities God hath lent him above others to vindicate silly, naked truth from the blemish craft and power might put upon her?' [7] This noble sentiment did not altogether appeal to those who, having hardly a fraction of Wentworth's income, had to make a living from the law. The fact that his friend George Radcliffe had been made King's Attorney for the North at about the time he himself became President might also cause comment. For the King's service, the appointment could not have been bettered, but however excellent Wentworth's motives were, he was certainly advancing his personal friends.

His next care was to establish his own position past question, a necessary task for the successor of the ineffective Lord Scrope. 'In relation to my own person,' he said, 'never President expected so little; in relation to this place, never any more jealous of the honour of his master, never any that looked for more.' [8] His conduct and that of his household must be above reproach. 'He is careful that as well his family as himself shall be exemplar in practice and ambition of good and honourable actions and employments', wrote an observer. 'He hath no favourite but his council which keeps off curtain and chamber motions, which he detests.' [9] The President represented the King and must therefore keep his distance from the overbearing nobility of the North; Wentworth fenced himself about with almost regal formalities and built a palatial new wing on to the Manor House at York. His intention was to create an official residence worthy of the King's deputy, but his action was, naturally enough, interpreted as an arrogant display of his own wealth and power. He had recently acquired the manor of Ledstone, a country house very much nearer to York than either Woodhouse or Gawthorpe, his other residences. This too he now began to enlarge to palatial dimensions. [10]

'Nature hath not given him generally a personal affability,' one Yorkshireman reported. He was cold and rough-mannered to his equals — even that easy-tempered young courtier Philip Warwick complained of his aggressive haughtiness — and he behaved easily only with his intimate friends. [11]

Harry Bellasis, the eldest son of Lord Fauconberg, was the first to repay the President in his own coin; on an official occasion he contrived to stand about ostentatiously with his hat on his head as Wentworth was passing. The insult to the King's representative could not go unpunished; the arrogant young man was summoned to London to explain it and realized his mistake too late when he found himself imprisoned in the Gate House at Westminster. The Privy Council at length agreed to let him go, after ordering him to apologize both to them and later, publicly, at York Sessions. Wentworth attempted to suppress this last humiliating punishment but the Council was firm and the proud young man, indignant at the prospect of having to accept mercy at his enemy's hands, agreed stiffly to the double disgrace, making only the request that it should be made clear to the world that he did not and would not apologize personally to Wentworth but only to the King's representative in the North. [12]

While young Bellasis was in trouble with the Lord President, his father, Lord Fauconberg, rashly attempted to bring Wentworth himself into disgrace by forwarding a petition to the Council charging him with deliberate injustice. The charge seems to have been fabricated between Fauconberg and Sir Conyers D'Arcy; all Fauconberg got for his pains was a reproof from the Privy Council and a command to apologize to Wentworth at York. He evaded this latter unpleasant necessity by staying in the South, which was probably wise as Wentworth was cogitating plans for imposing a punitive fine on him to teach him not to impugn the King's justice. [13]

The cases of Fauconberg and his son were typical. In both, Wentworth was undoubtedly right: right to insist on proper respect being shown to the King's representative, and right to overthrow a mischievous and groundless aspersion on the justice dispensed by the Council of the North. But in both cases he pursued his ends with a persistence that could be mistaken for personal spite and which was bound to make him (and hence the King's government) unpopular among the gentry of Yorkshire.

The whole four years of his active tenure of office as Lord President of the North was marked by attempts of men of influence in the county to call the power of the Council in question, and by Wentworth's persistent and sometimes deadly response to these challenges. One of the most outrageous defiances came from a Scotsman, Sir David Foulis, who had once been in the royal household, and who had retired to an estate in Yorkshire carrying off between five and six thousand pounds that he had quietly misappropriated. [14] His misconduct seems to have been, at long last, discovered, and it was possibly to divert attention from himself that he began to put it about in Yorkshire that Wentworth was also appropriating part of the royal revenue.

The King, in an attempt to raise money, had revived the medieval system by which a landowner of more than £40 a year was obliged to take on, at the coronation, the honours and duties of knighthood. By reviving this obsolete law, Charles was enabled to claim from most of the gentry either the fees payable in lieu of the old feudal knight-service, or, preferably, a 'composition' for them in ready money. This unwonted demand naturally caused widespread annoyance, and Sir David Foulis had ready listeners among the already irritated gentry when he told them that the quittances they had received for their money were probably worthless; it was most questionable whether money paid to the Lord President and his agents ever reached the Exchequer, and they would very likely have to pay all over again.

An accusation of this kind, given the primitive and complex nature of government finance under the Stuarts, was dangerous because it was very likely to be true. In the absence of any body of salaried officials to collect the revenue, the 'receivers' of the fees, fines, compositions and other dues of the Crown undertook the task on the understanding that they met the costs of collecting and paid themselves a reward by taking a percentage out of the money they received. It was Wentworth's boast that he was never late with the money and that he brought in a better yield than his predecessors. He was an inveterate self-praiser, but the figures he gave to Treasurer Weston and others, though they are often startling, cannot have been far from the truth because there would have been no point in making claims that a reference to the Treasury and Exchequer records would have disproved had they been false.

On the other hand Weston was always very suspicious of him and watchful to catch him out; it was sometimes his word against Wentworth's as to whether the money was late or not, and Wentworth certainly raised his own percentage on the recusants' composition money from sixpence in the pound to a shilling without asking leave of anyone. Challenged about this, he argued that unlike his predecessors he made no charge for expenses, and that the extent to which he had increased the total amount collected made the King enormously the gainer by the new arrangement. It was true, however, that while the money was in his hands he saw nothing reprehensible in using it as ready cash for his own affairs, usually for buying land, whenever it suited him. If he could pay the necessary sum into the Treasury when the money fell due, or when the Treasurer asked for it, that was good enough; and in a society where banks did not exist and the machinery of credit was awkward and primitive, his conduct was sensible and was indeed the normal practice.

Sir David Foulis, of all people, must have known all there was to know about misappropriating the royal revenue. He was a loud, indiscreet, talkative man and he very likely believed what he said about Wentworth. The dangerous rumour was apparently confirmed by an unfortunate mistake in the Exchequer, when a careless clerk reported to the Sheriff of Yorkshire that some of the gentry had not paid when in fact they had. The Sheriff, Sir Thomas Leighton, who happened to have married a daughter of Sir David Foulis, mulcted one victim a second time. Wentworth, to whom complaint was made, summoned him peremptorily before the Council to explain. The sheriff of a county was an important man, even if, like Sir Thomas Leighton, he was also an ass. Leighton was annoyed, and when his father-in-law (before a large company) told him that the Council of York, being a prerogative Court, had no authority to summon so much as a Justice of the Peace before it, let alone a sheriff, Sir Thomas boldly refused to come.

Sir David Foulis, with the help of his son-in-law, had struck a shrewd blow at the foundations of the Council itself, but the very disorders against which Wentworth was fighting unexpectedly came to his rescue. Leighton had hardly sent his refusal, when Lord Eure, who had sold his lands to pay his debts, fortified himself in a house no longer legally his and refused to be dislodged by the Sheriff's warrant. Leighton, humbled and suppliant, was forced to ask Wentworth's help, and it was only the cannon and soldiers of the Lord President, kept against such emergencies, which broke down the walls of the house and forced it to surrender. This brought about an unwilling truce to Leighton's feud with Wentworth and the knighthood business was settled, though not without some resentment on Leighton's part, which seven years later at Wentworth's trial he would amply demonstrate. [15]

Foulis, by now thoroughly frightened, hastened to Court and tried to ingratiate himself with the King. He asserted, with solicitous care for his Majesty's government, that he was a man of such importance in Yorkshire that if the Lord President lightly took offence at him the whole county would suffer for his fall; indeed, his support and industry were of far greater importance in the North, where he was much beloved, than all the good offices of a man so unpopular as Wentworth.

Wentworth was indignant at the impudence of this suggestion, which had indeed so little truth in it that few believed it. 'His Majesty shall contribute more to his own authority by making him an example of his justice than by taking him in again', he wrote, and continued with even greater fervour:

But this is an arrogance grown frequent nowadays which I cannot endure. Every ordinary man must put himself in balance with the King, as if it were a measuring cast betwixt them who were like to prove the greater loser upon the parting.... Let us not deceive ourselves. The King's service cannot suffer by the disgrace of him, and me, and forty more such. The ground whereupon government stands will not so easily be washed away.

To make an end of Sir David's slanders, Wentworth brought a libel action against him in the Star Chamber. He was found guilty, removed from all his offices, and ordered to pay £5,000 to the Crown and £3,000 damages to Wentworth. This the furious old gentleman refused to do, and was clapped into the Fleet prison until he came to his senses. He remained there for the next seven years. [16]

The real significance of the Foulis case was not so much that he had slandered Wentworth personally, as that he had questioned the authority of the Council of the North, and inspired his son-in-law, Sir Thomas Leighton, to do the same. For Leighton, Wentworth had only contempt. 'He is a fool led by the nose ... let him go for a coxcomb as he is', Wentworth had described him, when Foulis and he were both on trial in the Star Chamber, and Leighton had gone unpunished.

But he would not brook a sustained defiance of the Council's authority, and in the autumn of 1632 he asserted himself to crush the insolence of Sir Thomas Gower. Gower was a Justice of the Peace who had taken it upon himself, while on the bench, to say some very critical words about the King's attorney for the Council of the North. The King's attorney was Wentworth's friend Sir George Radcliffe. But Wentworth would have taken notice of Gower's conduct whatever the identity of the King's attorney. It was simply not to be tolerated that the conduct of so important an official of the Council of the North should be openly impugned by a Justice of the Peace in the course of his official duties. Fore-warned of a summons for contempt, Sir Thomas Gower removed to London, apparently taking a large family party with him. Here he lodged in Holborn, defied an attempt of the Lord President's officers to arrest him, and boldly petitioned the Privy Council to the effect that the Council of the North had no powers to arrest him once he had crossed the boundary of their jurisdiction. He also asserted that justice was no longer to be had in the North because no lawyer would appear in his defence for fear of the power of George Radcliffe. Meanwhile he behaved himself with such uproarious and confident defiance among his family and friends in Holborn that in the whole district — abutting on the Inns of Court and buzzing with young law students — he and his friends came to be 'wantonly termed the rebels of the North'.

This kind of behaviour, Wentworth fiercely but reasonably argued in a letter to the Privy Council, could not be tolerated:

Upon these oppositions and others of like nature, all rests are up, and the issue joined.... A provincial court at York or none? It is surely the state of the question, the very mark they shoot at; unless this court have in itself coercive power, after it be possessed justly and fairly of a cause, to compel the parties to an answer and to obey the final decrees thereof, all the motions of it become *bruta fulmina*, fruitless to the people, useless to the King, and ourselves altogether unable to govern a people sometimes so stormy as live under it. [17]

Gower was called before the Privy Council, where his case was argued. His counsel claimed that the Council of the North had no authority to arrest a man in the South, and opinion in the Privy Council does indeed seem to have been uncertain on the matter. But Wentworth, who was troubled by no doubts at all as to the legal position, seems to have thrown himself on his knees before the King, declaring that, without such authority, government in the North would become impossible. The case went against Gower, who was sent back to the North in custody and spent more than four months in prison in York. [18]

In the following March the King made the position clear once and for all by issuing a new Commission and Instructions for the Council of the North by which its powers were brought into line with those of the Star Chamber in the South. [19] Wentworth had been in London since January and was known to want the powers of the Council laid down in precisely this way, so that this Commission must logically be regarded as the outcome of his policy. It remains a matter of doubt how far it really increased the powers which the Council had originally been intended to exercise; Wentworth, who was after all a Yorkshireman bred up under the jurisdiction of the Council, was evidently satisfied that he had only restored in practice powers which had always been there in theory but had fallen into neglect. His critics and his enemies would always believe, with equal fervour, that he had enlarged the powers of the Court and thereby those of the royal prerogative in the North.

There was nothing out of order in the issue of a new Commission in the spring of 1633; it was the normal procedure whenever the secretary of the Council changed, and at this time a change had just taken place. The new Commission was, however, probably intended to tide over a rather more substantial change than that of the secretary. Wentworth himself had for some months past been preparing to leave Yorkshire for a more exalted and yet more difficult sphere of government. Though he was, with the King's consent, to retain his title as Lord President, the execution of the office would in the next years be in the hands of a Vice-President, and it was therefore for the instruction, enlightenment and guidance of Wentworth's deputy that the new Commission was issued. Wentworth himself never sat again in judgment as President of the Council under the new instructions of March 1633. The point was later to be of some importance, since the first and foremost charge against him when he was tried for High Treason was precisely this, of having procured the unwarranted, unwarrantable and illegal extension of his Presidential powers to satisfy his own ambitious lusts.

The most widely known activities of Wentworth as Lord President were inevitably those concerned with the status of his jurisdiction and the prosecution — or persecution as its victims would have called it — of those who challenged it. The cases of Foulis, Gower, and Fauconberg and his son, were all famous in London, the chief centre for legal discussion and political argument of the whole kingdom, and the mart whence news was distributed into every region of the countryside. Through reports and rumours brought from London, Wentworth's reputation as a hard, vindictive, ambitious man took root and grew, not only among those who, in principle or out of interest, disliked the King's methods of government, but also among many who, in the ultimate crisis which was to face King Charles, were wholeheartedly royalist.

Other and gentler aspects of his policy were known exclusively in the North where, though he had bitter enemies, he was also to find in the darkest time of his life some truly devoted adherents. It was his contention that by confirming the strength of the Council he would be able to enforce order and give justice, especially to the poor. The disappearance of the records of the Council of the North makes it difficult to prove, and impossible to disprove, that he actually did this. The most we can do is to deduce the sincerity, or otherwise, of his contention from such evidence as we have.

His measures to control the plague in the North had been efficient and administered with a constant care for the afflicted poor. His handling of the long and vexed problem of the drainage of Hatfield Chase stands out for his championship of the country-folk against Vermuyden and his shareholders. When he succeeded to the Presidency of the North, the quarrel was still in its early stages, and the King and Court were supporting Vermuyden, but by the summer of 1630 the King had been so far worked upon by the complaints from Yorkshire that he appointed a commission, naturally under the Lord President, to inquire into the matter. The trouble was twofold. In the first place Vermuyden and the shareholders in the drainage scheme were bitterly felt by the fen-dwellers to have taken too much of the drained land for their own as a reward; this was to be a common complaint about drainage whenever it took place. But the problem of Hatfield Chase was complicated by a second and more serious error. Vermuyden had undoubtedly miscalculated — it was his first big venture in England — and in draining the fens of Hatfield Chase he had partly directed the waters into three neighbouring villages which had hitherto been good, dry land. A pitiful report came to Wentworth at harvest time in 1630. The poor people were being compelled to wade away from their cottages carrying their children and goods on their backs. 'Their corn and hay which they had gotten standeth deep in water; their corn and meadow uncut is covered in water; that which was in stack, in cock, and in swathe is carried away with water.' [20]

Wentworth gave judgment by which Vermuyden was to repair the damage by cutting a new channel without delay, while the drained land was to be redistributed allowing a larger proportion to the fenmen and considerably less to Vermuyden and his share-holders. The scheme had not paid so well as the Dutch engineer had hoped, and this judgment of Wentworth would involve him and his company in heavy additional expenditure while further reducing their gains. He fought it by delay and disregard, presumably hoping that Wentworth would lose interest or take no steps to implement the judgment he had given. Wentworth hung on doggedly, as was his way, and Vermuyden was compelled, though not for another three years, to cut the so-called 'Dutch river' which prevented further flooding, and to accept the revised land distribution. [21] By that time Vermuyden was involved in the far more successful and far more extensive drainage of the Bedford level in East Anglia, where he had a stronger band of shareholders at his back, and the fenmen were championed not by the powerful Lord President Wentworth, but only by some of their local squires, Oliver Cromwell for one, who could achieve relatively little in their defence.

Wentworth's effective government of the North lasted for exactly four years. He had taken office in December 1628. In July 1631, shortly before the death of Lady Wentworth, the King had apparently decided to make him Lord Deputy of Ireland, a post requiring much the same strength of purpose and talent for civil and financial administration as Wentworth was showing in the North. The King's decision, at first secret, began to be generally known by the autumn of that year, [22] but Wentworth was unwilling to proceed to the new and unknown problems of Ireland until he had finally settled outstanding difficulties in the North. Not until the various cases of Fauconberg, Foulis and Gower were satisfactorily settled was he willing to withdraw so far from the Court, the Privy Council and the centre of affairs as he knew he would be in Dublin. Furthermore, he did not relinquish his Presidency. Confident in what he had achieved in restoring the effectiveness and prestige of the Council, he may have believed that his continuance in office as President would give an added strength to his successor, who would be more feared as his Vice-President than in his own right. But he was also, at this as at other times in his life, very unwilling to give up the power and the profits of any office that he had acquired.

This situation had never yet arisen in the North, but there was an exact precedent for it in the behaviour of Sir Henry Sidney, Lord President of the Council in Wales and the Marches, who had retained this important office through a Vice-President while he was intermittently absent as Lord Deputy of Ireland over a period of nearly fourteen years. [23]

The decision to repeat this pattern was open to criticism, but was probably on the whole a wise one. There were, of course, other candidates for the Presidency of the North who would have to be disappointed. The Earl of Newcastle was certainly one. But it is doubtful whether Newcastle or any other would have had the force of character to maintain the position Wentworth had built up. A Vice-President, somewhat in awe of his President, would be more or less bound to do so. The man chosen was Sir Edward Osborne: 'a discreet, generous gentleman', wrote Wentworth, 'and a person of entire affection to his Majesty's service.' Osborne was also the head of a family of considerable wealth and standing in the country, who proved scrupulously loyal to Wentworth, hardworking, capable and conscientious. The fact that he was married to Fauconberg's daughter gave him the opportunity of being conciliatory, without necessarily being weak, to the discontented faction. Had things gone smoothly with King Charles's policy and projects in the next ten years, this firm but rather negative man might have upheld the position that Wentworth had created in a manner that would have gradually gained a measure of acceptance even among those who disliked it. [24]

Wentworth himself, well pleased with his achievement in Yorkshire, hoped for greater successes and anticipated greater dangers in Ireland. He saw too clearly the weaknesses of the King's government, to be satisfied with the situation he left behind him in England, nor was he altogether confident that an appointment in Ireland, which would remove him a long way from the King's council and the King's ear, was the best thing either for the royal government or for himself. He had thought the matter over deeply and long before finally agreeing. He sailed from Chester in July 1633 with some doubts as to the future but with unshaken confidence in his own ability to battle in the King's interest with intrigue, opposition or adverse circumstance.

NOTES

[1] Knowler, I, p. 59.

[2] Ibid., II, p. 122; Holles, *Memorials*, p. 109; Collins, *Historical Collections*, p. 95; see also a relevant quotation from the Strafford MSS in Lady Burghclere, II, p. 101.

[3] Knowler, I, p. 145.

[4] For details of the kind of disorders that occurred see F. W. Brooks, *Yorkshire and the Star Chamber*, East Yorkshire Local History Society, 1954. An excellent brief account of the Council is to be found in the same author's pamphlet *The Council of the North*, Historical Association, 1953.

[5] *C.S.P.D.*, 1628-9, p. 585; *Academy*, June 1875; Tanner MSS, LXII, folio 300.

[6] Knowler, II, p. 433.

[7] Tanner MSS, loc. cit.

[8] Loc. cit.

[9] *Fairfax Correspondence*, I, p. 252.

[10] See an article on Ledstone in *Country Life*, LXXXIV, pp. 556, 580.

[11] *Fairfax Correspondence*, I, p. 252; Warwick, p. 112.

[12] Reid, pp. 414-15; Gardiner, VII, p. 230; Rushworth II, p. 88; Strafford MSS, XXI, No. 67, Wentworth to Marris, 8th April 1631.

[13] Reid, pp. 415-16; Burghclere, I, p. 146; H.M.C., Cowper MSS, I, pp. 420, 475; see also the petition of George Hall relating to this case in H.M.C. IV (*House of Lords MSS*) p. 61, which indicates the persistence with which Wentworth pursued his purpose of showing Fauconberg to be a liar. Strafford MSS, XXI, No. 72.

[14] See Wentworth to Carlisle, a letter quoted *in extenso* in the Introduction to *C.S.P.D.*, 1631-3.

[15] Strafford MSS, XII, No. 305; *C.S.P.D.*, 1631-3, pp. 425-6, 441; Rushworth II, p. 218; *Trial*, pp. 150-1; Knowler, I, pp. 89-90.

[16] *C.S.P.D.*, 1631-3, pp. xxiv-xxvi; Rushworth, II, pp. 215, ff.

[17] *C.S.P.D.*, 1631-3, pp. 450-1, 538.

[18] Rushworth, *Trial*, p. 139.

[19] Rymer, XIX, pp. 410-29.

[20] Strafford MSS, XII, No. 113, *Bridges to Wentworth*, 6th September 1630; this letter is quoted *in extenso* in Hunter, *South Yorkshire*, p. 164.

[21] Hunter, *South Yorkshire*, pp. 163, ff; a good account is given in L. E. Harris, *Vermuyden and the Fens*, London, 1953; much engineering detail is given in J. Korthals-Altes, *Sir Cornelius Vermuyden*, London and the Hague, 1925. It is an interesting comment on the confusion of interests and ideas in England at this time that, in the 'thirties, Strafford and Cromwell should both appear as champions of the fenmen. Cromwell's unsuccessful championship of the fenmen is, of course, well known; Strafford's part in a similar conflict has been largely forgotten.

[22] Knowler, I, p. 58; Strafford MSS, XII, folios 240, 249; Kearney, p. 27.

[23] Reid, p. 427; Skeel, p. 86.

[24] G. E. Aylmer, *The King's Servants*, p. 136, notices Wentworth's pluralism unfavourably in view of his avowed disapproval of the accumulation of offices in hands other than his own. Newcastle's desire for the Presidency is mentioned in *C.S.P.D.*, 1631-3, p. 395. Wentworth described Osborne's qualities in a letter to Ingram, 22nd August 1634, Strafford MSS, VIII, folio 137.

CHAPTER THREE

LORD DEPUTY OF IRELAND

God deal with me and my soul as I shall always seriously and honestly
intend the best for these affairs and public good of this people.
Wentworth to Sir John Coke, 1637

In the summer of 1633, at the time of Wentworth's departure
for Ireland, King Charles had been governing without Parliament for four and a half years. He had no intention of calling
Parliament again for an indefinite time, if ever. He had made
peace in Europe. English currency was underpinned by a steady
flow of bullion into the Mint secured through an advantageous
treaty with Spain of which the ingenious Cottington had been the
architect; the King's revenues also benefited by the 'seignorage'
that he took on every pound minted. In European politics the King
was neutral, with a strong bias in favour of the Spanish-Austrian
combine. His unfortunate brother-in-law, the exiled King of
Bohemia, had died of plague, and Charles, though he sent money
to his widowed sister and her children, scarcely now paid more
than lip-service to the idea of restoring her son to his hereditary
lands in Germany. The only effective Protestant champion who
had so far appeared to challenge the progress of Austrian and
Spanish arms in Europe, King Gustavus Adolphus of Sweden,
had been killed after eighteen months of victorious campaigning
in the autumn of 1632. It seemed unlikely that his generals and
their German Protestant allies would be able to maintain the
temporary advantage that he had won. In fact from a short-term
point of view, the King had gained for himself, and his subjects,
the economic advantages of neutrality combined with those of
being on the winning side.

Wentworth had always been in favour of peace with Spain. For
him politics and religion were strictly separate and he had little
patience with those who deplored the inactivity of the King while
one region after another of Protestant Europe was forcibly restored
to the Church of Rome. The fatal military and naval ventures of

the early years of the reign had shown beyond doubt that English intervention was useless. It might be regrettable that the House of Austria should come to dominate Europe, but there was no sense in refusing to face facts.

Wentworth was, in spite of the travels of his youth, not greatly interested in foreign affairs. His educational tour seems to have left him with a feeling of dislike for the French, and an enhanced belief in the value of a strong central government. King Charles needed years of peace in which to consolidate his government on a firm foundation of sound finance and good administration: that, to Wentworth, was the real importance of maintaining a neutral and cautious policy in Europe. It gave him no qualms that this meant friendship with Spain, coolness towards France, and a total disregard of the Protestant Cause.

The situation in England, or at least in the central government which meant the Court, was still for Wentworth extremely unsatisfactory. He lacked the qualities which would have brought him personally closer to his master. 'I looked upon my lord of Strafford as a gentleman whose great abilities might make a monarch rather afraid than ashamed to employ him in the greatest affairs of State.' This summing up in *Eikon Basilike*, whether or not it was written by Charles himself, lays bare the fatal weakness of Wentworth's position. The King was afraid of his 'great abilities'; Wentworth was, quite simply, too much for him. There could never be between them the mutual confidence that there was between Wentworth and Laud, or between the King and the easier, more amiable, more insinuating but very much lesser men with whom, by preference, he surrounded himself.

In the last four years Charles, as far as Wentworth was concerned, had grown only more remote. He had gained confidence not so much in himself as in his divine mission; a sinner before God, he approached the heavenly throne as the humblest suppliant, [1] and the God in whom he trusted answered his prayers, resolved his doubts, cast light on his darkness, and gave to Charles the King a firmness of purpose that was foreign to Charles the man. His government had been blessed, or so he thought: he had peace abroad and prosperity at home while the North in particular was advancing in civilization and order. In all good faith the King attributed these blessings to the favour of the Almighty bounteously bestowed on His chosen. He was not precisely ungrateful to Wentworth and his other servants; he was unseeing. He regarded all that happened as the due result of his own God-guided government, and he gave the glory to Heaven.

The King's cool acceptance of his labours did not yet rankle deeply with Wentworth; he could not, he said, be employed 'more honourably than in serving a King and his people'. [2] But the significance of Charles's manner could not be lost on him, and he was repeatedly shown that to the supreme height of his master he was no more than a subject and sometimes rather a demanding one. In theory Wentworth would have been the last to deny it, but in fact it meant that the Lord President of the North, in spite of his proven abilities, was very far from the political dominance for which he longed.

The most influential councillor at the Court of King Charles was undoubtedly the Queen, when she came to assert herself. She exercised her influence at this time capriciously and mostly in small matters. The only cause for which she deeply cared — the propagation of the Roman Catholic faith — was one to which she could not win her husband, or at least not beyond the point of tolerating her friends and relaxing the penal laws. Later, when the King's difficulties began, she became actively and disastrously concerned in English politics, but in the early part of his personal rule she used her influence with him chiefly to further the private interests of her friends. She was an admirable and persistent advocate for places at Court, for profitable grants, for wardships, patents and the like for all those who won her favour.

It would have been helpful to Wentworth had he been able to ingratiate himself with the Queen, but he was even less qualified to win her personal favour than that of the King. Instead he was to have a series of small clashes with her over the requests she made on behalf of her friends, some at least of which he felt bound to refuse. This difficult situation between him and the Queen had not yet fully developed, but he was experienced enough in the ways of Court to know that the witty, grasping, gay and unscrupulous who flocked round the lively little French Queen would be a serious block in the way of any man attempting a 'thorough' reformation of the government.

The word 'thorough' had come into use between Wentworth

and Laud in their private correspondence. Its two-edged implication — of driving through opposition, and of inquiring into
every corner — very well expressed Wentworth's exacting and
relentless attitude to the methods and processes of governing the
country and raising revenue for the King. But Laud was not so
optimistic as his friend about the prospects of success. 'For the
State, indeed my Lord, I am for *thorough*,' he wrote to him in the
summer of 1633, 'but I see that both thick and thin stays somebody,
which I conceive it should not; and it is impossible for me to go
thorough alone. Besides, private ends are such blocks in the public
way, and lie so thick, that you may promise what you will, and I
must perform what I can and no more.' [3] Laud did indeed here
put his finger on a cardinal weakness of the royal government.
Officials, high and low, who bought their places and treated them
as investments which were expected to pay substantial dividends
inevitably allowed their private ends to become blocks in the
public way. It was here, above all, at the centre, that a thorough
reform was most needed and was least practicable.

It was Wentworth's guiding conception that the personal
government of the King would justify itself by its evident virtues.
The commissions on debt and the Poor Law, the plans for supervising the conduct of Justices of the Peace, and his own use of
authority in the North, had all been manifestations of this policy.
But the King needed revenue and no one was more aware than
Wentworth that confusion in the collection of revenue and
extravagance in spending it would undermine the power of the
Crown, as much as the inefficiency and venality of the King's
servants, a problem which was closely linked to that of the
revenue. Wentworth's own methods of collecting the royal
revenues in the North — where he had been responsible for the
knighthood fines and the composition money of the recusants —
were efficient and profitable both to himself and the King. The
principal attractions that the Irish appointment held for him were
'the personal profit to be gained from the place' and 'the opportunity and means to supply the King's wants'. He believed that,
with skilful management, Ireland could be turned into a gold-mine
for himself and the Crown. He had, conceivably, learnt this idea
in the first place from Lord Treasurer Middlesex, who had been
one of his early patrons and who had always firmly believed in

Ireland as a potential source of revenue; or he may have learnt something of Irish possibilities from Sir Arthur Ingram, who, among his numerous undertakings, was deeply involved with the Irish customs. Difficulties and problems had increased since the time of Middlesex, but Wentworth was excited, rather than daunted, by the challenge of such a task. [4]

But in spite of the private profits that he made himself, or perhaps because of them, he had no illusions about the ruthless way in which officials and courtiers made money out of their positions regardless of the interests of the Crown. It seems at first sight hard to reconcile Wentworth's reiterated protests of selfless devotion to his master's service with the numerous profitable transactions that his correspondence reveals; but his theory and his practice were not wholly inconsistent with each other because he put the interests of the Crown at least on a level with his own, which was by no means the general practice of his contemporaries. It was understood that the King's servants, from the highest to the lowest, made a great part of their salaries from the perquisites of office. But the boundary could be drawn between legitimate fees and profits, and impermissible extortions. Wentworth knew very well what the boundary was and vehemently condemned in others any overstepping of it. He was not so quick to condemn his own trespasses, but given the standards of his time, given the extent to which his power to serve the King depended on his influence, his credit and his resources, he was an upright man. What he hated, suspected and, as the years went on, persecuted whenever he could were men of power and position who were less scrupulous than he took himself to be in furthering the King's interest at the same time as their own. [5]

There were plenty of these about the Court, and some of them, money matters apart, were loyal and loving servants who would later die for the King they had mulcted in the days of his power. But they were men without political vision, who sought profitable positions in the collection of import duties, who clamoured for monopolies of the sale of tobacco, or the manufacture of soap, or pins, or playing cards, with no real thought of anything but their own enrichment. Wentworth saw very clearly that if these locusts settled on the royal revenues it would be impossible to reform them in a 'thorough' or even a less thorough way. Furthermore, the multiplying of monopolies coupled with the incompetent and oppressive collection of duties, and the rather ostentatious extravagance of the Court — the new palaces, the masques, the dancing, the splendid entertainments — would create just that impression of greed and fecklessness most likely to irritate sober citizens and breed distrust of the Crown.

It was clear enough that Wentworth's fingers itched to have control of the royal finances. Though he protested that he had no designs on the place of Treasurer, the Treasurer, Weston, now Earl of Portland, never ceased to suspect that he had: [6] and with justice, for Wentworth's abilities admirably fitted him for the office, and he knew it. But Portland was a fixture; and it was the governorship of Ireland, not the Treasury, which was offered to Wentworth.

One of his friends, Sir Edward Stanhope, was convinced that the offer was a plot by his enemies to precipitate his ruin. It was certainly true that Deputies of Ireland were apt to return with their reputations damaged; neither of Wentworth's predecessors, Grandison and Falkland, had emerged scatheless. It was also true that the two councillors who had pressed for Wentworth's appointment were Portland and Cottington; the former was known to be hostile to him and the latter, though charming, was notoriously untrustworthy.

Wentworth in answer to Stanhope admitted that the Irish offer was 'the knottiest piece that ever fell into debate with me' but refused to believe that the intention was to ruin him. 'The worst sure that can be', he wrote, 'is to set me a little further off from treading upon anything themselves desire.' [7] *That* he certainly suspected. His colleagues found him too exacting, too strenuous and too interfering, and at times also too grasping. If Portland died or withdrew, Cottington as Chancellor of the Exchequer might well prefer to be at hand when there was talk of his replacement, and to have Wentworth far away in Ireland. On this, Wentworth had no illusions. But that was a risk he felt willing to take, for a time at least, because the possibilities of Ireland fascinated him.

It had for him, evidently, two great attractions. He would be able to exercise on an entire nation, a country self-contained, having its own Parliament, its own laws and very much its own problems, his abilities for government. He believed he would be able to build up the economic life and the revenues of Ireland in a way that would be advantageous to the inhabitants and profitable to the English Crown. If he could succeed in Ireland, where others had failed, he would enormously enhance his reputation, and so his power, with the King.

Soon after his official appointment to Ireland, Wentworth put before the King a number of propositions concerning his new post to which he secured agreement. He asked that no further grants be made by the King out of the Irish revenue until all debts had been cleared; he asked that his right to appoint to the principal offices in Ireland be established, that no grants be passed without his knowledge, that no complaints of injustice be brought to England, by-passing his Court in Dublin. Furthermore he asked for the right to discuss the Irish revenue, when necessary, privately with the Lord Treasurer instead of with the larger Committee of the Privy Council for Irish affairs. Finally, he wanted one Secretary of State, and one alone, to be the recipient of all his dispatches from Ireland. These were necessary precautions against the intrigues of place-hunters at Whitehall and against leakage of information and revenue. They were designed, as well, to keep the Deputy, and thereby the government of Ireland, in direct touch with the King. Wentworth had also taken the precaution of finding for himself among the lesser officials about the Court a personal agent whom he entirely trusted. This was William Railton, who in his absence acted for him in many of his private and public affairs — making purchases, supervising business deals, carrying messages. This industrious, observant and faithful man was in the next years to be a frequent visitor at Lambeth Palace and in the palatial houses of Wentworth's fellow ministers.[8]

These preliminaries being settled to his satisfaction, Wentworth was at last ready to cross over into Ireland in the summer of 1633. He had sent a part of his family in advance of him. His youngest brother George, who had grown in the last years into his devoted and efficient shadow, was in charge of the household which had already been established in Dublin Castle, and was making all ready against his arrival. The presence of a mysterious young woman in the new Deputy's residence gave rise to some speculation. She had in fact been Wentworth's wife since the previous autumn. There was nothing very extraordinary in his having married again less than a year after Arabella's death; a man in his position, with a large household to control and three young children, would have been expected to marry again without much delay, though perhaps he had done so a little soon. There was nothing extraordinary in his choice of bride. Elizabeth Rodes, daughter of his near neighbour Sir Godfrey Rodes of Great Houghton, was not an heiress; he did not wish for another heiress, because in the event of his death the jointure suitable to an heiress might have been a burden on his son's estate. He had wanted a wife with a respectable but not excessive portion; the dowry of Elizabeth Rodes was £1,000. [9] She was about eighteen years old, to his forty, and was at first more overawed than gratified at being suddenly and surreptitiously married by the greatest man in the county.

The only mystery about Wentworth's third marriage was the mystery he made himself. He married her secretly, kept her in his house in Yorkshire as, officially, a gentlewoman in charge of his children; sent her to Dublin with no explanation of her position, and only publicly acknowledged her as his wife a year after the marriage. Long before that, the scandal was loud enough to reach Whitehall, and to induce from William Laud a letter of cautious, slightly pained inquiry about the pretty young woman who was said to be looking after Wentworth's children. [10]

Wentworth's probable reasons for concealing his marriage show that curious mixture of shrewd calculation and lack of ordinary human insight which so often marked his behaviour. Arabella's death and his ensuing need to marry again for his own and for his children's sake had fallen at an awkward time in his political career. In the autumn of 1631 when Arabella died he had just been appointed Lord Deputy of Ireland; in the autumn of 1632 when he married Elizabeth Rodes he was on the point of leaving Yorkshire for some months in London to settle the affairs of the North and some of the affairs of Ireland with the King. At such a time of prolonged absence his children, the eldest of whom was only six, would need a mother and his domestic household a mistress. Hence, presumably, his haste to complete the marriage and settle his young wife into her new surroundings. When talk began in Yorkshire, instead of publishing his marriage, Wentworth simply hurried her off to Ireland to await his arrival.

Elizabeth Rodes, unlike Arabella Holles, had not been brought up in a political family on the edge of the Court. She was a country gentlewoman with no experience of the world. Had she lived in Yorkshire, and later for some months in Dublin, as the wife of the absent Lord President and Lord Deputy, she would undoubtedly have been courted by all those who wanted to gain favours from her husband. To expose an inexperienced young woman, without help or guidance, for weeks together to the attentions of such people would have been to invite trouble. This seems the likeliest reason for Wentworth's concealment of the marriage, and, politically speaking, he was wise. In fact before he reached Dublin no one paid any court to the lady who lived so quietly and whose status was in doubt. Whatever problems later assailed him, he was not to be plagued by suitors who had wheedled half-promises out of his wife or placed her under supposed obligations to them by offering her their attention and services.

What he gained politically, he lost in his private reputation. The sudden death of Arabella, the hostility of her family, the secret and too early remarriage: all these things together enhanced the ugly rumours about him. It would become a common scandal that he had struck and killed his second wife to marry his whore. The rather ponderous gallantries that he permitted himself with the ladies of his acquaintance would be exaggerated into the expressions of an indiscriminate and uncontrolled lust. The scandals which grew up about him, and they grew thickly in the next five years, were set going in the first place by the ill-managed business of his third marriage. It was typical of Wentworth that, in planning this elaborate deception, he never seems to have realized that it would start scandal or that it mattered if it did.

Though forethought and calculation had governed Wentworth's choice of his third wife, the speed with which he contracted this new marriage suggests that something more was involved. There was never any question for him but that Arabella had been the quintessence of perfection, the only intense and all-satisfying love he had ever known. His friends, little by little, came to fill the place of her companionship and after her death he poured out to them in his frequent letters those anxieties and hopes which he must in happier times have confided to her. But his neighbour's pretty daughter, gentle, clinging and rather silly, had undoubtedly aroused in him a measure of protective and demanding love.

Elizabeth Rodes was a kind mother to her stepchildren and a submissive wife to a man whose transcendent greatness filled her with awe. 'The fellowship of marriage', he told her gently, 'ought to carry with it more of love and equality than any other apprehension. So I desire it may ever be betwixt us, nor shall it break of my part.' [11] It did not break on either part; she kept for him always in his restless political life the undisturbed certainty of domestic peace. He liked to linger with her, he teased her gently for forgetting to sign her letters, he gravely discussed with her the personal charms of the ladies of their acquaintance, and though there was no intellectual equality in his words to her there was deepening tenderness; the formal 'Madam' of his first letter to her became in a little while 'Dear Bess', and last of all 'Sweet Heart'.

Whatever his private happiness the union was not otherwise helpful to him. Elizabeth was too young and inexperienced to fulfil any difficult public duties. He kept her always in the background, never even presenting her at Court, while her family were strongly Puritan and never very helpful to him in Yorkshire. [12]

In July 1633 Wentworth at last left for Ireland, taking with him thirty coaches of six horses apiece — an equipage fit for a king, which provoked some unfriendly comment. Before he left English soil he fired a parting shot in the battle for the Council of the North. Sir George Vernon, a crotchety old judge, had questioned the judicial powers of the Council, and this in spite of the new Commission to which his attention had been drawn. This was outrageous, wrote Wentworth; Vernon must be prevented from riding the northern circuit in future. Having settled this business, he embarked at Chester and reached Dublin Bay early in the morning of July 23rd. [13]

Great preparations had been made for his official welcome. The nobility of Ireland had ordered new liveries for their servants and prepared trains of nearly two hundred horses apiece to bring him in state to the city; so brave a show might well impress him with their power and his due obligations. But Wentworth, who had left London with such pomp, now changed his tactics; he came ashore some distance out of the city and walked thither on foot with only a small attendance, though the Earl of Cork got wind of his coming, bustled into his coach and contrived to meet him half way. [14]

Richard Boyle, Earl of Cork, who had been co-governor with Lord Loftus since the recall of the last Deputy in 1629, now withdrew, declaring confidently that 'the kingdom was yielded up in general peace and plenty'. [15] Wentworth had however resolved 'not to deliver any opinion concerning his Majesty's affairs within that kingdom' till he could judge for himself; from other sources than Cork's account he had less sanguine reports, which his immediate observation confirmed. 'It doth almost affright me at first sight', he wrote to Portland, and with cause enough, [16] for the politics and problems of Ireland made the difficulties that he had confronted in the North seem trivial.

The Irish problem only superficially resembled the problem of the North. There Wentworth had had to deal with headstrong landowners who put their own quarrels and their own interests before the commonweal; and men like these he was to find again in Ireland. But there was no colonial problem in the North, no antagonism between different races or between settlers and natives. This was the central problem of Ireland.

Ireland had belonged to the English Crown since the reign of King Henry II, but the descendants of the Norman families who had then crossed over had in many ways assimilated themselves to the predominating Irish. They had intermarried with them, and their leading nobility had often acquired some of the characteristics of the chiefs of Celtic clans. The Earl of Clanricarde (de Burgh) and the Earl of Ormonde (Butler), of Norman descent, both enjoyed much the same prestige and much the same power with their people as, for instance, such ancient Irish chieftains as the Earl of Inchiquin (O'Brien) or the Earl of Antrim (Macdonnell). Moreover the Norman-Irish, or the 'old English' as they were then more often called, like the native Irish, had remained on the whole true to the Roman Catholic faith.

The trouble between England and Ireland had entered upon a new and bitter phase when the Reformation was followed by a sudden burst of English colonial expansion. When the population of Ireland, by and large, rejected the official religion of the English, difficulties were bound to follow. Then, in the latter part of Elizabeth's reign, came the influx of a new kind of English settler — not warriors like the Normans, but men who were resolved to exploit the agricultural possibilities of the land, to build towns, to create sea-ports, to develop a new and more profitable way of life, out of key with the temperament and civilization of the Irish. The story would be repeated in later centuries in many different quarters of the globe, with the same misunderstandings and bitterness. Irish civilization was primitive and nomadic, based on the tribe, and on herds of cattle driven from pasture to pasture. The poor people built neither houses nor barns but pitched tents of hide in the open country. In spite of generations of contact with the English, the English system of land tenure had only taken root in the so-called English Pale, near Dublin. Irish inheritance went by tanistry, in a criss-cross of nephews and cousins; primogeniture was an Anglo-Norman scheme, but the Irish stuck to their old method of dividing all between brothers. But now land-hungry settlers flooded in to the unexploited lands of Ireland, refused to accept Irish customs in the use and possession of land, staked out their claims, built farms, stored their surplus corn in barns, and introduced new kinds of agriculture which took the pasture away from the cattle, and curtailed the wide regions over which the creaghts had wandered.

The clash of two civilizations, exacerbated by the clash of two religions, culminated in bloody wars. The so-called pacifications of Ireland by the English government became suppression by massacre and confiscation. Things were further complicated by the religious wars in Europe, so that Ireland was stimulated to play the part of champion of the Church against the heretic English. After the wars of Elizabeth's reign, in the early years of the seventeenth century the 'new English' — as these later settlers were called — were strongly established. Munster had been developed largely by English settlers; Ulster by English and Scots. In both regions the native Irish felt themselves to be, and indeed were, grievously wronged. Their land was certainly seized from them on the pretext of a 'defective title', meaning that they could show no documents acceptable in English law to prove that it was theirs. There was wild and enthusiastic forgery but it did not often work. The situation was chaotic. The English settlers, whatever they made it look like by law and on paper, held what they had taken by force, or the threat of force. The Irish, defeated in the wars, did not consider the matter closed. Certainly there would be rebellion again; in the meantime they raided and robbed the settlers whenever possible. Their religion, though in theory prohibited by English law, was generally and openly practised since no Deputy in his right senses could risk suppressing it. It was as strong among the 'old English' landowners and among the small but important middle class — lawyers and merchants who on the whole supported law and order — as among the so-called 'wild Irish' and their chiefs.

In the confusion of Irish politics three groups could be distinguished, although 'group' is too compact a word for such disparate and various conglomerations. There were on the one side the irreconcilable Irish whose chiefs were either in exile or temporarily pacified and loyal to the government: they were deeply opposed to the English order and had faith in some ultimate resurgence of Ireland and the Irish and in the expulsion of the greedy intruders, linked perhaps with support from Roman Catholic powers abroad. This group had appeared to be politically quiescent since 'the Flight of the Earls' in 1611, but its leaders still lived abroad and it was far from dead at home. In extreme opposition to these were the 'new English', the settlers of the last fifty years, who wanted to see the whole of Ireland allotted to those who would work the land to the best advantage, develop commerce and manufacture and get rid once and for all of primitive ways of life, raiding, robbery and disorder, and of course the old idolatrous religion. Their ideal was a prosperous, orderly, Protestant Ireland which they would be free to develop for their own benefit.

Between these extremes was a numerically very considerable group which included the 'old English' and some of the native Irish landowners, and merchants, lawyers, ship-owners and manufacturers (such as they were) of the cities and sea-ports. These were willing to accept and profit by the law and order imposed by the government, provided they were left in peace to practise their religion and provided their property was secure against further encroachment by the 'new English'. At this period the 'old English' and the Irish still owned between them a much larger part of the territory of Ireland than the incoming settlers had

H   129

managed to engross. With the support of the 'old English' something might have been done to achieve a permanent pacification of Ireland. But the situation was bedevilled by the religious question. Because these loyalists were Roman Catholic, the 'new English' were constantly able to represent themselves as the champions of true religion against the old idolatry; land-grabbing was speciously disguised as an enlightened process for civilizing and converting the superstitious Irish. Again, because the loyalists were Roman Catholic, their right to hold office, to practise at the bar, to sit or vote in Parliament (all of which things, in fact, they did) could always be called in question. Any Deputy who supported them too strongly might find himself accused of dangerous Roman Catholic sympathies by the powerful 'new English'.

This was the trap into which Wentworth's predecessor Lord Falkland had fallen. He had hoped, in a severely practical spirit, that the situation could be solved to everyone's satisfaction if this middle group in Ireland could be officially granted the security it craved in return for a handsome vote of money to the Crown. He had thus arranged to barter the so-called 'Graces' to the Irish, in return for a number of subsidies. The most important of the 'Graces' was the guarantee that sixty years' possession of land should be recognized as constituting legal tenure, and that Roman Catholics should be officially permitted to hold office. But the sixty-years clause would have put a stop to the land-grabbing of the new settlers, while the suggested favour to Roman Catholics gave the 'new English' the opportunity to fight the 'Graces' on religious grounds. The 'new English' were not numerically dominant, and they held less land than their opponents, but a group of them, owing to their now very considerable wealth, had secured key positions on the Lord Deputy's Council in Dublin. The hapless Falkland, entangled in quarrels with his Council, was recalled to England where the King, harassed by the 'new English' councillors and their friends, found himself unable to confirm the 'Graces', though the money that had been voted in return for them was steadily being paid in to the Irish exchequer.

This then was the situation which Wentworth faced in Ireland. Though he did not know yet how he would handle it, his purpose and his policy were clear to him from the start. He showed the beliefs and prejudices of Englishmen of his epoch. He could see in ancient Irish civilization nothing good whatsoever; it was to him self-evident that the wild Irish would be better men, more pleasing to God and happier in their lives, if they gave up their savage ways, learnt more sensible and profitable methods of tilling the land, were grouped into villages and towns, apprenticed to trades, and turned as fast as possible into clean, industrious Protestants. Since they were themselves lazy and backward — their deplorable standards of living showed him that — it was necessary that these changes be wrought for them and even in despite of them. They must be wrought either by recent energetic settlers from England and Scotland, or by 'old English' and law-abiding Irish willing to work with the English. Under such a dispensation the Irish people would be materially much better off than they could ever hope to be under their native chiefs in a state of primitive and savage independence.

Wentworth was in effect on the side of the settlers, and was to show himself in favour of greatly increasing their number and of enlarging yet further the area of English plantations in Ireland. But he was not in favour of the particular group of settlers who had gained control of the Council Board in Dublin, and he was prepared, to reach his ends, to play the 'old English' against them if need be. For him, moreover, projects for material improvement were sincerely combined with a sense of mission; he took it as natural, indeed almost as the divine will, that the Irish ('a conquered nation' as he called them) could be dispossessed and treated as a subject race; he also held it to be important that the Irish should, for certain essential commodities, remain dependent on England so as to compel them to obedience to the Crown. [17] But, these things once settled, he also held that the people of Ireland, of whatever race or religion, must be governed justly, that their rights, once established, must be assured, and that all must be encouraged to participate in the material blessings which improved agriculture and expanding commerce would bring.

The 'new English' in the Council at Dublin were not troubled by any such considerations; even their parade of Protestant devotion was (as he was soon to find out) often a cover for making private profit. Wentworth was to come, as the years went by, to hate them with an obsessive hate, not because their open aims in Ireland were different from his, but because their behaviour was a corruption and a parody of those aims. They, for their part, were to pursue him with a vindictiveness that owed much to their sense of rage and betrayal. He should have been one with them: instead he, severally and collectively, checked and humiliated them all.

These developments were still in the future, although Wentworth was not long in deciding what kind of people he had to deal with. In a letter to Lord Treasurer Portland, ten days after his arrival in Dublin, he described his Council as 'a company of men the most intent upon their own ends that ever I met with'. A few days later he was writing to Arundel: 'I find myself in the society of a strange people. Their own privates altogether their study without any regard at all to the public. Great cures to be wrought but where the medicines or the persons faithfully to apply them are to be found I know not.' Two of these 'strange people', the Chancellor Loftus, and the Vice-Treasurer, Lord Mountnorris, had become involved in trouble with the preceding Deputy which ended up before the King's Council at Westminster, but it was the Deputy Falkland who had lost the game, not his Councillors. 'It is the genius of the place', wrote Wentworth, 'to soothe the Deputy, be he in the right or wrong, till they have insinuated themselves into the fruition of their ends, and then after to accuse him, even of those things wherein themselves had a principal share.' [18]

The strongest man on the Council was the Earl of Cork, Lord Treasurer of Ireland; he was of a north country family, had come over from England with the Earl of Essex and built his future largely out of the ruin of Sir Walter Raleigh, whose Irish properties he had acquired. In unscrupulous and astute speculation, in bold ventures and energetic pursuit of gain, Cork was outstanding, and he had the coarse virtues that go with such gifts. He was generous, jovial and tyrannously affectionate, a good master and a good friend to those who served him well, and a proud and careful father to his fourteen children. Good or bad, he was impressive in his own sphere and not unworthy to be called the 'great Earl of Cork', as he came to be known in Munster, where he had indeed done wonders for commerce and agriculture.

It was typical of Lord Cork's quick eye to advantage that almost as soon as he heard of Arabella Wentworth's death he had written to the newly-appointed Deputy, offering him his eldest available daughter. It was also typical of Wentworth that in evading this offer for himself, he managed to capture Lord Cork's eldest son for his niece Elizabeth Clifford. He calculated that the glorious antiquity of the Cliffords would so dazzle the parvenu Cork that he would be prepared to accept a relatively modest dowry. By this alliance he did an excellent stroke of business for the impoverished Cliffords, and created a bond of relationship between himself and Cork that was close enough to be useful but not so close as to be stifling. [19]

The Chancellor, Lord Loftus, also of northern origin, was a very different kind of man, crafty, cunning and mean. He had very considerable legal abilities of which he was inordinately vain, but had risen in Ireland largely through the influence of his immensely powerful uncle who had, in Queen Elizabeth's time, combined the offices of Archbishop and Lord Chancellor. For a time it had looked as though the nephew had the same dual ambitions, for he had taken deacon's orders, and though he soon abandoned the Church for the Law as a career he held on, till the day of his death and in spite of efforts to dislodge him, to an archdeaconry to which he had been appointed in his earlier years. Cork and Loftus each greeted Wentworth after his own fashion, Cork with exuberant cordiality, Loftus with an insinuating show of good-will.

Lord Wilmot, President of Connaught, was a veteran soldier of the Elizabethan wars who had felt very sure of becoming Deputy himself, an ambition in which he probably had the backing of Loftus. [20] Envy of Wentworth predisposed him to opposition, though he was less politic than Cork or Loftus, of a tough, boisterous and turbulent humour. He had been in trouble ten years before for alienating Crown land in Athlone and keeping the proceeds; at that time he had had influence enough to escape trouble and keep his gains. [21] Under the keen-eyed Wentworth, this kind of dishonesty towards the Crown would not be so easy.

Francis Annesley, Viscount Mountnorris, who had recently procured himself the profitable place of Vice-Treasurer of Ireland, was potentially the most dangerous of them all. He was almost a professional trouble-maker for Deputies of Ireland and an inveterate tale-bearer to Whitehall. He, more than anyone, had made Falkland's position intolerable and had been chiefly responsible for his recall. He was also singularly unsuited to his post of Vice-Treasurer, dilatory in business, interfering, and even insolent. 'He disorders the proceedings of the whole court through his wilfulness and ignorance', complained Wentworth. Moreover he was 'given to good fellowship', and when he was a little drunk, which was often enough, could be criminally indiscreet. He gambled heavily and pursued 'his advantage upon young noblemen and gentlemen not so good gamesters as himself'; if he could get security enough he often advanced them money in order to win the more for himself. As for the funds of which he had control, he was apt to pay in or out where and when he chose, sometimes only after receiving a bribe through one of his servants. [22]

Wentworth's hope was in the notorious disagreement of these councillors among themselves. Cork was playing the game of the new Protestant settlers and his own interests pretty openly. Loftus and Mountnorris had built a rival faction by playing in with the 'old English' and Roman Catholics when it suited them. One day as Cork and Loftus were accompanying him to church, Loftus noisily accused Cork of dishonesty, Cork retaliated that he 'never did anything that was not both honourable and honest and wished that his lordship had been as careful', Loftus rounded on him, Cork hurled back the insult, and in this righteous mood they alighted and entered the church. Even at the Council they could not be quiet. 'I care not for your opinion,' sneered Loftus. 'Nor I for yours,' retorted Cork. 'I care not a rush for you,' shouted Loftus, and so they continued multiplying 'unkind conceits one upon the other' until Wentworth first asked and then commanded them to silence. Mountnorris, though he belonged politically with the Loftus group, detested them both, and refused to honour their warrants on the Exchequer, rudely shouting in their faces: 'I'll pay when and to whom I please.' On another occasion, however, a lesser Councillor, Lord Ranelagh, Cork's son-in-law, publicly called Mountnorris a liar, and the quarrel had had to be smoothed out in a hearing before the Council board. [23]

'Without the arm of his Majesty's counsel and support', wrote Wentworth to Portland immediately on his arrival, 'it is impossible for me to go through with this work.' [24] He had good reason for asking the direct support of his master, for he could foresee one very serious danger. If the Queen's party and the Irish Council should begin to intrigue together against him, he might well be lost. His

fears were justified, for most of these men had important connections at Court. Lord Wilmot had sons at Court, and when one
of them killed his man in a duel, the father had influence enough
to get him a pardon. Mountnorris had a ramification of friends at
Court. Lord Cork had lost no time in marrying his daughter
Lettice, after Wentworth's refusal, to the eldest son of Lord
Goring, one of the Queen's especial favourites. The bridegroom
turned out so unsatisfactory that Wentworth's good offices were
sought by both families to call the young man to order. [25] But
though they could not control their son and son-in-law, Lord
Goring and Lord Cork knew very well how to order their own
affairs to mutual advantage.

On the other hand, one recent development in England greatly
cheered the Deputy. He heard almost immediately on his arrival
in Dublin that Laud had been elevated to the Archbishopric of
Canterbury. It was a foregone conclusion that this would happen
as soon as the see became vacant, but it was none the less a source
of pleasure and reassurance. Although Laud responded rather
gloomily to his joyful letter of congratulation, Wentworth continued to trust that Laud's influence in the King's affairs would
grow continually stronger. [26]

Surrounded by hostile and untrustworthy colleagues in Ireland,
Wentworth was himself supported by the friends and servants he
brought with him. He had chosen a small group of assistants with
some care. He had secured for Christopher Wandesford the
Mastership of the Rolls and a place on the Irish Council; George
Radcliffe too was given a seat a few months later. He singled out
as his principal Secretary of State Philip Mainwaring, a court
hanger-on who had in the past been a useful and intelligent
informant to him especially on foreign affairs; Laud and Cottington did not care for the man but Wentworth's choice was justified,
and he proved a trustworthy assistant. [27]

His great strength, however, lay in the authority he had got
from the King, which confirmed to him direct powers not exercised,
or at least not unquestionably, by his predecessors. In effect
Charles had, by the instructions passed at Wentworth's request in
the Privy Council, given to his Deputy vice-regal powers, made all
his subjects of Ireland answerable to him, while he himself was
answerable only to the King. This was an attempt, in line with the

present policy of the monarchy, to concentrate authority and to prevent the circumvention and cross-purposes which had weakened the royal government in England and made it almost a dead letter in Ireland. It remained to be seen whether the King would stand, in practice, to what he had promised Wentworth on paper. [28] Wentworth's control over the appointment of the principal offices in Ireland had additional significance because it put into the Deputy's hands an unrivalled power of patronage which would certainly be useful in strengthening his hand in Irish politics. Also — since every office-holder paid for his appointment — it gave him a considerable extra source of personal revenue.

Wentworth's letters on the eve of his departure for Ireland had shown him hopeful and full of projects. His idea was first and foremost to make the country profitable to the Crown and to itself by increasing trade and manufacture, naturally of a kind not to compete with England. He would, he promised the King, 'leave your subjects there in much happier condition than I found them, without the least prejudice to your subjects here'. He was hopeful about an agreement with Spain by which Ireland should be a regular victualling station for the Spanish fleet: a most profitable business. But secure government was the *sine qua non* of economic prosperity. Planning for the revenue on the one hand, he was also planning to consolidate the authority of the King in Ireland, to weaken the power of the magnates, to strengthen that of the Crown, and to bring the people — wild Irish, tame Irish, old and new English alike — into a state of suitable docility. This was to be done by combining the rigid exercise of authority with an impartial and universal administration of justice, within the reach of all. He would make the King 'more absolute master of this Kingdom by his wisdom than any of his progenitors were ... by their swords'. [29] This was a large promise because Ireland, in the words of a modern historian, 'presented the paradoxical spectacle of a country in which royal interests were systematically disregarded, royal possessions systematically filched away, and royal revenues steadily diminished, but in which royal power was potentially immense'. Wentworth's resolve was to convert potential into actual power. [30]

It was no use to begin by quarrelling, and Wentworth was conciliatory at his first coming, paying his respects separately to

Cork and Loftus the day after he landed, a courtesy which flattered them. On July 25th he was formally installed: Cork and Loftus with some other Councillors came to the Castle, where he met them, and taking them one on either hand proceeded to the Council Chamber, scrupulously giving them precedence at each doorway. There he took his seat at the head of the table and after hearing the King's commission read, took the Sword of State from the hand of the Chancellor's son, Sir Robert Loftus. Later he proceeded to the Presence Chamber and after making a solemn obeisance to the chair of State, the symbol of his master's sovereignty, took his place on the dais and conferred the honour of knighthood on his youngest brother. The Sword of State, long left in the scabbard, yielded only with difficulty to his powerful hand. [31]

His first sight of his new sphere of activity depressed him. Dublin, the capital of Ireland, did not make a favourable impression on a man who had lived in huge and busy London or the stately and well-built city of York. The unplanned streets sprawled vaguely out from the grey waters of the Liffey to a rather indefinite boundary on the muddy St Stephen's Green. Few of the streets were paved and much of the town appeared, to Wentworth's critical eye, to be rapidly sinking into the mud. He saw no prospect of his favourite sport of hawking, as not a partridge had been seen near Dublin within the memory of man, and what with bogs, mud and ditches, he could not find even space enough for 'taking the air' on foot. The Castle where he was to live was partly derelict and murderously damp. From his study window he looked out on a neglected field, half under water, where an old horse fetlock deep in ooze woefully cropped the muddy grass. Writing to his brother-in-law, Lord Clifford, Wentworth described the poor beast's dejected stumblings, feeling perhaps in that moment that the outlook from his window was a parallel to the outlook before him in Ireland. [32]

Revenue was the immediate problem, and Wentworth's relations with his Council, and with the rival groups in Ireland — the Irish, the 'old English' and the 'new English' — were closely bound up with this. Everyone knew that the Irish army such as it was (and Wentworth thought poorly of it when he saw it) was the only force that could maintain order. But finding money to pay it was an acute problem. Fiscal reforms initiated in the time of King

James I had made it possible for Lord Grandison, Deputy from 1616 to 1622, greatly to reduce the deficit in the Irish budget. Then, from 1624, had come the folly of the European wars in which Buckingham had involved the King. For the defence of Ireland, always vulnerable to attack from England's enemies, a much larger army had to be kept on foot, and although this had been reduced again by the time of Wentworth's appointment, the havoc wrought in Ireland's finances had not been wholly repaired. Apart from a debt of £76,000, there was a gap of £20,000 between ordinary revenue and ordinary expenditure. The additional subsidies voted in return for the Graces were approaching exhaustion, and if a crisis was to be averted some permanent source of revenue must be found, as well as an immediate extra subsidy. [33]

Wentworth had been wrestling with the problem for a full year before he sailed for Ireland. The Council was, of course, divided. Cork, true to the policy of the Protestant settlers, was in favour of reinforcing the recusancy fines and thus, logically enough, compelling the Roman Catholic population to pay for the army which their own potential rebellion rendered necessary. Mountnorris was opposed to this policy, and Wentworth, after consideration, even more so. Recusancy in England and recusancy in Ireland were very different things, and Wentworth, even before he reached Dublin, could see that the enforcement of recusancy fines in Ireland would be a massively unpopular task liable to lead to serious trouble. He probably had the foresight also to see that if, as Cork and other Protestants piously argued, the fines had the result of converting the population, the King's revenue would dry up. Wentworth much preferred to solve the Irish revenue problem through the better collection of the customs. His confidence that he could and would also increase Irish trade fitted into this scheme. He would make Ireland prosperous and he would make Ireland pay. This was better politics and better economics than to penalize the Roman Catholics. So much for the future.

In the meantime an immediate subsidy had to be conjured from somewhere. Wentworth, partly through the services of an agent whom he sent into Ireland in the summer of 1632 and partly through the support of Mountnorris on the Council, persuaded the leading Catholic nobility to agree to a further year's payment of the subsidy fixed under the Graces, in the hope that Wentworth would favourably consider the confirmation of them when he came, and would in all probability not enforce the fines against the recusants.

In this struggle Lord Cork representing the 'new English' had been obstructive on the Council. It certainly looked as though Wentworth intended on his arrival to support Loftus and Mountnorris, and to favour the 'old English' and the Roman Catholics more than his immediate predecessors had done. He showed himself no respecter of new settlers or Protestants in taking action against a group of them who, encouraged by a member of the Council, Lord Balfour, had worked up resistance to the subsidy plan in the county of Fermanagh. Two months before his arrival, he had had the ringleaders from Fermanagh imprisoned and Balfour arrested. Immediately on his arrival they were tried before the Council; Balfour was dismissed from his seat on the Council and sent over to England to answer for his misconduct to the King; the others were released on apology. It was, all told, an effective demonstration that Wentworth was not to be defied with impunity. [34]

The subsidy had only another six months to run, and Wentworth immediately raised in the Council the question of extending it for another year, thus keeping the finances of the government in a reasonably healthy condition until the end of 1634, during which interval a Parliament should be called to reconsider the position. In this move for an extended subsidy he was supported strongly by Loftus and Mountnorris, while Lord Cork said nothing until Parliament was put forward as a bait, when he gave in with a good deal of emphasis on the necessity of calling it. [35]

Soon after this, Wentworth sent for Mountnorris's accounts and, with the help of Radcliffe and his brother George, checked them carefully. [36] Under Mountnorris and his predecessors the custom of paying by paper assignments had arisen; these were optimistically drawn on the expected yield of the revenue, without any real security. Sometimes they were not presented for years but passed from hand to hand and became, temporarily, part of the Irish currency. When they were at length presented, they could not always be met. In the meantime the Treasurer was often ignorant what assignments had been made by his predecessors or subordinates. As Wentworth graphically explained, 'no man knows where or how to come to his money', while the Deputy himself was 'being eternally led blindfold along'. [37]

From the account books of Lord Mountnorris Wentworth turned to the Irish army. Lack of pay was the root of indiscipline, the soldiers lived precariously 'fetching in every morsel of bread upon their swords' points', a situation which, it must be admitted, was not at all uncommon in seventeenth-century armies. The officers bought their commissions and executed them indifferently or not at all. Some troops had never seen their commanders; they were seldom called to their colours, rarely drilled and scarcely armed. 'Their horsemen's staves', commented Wentworth on first seeing some of his cavalry, '[are] rather of trouble to themselves than of offence against an enemy.' [38]

Great was the consternation when three months after his coming Wentworth set up a commission to 'lay open the naked truth of all things'; 'the captains', he wrote with sour amusement, 'begin to fear they may be called upon to do their duties, which will be to their loss.' The fears of the captains were realized in the following spring when an order went out to officers to set their troops in order and recruit them to their full strength within six months. 'Assuredly I will not jest with them,' said Wentworth grimly. The army was small, consisting of two thousand foot and a thousand horse; Wentworth arranged that besides the Deputy's own troop of a hundred horse, two foot companies and a troop of horse were always to be in Dublin for a month at a time in rotation, so that every two years the whole army should pass under his eye. The worn-out and useless arms of the foot soldiers were to be replaced by equipment bought in the Low Countries, at Wentworth's own expense if necessary: he did not trust the Ordnance office in England. One day a week was to be set apart for exercising. [39]

He himself gave an example; in the fine spring of 1634 he rode out as often as his other duties allowed him, to superintend the training of his own troop 'on a large green near Dublin', an impressive figure 'clad in black armour with a black horse and a black plume of feathers'. As his military knowledge had all been acquired from books, his assumption of this martial character, and the black armour in particular, was the subject of some ill-natured jesting. [40] But his idea was sound, none the less; it showed him to have a personal concern for the state of the army.

Over the reorganization of the army Wentworth tested the value of the King's promises. He had assigned the captaincy of a horse troop to Lady Carlisle's brother, Harry Percy, when to his indignation he received a command from the King asking him to keep it for a kinsman of the late Deputy Falkland. Wentworth protested in vain, and at length, seeing he was to have no choice in the matter, gave way with a poor grace, complaining that 'where once the power of reward and punishment is taken away, there respect and obedience are not in any judgment to be expected, or by any means to be enforced', and adding pointedly that he had told the King of Percy's appointment long before any other name was mentioned. [41] The King was moved by his arguments and promised almost apologetically never to let such a thing happen again. But Wentworth was not wholly reassured.

From the army he turned to the navy; Ireland was dependent on the English navy to defend her coasts, and the Admiralty made difficulties in paying and providing the sailors. 'Thus are we used by your officers of the navy', dictated Wentworth stormily to his secretary,

> and have no power to help ourselves, the King's guard for the trade of this Kingdom lying idle in harbour in this busiest time of the year, whilst the subject is pilfered hourly in every creek; it makes no matter, the Deputy must have nothing to do in the Admiralty, it were a strange usurpation for him to trench upon it, nor, by my faith, dare I do it; ... it grieves me to the soul to see the commerce of the Kingdom run immediately and fatally thus to ruin before mine eyes, and that there should be no means afforded me at all to remedy at least as far as I might be able. [42]

With such outbursts he drove the English Admiralty to action, meanwhile advancing his own money to meet the crisis. He had not been in Ireland a week before the first pirate vessel was triumphantly brought in and he welcomed the victorious captain with the well-won honour of knighthood. [43] In the course of the winter a piratical base in the Isle of Man was smoked out and the ringleaders brought in; some of the prisoners were sent to England for justice and Wentworth advised the King to proceed sternly with them. 'The warmer and rounder you seem to be in your resolution to hang them, the better', he wrote to Sir John Coke, but added the moderating advice that only the English-born pirates should suffer death, all others being set free for fear of ill-feeling with foreign governments. The pirate question was indeed beset with diplomatic problems, since many of the rovers were either 'Dunkirkers' or 'Biscayners' and it was not always easy to distinguish between them and seamen claiming to be honest subjects of the King of Spain. Once at least Wentworth arrested a captain and crew who turned out not to be pirates at all; he hastily expunged the error by letting them go with a present of clothes and money for every man. But even to pirates he was reasonably humane, saw to it that the prisoners had warm clothes provided against the cold of Dublin Castle and nagged the dilatory Admiralty to make a decision about their fate instead of leaving them to rot. [44]

For the first half-year in Ireland, Wentworth was busy 'ingathering with all possible circumspection observations where, upon what, and when to advise reformation'. In this task he was not much helped by his Council. 'It is a maxim amongst them', he wrote to his friend the Earl of Carlisle, 'to keep the Deputy as ignorant as possibly they can, so albeit not in place yet he may be subordinate to them in knowledge.' In spite of their resistance, he assured Carlisle, he would 'sound the depths' and reveal their secrets. Making allowances for Wentworth's suspicious and critical temperament, his account of their behaviour is convincing; the technique is not unknown between a minister and his senior civil servants today. [45]

Besides the pressing question of revenue, the administration of justice would certainly need attention. There was trouble at the time of Wentworth's arrival about the Lord Chief Justice, Lord Kilmallock. It appeared that in trying one Philip Bushin for the murder of his wife, he had admitted no witnesses for the defence, had heard the case *in camera*, had empanelled a second jury when the first refused to convict, and after the accused man had been duly hanged had appropriated half his estate, the other half going to the sheriff who had brought the charge of murder. Even if it is assumed that Kilmallock was convinced of Bushin's guilt, his conduct was distinctly questionable.

The case reached the English Privy Council, because rumours went so far as to involve Lord Deputy Falkland in the unsavoury business. Falkland brought an action for slander in the Star Chamber, and the case (which was heard while Wentworth was among the Councillors present) made an inquiry into the conduct of the Lord Chief Justice essential. Kilmallock was sent for and questioned. Of fourteen English judges, twelve declared him guilty, on the evidence, of a deliberate perversion of justice; one thought the matter only a miscarriage, and one, on technical grounds, did not think his case should have been brought before the Privy Council. He was made to restore Bushin's estate to his family and to pay £5,000 fine; he was also, very properly, deprived of his office. [46]

The appointment of the new Lord Chief Justice was in Wentworth's hands. In the accepted manner of the time he sold the place, doing rather better than usual because Lord Cork paid him an additional £1,000 to appoint Sir Gerard Lowther. Lowther was one of the 'new English', a north country man, which accounts for Cork's desire to have him in a key position to support the 'new English' interest. It should be added that he was also a strong and able man, well-fitted for the post. Another name put forward by Cork for legal preferment, with a substantial fee attached, was turned down. [47]

Kilmallock's case was symptomatic of a widespread evil. He had been drawn into it by the sheriff, who having a mind to Bushin's land had willingly listened to the tale of murder put about by one of his personal enemies. Throughout the country men in official positions, men with wealth and power, thought it natural to get what they wanted by intimidation, or process of law heavily tilted in their own favour. This was not a trick confined to the settlers. (Kilmallock was incidentally of Irish stock, and had tried the case in the Irish language.) Native Irish chiefs — like clan chiefs in Scotland, like feudal barons in England of old — naturally packed juries with their clansmen, their tenants or their dependants. For a single man, a poor man, or a stranger, to get justice against a local magnate — be he Irish, old English or new English — was extremely difficult if not impossible.

Ireland had a Court which was supposed to control the magnates, like the Star Chamber or the Council of the North. This was the Court of Castle Chamber, a committee of the Privy Council under the presidency of the Deputy. Its powers were vaguely defined; but it had the right to try cases on petition: in theory this should have enabled Wentworth to right the wrongs of any supplicant who could make out an intelligible petition to the Court. But in practice his powers were much curtailed by a considerable doubt as to whether the Court could hear cases between party and party or only cases directly affecting the Crown.

Wentworth accordingly wrote to the King, emphatically representing that the Court must have authority to try cases between parties, as the Court of Star Chamber did. The King, who was hesitant about breaking precedent, compromised by giving him during his term of office a special dispensation to try cases between parties. Wentworth made full use of it, and as time went on, the Court met sometimes as often as four times in the week and became an important instrument of his plan for securing a system in which 'the poor knew where to seek and to have his relief without being afraid to appeal to his Majesty's Catholick justice against the greatest subject.' It went without saying, of course, that Wentworth also freely used the Court to enforce his Majesty's authority more especially against the greatest subjects. [48]

For a general reform of the abuses in the law courts and the disorders of the revenue, the remedy was through act of Parliament. After six months in the country Wentworth felt that he had the measure of the powers opposed to him and of those on his side. He who had sat through so many abortive Parliaments at Westminster believed that he could call, and manage, a Parliament in Ireland to his own, and the King's, satisfaction. In January 1634 he had drawn up his reasons for an Irish Parliament in a memorandum to the King. On March 1st his youngest brother George Wentworth arrived at Westminster on urgent business from the Deputy. He called on Cottington, dined with Archbishop Laud, visited Lord Treasurer Portland, whom he found ill in bed, and then posted down to Newmarket, where the King was hunting. On the King's return from the chase, he was led into his presence by the friendly Earl of Carlisle, and on his knees presented his brother's dispatches. [49]

NOTES

[1] A revealing prayer in King Charles's hand is in *C.S.P.D.*, 1631-3, p. xvii.
[2] Knowler, I, p. 74.

[3] Ibid, I, p. 111; this is the earliest use of the term 'thorough' in the political sense given in the *Oxford English Dictionary*. See Aylmer, *The King's Servants*, pp. 238-9.

[4] Strafford MSS, XXI, No. 79; Tawney, *Business and Politics under James I*, p. 97; Upton, *Sir Arthur Ingram*, p. 219.

[5] The question of fees and perquisites is fully discussed by Aylmer. He attributes to Wentworth a sinister 'double think' in his attitude to legitimate gains. This is a little hard. Wentworth certainly did things himself that he condemned in others, but I doubt if there was more in this than a rather unusual degree of self-deception.

[6] Strafford MSS, XXI, No. 98; XL, No. 51.

[7] Strafford MSS, XXI, No. 79; Knowler, I, p. 60.

[8] Ibid, I, pp. 65-7; see also Aylmer, pp. 70-1. Mr Aylmer notes in his index the status of William Railton as Keeper of the Council Chamber and later Clerk of the Privy Seal.

[9] Cooper, pp. 232-3; Birch, I, p. 195; *C.S.P.I.*, 1633-49, p. 15.

[10] Strafford MSS, XX, No. 112, Laud to Wentworth, 1st October 1632; Wentworth to Laud, 9th September 1633, both quoted in Lady Burghclere, I, p. 170; Knowler, I, p. 125.

[11] *Biographia Britannica*, VII, p. 4182 n.

[12] *Private letters from the Earl of Strafford to his third wife*, ed. R. Monckton Milnes, *passim*; Elizabeth's brother Edward fought on the Parliamentarian side in the Civil War and became one of Cromwell's major-generals.

[13] *Knyvett Letters*, ed. Schofield, p. 81; Knowler, I, pp. 129-30.

[14] Knowler, II, p. 430; Carte, I, p. 55; *Lismore Papers*, Series I, III, p. 203.

[15] *Lismore Papers*, loc. cit.

[16] Knowler, I, pp. 89, 96.

[17] Ibid., I, p. 93.

[18] Ibid., I, pp. 96, 120; Strafford MSS, VIII, folio 11, Wentworth to Arundel, 19th August 1633.

[19] Strafford MSS, VIII, folio 20, Wentworth to Clifford, 28th September 1633.

[20] Knowler, p. 61; see also Kearney, p. 11.

[21] *C.S.P.I.*, 1615-25, pp. 436-7; Knowler, I, p. 399.

[22] Knowler, I, p. 403.

[23] *Lismore Papers*, Series I, III, pp. 7, 205 ff; IV, p. 110.

[24] Knowler, I, p. 96.

[25] Strafford MSS, XIII, Nos. 20, 23.

[26] Strafford MSS, VIII, folios 13-14, Wentworth to Laud, 28th August 1633; Knowler, I, pp. 110-11.

[27] Knowler, I, pp. 54, 115, 134, 211, 263.

[28] Knowler, I, p. 67; see also Kearney, *Strafford in Ireland*.

[29] Knowler, I, pp. 93, 414; II, pp. 19-20.

[30] Terence Ranger, 'Strafford in Ireland: a Revaluation', *Past and Present*, April 1961, p. 33.

[31] Knowler, I, p. 114; *Lismore Papers*, Series I, III, p. 203; Carte, I, p. 56.

[32] Strafford MSS, VIII, folio 20, Wentworth to Clifford, 28th September 1633.

[33] Kearney, pp. 33-5.

[34] The mechanics and the finances of this very complex incident are to be found in Kearney, pp. 35-41; the judicial and legal aspect of it in O'Grady, pp. 23-4; Knowler, I, 71-2, 77-8, 88, 97, 133, 146-9; see also H.M.C., *Cowper MSS*, I, pp. 481-2.

[35] Knowler, I, pp. 99, 114 ff.

[36] H.M.C. *Various*, VIII, p. 40.

I

[37] Knowler, I, p. 190.

[38] Ibid., pp. 75, 195.

[39] Ibid., pp. 132, 144, 195 ff; Strafford MSS, V, folio 179, Wentworth to Coke, 2nd March 1635.

[40] H.M.C. Report II, p. 283.

[41] Knowler, I, pp. 138, 205.

[42] Ibid., p. 107.

[43] Ibid., pp. 198, 101.

[44] Ibid., pp. 107, 135–7; Strafford MSS, IX, folio 36, Nicholaldie to Wentworth, 25th January 1634.

[45] Ibid., p. 120; Strafford MSS, VIII, folio 12, Wentworth to Carlisle, 27th August 1633.

[46] *C.S.P.I.*, 1633-47, pp. 26-31; *Rawdon Papers*, p. 406; S. R. Gardiner, *Reports of Cases in the Star Chamber*, Camden Society, 1886, pp. 27, 37, 49, 56-7.

[47] F. E. Ball, *Judges of Ireland*, I, pp. 254-5; *Lismore Papers*, I, iii, p. 220; iv, p. 25.

[48] *C.S.P.I.*, 1633-47, p. 253; Knowler, I, p. 201; II, p. 18; Rushworth, *Trial*, pp. 208-11; H.M.C. *Various*, III, p. 155.

[49] Knowler, I, pp. 183 ff; 218 ff.

CHAPTER FOUR

THE PARLIAMENTARY EXPERIMENT

*I take it to be no less than the ground-plot whereon to set and raise safety
and quiet to this kingdom, as it stands with relation within itself, security
and profit as it is in dependence upon the Crown of England.*
Wentworth to the King, January 1634

FOR as long as Wentworth could remember, parliaments had
been called as a last resort when the government was in straits
for money. This had given them their power to try conclusions
with the King. The Irish government was in no such difficulty,
because the subsidy, which he had organized in the previous
summer, still had several months to run. This put the Deputy in a
strong position.

The King considered in detail Wentworth's lengthy propositions
for the managing of Parliament and the probable business to be
set before it. He explained that he would prevent grievances and
supply becoming so interwoven as to give Parliament any bargaining power, by having two sessions, the first for the granting of
money, the second for legislation, and the second wholly dependent
on the success of the first. [1]

On the other hand he was anxious that the Irish should not be
overburdened with taxes if they did their duty by giving freely in
the first place. For the rest he was a good deal concerned about the
tricky business of the Graces, the confirmation of which was sure
to be raised by this Parliament, although not — if his purpose
held — until after the money had been voted. The management of
this difficult question he hoped to organize by having the Protestant
and Catholic interests fairly well balanced in the House, so that
he could, in his own words, 'poise one by the other ... which single
might perchance prove more unhappy to deal with'. He also
suggested that a great number of army officers might be included
'who, having immediate dependence upon the Crown, may almost
sway the business betwixt the two parties, which way they please'.
But this piece of cunning the King rejected, asking Wentworth

'to make choice rather by particular knowledge of men's interests and good affections'. [2]

Wentworth as an instructor on how to manage Parliament tickled the humour of some of the King's councillors. When, in another letter, which Secretary Coke read aloud to them, he was emphatic about preventing troubles like those which had arisen in 1628 through the prearranged plans of the King's opponents, Cottington smoothly interpolated '*quorum pars magna fui*,' and got a laugh, which Laud reported to Wentworth, who failed to see the joke. [3] But in general he had every reason to be pleased with the royal response: Charles fixed the calling of the Irish Parliament for the following Trinity Term, assured Wentworth that he left all to his 'courage and dexterity', and added to his official approval a private letter in which he hoped (though not very sanguinely) that in this matter of Parliaments 'you would set me down there an example of what to do here.' George Wentworth was back in Ireland with the royal commission and a sheaf of letters before the end of April 1634. [4]

All this while Wentworth had kept very close about his plans for the legislative business of the coming Parliament. The crux of the matter would be the fate of the Graces; legislation had been promised to make them statute law in Ireland. There had been no attempt to fulfil the promise because no Parliament had been called, and this, the first Parliament to be called since the King agreed in principle to these concessions, was bound to be faced with the awkward problem of either rejecting them or turning them into law. The Earl of Fingall, a prominent proprietor among the old English of the Pale, quite legitimately called on Wentworth and tried to sound him about the proposed legislation, and was snubbed for his pains. [5]

Wentworth's particular trouble was that he had, hitherto, appeared to favour the 'old English' and the Roman Catholics. But in his own mind he was quite certain that a continued expansion of the area of English settlement was desirable for the civilization and Protestant conversion of the benighted Irish. His ultimate and fixed project was to organize a plantation of Connaught as thorough as that of Ulster had been a generation earlier. He therefore had no intention of confirming any of the Graces which, by leading to the recognition of existing land tenure, would prevent the plantation. Once he had shown his hand on this vital question he was bound to lose the support of the 'old English' and the Irish, all of whom resented the Protestant newcomers and many of whom would find their property affected. His only real hope of getting his subsidies without trouble was to lead on the 'old English' and the Irish in Parliament with the hope that he was their friend.

The nature of the Irish Parliament had been radically altered in the last fifty years. In 1585 in the last Parliament to meet before the furious wars which ended Queen Elizabeth's reign, there had been a large Roman Catholic majority. English policy had altered this by the time the only Parliament of King James's reign met. The creation of a number of new boroughs in the interests of Protestant settlers, and the plantation of Ulster, gave the Protestants the majority in the Parliament of 1613 — 132 members, as against 100 Roman Catholics. In the House of Lords, the Anglican bishops and the few Protestant peers had only a narrow majority over the predominantly Roman Catholic nobility. But the number of peers in Ireland had been very nearly quadrupled since then by the reckless operations of King James and King Charles, selling titles for cash. The great majority of these new peers were Protestants. Some of them, moreover, were permanent absentees. This gave the Deputy the chance to allot proxies for them, and as he naturally chose for these the nobility likely to support him, it gave him a strong government majority in the Lords; 'rather their Proxies than their company', he wrote cheerfully to Sir John Coke. [6]

With his twenty years' experience of English Parliaments and elections he was busy organizing support for the government in the weeks preceding the elections. It was important, of course, to have a sufficient number of officials and government dependents in the House to inspire and guide the debates. This had been the Elizabethan method, and the neglect of it had been largely responsible for the trouble under the Stuarts. He sent out about a hundred letters to persons of influence, recommending candidates for election, not always with the hoped result. The town of Dundalk obstinately rejected both his Protestant nominees and returned Roman Catholics of their own choice. Lord Cork — who was told to his annoyance that his sons, aged twelve and sixteen, though peers in their own right, could not take their seats in the House of

Lords — was asked to secure the return of six government candidates for boroughs known to be in his control. To show his independence, he compromised by returning only three of them. They were Philip Mainwaring, the Secretary of State; George Wentworth; and the Deputy's physician, Maurice Williams. He failed to secure the election of Thomas Little, Wentworth's private secretary, who was found a seat elsewhere. Christopher Wandesford and George Radcliffe, those twin pillars on whom Wentworth always relied for support, were accommodated with the boroughs of Kildare and Armagh respectively. [7]

The Speaker, though in theory chosen by the House of Commons, was the nominee of the Deputy. Here Wentworth was ingenious, for he chose an able Irish lawyer, the Recorder of Dublin, Nathaniel Catelin. If not a Roman Catholic, he was certainly of Catholic sympathies, and had some years before been involved in a quarrel between the Dublin Corporation and the Lords Loftus and Wilmot which had lost him his seat on the Council. The choice was therefore likely to be popular with the Roman Catholics in Parliament, and showed that independence of his Council's feelings which had already been very noticeable in Wentworth's conduct. [8]

Parliament met on July 14th, 1634. Wentworth rode down in state surrounded by all the peers of Ireland and officers of the vice-regal Court in due order, the young Earl of Ormonde carrying the Sword before him. 'The meeting was', he wrote afterwards, 'with the greatest civility and splendour Ireland ever saw.' Next day before both Houses he emphasized the power of the King and the duty that they owed him. 'The resolutions set in assembling of Parliaments,' he began, 'are the hidden secrets, the privileged peculiars of Kings, for which they are in no kind accountable.' Changing his tone he grew more confidential, and rapidly outlined in general terms what he hoped they would achieve for the good of Ireland. He emphasized how much they owed to the King 'under the well-pleasing shade of whose greatness and goodness you enjoy all that you have'. After this possibly tactless reminder of the King's power, he enlarged on the theme of supply. Let them vote the subsidies in this session, and in the next 'his Majesty, above all you can think, will go along with you in that latter session ... but still according to the order of good manners, Reason and Nature, himself first, his people afterwards.' Having, as it were, promised and withdrawn in one breath, he now seemed to promise again: 'Lay your hands upon your hearts and tell me if ever the desires of a mighty and powerful King, were so moderate, so modest, taking, asking nothing for himself, but all for you.' Bargaining with the King was not to be thought of: 'It is far below my great master to come at every year's end, with his hat in his hand, to intreat you that you would be pleased to preserve yourselves.'

Lastly he exhorted them to unity.

'Divide not between Protestant and Papist, divide not nationally, betwixt English and Irish. The King makes no distinction between you, reputes you all without prejudice and that upon safe and true grounds … his good and faithful subjects…. Above all divide not between the interests of the King and his people, as if there were one being of the King and another being of his people. This is the most mischievous principle that can be laid in reason of State…. You might as well tell me an head might live without a body, or a body without a head, as that it is possible for a King to be rich and happy without his people be so likewise, or that a people can be rich and happy without the King be so also…. Their well-being is individually one and the same, their interests woven up together with so tender and close threads, as cannot be pulled asunder without a rent in the Commonwealth…. Remember therefore that I tell you, you may easily make or mar this Parliament.' [9]

Like all Wentworth's speeches, the address to the Irish Parliament was delivered with great histrionic skill, which was not lost on an audience which appreciated eloquence. On earlier occasions, before the Commons at Westminster and the Council of the North, Wentworth had been not only eloquent but extremely lucid. On this occasion he was only lucid where he could afford to be — in making it clear that nothing whatever would be done in the way of legislation until the subsidies had been voted. As for what he would allow to be done thereafter, in the King's name, that — by the time he had finished speaking — was anybody's guess. The 'old English' were not deprived of hope, but they were not much encouraged in it either.

They made a rather feeble demonstration of their rights against the overriding claims of the Deputy by trying to question the rightful election of some of the government nominees, as being absentees unknown in the places they were supposed to represent. But this was felt by the Protestant majority in the House to be a dangerous move in favour of stronger Roman Catholic representation, and a motion, put by Christopher Wandesford, resulted in a majority of twenty-eight in favour of shelving inquiry until the more important business of the session had been discussed. [10]

Wentworth was fairly sure, none the less, that the 'old English' and the Roman Catholics generally would vote for the subsidies in the hope that the Graces would be ratified. In the Council there was a faint stirring of opposition in another quarter. Sir William Parsons and Lord Ranelagh — both of the Protestant interest — were against his pressing immediately for a subsidy vote. Their reasons remain a little mysterious. He himself thought it was 'a design to gain time, to frame parties, and to grow into full understanding among themselves'. [11] It may have been something like this, a desire to take stock of the bargaining possibilities offered by a Parliament, possibilities which Wentworth was so evidently intent on choking.

He acted with his usual ruthlessness. Having got most of the Council to agree with him, he then charged them all to support the vote in Parliament. He was not going to have members of the government, either openly or privately, opposing government measures. As a result Parliament, within a week of its opening, voted six subsidies unanimously: no group in Parliament felt strong enough or sure enough of the position to risk alienating the Deputy. Too much was at stake. The Graces were yet unconfirmed, and while they continued in this state the Irish and the 'old English' had every reason to try to please the new Deputy in the hope that their titles to their land would be recognized. The 'new English', on the other hand, wooed his support for the opposite reason: in the hope that he would abrogate the Graces which protected existing landowners, and throw open more land for plantation.

The remaining fortnight of the session was filled in with trivial legislation; in Wentworth's words, 'we have entertained and spun them out in discourses but nevertheless kept them from concluding anything.' He was thus, though with a good deal of artificial delay, able to postpone the open decision on the Graces until the second session. Parliament was adjourned on August 2nd, with considerable ceremony, and Wentworth wound up the subsidies question by undertaking that none of the money should be used outside Ireland. [12]

On this last point he had already written to Portland: 'We are but now entering here upon our spring and let us not be nipped in the head so soon as we peep forth.' At the close of the session he repeated his opinion that the diversion of Irish subsidies would 'utterly shipwreck my credit and estimation amongst them'. But his anxiety was not allayed by Portland's assurances of agreement. He wrote to Laud: 'My Lord Treasurer promises not to fetch any of them [i.e. moneys] hence, but I see them on that side driven to such streights as like sinking men, they catch hold of each twig to keep themselves above water, and I am still in mortal dread of them.' [13] It was his ultimate intention to increase the King's revenue through the Irish customs; but that lay in the future. In the meantime he was right to believe that any diversion of the subsidies away from the objects for which they had been voted would undermine confidence in his government.

As far as good management was concerned, Wentworth had a right to be pleased with the outcome of the first session. His personal hopefulness and confidence in his future were heightened when, on September 17th, his wife gave birth to a son, 'a young Irishman' as the proud father described him. [14] In this buoyant mood he wrote privately to the King asking for an earldom. There had been talk of an earldom when he accepted the post of Deputy, and such a mark of the royal favour would have greatly strengthened him for the coming and far more difficult Parliamentary session that lay ahead. But Charles did not care to be pestered for advancement. He had given, for cash and for services much less than Wentworth's, a number of peerages, but he had an objection to gratifying this too insistent servant: possibly it arose from his memories of Wentworth's tedious angling for ennoblement for at least ten years before he was taken into the royal favour. He had waited then; he could wait again. 'I am certain that ye will willingly stay my time,' wrote the King, 'now that ye know my mind so freely, that I may do all things *a mi modo*.' [15]

Without any special mark of the King's favour, therefore, Wentworth re-opened Parliament on November 4th, 1634. The position was now extremely delicate. On November 6th the House appointed a Committee to receive and report on the Deputy's pronouncement on the Graces. Though he had dropped hints that he might not be able to confirm all of them, the 'old English' and the Irish were still very hopeful. One forewarning there had been which they did not seem to have taken too seriously. This was the establishment at the close of the last session of a Commission for Defective Titles. In theory this Commission was to confirm ownership of land by straightening out the tangled claims of landowners who appealed to it. It was not yet absolutely clear how it would work in practice, and this may account for the fact that it had been confirmed in Parliament without serious opposition. In effect, Wentworth's plan was that the Commission should straighten out tenures wherever possible by making landowners hold *in capite* from the Crown. The salutary effect of this would be to confirm them in their possessions against further encroachments or claims; but the reverse side of the process was that it made them liable to all the irksome dues which King Charles's government sought to extract from tenants of the Crown, and brought them within the jurisdiction of the Court of Wards so that the guardianship of their heirs, and all the notorious profits to be made out of these, went to the Crown whenever a proprietor died before his son was of full age. The Irish Court of Wards, reorganized about fifteen years earlier, was one of the few institutions in Ireland which consistently made money for the Crown.

If the Commission for Defective Titles was to work at all, it was evident that one of the most important concessions in the Graces would have to be withdrawn: namely that which assured to the landowners of Ireland that sixty years' possession would be admitted as a valid title to land without further trouble. Apparently those who were liable to be worst affected by the Commission, the 'old English' and the Irish landowners, had not fully taken in the contradiction between it and the concession in the Graces, or else believed that the Deputy, who had always been so favourable to them, would find some way round it.

For the first ten days of the new session Wentworth played for time. But on November 17th one of his numerous government bills for improving social and public morality was defeated by seventy-eight votes to sixty-nine. As it was a bill against bigamy it is interesting that the Roman Catholic side of the House voted it down, but the vote had little to do with the content of that particular bill. It was a provocative gesture by the Irish and the 'old English' to show their dissatisfaction with the government. The numbers involved in the voting also showed that the government groups were not effectively performing their task of holding their supporters together and making sure they attended the House.

Another incident had meanwhile occurred to make further argument between Wentworth and the Commons. An eccentric English settler in Munster named Sir Vincent Gookin had composed a long address to Wentworth on the state of Ireland. Like many settlers, he found the Irish very trying: 'They are full of words but to little purpose ... their delights are in nothing but idleness.' Where Gookin differed from other Englishmen was that he disliked not merely the Irish but everyone else as well, 'new English' and 'old English', lawyers, clergy, soldiers and sea-captains — all were villainous, dishonest, grasping and in conspiracy to deceive the virtuous, hard-working and honourable Sir Vincent, who had contrived, somehow and in spite of them all, to amass a considerable fortune. He never sent his address to Wentworth, but he contrived to have it scattered abroad among members of Parliament, who were naturally very much annoyed and 'would have hanged him if they could'. Wentworth, when he saw the paper, rather agreed with their annoyance, but was quite certain that he did not want the Irish House of Commons claiming the right to try Sir Vincent, which they were on the point of doing. He was not going to see them make the judicial claims that had proved so troublesome when exercised by Parliament in England. Consequently he took steps to call Sir Vincent to order himself, and on November 26th informed the House that he had done so. [16]

The timing of this check to their pretensions was not very fortunate. The very next day, he issued the long awaited results of his deliberation on the Graces. Presumably he thought that the Protestants and 'new English' would be present in sufficient strength to control the House, but evidently not enough had been done to assure their attendance and his decision on the Graces was very ill received. Of the fifty-one detailed demands which were comprised in them Wentworth agreed that ten only should become statute law, and that all the rest, with the exception of two, should be continued at the discretion of the government. The two exceptions, articles 24 and 25, affected land tenure, especially in Connaught, and in the region where the 'old English' and Irish proprietors were predominant; here sixty years' occupation was not to be regarded as conferring a sufficient title to land. The meaning of the rejection of these two clauses was abundantly clear: Wentworth would support and extend the plantations, and Connaught would be colonized as Ulster had been. On top of this threat to the Irish and the 'old English', the Deputy was only willing to continue the toleration of Roman Catholics in legal and official positions at discretion. It remained open to him to suspend any Catholic lawyer or office-holder by the simple process of calling him before the Council and tendering to him the Oath of Supremacy. This oath, recognizing the King as head of the Church, no Roman Catholic could or would take. Even if this was never done, the threat of it was a heavy blow to the Irish and the 'old English', and above all to the great number of lawyers and office-holders now in the House of Commons.

The response to the announcement on the Graces was immediate and more troublesome than Wentworth had expected. 'The refusing their two darling Articles', he wrote to Secretary Coke, 'did much unsettle them, which, together with the apprehension of the plantations (which of all things the Friars and Priests abhor) so far stirred the Popish party as they grew very peevish; and having by the negligent attendance of the Protestants gained two or three questions upon the Dividing of the House ... they grew upon it to such a wanton insolence, as they rejected Hand over Head all that was offered them from his Majesty and this State; the bill against bigamy they would not should be engrossed; the law for corrective Houses they absolutely cast out; the law against fraudulent conveyances ... they would have none of; ... in all these things never gave or answered reason but plainly let us see their wills were met together to refuse all, but to refute nothing.'

Wentworth, for two or three days, considered the possibility of an adjournment, but fortunately for him the Roman Catholic party over-played their hand and the negligent Protestants — presumably whipped in by some government supporters, though

Wentworth does not specifically say so — came back to their Parliamentary duties. The real error was made by Sir Piers Crosby, an unscrupulous tough with 'old English' connections, who was a member of the Council. 'Vanity and forgetfulness of duty', wrote Wentworth, 'transported him so far, as that in the bill for repressing of murders, by a strict punishment of the accessories, wherein the law here before was defective, he declares himself as it were the ringleader of that party, passing his vote not only against the bill, but (when some endeavoured to save it by that means) even against the recommitment too.'

At this, Wentworth took action. At a Council meeting with twenty-eight members present he put Crosby's conduct before them and secured a unanimous vote for his sequestration from that body. (Though later this was to be raked up as a tyrannous act, it is — on the whole — the general practice of governments to object to strong opposition in Parliament from one of their own members, though the modern practice more often takes the form of the voluntary resignation, rather than the expulsion, of the dissident.)

Wentworth followed this with a harangue to the Council on the feeble conduct of the Protestants in the House of Commons. The effect of this was to bring them to the House in larger numbers, and on December 3rd Christopher Wandesford moved for the expulsion of Geoffrey Barron, the member for Clonmel, a very vocal leader of the Roman Catholic group. The previous day a similar motion had been defeated, but on December 3rd it was carried by sixteen votes. From that time on, business fell again into a course more pleasing to Wentworth. The Roman Catholics continued, as a demonstration, to dispute most measures, but the Protestants were now at full strength and in the remaining ten days of the session all the important government measures were, by one means or another, hurried through the House. The crisis of the Graces was over and Wentworth had his way. [17]

When Parliament was adjourned over Christmas, Wentworth was pleased with everything except the 'peevishness' of the 'Popish party'. He was wilfully blind to their very real grievances, and put down their opposition to the influence of the Friars and Jesuits who worked them up against the idea of further colonization — which Wentworth called 'civilization' — and to their own 'insolent forwardness' and other faults of temperament. [18] His use of words

157

reflects the comments he had made on the Catholic French when, as a young man, he had characterized them in his diary as sullen, dogged and superstitious.

A bigoted Protestant, he felt, at best, contempt, and at worst a real hatred, for the Papists, and took a sour pleasure in retailing their quarrels, their delinquencies, or even their poverty. When the secular and regular priests had one of their habitual squabbles, Wentworth summoned the Catholic Archbishop of Dublin before him for consultation. He unkindly described him to Laud as a fat, florid man who would not have looked out of place marketing a bale of cloth in Leadenhall. (The same would incidentally have been true of Archbishop Laud.) For the rest, he was clothed in a black suit, a brown cloak, and blue stockings, and all his legal advisers in coarse brown cloth with most of the buttons off their doublets. [19] That his shabby appearance was the effect of a poverty very suitable in a follower of Christ did not occur to Wentworth. Later on he recorded with irritation that a Carmelite friar, prosecuted for seducing a young girl, was being made into a martyr by the faithful. [20] What was to be expected, he hinted, of such backward and superstitious people?

In his curiously hard indifference to anything but the material issues, he seems sincerely to have thought that opposition to the benefits of English and Protestant civilization could arise from nothing but wilful stupidity. In the modern phrase, he might be called an advocate of social engineering; he expected those who in the process of improvement were bulldozed out of their estates, their religion and their way of life to recognize the benefits conferred on them. For the rest, Catholicism was, for him, with his Calvinist and Elizabethan background, the religion of traitors and rebels. 'So long as this Kingdom continues Popish they are not a people for the Crown of England to be confident of', [21] he wrote. The statement was, of course, true, so long as the Crown of England continued a policy of taking away their land to give it to Protestant strangers. But that, Wentworth did not add — and did not even think.

During the last months Wentworth had noticed and brought on to the Council a valuable supporter. This was the Earl of Ormonde. This high-hearted nobleman, twenty-four years old and head of one of the greatest 'old English' families, the widespread and territorially powerful Butlers, had been brought up as a royal ward and a Protestant, though the rest of his kindred were of the old religion. Handsome, intelligent and valiant, he was also to the very core of his being a man of honour: loyal, chivalrous and just. His first contacts with the Deputy had been typically spirited. He had taken strong exception to Wentworth's tactless description of the Irish, in his address to Parliament, as a 'conquered nation'. That evening he told him, face to face, that such words 'were not well'. Wentworth never cared for criticism, and he was further provoked when Ormonde defied his express order against the wearing of swords in Parliament and smartly told an official who tried to take it from him that 'if he had his sword it should be in his guts'. Wentworth summoned him before the Council. He appeared with his Earl's patent and threw it on the table as proof that the King had made him an Earl *per cincturam gladii* and for less than the King he would not ungird his sword. Wentworth conceded the force of the argument.

George Radcliffe, consulted about this young firebrand, urged Wentworth to make a friend and not an enemy of him. This was good advice, but Wentworth could hardly have followed it with success had there not been, in spite of these early clashes, a considerable natural sympathy between him and Ormonde. They shared the same energy, the same regard for efficiency, even in some degree the same hopes for a more orderly and more prosperous Ireland. In January 1635 Ormonde was sworn of the Council. It was the official beginning of a career in Irish politics that was to extend over fifty years.

The winning over of Ormonde was something more than a personal triumph. Ormonde was, by right of his position, the natural leader of the 'old English'. His Protestant upbringing divided him from them on the religious question and his loyalty to Wentworth deprived them of his support when, within the next years, the land question became acute. Quite apart from his ability and character and positive influence, all of which stood Wentworth in good stead, this negative effect of his dissociation from the interests of his own people was to be, for a time at least, a source of strength to the Deputy. [22]

Parliament met for a third session on January 26th to complete the legislative programme and allot the sums of money to be paid by each region towards the subsidy. Once again Wentworth's logic was greater than his political cunning. He insisted that the burden be distributed according to the relative wealth of the provinces and of the landowners. The great men, he wrote to Sir John Coke, had hitherto been apt to lay 'the burden upon the poor tenants most unreasonably freeing themselves; as for example, my lord of Cork, as sure as you live, paid towards the £20,000 yearly contribution, not a penny more than 6/8 Irish a quarter.' [23] It could hardly be expected that Lord Cork, and others who had behaved in the same way, would applaud the Deputy's plans for equalizing the burden. But if individual settlers were irritated by an increase in their liabilities, the 'old English' were once again the chief sufferers. Leinster, which had been longest in cultivation, was the richest province and was assessed for the largest contribution, and in Leinster the 'old English' predominated. The new assessment was none the less generally accepted, and the Irish revenue assured for the next four years at a rate that would meet current expenditure, especially the army, and go far to wipe out the existing debt. [24] Later, when his need was greatest, in the Parliament of 1640, Wentworth would reap the harvest of the discontent that the new arrangement had sown.

When Parliament rose on April 18th, 1635, Wentworth had every reason to congratulate himself. Not only had money been secured but highly satisfactory legislation had been passed. The new laws were printed soon after in a small but stately volume, bearing cherubs and cornucopia on its title page, followed by the royal arms and, on the next page, the arms of Wentworth handsomely set out.

The new acts were the clear expression of Wentworth's policy. As in the North, so also in Ireland, he tried to implement the paternal and moral responsibilities of government and attempted at the same time to regulate and improve the conduct of the people while protecting the poor against exploitation and gross injustice. Hence therefore the acts against bigamy, sodomy and blasphemy; hence also the act for setting up houses of correction for vagabonds. But there was an evident intention of protecting the poorer sort in the acts limiting the interest to be taken by usurers, curtailing the blackmailing activities of informers who preyed on the humble and ignorant, forbidding landlords from taking heriots illegally, and increasing the penalties against those who bribed or intimidated juries. Acts intended to facilitate the bringing of murderers to justice and to prevent the forcible abduction and marriage of young heiresses were evident reflections on the still uncontrolled and unpoliced conditions of great parts of Ireland. Another group of acts, some of which earlier Parliaments had also passed, dealt with agriculture and the countryside and were an attempt to improve and modernize conditions. Roads and bridges were to be kept in repair; penalties were threatened against those who robbed orchards, barked trees and injured young crops; measures were to be taken to maintain and increase the number of fish. The primitive methods of farming prevalent among the Gaelic population were denounced: these included ploughing with the plough attached to the horse's tail, plucking sheep instead of shearing them, and burning the corn to divide straw from grain, a remarkably inefficient method which destroyed the winter fodder and bedding of the cattle and left the grain singed and ill-tasting. This last act was phrased with some fierceness against those of 'a natural lazy disposition ... that will not build barns to house and thresh their corn in, or houses to keep their cattle from the violence of the weather'.

The government was legislating against the customs of a nomadic civilization which survived in desperate poverty. Ploughing by the tail and pulling the wool off sheep were the habits of a peasantry too poor and too primitive to possess or to make proper instruments. In the circumstances it was not remarkable that Wentworth, in common with the new settlers, saw an obvious remedy in taking over as much as possible of the agriculture of Ireland themselves. The kind of paternalism that strives to improve agriculture by educating the natives and distributing better instruments among them had hardly been thought of in the seventeenth century; and besides it would have been far too expensive. All Wentworth could do was to legislate against bad farming, probably with little effect, and continue with his plans for 'civilizing' Ireland by further plantations.

The most effective and significant of the laws passed by this Parliament were however the group which clarified the laws, especially those related to land and inheritance. Here the emphasis was consistently on increasing and centralizing the powers of the Crown, making more landowners hold direct of the King, and enlarging the scope of the Court of Wards in relation to the estates and education of minors. In the vital question of the possession of land, the legislation of Wentworth's Parliament tended to consolidate the power of the Crown and to make the way clear for a still further influx of 'new English' settlers. [25]

Though the interests of the English Crown and the Protestant settlers came first with Wentworth, his protestations about justice for the poor and a measure of economic consideration for Ireland were not mere words. He continued to prevent the taking of Irish subsidies away from Ireland. He was successful in getting an export duty on English coal removed because of the distress and shortage it caused in Ireland. He held out firmly against an English attempt to curtail the export of tallow — an important article of Irish commerce — in the interests of English soap monopolists. He had moreover set in motion a plan for revising and reducing all the fees to be charged in law courts; lists of the standard rates were to be put up in public places and overcharging was to be punished. When word came from England, where a parallel scheme for the revision of fees had been mooted, that the Irish plan could be postponed till the English one was ready, he replied caustically that he saw 'no ground why the reformation of fees here should wait expectant upon that of England'. In his view the English reform would, at the present rate of progress, not be complete in his lifetime. [26]

It seemed to Wentworth in the spring of 1635 that he had achieved great things. He had called and managed a Parliament and got from it the revenue and the legislation he needed. 'This is the only ripe Parliament that hath been in my time,' he wrote, 'all the rest have been a green fruit broken from the bough.' On consideration he believed that plucking fruits from the tree of Parliament might be made even easier by a stealthy disfranchisement of the Roman Catholic burghs. After all, what was the use of a seat in Parliament to these 'obstinate, senseless creatures ... who had no more wit nor will than to do just as their Jesuits and Friars appointed them'. He thought about twenty towns could probably be disfranchised by finding faults in their charters. [27]

On the other hand he would not allow Parliament to have a monopoly of legislation. 'I purpose to revive all the laws they have refused,' he wrote to Secretary Coke, 'and to establish by Act of State as many of them one after another as this Council shall think fit, it being necessary this people should see his Majesty will be without more ado obeyed and have his subjects governed and carried those ways which he in his own wisdom shall most approve and prescribe for them.' [28]

Wentworth's proceedings were noticed with a certain awed amazement in England. Sir Thomas Roe, the veteran diplomatist who, thirty years before, had led a pioneer embassy to the Court of the Great Mogul, reported on him perspicaciously: 'He does great wonders; he has called and managed a Parliament and made a firm understanding and love between the King and his people, besides getting money. He is severe abroad and in business and sweet in private conversation; retired in his friendships, but very firm; a terrible judge and a strong enemy; a servant violently zealous in his master's ends and not negligent in his own; one that will have what he will, and though of great reason, he can make his will greater when it may serve him, affecting glory by a seeming contempt; one that cannot stay long in the middle region of fortune, being entreprenant, but will either be the greatest man in England, or much less than he is.' [29]

Roe saw both sides of the situation. He realized at once Wentworth's strength and weakness; he saw that success would make a man of his nature over-confident when his greatest need would be caution, for Wentworth's success provoked hostility and criticism almost at the same time as admiration and he did not bear his achievements with ingratiating modesty. He had even boasted to the King that none of the last five Deputies could compare with him, an opinion which would do him no good if repeated to the relations and friends of his predecessors. The King graciously declared to him that 'the accounts that you give me are so good, that if I should answer them particularly, my letters would rather seem panegyrics than dispatches.' Cottington was convinced that Wentworth had won a complete victory; 'My Lord Marshal', he declared, 'is your own, my lord of Canterbury your chaplain, Secretary Windebanke your man, the King your favourite, and I your good lord. In earnest you have a mighty stock of opinion amongst us which must of necessity make you damnable proud if you take not heed.' [30]

The astute Roe had uttered a profound truth when he said that Wentworth might become 'the greatest man in England'. The

Lord Deputy, absorbed as he now was in Irish politics, still looked to England as the ultimate scene of his operations and seat of his power.

In March 1635 the Lord Treasurer Portland died, and the King, pending a new choice, consigned the office to commissioners. Already Wentworth's friends were congratulating him; even before Portland's death one of the Privy Council wrote pressing him to come to England. 'I know none so fitting to succeed, or so able to fill the place,' he urged, 'my great master's service needs such an Atlas.' Cottington and Newcastle added their entreaties. [31] With the wind apparently set in his favour, Wentworth charged Cottington to prevent his appointment, and declared to Newcastle that nothing would make him stir from Ireland till the post was otherwise bestowed. More emphatically he wrote to one of his agents:

> I do not serve the King out of the ordinary ends that the servants of great princes attend them with; great wealth I covet not; greater powers than are already entrusted to me by my master I do not desire; I wish much rather abilities to discharge those I have, as becomes me, than any of those I have not. Again I serve not for reward, having received much more than I shall ever be able to deserve. [32]

Wentworth's reasons for this rejection of the post for which he was so eminently fitted, and which three years before he had so evidently desired, are not easy to fathom. He fully trusted only one of the numerous associates to whom, from Ireland, he wrote his lengthy letters. He was wholly frank only to the Archbishop, and frank to him under the double cover of a code and of an oblique method of expression. The cipher which he used is preserved among his papers and the sheets covered with close and clearly written numbers can be easily turned back into English; but when this is done there remains the additional problem of discovering precisely what he meant by the allusive, elusive phrases and the sidelong references to past conversations and the private jokes that make up a large part of his letters to Laud.

In his letters to the Archbishop there are indications that he did indeed want the post of Treasurer, or would have wanted it had circumstances been propitious. But the amiable Cottington, who declared both in letters to Wentworth and in talks to Wentworth's friends that he had not the least desire to be Treasurer himself, that he thought none fitter for the post than Wentworth, and a dozen other such protestations — Cottington in spite of all this was hoping for the appointment himself. Wentworth suspected therefore that a network of intrigue and secret jealousy would entangle him if he were promoted to the vacant place. [33] If he left Ireland with his work half done, with resentful enemies like Piers Crosby and the Earl of Cork in close touch with other potential enemies in England, he might find himself in the kind of trouble that had met Lord Falkland on his recall from Ireland. He was not by nature a cautious man, but he was quite perceptive enough to see that he would be unlikely to do himself or the King any good if he took the office of Treasurer in the teeth of widespread and insidious hostility which would cripple his action and perhaps achieve his ruin.

If the King had wanted Wentworth for Treasurer he could have had him, and it is possible that Wentworth hoped for some such overriding command to give him the office that he declared, officially, he did not want. But the King did not want him for Treasurer, for reasons which can easily be deduced. Charles, with no gift for finance, was surrounded by courtiers who put up to him innumerable ideas for raising money, usually by monopolies, and always in ways which would fill their own pockets first. Charles was easily deceived by these ideas and hated to be undeceived. Moreover, as he lived surrounded by these buzzing gnats — who were often very amiable gentlemen — he disliked having to refuse them their requests. Wentworth had been, and was still being, extremely obstinate over a project much talked of at Court, which enjoyed strong support from the Queen's friends. This was a soap monopoly by which a large income was to be made both for the monopolists and for the King by the manufacturers of a new kind of soap. One of the concessions they needed to ensure success was a restraint on the exportation of Irish tallow, and this Wentworth had blocked, [34] behaviour which the soap monopolists, to their own satisfaction, ascribed to his interest in the yield of the Irish customs, of which he was a farmer. He had also been difficult about lesser requests, and was permanently troublesome about royal grants affecting the Irish revenues or Irish land. 'Ten thousand pounds for my Lord of Nithsdale', he wrote ungraciously to the King, 'strikes deep into this exchequer. Yet it shall be paid as your

Majesty appoints. I do nevertheless most humbly supplicate your Majesty that no more of this kind be fetch forth of your subsidies, till the debts of the Crown be discharged.' [35]

The Treasurer was never — or rarely — a popular character at Court, but Wentworth as Treasurer was likely to be a constant drag on everyone's pleasures. It is conceivable also that Charles, who had a very long memory for his enemies, recalled that Wentworth had been a friend and protégé of Lord Middlesex, that most successful and most unpopular of Treasurers, whom Charles, as Prince of Wales, had vindictively hounded to destruction because he opposed the Spanish War with which he and Buckingham had become besotted. [36] Whatever the reasons, Charles did not want to have Wentworth for Treasurer, or at least not enough to challenge Wentworth's official parade of unwillingness.

At moments Wentworth himself felt unequal to the conflicts in which the office of Treasurer would have involved him. He found his post in Ireland far more exhausting than anything he had yet undertaken, and his nerves and his health were affected. His letters reveal, to the twentieth-century reader, a certain lack of balance, something which recalls Dryden's 'great wits are sure to madness near allied'. In his energetic and active mind there was a tenseness, a suggestion of hysteria, that grew more marked with the years. His desire for approbation and applause was above the normal, and it is not surprising to find in him, therefore, a tendency to nervous, but by no means imaginary, illnesses calculated to secure him the cherishing and sympathy of which he could never have enough. In Ireland there were good reasons, other than those of temperament, for the decline of his health. He suffered from an evident predisposition to rheumatism and the damp climate seeping into his joints racked him with aches and pains. His hands and feet were intermittently crippled by gouty swellings; he was tormented by insomnia and migraine; he had occasional fainting fits. He wrote despondently to Cottington, 'I grow extremely old and full of grey hairs ... and should wax extremely melancholy were it not for two little girls that come now and then to play by me. Remember I tell you I am of no long life.' But he could still laugh at times, even at the detestable climate, and at the tiresome Dean of St Patrick's who persistently prayed for rain, 'which is a thing of all others we ... may best spare in this kingdom.' [37]

He was forty-two, no great age even in that epoch of quick ripening and early death, and certainly no one except himself thought his energy was flagging. His three elder children were all healthy; but his third wife's child, 'little Tom', died in the summer of 1635. She was to have two more children in the next three years who did not survive. His hopes of an heir to his name remained concentrated on his only son, Will, to whom any accident threw him into a desperate anxiety. He did not see much of his children and was delighted with them when he did. Between his indulgence and the respectful kindness of their timid, devoted stepmother the little Wentworths must have had a most enjoyable childhood.

Their father, writing at his desk, or brooding over columns of figures, planned for himself and for them as well as for the King his master. The two little girls quietly playing beside him would have each a dowry of £10,000; Will — who was presumably excluded from the study because boys have not the art of playing quietly — would inherit, if all went well, one of the greatest fortunes in England. He must also be started early on the road to Court favour; his father selected a noble present of hawks from his own mews and sent them over to England, fitted with all the necessary appurtenances of the most expensive kind — an impressive gift in the name of his only son to the little Prince of Wales. [38]

Wentworth was not merely a minister of the Crown; he was, in a manner of speaking, director and shareholder in the Crown as a business concern. He was, in practice, entirely aware of this, although he preferred to think of his duty exclusively in nobler terms. 'I trust God,' he wrote to Newcastle, 'so to demean myself as his Majesty shall not at all alter his good opinion towards me, and then welcome what God sends, I am not too good to die for him'. [39] He did not think the words were prophetic; yet they were something more than a flourish. He was ready, when the crisis came, to stake his life as well as his fortune for the kind of government in which he believed.

NOTES

[1] Knowler, I, p. 186.
[2] Ibid., p. 187.
[3] Ibid., pp. 255, 300.
[4] Ibid., pp. 186, 233, 415 ff.

[5] Ibid., p. 246.

[6] Ibid. ; for a full analysis of the membership of this Parliament see Kearney, pp. 45-52, 223-59.

[7] Brereton, p. 133; Knowler, I, p. 240; *Lismore Papers*, Series IV, I, p. 30; Kearney, pp. 46-8, and Appendix I.

[8] For Catelin's past career see O'Grady, p. 122.

[9] Knowler, I, pp. 273-4, 286-90.

[10] *Commons Journals, Ireland*, I, p. 106; Kearney, p. 54; Knowler, I, pp. 277-8.

[11] Knowler, loc. cit.

[12] Ibid., pp. 278, 292.

[13] Ibid., pp. 274, 296-7, 300.

[14] H.M.C. *Various*, II, p. 371.

[15] Knowler, I, pp. 331-2.

[16] Ibid., I, p. 349; *C.S.P.I.*, 1625-60, pp. 181-6.

[17] Knowler, I, pp. 347, 350-1; *Commons Journals, Ireland*, I, pp. 121-55; on the Graces see Knowler, I, pp. 310-28; Kearney, pp. 61 ff.

[18] Knowler, I, pp. 350-1.

[19] Strafford MSS, VIII, folios 13-14, Wentworth to Laud, 28th August 1633.

[20] Ibid., V, folio 190, Wentworth to Coke, 2nd March 1635.

[21] Knowler, I, pp. 350-1.

[22] Carte, I, pp. 129-32; Rushworth, *Trial*, p. 167; Kearney, p. 52.

[23] Knowler, I, pp. 399-401, 407.

[24] Kearney, pp. 65-6; *Commons Journals, Ireland*, I, pp. 179-81.

[25] *Acts of Parliament*, Dublin, 1636.

[26] Strafford MSS, IX, folios 38-9, Wentworth to Coke, 19th May 1635; Ibid., V, folio 177, Wentworth to Coke, 2nd March 1635.

[27] Knowler, I, p. 470; Strafford MSS, IX, folio 35, Wentworth to Coke, 18th May 1635.

[28] Ibid., folio 33.

[29] *C.S.P.D.*, 1634-5, p. 350.

[30] Knowler, I, pp. 128, 139, 365, 430.

[31] Ibid., pp. 387, 439.

[32] Ibid., pp. 343-4, 410, 420.

[33] Strafford MSS, VI, folios 263-75, Wentworth to Laud, 2nd November 1635.

[34] Knowler, I, pp. 342, 393; Laud, *Works*, VII, 144; Strafford MSS, VI, folio 265, Wentworth to Laud, 2nd November 1635. For a summary of the soap project see *The King's Peace*, pp. 160-1.

[35] Knowler, I, p. 492.

[36] For the attitude of Charles to the impeachment of Middlesex see R. H. Tawney, *Business and Politics under James I*, pp. 234-8, 247.

[37] Knowler, I, pp. 294, 370, 378, 391; Strafford MSS, VI, folio 121, Wentworth to Laud, 19th November 1634.

[38] Strafford MSS, XXI, No. 179.

[39] Knowler, I, p. 412.

—◦❧ ⋆⋄❧❦❁⋄✦ ❦◦—

CHAPTER FIVE

THE LAND AND THE CHURCH

And so, thorough let us go and spare not.
Wentworth to Laud, May 15th, 1634

'HE rules Ireland like a King', Sir Thomas Roe had said, and this was no more than the truth. Although Wentworth jealously suspected that there would be interference from interested parties at Court, the King on the whole held to his agreement for giving him unimpeded control, and when attempts were made to circumvent him through Court influence they were rarely successful. In spite of this, Wentworth never ceased to be anxious lest his plans should be thwarted from England, and a muttering fear of Court intrigue runs through all his dealings with his master, still more through his correspondence with Archbishop Laud.

This distrust was especially evident in Wentworth's handling of the land question. This was the basic problem in Ireland and the one over which he made his bitterest enemies. It was evident by the time that his first Parliament dispersed that the Deputy was resolved to proceed apace with the further colonization of Ireland. The Commission for Defective Titles, under his care, would be an organization for converting all doubtful and confused claims to land into tenures from the Crown, so that the royal revenues would be increased at the expense of landowners in Ireland. It was also clear that he intended that the King's title should be 'found' for most of the province of Connaught, thus making it possible to 'plant' it by royal grant, as Ulster had been planted. The practical defence for the morally indefensible process by which Irish land was appropriated was — as Wentworth and others frequently argued — that the country, under English forms of tillage, would support a greater number of inhabitants in much better conditions than it did in its primitive state. This argument, though it is often true, rarely makes much appeal to an indigenous population about to be dispossessed.

In this respect Wentworth was wholeheartedly in favour of colonializing Ireland, and had neither doubts nor inhibitions about the matter. But he vehemently disapproved of speculation in Irish land by absentees, and still more of the atrocious way in which men of power and position made money by harassing the numerous unfortunate small proprietors whose titles to their land were dubious or illegal. If on the one hand the Commission for Defective Titles would increase the revenues of the Crown and lay open new regions of Ireland for 'plantation', it would on the other create, in the ultimate event, some recognized security of tenure.

This idea was not a mere flourish to give an appearance of justice to a rapacious and unjust proceeding. It had a meaning for Wentworth, and he showed that it had by proceeding with considerable rigour against the 'great ones' whom he found making a profit out of the existing confusion of tenures. Lord Balfour, the nobleman whom he had expelled from the Council on his first coming, was fined £200 for offences of this kind. [1] He compelled Lord Mountnorris, who had appropriated the estate of another man on the strength of a flaw in the title, to return it to the victim. [2] He wrote scathingly to the Earl of Arundel, when he discovered that he employed two agents in Ireland for no other purpose than to make money for him out of the legal anomalies of land tenure. 'I judge it no ways, under favour, comely in your lordship', he wrote, ' ... to hunt at random all over the province of Leinster, searching and prying for extremities upon legal advantages, turning the ancient owners forth of their estates, separating the subject from the promised and princely protection and grace of his Majesty.' [3] Arundel, who had been friendly to Wentworth, was henceforward an enemy.

Wentworth showed the same concern for the ignorant victims of legal quibbles when he turned on Wilmot for having alienated Crown land. He wanted the land back for the Crown but he also insisted that those who had bought it from Wilmot in good faith should not suffer, but should have their money refunded to them. [4]

As for the new plantations, he gave out as his policy that land which was successfully claimed by the Crown should be granted first to settlers who would 'upon the place industriously attend their own undertakings'. Furthermore, he was in favour of granting the land in numerous small estates, so that there would be 'more people to breed civility, more shoulders to undergo the public service and charge of the country, and the covenants of plantation better complied withal than I usually find they be, when there are great proportions given to any particular man'. [5]

In the Ulster plantation there had been much mismanagement. The Corporation of London had received an enormous grant of land round Derry and Coleraine for a very low rent, and had then leased it to agents who failed to honour the various obligations about guarding the coasts, building strong places and cultivating the land, which had been a part of the contract. For many years a public-spirited gentleman named Sir Thomas Phillips, with the interests of the plantation at heart, had tried to get this matter put right. It was not until Wentworth came that the question was at length opened up, not in Dublin, but before the Privy Council in England. In March 1635 the neglectful Corporation were found to have broken their contract, were fined £70,000, and threatened with the loss of their possessions in Ulster. The King and his Council were unwise in proceeding to extremities with so influential a body as the Corporation of London and Wentworth was himself in favour of moderation once the case was proved. But whatever ultimate decision was reached about the Londonderry plantation — and the final settlement dragged on for years — he made it clear that his principal interest in the matter was to get security for the tenants, provided they paid their rents, and an increased income to the Crown, especially from the customs revenues of the ports. [6] Although the Corporation regarded him with cordial dislike for the part he had played in losing them their lands in Ulster, he was more moderate in the whole matter than the King his master.

The delinquencies of the Corporation of London had been revealed in the spring of 1635. In the summer, soon after the dissolution of Parliament, Wentworth at the head of the Commission for Defective Titles set out towards Connaught. Christopher Wandesford, who accompanied him, had no doubt of the virtue of his proceedings. 'The King's title is found to a principal part of the county of Connaught', he wrote contentedly to Sir Gervase Clifton in England, 'and so will be, I hope, for the whole, there being nothing but justice and honour intended to them. All things my Lord doth, being of a piece, he prospers the better.' [7] Juries empanelled in the counties of Sligo, Mayo and Roscommon had indeed, without a murmur, declared that the land belonged legally to the English Crown. The reasons for this docility were clear; there had been no organized resistance and the jurors had been carefully selected from those whose chief interest was to stand well with the government. Wandesford was right, according to his lights, that 'justice and honour' were intended: some land would of course be taken away to grant to new settlers, but much (three-quarters in fact) would be left to its present tenants on a secure, if rather expensive, form of tenure. This was obviously better than the expropriation which might be expected if there were resistance to a strong and determined government; some, with shaky titles, probably thought it better anyway than living in continual insecurity.

When the Deputy proceeded into Galway he met with a very different reception. Here the influence of one landowner was paramount. This was Richard de Burgh, Earl of Clanricarde, who was, after Ormonde, the most influential of the 'old English' nobility. Clanricarde was by now well advanced in years and lived very much in England. He had married, long since, Frances Walsingham, that quietly adaptable lady who had been left a widow in 1586 when her first husband Sir Philip Sidney had died of wounds in the Netherlands, and a widow again when her second husband the Earl of Essex had been beheaded in 1601. Clanricarde's connections with the English Court and nobility were therefore deep-rooted and of long standing. So were his connections with the Irish lands over which his family had exercised a patriarchal chieftainship for generations. The sheriff empanelled a jury which contained ten of Clanricarde's kindred; furthermore, the county had been prepared in advance by the dexterous canvassing of Patrick Darcy, one of the ablest men at the Irish bar, whose forensic skill — when exercised in his own favour — Wentworth had much admired in the recent Parliament. It must have needed courage, on Darcy's part, to campaign against the Deputy, because the fate of the Galway jurors was to show that their three more docile neighbouring counties had acted with greater wisdom in giving in to a governor who would not in any circumstances agree to take no for an answer. [8]

On August 25th, 1635, Wentworth was reporting wrathfully to Sir John Coke in England that the county of Galway 'most obstinately and perversely refused to find for his Majesty'. There had been some pleasantly Irish incidents during the hearing; one of the twelve jurors, not related to Clanricarde, had apparently been about to give his opinion in favour of the King's claim, when his neighbour had tugged him significantly by the sleeve. Wentworth indicated his displeasure at these manoeuvres and at the verdict by fining the sheriff who had empanelled the jury, citing the jurors before the Castle Chamber and fining all of them for giving a wrong verdict, summoning Patrick Darcy to take the Oath of Supremacy and debarring him from practice when, as a Catholic, he refused, declaring Galway exempt from all the Graces, moving a garrison into the town, and finally having a new jury empanelled which obediently gave a verdict for the King. (9)

It was perhaps unfortunate for him that old Lord Clanricarde almost immediately died — broken-hearted, said his family. 'They might as well have imputed unto me for a crime, his being three score and ten years old', wrote Wentworth irritably. (10) But he had got his verdict and hoped soon to begin on his project of lining Galway 'thoroughly with English and Protestants'. (11)

His schemes for Connaught were, however, not fully implemented, partly because the new Lord Clanricarde was extremely tenacious of his family's rights and succeeded in hampering his intentions, partly because the attempts of the courtiers in England to acquire profitable concessions in the new plantation caused him to spend as much time in refusing and blocking requests as in gratifying those whom, for one reason or another, he thought it wise to assist, and in distributing the rest of the land to suitable settlers. There was, in truth, some difficulty in finding those 'able and industrious' colonists on whom Wentworth had counted, and he was himself, though he did not realize it, responsible for this shortage. Because it was widely believed that to colonize Ireland was to strike a blow against Popery, the most energetic settlers for the last generation had been predominantly Puritan. But since Puritan views were associated with opposition to the centralizing power of the Crown, and since Wentworth now represented to the Puritan gentry of England the kind of government they most feared and hated, few were willing to venture to Ireland while he governed there. The most 'able and industrious' colonists were now crossing not the Irish Sea but the Atlantic Ocean, and the men

173

whose energy and talents Wentworth could have used in Ireland were instead building an austere, sober and vigorous civilization in New England.

Christopher Wandesford could hardly have uttered a more inept judgment than he did when he described all Wentworth's doings as 'being of a piece'. His policy in Ireland had a superficial consistency, but it was fundamentally incoherent. In his pursuit of justice for the 'meaner sort' and power and revenue for the King, he had begun by alienating the 'new English' magnates; he had already offended Wilmot and Mountnorris as well as lesser men like Balfour. He was soon to be involved in a prolonged struggle with the greatest of them all, the Earl of Cork. Such an onslaught on the leaders of the 'new English' could only have been politic if he had consolidated his position by gaining and keeping the 'old English' and the Irish for allies. But his land policy was a 'new English' land policy, and though the 'old English' and the Irish might bow before it, it could never be welcome to them. The new Lord Clanricarde, a popular and powerful man, contesting every inch of the way with the Deputy for the next five years, kept animosity against him quietly smouldering, not always underground. [12]

It is possible that, had Wentworth been able to prolong his government in peace for another ten years, he might by virtue of sheer strength and efficiency, by the softening effects of economic prosperity and a reliable system of justice, have established a colonial power in Ireland that could have survived. As it was, he made the error of attacking too many problems at the same time, so that he alienated simultaneously every powerful interest in Ireland. Considering the nature of some of those interests, this was by no means to his discredit, but it was greatly to his disadvantage, and it was the cause of ultimate disaster not only to him but to Ireland. His government was a period of greater economic prosperity, and of more just and orderly administration than Ireland had enjoyed for generations: but when the crisis came, in the eighth year of his power, almost every vocal and influential group in Ireland wanted to be rid of him.

His position would have been morally stronger if he had been consistent in his own conduct. But Wentworth was apt to make exceptions to the excellent principles he so often enunciated. If he resisted many requests for land from courtiers who would be absentees, he was none the less prepared to overlook this drawback in the case of his particular friends. He secured land for Sir John Coke, the amiable old Secretary of State. He was helpful to Endymion Porter — a favourite attendant of the King whom it would perhaps have been folly to offend. Rather more unwisely he bought in land for the beautiful Lady Carlisle, the widow of his old friend; scandal later linked his name with hers. [13] The lands that he bought for his brother George, and the very large estate — 20,000 acres — that he allowed Wandesford to acquire, [14] were not so inconsistent since presumably both these landowners would be in Ireland to look after their affairs, if hardly in a position 'industriously upon the place to attend their own undertakings'.

Later, Wentworth was to act in a manner even less consistent with his own views about land by indulging in purchase on a large scale himself, but that conduct, with the odium it was to arouse, lay still in the future. When the plantation of Connaught began he was still too little attracted by the prospects of Ireland to have departed from the resolution he had once imparted to Arundel: 'landless I came hither and landless I shall go hence.' [15]

While he had alienated the 'old English' and the Irish by his land policy, he had, during the same year, entered into a struggle with the greatest of the 'new English' magnates, with the Earl of Cork, which was to be literally a fight to the death. It can be traced in the pages of Lord Cork's diaries from its beginnings at a ruffled interview over a dinner table, through the storm of legal proceedings, to a final grim entry on May 12th, 1641: 'the oppressing Earl of Strafford ... was beheaded on Tower Hill, as he well deserved.' [16] Cork did not win his battle single-handed, but in the end he won it.

The cause of it all was the reform of the Church. The King and Archbishop Laud were anxious to bring Ireland into conformity of religion with England, a scheme to which Wentworth gave a modified consent. 'Tis true', he wrote to Cottington, 'I said his Majesty had power to pass upon the people all the laws of England concerning religion, which I say still, howbeit I judge it a point in no case to be stirred at this time. The Roman Catholic Church hath many a root lying deep and far within ground; which would be first thoroughly opened before we judge what height it may shoot up into, when it shall feel itself once struck at to be loosened and pulled up.' [17]

The conversion of the Irish would have to wait until the English Church in Ireland enjoyed greater moral prestige and economic security than was at present the case. On his arrival Wentworth wrote to Laud that 'there is hardly a Church to receive, or an able minister to teach the people'. One parish church in Dublin was used as a stable, another as a tennis court; the crypt of Christ Church Cathedral was leased as an ale-house, and St Patrick's was frequently flooded by the nauseous overflow of neighbouring slaughter-houses. The country churches were decayed, the clergy lewd and ignorant, and the Earl of Cork had appropriated four hundred livings and rented the bishopric of Waterford for forty shillings yearly to an obedient kinsman of his, subletting the vicarages for a handsome profit. Wentworth mentioned among other abuses 'abominable polygamies, incests and adulteries' as well as poverty and ignorance throughout the land. 'To attempt [the conversion of Ireland]', he wrote to the Archbishop, 'before the decays of the material churches be repaired, and able clergy be provided, that so there might be both wherewith to receive, instruct and keep the people, were as a man going to warfare without ammunition or arms.' 'You know my ground,' he added a little later, 'not to attempt at all till we be provided to drive it thorough.' [18]

The Deputy was on the whole supported in his policy by the Archbishop of Armagh, the Primate of Ireland. James Ussher was a learned, independent man in later middle-age; his temper was cold and confident and his philosophy of life an unforgiving fatalism. Wentworth was at first baffled by his manner, but Laud urged him to try again and in course of time he began to respect Ussher for his courage and integrity. At first he had thought him too subservient to the 'great ones', especially Lord Cork, and had argued with him on the point, apparently with success. Even later when the reform of the Church was well under way, he sometimes found Ussher infected with the easygoing Irish habit, 'the genius of the country' as Wentworth called it, for covering up the faults of their friends. But in general Ussher was an upright man and no respecter of persons; he reproached Wentworth himself with considerable severity for licensing a playhouse in Dublin. [19]

It was perhaps with a certain malicious pleasure that Wentworth subsequently chaffed the Archbishop on the magnificence of his establishment. 'My lord,' he said, as they sat at dinner in Ussher's house, 'you live very splendidly.'

'Yet,' replied Ussher gloomily, 'I shall live to want necessaries.'

'You must live a long time,' Wentworth mocked him, 'for no such thing is in prospect.'

'I shall live to close your eyes,' said Ussher, with which reassuring prophecy the conversation presumably died. [20]

The English Church in Ireland leaned of necessity towards Puritan-Protestantism because it was placed in a state of constant opposition to the Roman Catholic inhabitants. Wentworth was prepared to argue with Laud that, in the special circumstances of Ireland, such forms as bowing at the name of Jesus might be really inadvisable. [21] In questions of Church government, on the other hand, he was for crushing Puritanism wherever he found it, and was exasperated at finding it rife among the Protestant clergy in Ireland. [22] In Ulster in particular many of these clergy were Scotsmen, practitioners and advocates of Presbyterian church government, though working within the framework of an episcopal church.

Wentworth secured the appointment of two bishops very much after his own heart in this difficult region. John Bramhall, an able and vigorous Yorkshireman, was appointed Bishop of Derry in 1634, and a year later when the still more Scottish Calvinist diocese of Down fell vacant Wentworth pressed for and secured the appointment of Henry Leslie, an Episcopalian Scot who knew how to handle his own countrymen. Gradually he was to influence other appointments, so as to eliminate bishops who were dependents of the great landowners, or other undesirable characters like the Bishop of Killaloe — 'his name is Jones, a very wretch, betrays the church at every turn.' [23] Poor Bishop Jones was perhaps not as blameworthy as Wentworth thought. He constantly sold Church land on the sly for ready money; but it is possible that the revenues of his see were so diminished that he could live no other way.

The economic state of the Church in Ireland was even more deplorable than that of the Church in England at this time. [24] Writing to Laud, Wentworth planned for uniform and properly conducted Anglican worship all over the country — the same ideal towards which Laud was working in England. He imagined that such a Church would attract the common people into the fold; alongside this, there was to be better education; he agreed with Laud that it was important to 'set able men in the free schools', and so, gradually, by the 'virtuous education of youth ... soften them in that barbarous malignity the generality of this nation still retains for the English'. [25]

Queen Elizabeth had founded the most famous educational institution in Ireland, Trinity College Dublin, in 1601. Archbishop Laud had his eye on this as on all other sources of intellectual life in the King's dominions. He was not satisfied, and neither was Wentworth. The amiable Provost, a kinsman of Archbishop Ussher, had not the character to control the Fellows, few of whom were conscientiously performing their tasks. His only valuable scheme — by which students in theology were taught to read the Bible in Irish — did not commend itself to Wentworth, who regarded the ancient language as a barbaric survival not to be encouraged. It was not, however, his interest in Irish but his obvious incompetence that caused the removal of Provost Ussher, who was consoled with an archdeaconry.

The successor, approved by Wentworth and Laud, was William Chappell of Christ's College Cambridge, whose principal claim to immortality is that he was, briefly, John Milton's tutor and was cordially disliked by him. Chappell was a disciplinarian and had the character and drive necessary for the planned reorganization. Wentworth secured his election, as he usually secured what he wanted, by instructing the Fellows to vote for him, which, however unwillingly, they obediently did. His election was followed by the recasting of the College charter; in future the Provost was to be appointed by the Crown, and in all essentials, Trinity College was to be under direct state control. In return for obedience, the Fellows had security of tenure for life. Trinity College was to be a centre of classical and theological education, as then practised in England, and was to be made intellectually strong enough to fulfil its function as a principal influence for civilization, in the sense in which Wentworth understood it.

An effective code of discipline which prevented students from idling their time away in ale-houses or more vicious places, combined with a good standard of learning, was to encourage families of all ranks to send their hopeful sons to it. Wentworth gave an example by placing his cherished Will there as soon as he was old enough. In theory the advantages of the College were open to any boy of whatever race or religion who could pass the oral entrance tests. No questions were asked. But as the accepted student had to take the Oath of Supremacy, and to sign a statement condemning the doctrine of transubstantiation, the College was almost exclusively a centre of education for Protestants, which meant predominantly the 'new English'. Whatever the limitations of this plan, Trinity College became in the next years an efficiently run centre of learning, if not precisely of enlightenment. [26]

The reorganization and improvement of the Protestant Church in Ireland was a more complex problem. Convocation, which met early in 1635, gave some trouble owing to the Puritan temper of the Lower House, who attempted to resist the Thirty-Nine Articles of the English Church which were now to be imposed on them. Ussher, who knew the temper of the ministers and settlers of Ulster in particular, handled the matter somewhat gingerly. He had himself stabilized the worship and doctrine of the Reformed Church in Ireland by a series of articles passed in 1615; these were markedly more Calvinist than those now offered to them. In theory the plan was to keep both sets of articles in operation, thus broadening the basis of the Irish Church. In practice, given the views on uniformity shared by the King, Wentworth and Archbishop Laud, the passing of the Thirty-Nine Articles would make things increasingly difficult for the Puritans.

Wentworth overruled Ussher's doubts. On hearing that the Lower House of Convocation was presuming to criticize the Thirty-Nine Articles, he sent down a brief and typical command to the Prolocutor of the House.

I send you here enclosed the form of a canon to be passed by the votes of the Lower House of Convocation, which I require you to put to the question for their consents, without admitting any debate or other discourse, for I hold it not fit nor will suffer that the articles of the Church of England be disputed. Therefore I expect from you to take only the voices consenting or dissenting, and give me particular account, how each man gives his vote. The time admits no delay, so I further require you to perform the contents of this letter forthwith.

The Prolocutor, who was Henry Leslie, soon after to be made Bishop of Down, was on Wentworth's side, and peremptorily put the Articles to the vote without debate. In the face of this mood of the Lord Deputy, only one of the Puritan clergy had courage enough to vote against them. [27]

Reorganization from the top could, however, serve no purpose until something was done to curb the power of laymen over the Church — Wentworth was in favour of limiting the livings in any one man's gift to a maximum of two — and to restore the endowments which had been engrossed by rapacious landowners, or were being traded for cash by impecunious churchmen. Wentworth went about it with his usual grim pleasure. 'I had it in mind to trounce a bishop or two in the Castle Chamber', he wrote to Laud, and came down heavily on the peccant Bishop of Killaloe. A dean who had sold a parsonage was also, in Wentworth's favourite phrase, 'soundly trounced'. [28]

But it was against the Earl of Cork that he planned a major attack, for in systematic plunder of the Church he was the greatest culprit in Ireland. There he stood with his shining, jovial face — eating heartily, laughing heartily, quarrelling heartily. The Earl of Cork allowed his younger daughters a hundred pounds a year pin-money, he gave handsome tips to his servants on New Year's Day, and he entertained like a king; but when one of his tenants committed suicide, he enforced the law upon the widow, drove off her kine, and congratulated himself on his charity for not taking her few chattels as well. The Earl of Cork attended two sermons every Sunday; he had plausible account books retailing the churches he had rebuilt, the vicarages he had repaired, the parishes he had provided with ministers; but he had acquired a large part of his wealth by browbeating poor vicars into making over the tithes to him in return for an annual pittance, perhaps as large as the Christmas box Cork might give his little daughter Peggie. [29]

He had been assisted in his machinations by a numerous family who could be placed in key positions. Two of the Boyles had been successively Bishops of Cork. Another was Bishop of Waterford.

His predecessor in that diocese, labouring under the oppressions and encroachments of the mighty Earl, had once declared that he had heard of bishops burnt to death but never till now of one 'boyled to death'. [30]

Wentworth was resolved to have no more 'boyling to death' of churchmen, and even to resuscitate earlier victims of the process. He set on Sir George Radcliffe to detect irregularities in the Earl of Cork's titles to possession. He avowed his intention of encouraging the clergy to present petitions in the Court of Castle Chamber. [31] Other peers of Ireland, among them Clanricarde, tactfully restored what had been wrongfully taken before things went any further. But Cork had too much at stake. He ignored the threat and was enraged when he found what he considered his private affairs openly discussed at the Council table. By the intervention of a friend, Cork arranged a pleasant little dinner party for the Deputy, who enjoyed himself and was 'pretty merry'.

But this was not, as he had hoped, the end of the prosecutions. They went on. He was scornful, indignant and neglectful. When he failed to come, Wentworth charged him six pounds for costs — a culminating insult. 'God forgive the Lord Deputy', he scribbled in his diary, but later on the pious prayer became a curse: 'God never forgive the Lord Deputy.' [32]

Writing to Laud, Wentworth compared the Church lands that Lord Cork had swallowed to a three-course dinner with 'a dessert besides'. A little later, when he had more accurate information, he estimated the probable gain to the Church from the various prosecutions of Lord Cork at about £30,000. [33] He was doing good service to the Church in forcing the old scoundrel to disgorge, but he showed his usual awkwardness in giving the proceedings an air at once tyrannical and personal. The first case concerned a timorous clergyman named Beresford, who had been prompted to bring this action. Though Cork was agitating for a hearing in camera, Wentworth wanted to have the matter out in public, as 'an open example to lead on and encourage the poorer clergy to exhibit their just complaints against persons how great so ever'. Poor Mr Beresford was already in such a panic that he fainted away from sheer fright as soon as Wentworth raised his voice, and when he had recovered himself, asked in a bewildered way for a private hearing. Wentworth overruled him, saying fiercely that he was not going to give Mr Beresford or anyone else 'ground to clamour against me for anything done in secret'. Mr Beresford, more dead than alive, won his case, which was just what Wentworth intended, but it was an odd way to encourage the poorer clergy to appeal to him: by frightening the first plaintiff almost out of his wits. [34]

At the same time, he was pursuing the Earl of Cork about another less important and more delicate matter, involving his personal pride. The Earl had set up, just in the place of the high altar in St Patrick's Cathedral, a huge family tomb. A coarse and pompous piece of provincial baroque, the tomb, which is still to be seen in a more discreet place in the cathedral, is rather an historic than an artistic monument, though visitors to Dublin at the time found it 'famous, sumptuous and glorious'. Wentworth for his part did not think much of it, although it was not for aesthetic reasons, but for religious ones that he set out to have it removed. Those who attended the Cathedral, he complained, could not 'do reverence to God' without also 'crouching to an Earl of Cork and his lady … or to those sea-nymphs his daughters, with coronets upon their heads, their hair dishevilled, down upon their shoulders'. [35]

The clergy were divided in their feelings. Some of them had no objection to the tomb, but Wentworth's supporter Henry Leslie gave great offence to the touchy Earl by preaching on a text from Isaiah: 'What hast thou here and whom hast thou here, that thou hast hewed thee out a sepulchre here, as he that heweth him out a sepulchre on high.' [36]

Cork was angry and obstinate, but Wentworth was persistent, and in the end the tomb came down, piecemeal, 'put up in boxes as if it were marchpanes and banqueting stuffs going down to the christening of my young master in the country', wrote Wentworth, who had never taken Cork's feelings in the matter at all seriously. [37] He was mistaken to underestimate them. The attack on his expensive tomb wounded Lord Cork in a very sensitive place; he was immensely proud of the tomb, which had cost him a thousand pounds; he was immensely proud of his family, his daughters with their beautiful long hair and his clever sons. (Of one of them, the youngest, Robert, he had immortal reason to be proud, though he was not aware of it.) Wentworth's action in checking his patriarchal pleasure seemed to give to all the rest of the prosecutions a tang of personal spite; this at least was Cork's reading of it and he now began to say that all his troubles were caused by the Deputy's annoyance at a misunderstanding over the marriage settlement of his niece Elizabeth Clifford, who had become the wife of his eldest son Lord Dungarvan. [38]

This was not the last that was to be heard of the Dungarvan marriage settlement. Lord Cork had set aside for the young couple revenues derived from an ancient charitable foundation, the College of Youghal. He had got this property at a low price from the wreck of Sir Walter Raleigh's Irish estates after his fall. Since then he had made his cousin, the amenable Bishop of Cork, head of the so-called College of Youghal while he appropriated most of the revenue. The College was supposed to be a charitable foundation for the sick, but the income of the place had been 'reduced from one thousand to fifty pounds a year', so that the poor were 'turned naked and empty away from the reliefs provided by the piety of former times'. [39]

Evidence of these misdeeds was procured from the Bishop of Cork — 'my faithless and unthankful kinsman whom I have raised from being a poor schoolmaster at Barnet', raged the indignant Earl. [40]

He none the less assumed that, in this particular case, the intolerable Wentworth would let matters rest, since he was himself a trustee of the marriage settlement of which Youghal was the basis. Wentworth thought otherwise. 'Neither alliance nor any other thing or reason, shall be ever able to separate me from the service of God and my master or persuade me to quench the flame in another man's house by taking the fire of that guilt into my own bowels', he wrote to Laud, 'which my conscience cries upon me I do if I silently pass over this profanation and so become *particeps criminis* with him.' [41]

On March 20th, 1635, the case was before the Castle Chamber and Cork was peremptorily asked to explain his possession of the College of Youghal. With unconscious humour he protested that he had done nothing that was not a common custom in Ireland, and when this was rejected as inadequate, he asserted truculently that his seizure of Church land was only illegal by an act of State promulgated by a Deputy now dead and never ratified by Parliament. Wentworth cut him short. 'Great as you are, my lord,' he said, 'I will make you and all the subjects of Ireland know that any act of State, made or to be made, shall be as binding on you and the subjects of Ireland during my government as any act of Parliament.' (42) Cork was temporarily silenced, but he did not forget the outburst.

It was now the summer of 1635, and Wentworth would soon have the Earl of Clanricarde's enmity to contend with as well as that of Lord Cork. At first, however, Cork tried subtler methods. On Wentworth's progress into Connaught, Cork joined him at Portumna in Galway, bringing with him Lord Clifford, Wentworth's amiable brother-in-law, who was of course, through his daughter's marriage settlement, also somewhat concerned about the case. Wentworth was not pleased at this attempt of Cork's to exploit his affection for Clifford in his own interest. (43) It was clear to him that this was only a beginning; the Earl's next move would be to mobilize all his friends at Court to persuade the King to stop the case.

He took steps at once to outflank the Earl of Cork's approach to the King by writing very explicitly himself to Archbishop Laud, well knowing that his words, retailed by Laud, would work more effectively on Charles than if he wrote direct.

> If now after all this, the Earl by pressure of his friends on that side should stop the proceedings in the Castle Chamber, escape the punishment in this cause, and shake his Majesty from his former councils and resolutions, the consequence of it would be passing bad. The Church would not only be dispossessed of Youghal, but those endeavours, which have kindled of late for the restoring thereof, be again altogether quenched and smothered under the apprehension and pressures of great and powerful adversaries.... It will be a blemish upon the administration of his Majesty's justice in this kingdom and raise an overweening in persons of power, as if our authority were set rather over the poor than over them, a belief they are upon all occasions ready to flatter themselves into, and hath hitherto been a great stop and disturbance to the free and steady course of justice on this side.

In the Earl of Cork's especial case, he went on, if proceedings were stopped the Commonwealth shall lose a public example, which is more than needful to stay the stomachs of these eaters ... to the joy and comfort of this people, who naturally are in no case better pleased, than where they see right may be had against one of their great lords, a blessing, God knows, which they have seldom heretofore been acquainted with. [44]

Archbishop Laud pressed this eminently sensible and just opinion on the King at much about the time that the news of Wentworth's punitive measures against the obstinate sheriff and jury of Galway reached the Court. King Charles therefore in the autumn of 1635 found himself at one and the same time approached by the indignant friends of the Earls of Cork and Clanricarde. There had been murmurs earlier in the same year from the indignant friends of Sir Piers Crosby, while Lord Wilmot all that summer had been lamenting at Court about the Crown lands he had had to give up. All together it was beginning to be said rather too loud and too frequently by those on whom Wentworth laid a strong hand, that his Majesty's Deputy in Ireland behaved like a Caesar, a Nero, or a Basha of Buda, rather than the representative of a Christian King.

Charles agreed in theory with all that Wentworth had written to Laud, and Laud informed Wentworth, who was duly gratified. But a month later, at the end of October, the King had doubts, and a letter came from Secretary Windebanke (who did not normally deal in Irish affairs) to inform the Deputy that the King was removing the case of the Earl of Cork for examination in England. Wentworth's eloquent anger was not stemmed by the necessity of putting it all down in cipher when he wrote to Laud. His rage vibrates even through the hailstorm of numbers:

It is likewise over all the town already by way of great boast and exultation that Cork hath procured letters for the stay of all proceedings here and that he and his cause is to be transmitted there which I protest I find sinks the best affected in this state ... and it would I fear ... be the beginnings of great disservice to the Crown and an absolute let of all endeavour for restoring this poor church.

Once let Cork take the case to England, he predicted, and 'believe me he will have so many windings and turnings, strow and throw his golden apples with such art in the way, as he will infinitely delay the cause ... and in conclusion win the race.' In fact, he would bribe and wangle himself back into the possession of his illicit gains. [45]

The Earl of Cork's principal friend at Court was the Lord Chamberlain, the Earl of Pembroke, whose influence at this time was considerable. In a final effort to get his way, Wentworth enclosed with his letter to Laud a direct appeal to the King which he asked his friend to pass on at his discretion. It was indeed very well phrased, and Laud conveyed it to the hands of Charles. In this brief and respectful note Wentworth denied any personal animosity to those whom he had prosecuted, reiterated his zeal for the King's service, and pointed out that he had now received two quite contradictory directives about the Earl of Cork — first, one telling him to go on with the case, and now one from Windebanke telling him to desist, 'so as I am altogether lost how to proceed in the matter and ... humbly beseech the light of your full and determinate pleasure whereby to wind myself out of this labyrinth.' [46]

In the midst of his anger and his worries, Wentworth seems as usual to have been amusing what leisure moments he had with Ovid's *Metamorphoses* — apparently the Eighth Book — so that his figures of speech recall a world of legend strangely unrelated to the sordid facts before him, with the Earl of Cork transfigured into Atalanta's lover strowing golden apples and the King cast as Ariadne to his own Theseus.

Charles, exhorted by Wentworth and pestered by Pembroke, decided on a compromise. He left the case of Youghal to be dealt with in Ireland, but asked that every reasonable effort should be made to settle the matter out of court. Lord Cork still resisted furiously, but in the end he was worn down by the alternate threats and persuasions of Wentworth, the arguments of Archbishop Ussher, the tearful pleading of his son Dungarvan, and the serious illness (perhaps psychosomatic?) of Dungarvan's wife. He agreed to pay £15,000 indemnity and return the lands on condition that Wentworth appealed to the King for a re-grant on a legal title. [47]

'No physic better than a vomit,' wrote Laud cheerfully to Wentworth, 'if it be given in time; and therefore you have taken a very judicious course, to administer one so early to my Lord of

Cork.' [48] But the Earl of Cork, who had been made to disgorge in all about forty thousand pounds for his various misdeeds, may be forgiven for finding the dose too stiff. He could not even be sure that Wentworth had done with him. When the bishopric of Waterford fell vacant, it was not one of the Boyles who was appointed to it, but John Atherton, a young nominee of the Deputy. Cork would have been annoyed but not much surprised to hear the strangely uncanonical account of this young man that Wentworth gave to Laud. 'There is not such a terrier in England or Ireland for the unkennelling of an old fox', he wrote: Cork 'will think the devil is let loose upon him'. [49]

Judged by his immediate achievements Wentworth appeared to be winning on every front. But he had made dangerous enemies: in Ulster, Lord Balfour, Sir Piers Crosby, all the surplice-hating, anti-episcopal Scots ministers and their flocks, not to mention the Corporation of London, smarting at the loss of their profits in Derry; in Connaught he had Lord Clanricarde and the whole Burke and de Burgh kindred against him; in Munster he had an unforgiving and powerful enemy in the Earl of Cork; in Leinster he had angered the 'old English' gentry by increasing their share of the subsidy. He went confidently on, pleased by the evident signs of his success, never fully realizing how many of those that fawned upon him in Ireland were 'sheathing in flattering looks the deadly knife'. [50]

NOTES

[1] C.S.P.I., 1633-47, pp. 158-9; Knowler, I, p. 345.

[2] Rushworth, Trial, pp. 205-8.

[3] Knowler, II, p. 30.

[4] Ibid., I, pp. 399, 496.

[5] Ibid., I, pp. 258, 339.

[6] T. W. Moody, The Londonderry Plantation, pp. 368-9; Knowler, I, p. 174; II, p. 25; Rushworth, II, ii, pp. 1052 ff.; Carte, V, pp. 223-4, 230.

[7] H.M.C. Various, VII, p. 410.

[8] Mr Kearney (p. 95) attributes the behaviour of the Galway jurors in part to a belief that Wentworth was likely to be recalled. The work of undermining him had of course begun in England by the summer of 1635 and he already had Wilmot, Mountnorris and some other notable mischief-makers lined up against him.

[9] Knowler, I, p. 450.

[10] Ibid., p. 492.

[11] Ibid., II, p. 33.

[12] On the incoherence of Wentworth's policy see Moritz Bonn, Die Englische Kolonisation in Irland, p. 373.

[13] Cooper, pp. 241, 245.

[14] MacColl, Wandesfordes of Kirklington and Castlecomer, pp. 78-9, 140-3.

[15] Strafford MSS, VIII, folio 49, Wentworth to Arundel, 4th November 1633.

[16] *Lismore Papers*, II, V, p. 106.

[17] Knowler, I, pp. 370, 375.

[18] Ibid., pp. 172, 187 ff; Harleian MSS, 4297, folio 35; *C.S.P.D.*, 1633-4, p. 179.

[19] Strafford MSS, VI, folio 37, Wentworth to Laud, 18th March 1634; folio 43, the same to the same, 12th April 1634; VII, folio 39, the same to the same, 10th July 1637.

[20] *Camden Miscellany*, XI, p. 54.

[21] Strafford MSS, VI, folio 201, Wentworth to Laud, 14th July 1635.

[22] Ibid., folio 123, Wentworth to Laud, 9th December 1634.

[23] Ibid., folio 28, Wentworth to Laud, 7th March 1634; folio 76, the same to the same, 3rd June 1634.

[24] See Hill, *Economic Problems of the Church*, Oxford, 1956, pp. 230-1.

[25] Strafford MSS, VI, folio 45, Wentworth to Laud, 12th April 1634; folio 56, the same to the same, 15th May 1634.

[26] Maxwell, *The History of Trinity College, Dublin, 1591-1892*, pp. 38 ff. A more critical account is to be found in H. L. Murphy, *A History of Trinity College, Dublin*, Dublin, 1951.

[27] Knowler, I, pp. 342, 345; Reid, *Presbyterian Church in Ireland*, I, p. 172; D. Wilkins, *Concilia*, IV, pp. 495-7 n.

[28] Strafford MSS, VI, folio 44, Wentworth to Laud, 12th April 1634; folio 23, the same to the same, 31st January 1634. See also Hill, op. cit., pp. 334-7.

[29] *Lismore Papers*, Series I, contain Cork's daily jottings, which are extremely revealing.

[30] Strafford MSS, VI, folio 23.

[31] Ranger, 'Strafford in Ireland', pp. 39, 43. Full details of Cork's troubles may be expected in Mr Ranger's forthcoming biography of the Earl of Cork.

[32] H.M.C. *Various*, VII, pp. 292-3; *Lismore Papers*, I, IV, p. 143.

[33] Strafford MSS, VI, folio 4, Wentworth to Laud, December 1633; folio 47, 12th April 1634.

[34] Ibid., VI, folios 3-4.

[35] Brereton, p. 138; Strafford MSS, VI, folio 35, Wentworth to Laud, 18th March 1634. Wentworth was curiously unobservant; though Lord Cork had captured peers for several of his daughters, they are not, in fact, wearing coronets.

[36] Isaiah, xxii, 16; Laud, *Works*, VII, 70; Strafford MSS, VI, folio 28, Wentworth to Laud, 7th March 1634.

[37] Knowler, I, p. 379.

[38] *C.S.P.I.*, 1633-47, p. 43; Strafford MSS, VI, folio 33, Laud to Wentworth, 11th March 1634.

[39] Ibid., folios 10-12, Wentworth to Laud, 29th January 1634.

[40] *Lismore Papers*, I, IV, p. 185.

[41] Strafford MSS, VI, folio 9, Wentworth to Laud, 29th January 1634; H.M.C. *Various*, VII, p. 293.

[42] Rushworth, *Trial*, pp. 175-6.

[43] *C.S.P.D.*, 1635, pp. 385 ff; Knowler, I, p. 459.

[44] Knowler, I, pp. 459-60.

[45] Strafford MSS, VI, folios 271-2, Wentworth to Laud, 2nd November 1635.

[46] Knowler, I, p. 477.

[47] H.M.C. *Various*, VII, p. 414; *Lismore Papers*, I, III, pp. 183-5.

[48] Knowler, I, p. 156.

[49] Strafford MSS, VI, folio 331, Wentworth to Laud, 9th March 1636.

[50] The quotation is from Fanshawe's poem, 'The Fall', long thought to be about King Charles I. Professor Cleanth Brooks has however shown that Fanshawe had Wentworth, and not the King, in mind.

CHAPTER SIX

COMMERCE, REVENUE AND THE CASE OF LORD MOUNTNORRIS

The reasons which moved me were the consideration of our commodious situation; the increase of trade and shipping in these parts of your dominions, which seem now only to want foreign commerce to make them a civil, rich and contented people; and consequently more easily governed by Your Majesty's ministers and the more profitably for your Crown than in a savage and poor condition.

Wentworth to the King, 1633

As soon as he knew he was to go to Ireland, Wentworth had begun to reflect on the condition and the prospects of Irish trade. The 'commodious situation' of the country in the sea-traffic of the West was apparent and had indeed long been apparent to others besides himself. His opponent Lord Cork, who in his energy and the acuteness of his business acumen had much in common with him, had greatly developed the commerce of the Munster ports, from which ships sailed, when the seas were safe, not only to Bristol, Minehead, Barnstaple and Bideford but to France, Holland and Spain. While England remained the country with which Ireland had her principal trading connections and Scotland was the chief customer of Ulster, Irish merchants had also long-standing connections with Spain and France and more desultory exchanges with the Low Countries and the Baltic. [1] The largest and most important port of the Kingdom was Dublin; the most disappointing, to Wentworth's active mind, was Limerick, with a fine deep harbour which could take a ship of three hundred tons burden, if only the people would set their minds to developing it. [2]

Kinsale had great possibilities as a port of call for revictualling — whether for the Spanish navy as Wentworth suggested, or for merchant ships bound on long journeys. Wentworth wished also to see it developed as the permanent base for the ships sent by the Admiralty to patrol the Irish Sea. Once, during his government, Kinsale was enlivened by the visit of a Danish East Indiaman, under convoy of a warship commanded by one of King Christian's numerous bastards. The young admiral challenged the local Irish to drinking bouts, Wentworth reported, and 'laid them down on all sides before him, till at last they set a mine against him, mingled the sack he drank with usque-baugh which utterly blew him up'. [3]

Ireland was not a self-supporting country. For luxuries like wine and all the finer sorts of cloth, she depended on imports from France, Spain and England; more serious was her dependence on English and continental sources for the salt essential for preserving fish, butter and meat. Her chief exports were hides, tallow, timber, wool, corn, livestock consisting of cattle and sheep, a little iron (Lord Cork was developing mines in the south), and a great deal of fish, especially salmon, eels, herrings and pilchards. [4] But another source of possible profit lay in the carrying trade for which Ireland was very well placed, and which had apparently begun to develop before the recent wars and the increase of piracy checked it again. Shortly after Wentworth's coming he averred that the Dutch were in command of most of the carrying into Ireland. [5] This dependence on Dutch vessels was dangerous on account of the war between Spain and Holland. Wentworth himself believed that the best opportunities for Irish commercial development lay in nourishing that trade with Spain which had been interrupted by the war of 1625-30. But the Spanish privateers, the 'Biscayners', were authorized by their government to prey on Dutch vessels as belonging to an enemy nation. Unhappily, while the Dutch controlled the bulk of the carrying trade across the Irish Sea, the 'Biscayners' were 'continually riding betwixt headland and headland, watching the outlets of our mouths and harbours', and thus threatening and preying on Irish imports and exports because they were carried in Dutch bottoms. [6]

Wentworth's representations on this point to the Spanish Resident in London, together with his far better organization of a naval guard for the Irish coasts, put a stop to this menace. He was not quite so successful in his measures against the so-called 'Turks', the raiders from the Barbary coast. Although there do not appear to have been any landings during his government, they still from time to time captured fishing boats, once actually in the harbour of Cork, and carried off the crews into slavery. It was a matter of indignation to Wentworth that this slave trade was materially assisted by the French, who permitted the pirates to come into their ports and send their human cargo overland for reshipment at Marseilles in utter defiance of supposed treaties of friendship with King Charles and his subjects. [7]

In general, however, Wentworth was successful in making the seas of Ireland reasonably safe. His methods were simple. He insisted that the Admiralty dispatch the ships for the Irish guard before the end of March, and not — as hitherto — only in July. [8] He saw to it that arrangements for victualling, pay and equipment were reasonably efficient and made an example of a quartermaster who was caught selling the men's provisions. [9] He got the most efficient of his sea-captains to go over to the Isle of Man and take measures to check the brisk traffic that was being done there in receiving cargoes plundered by the pirates in the Irish Sea. [10] He asked — or rather instructed — the Admiralty to send smaller and more manoeuvrable ships of war than they had apparently been in the habit of doing, [11] and he tried, by preparing Kinsale as a permanent base and store for the navy, to cut out the waste of time and the confusion which arose from the Admiralty system of paying the men and refitting the ships exclusively in England. [12]

The ultimate benefits to be expected by the English Crown from these methods were twofold. Not only would Irish trade increase when the seas became safer, but the great amount of smuggling that went on, often with the help of the pirates, [13] would also be checked. Either way, or both ways, the customs revenue would benefit.

Wentworth's economic policy was clear rather than original. His conception of commerce as a principal influence in making the Irish 'a civil, rich and contented people' was the classic belief of the planters who for the last fifty years had been trying to adapt the Irish way of life to the demands of the modern world as they saw them. With equal firmness, he stated his belief that the resources of Ireland might be developed in such a way as not to interfere with English trade and to keep Ireland dependent on England for necessities. This belief too was widely held in England at that time and put into practice by the government. Throughout his Deputyship, Wentworth never had the initiative in fundamental matters of commercial policy because all major decisions were taken by the Council in England in relation to the general economic policy of that country. [14] There was not at this time any deliberate attempt from England to choke Irish trade: that would have been folly, since it was important that Ireland should not become a financial burden. But the necessities of English trade and diplomacy governed economic decisions without any special thought for Ireland, where trade often suffered as a result. There were also from time to time ill-considered interferences with Irish commerce in the interests of English monopolists.

Wentworth's services to the Irish economy did not therefore consist in any new policy, since he was in no position to impose one; furthermore everything that he did was subordinated to the main object of his economic administration, that of increasing the revenue of the Crown. But he was, within these limitations, a more far-sighted, a bolder and a far more active governor than his predecessors. His success in checking the pirates alone was a great service to the peaceable development of trade, and he was capable of holding out against any measures of the English Privy Council which he felt to be unsound.

Thus he had objected strongly to the limitation on Irish exports of tallow, in the interests of the proposed new monopoly in soap which was being mooted in England. This was not an objection on principle, but simply to a particular project which he recognized from the beginning as fraudulent and foolish. He objected equally strongly and for the same reason to a proposed English monopoly in salt, because England alone could not possibly supply enough salt for Irish needs. At other times he stood out against proposed impositions on Irish imports and exports because he thought they would, in the end, lower the revenue by reducing the volume of trade, or otherwise do more harm than good. He persuaded the King to take off the additional duties which he had imposed on the importation of English coal. Coal was an essential import and the high price caused great hardship. On another occasion Wentworth fined the Mayor of Dublin for buying coal at a privileged rate, then fixing the market price at a much higher figure and reselling his large stocks. [15]

He stood out too against duties imposed from England on horses sent into Ireland. The breed had seriously declined in Ireland in the recent wars, and he was anxious to import horses not only for essential uses, but to improve the stock. It would be an exaggeration to give Wentworth any credit for Ireland's later fame for its horses, but at least he stopped the decline and took steps to improve the breed. At about the same time as his intervention about coal and horses, he checked the imposition of import duties in England on Irish cattle and sheep, on the grounds that this would gravely discourage a country where the improvement of livestock was one of the most potentially valuable sources of wealth. [16] He also later opposed the raising of the Irish customs rates on the grounds that their commerce was not yet well enough established to bear any heavier charges than they already paid. [17]

It is an old and still popular belief that Wentworth destroyed Irish woollen manufacture in the interests of England but created the Irish linen industry to replace it. Neither proposition is born out by the facts. Very little fine woollen cloth was made in Ireland, and the English prohibition on the export of fuller's earth, essential for its manufacture, was in force before Wentworth became Deputy. On the other hand, coarse Irish woollens — rugs, blankets and friezes — were exported to England, mostly to the north Devon ports, throughout Wentworth's government rather more extensively than before, without apparently causing any protest from English clothiers. [18] But far more important than the relatively small trade in coarse cloth was the trade in raw wool. This had been, of late years, a serious problem because the English clothiers, suffering under a long depression, were very unwilling that Ireland should sell raw material to their rivals abroad, but were unable themselves to absorb all the wool which Ireland could sell.

A system of export by licence only, through certain staple ports, had grown up. Wentworth condemned this system because it had undoubtedly led to a great deal of corruption, the merchants of the staple working the arrangement largely to serve their own interests, and the Deputy, or rather his agents in the ports, becoming very deeply involved in bribery and other corrupt practices. Evasion of the regulations by large-scale smuggling was also widely practised. Wentworth disliked the staple system and much preferred the method of granting licences direct to merchants, partly because this could be better controlled by the government and partly because the licence fees accrued directly to the profit of the Deputy and the King. Under his rule the staple system was greatly modified and the efficiency of the licensing plans much improved. It was his good fortune, and not his good management, that the English demand became during the years of his rule sufficiently large and steady to absorb Irish wool in large quantities, so that, in spite of the expense of licensing and the tightened administration which cut off the smugglers' trade, Irish wool exports increased during these years. Later, there was to be much retrospective complaint by merchants of the harshness of the system, but at the time trade was undoubtedly good, if less profitable to individuals than it would have been without the duties or licence fees. [19]

Wentworth's attitude to revenue was clearly reflected in his argument for the export of Irish wool to England: the licence fees and customs duties on wool, which went out raw and came back as finished cloth, might enrich the King as much as four times on every fleece. [20] But the statement of an opinion apparently so indifferent to the welfare of the Irish merchants and the Irish consumer must be measured against Wentworth's unwillingness to have duties, in general, raised too high. He seems always to have been a very competent judge of what the market would bear. It must also be remembered that this complexity of inward and outward duties, this network by which restrictions were first imposed out of economic policy and then exemptions granted as a means of raising revenue, was only one of the numerous confused schemes found by an epoch when no adequate method of taxation had been evolved to meet the needs of the state.

Wentworth's encouragement of linen manufacture, though a relatively minor matter, has received far more attention than it deserves, presumably because of Ireland's later fame for this commodity. Wentworth noticed at once the suitability of the Irish climate for the development of linen weaving. A good deal of flax was grown, particularly in the north; linen yarn and some linen, neither of very good quality, were being produced. The yarn, however, was increasingly exported to Lancashire for its growing textile industry. Wentworth's plan was to restrict the exportation of yarn by making stipulations as to its quality and stopping all that his agents thought to be below standard; at the same time he set up looms at his own expense and developed the manufacture of linen cloth with the help of French and Flemish workmen brought over for the purpose. He also imported a great quantity of flax seed for growing a better kind of flax, and planned in time to undercut the Dutch and French manufacturers by as much as twenty per cent. But the scheme was misconceived. The confiscation of the yarn caused considerable outcry and Wentworth abandoned the project after losing a good deal of money. [21]

His correspondence reveals other projects for developing industries in Ireland. He had ideas for making the Irish army independent of England for cannon by starting iron foundries, and a plan for manufacturing gunpowder was abandoned regretfully when surveyors reported that there was too little prospect of digging saltpetre in Ireland in large enough quantities. The 'saltpetre-men' — privileged to dig for His Majesty's manufacture of gunpowder — always caused so much resentment and disturbance in England that it must be held to Wentworth's credit that he decided, though regretfully, to spare Ireland this nuisance.

He had a hopeful project for the manufacture of glass; he developed a quarry for black marble in Ulster, and at one time he seems to have entered on a plan for bringing over workmen from the famous Mortlake factory and starting the weaving of tapestry in Ireland. These projects, which had little time to mature, vanished in the wars of the next decade, and his plan for improving water-transport by clearing the fairway of the Shannon also came to nothing. [22]

The money for his schemes came largely from the profits of his place as Lord Deputy of Ireland, and his plans for the extension of Irish industry were closely knit with plans for increasing his own fortune. In this way he did not greatly differ from entrepreneurs like the Earl of Cork who had, according to their own lights, been 'civilizing' Ireland in precisely this way for the last thirty years. It is, however, apparent from his correspondence and from the nature of some of his ventures — the linen, the glass and the tapestry for instance — that he was prepared to risk more than Lord Cork and others had been on long-term ventures and on projects which had more prestige value for Ireland than immediate and evident profit for him. There are certainly traces in his policy of an outlook that was neither purely personal nor purely materialist, and if it is praising him too highly to give him unqualified honours as a pioneer and enlightened industrialist with a clear-sighted vision, it is doing him less than justice to put him on the same level as the get-rich-quick settlers whom he disliked and opposed.

His weakness did not lie in his ideas, which were often good. It cannot be wholly accidental that many of those industries which he either started or stimulated were, at a later date, to become important for the Irish economy and for Irish prestige. Linen and glass and the breed of horses — these were all things in which Wentworth at least foresaw the possibility of Irish pre-eminence.

It was not his ideas that were at fault, but his management. He understood land much better than he understood manufacture, and his outstanding gifts were for administration, for stopping up leakages in the collecting and spending of money, for saving and even for multiplying money by processes of orderly and exacting management. His greatest triumph, therefore, was in the increase of the revenue from the customs.

Like the English customs, the Irish customs were farmed out for an annual rent; any profits over the rent and the costs of collection were evenly divided between the King and the farmers. Owing to the decline in Irish trade during the war with Spain from 1625 to 1630 the customs had become very unprofitable, and even though the duties were raised early in 1632 the King was having difficulty in renewing his contract with the farmers on advantageous terms. This was the situation at the time of Wentworth's appointment, and he at once threw himself into the task of finding new customs farmers who were willing to pay a rent as large as before, or larger. Although he was successful in his quest he was at first very unwilling to become personally involved. It was, however, normal for a Deputy to have some stake in the customs, and finally he came in, bringing George Radcliffe with him. The new contract looked extremely speculative, as the farmers offered the substantial annual rent of £15,000 together with half the profits to the King. Everything depended on the improvement of Irish trade as the outcome of European peace. In fact, owing to Wentworth's suppression of piracy and his more efficient management of the ports, the customs rose extremely fast. In the year in which Wentworth first came to Ireland (March 1633 – March 1634) the profits were £25,846, an increase of about £3,000 on the previous year. But in the following year, as the effect of better order by sea and land became apparent, they rose to £38,174. It would be reasonably safe to predict a further rise in the coming years. (23)

As a result the most devious intrigues began among the farmers. Wentworth no longer felt that the King was being justly treated in getting only a half share of the profits; he wanted to see the royal revenue benefit by at least five-eighths, as against three-eighths to the farmers. It was, however, typical of him that, while he wanted the King to have this extra eighth, he also wanted to secure as much as possible of the remainder for himself, by making a new contract and getting rid of the rest of the syndicate. His motives were not wholly those of personal greed. Money meant power, and Wentworth wanted the power quite as much as he wanted the money; his faith in his capacity to use power well, and in the King's interest, grew stronger every year. Furthermore, if he did not himself take over the bulk of the customs farm, in whose hands would he be leaving these expanding opportunities of wealth and influence? There were one or two customs farmers in England, among them Sir Arthur Ingram, with whom he had recently quarrelled; but though he wanted them bought out they were not very dangerous men. The dangerous man was Lord Mountnorris, holding a substantial share in the syndicate, holding also the office of Vice-Treasurer of Ireland, and — by the spring of 1635 — no longer either a friend or a supporter of Wentworth. To get him out of his Treasurer's office and out of the customs syndicate had now become of prime importance.

Wentworth had begun by trusting Mountnorris rather too freely. He had been almost in alliance with him before he came to Ireland, exchanging confidential comment and advice. Almost as soon as he reached Dublin he had begun to revise his views, and by the spring of 1635 he found few things more inconvenient than having Mountnorris as Vice-Treasurer. He described him, justly enough, as dishonest and incompetent, but this was not the only reason he wanted to be rid of him. The Vice-Treasurer was in a position to know a very great deal about the Deputy's revenue as well as the Irish revenue. For Wentworth, who never saw any reason why he should not use public money to advantage when he had it in his hands, it was essential to have as Vice-Treasurer a man who trusted him at least as far as he trusted himself. He would never default when it came to paying over what was due to the Crown; in the interim, he was the King's banker rather than his cofferer, and arrogated to himself a certain freedom in using cash balances in hand to meet the instant needs of government or to finance ventures which might be profitable both to himself as Deputy and to Ireland and to government.

In a financial situation at once so primitive and so delicate as that which obtained at this epoch it is difficult to draw the line between the permissible and the impermissible. Wentworth took very big risks, but in the last resort he knew what was the King's and what was his own. Lesser operators — of whom Mountnorris was one — might not take such risks, but they regarded as their own anything they could get and keep without danger of discovery. [24]

It was therefore from the early months of 1635 Wentworth's intention to get Mountnorris removed from his post as Vice-Treasurer and to oust him from the customs farm with all its glorious possibilities of wealth and power. Mountnorris was no less resolved to stand his ground, indeed to do more: to increase his share of the customs at Wentworth's expense. The tussle was long and was complicated by Wentworth's simultaneous quarrel with Lord Clanricarde over the plantation of Galway, with Lord Cork over the possessions of the Church, and with Wilmot over the alienation of Crown land in Athlone. Mountnorris was well-friended at Court in England; his plans were carefully laid, and Wentworth had many enemies. He might easily have won, had he not made a foolish error in discretion, which enabled Wentworth to annihilate him when he least expected it.

The fatal story began with some foolish indiscipline in the army and some crude ill-manners in the Deputy's household. A brother of Mountnorris, a lieutenant in the army, behaved insubordinately to Wentworth at a review and was reprimanded. As soon as the Deputy's back was turned he showed how little he cared for the reproof by making an insulting gesture at his commander-in-chief. Wentworth, who saw this out of the tail of his eye, wheeled instantly about and fetched him a smart blow with his cane. To strike an officer and a gentleman was, in the circumstances, unwise, though it was not unusual in the armies of the time. A few days later one of Wentworth's attendants dropped a stool, more on purpose than accidentally, on his gouty foot. The boy was also a kinsman of Mountnorris.

The indiscreet Mountnorris, not long after, at a dinner party at the Lord Chancellor's was heard loudly to announce that the incident of the stool had been an act of vengeance for the public affront given by the Deputy to the family, but his brother — Mountnorris bragged — would not be content with so slight a revenge. It was generally felt at the dinner party that Mountnorris had gone too far, had even implied that his insulted brother ought to wipe out the blow he had received by sticking a knife into the Lord Deputy. (25) No one thought it wise of Mountnorris to talk in this way, but Wentworth, to whose ears it came in due course, took no immediate action.

He had other plans for ridding himself of Mountnorris. He had reported to the King that the Vice-Treasurer was, contrary to express command, levying sixpence in the pound to himself on every sum to be paid out of the Treasury, and still winking at the good business that his servants did in refusing all payments unless bribed in advance. Wentworth asked for powers to institute an inquiry into this behaviour; he also asked for permission to summon a Court Martial, if he thought necessary, to try Mountnorris for his indiscreet remarks at the Chancellor's dinner party. Pending the outcome of either or both of these he wished to suspend Mountnorris from his office as Vice-Treasurer. The King sent him the powers for which he had asked, but refused to countenance the suspending of Mountnorris at least until the financial charges against him were proved. (26) This restriction did not altogether suit Wentworth, but for the time being he merely went ahead with the inquiry into his behaviour at the Treasury, kept his more drastic power to call a Court Martial secretly in reserve, and hoped that Mountnorris would resign of his own accord when he found his accounts questioned.

Nothing of the kind happened. Mountnorris was aware that Wentworth had Cork and Clanricarde against him, with all their friends at Court to help them. He now also began to attack the Deputy through friends in England. His mouthpiece, the persuasive barrister Patrick Darcy, offered to the King figures which seemed to indicate both that Wentworth was doing too well out of the customs and that he was spending too much money on the ships guarding the Irish sea; Darcy advised the King to resume the customs to himself and consider a much more advantageous way of farming them without the assistance of Wentworth. The King was not at first impressed. [27] He must have been aware that Darcy had been a prime mover of Clanricarde's case against the Crown in Galway, and that he had also defended Lord Cork in the case about the College of Youghal. These associations were not altogether reassuring. It seems to have been only later that Mountnorris was named as the man behind Darcy and the real author of the new customs scheme.

In November 1635 Mountnorris wrote openly himself to the King; he implied very clearly that the Deputy had been cheating over the customs, that he could supply all the necessary figures, and that he would himself make a much more profitable offer to the King if he were not prevented from leaving Ireland. [28] The implication was that Wentworth was holding him up.

Wentworth cannot have been ignorant of this appeal to the King; at least the drastic speed with which he now acted suggests that he was resolved to prevent his journey to Court at whatever cost. Quite suddenly, in December, he used the King's authority to set up a Court Martial. In his character of commander-in-chief he arraigned Mountnorris for the words he had spoken at the Chancellor's dinner table in the previous spring. They could be construed as treason. Faced by so shocking and so unexpected a charge, Mountnorris asked for time to consider and for a trial by his peers. He was told that a military court knew nothing of trial by peers, and after about an hour's discussion he was unanimously condemned to death.

None of those who voted for a capital sentence thought that it would be carried out. It seems to have been understood that this was merely a gesture, and Wentworth himself assured the stunned victim that he would intercede with the King for a pardon. He would rather, he said, lose his hand than that Mountnorris should lose his head. The phrase might have been better chosen; even in the turmoil of his dismay, Mountnorris felt a special resentment that Wentworth's hand and his head should be put in balance together. [29]

The Deputy had gained his principal purpose. Mountnorris, under sentence of death for treason, could no longer hold office as

Vice-Treasurer, and while he remained in prison awaiting pardon, he could not of course go to England to interfere with Wentworth's plans for the farm of the customs.

The incident showed Wentworth's reckless ingenuity in gaining his ends, but it also showed his lack of human insight. He had removed Mountnorris from his path at a critical moment and had dealt a blow at his reputation from which he would scarcely recover. But a Court Martial, in peacetime, when no imminent danger threatened, was altogether too provocative a measure.

The news, when it reached the Court, produced a hubbub of protest. Already there was strong feeling against Wentworth's aggressive conduct. Lord Wilmot was smarting under the treatment he had received; Lord Cork had bought an estate in England, it was said, to escape from the Deputy; Sir Piers Crosby had been expelled from the Council and the amiable Patrick Darcy had been hounded for his defence of the Galway proprietors. All these men were either about the Court in person at this time, or had friends who were. In November poor old Clanricarde had died, heartbroken, it was said, by the Deputy's ruthlessness. And now, in December, Mountnorris was sentenced to death. Rumour ran ahead of events, and there were those at Whitehall who could precisely describe the exact manner of his shooting in the courtyard of Dublin Castle.

Wentworth's friends were greatly troubled. They trusted that he could justify his conduct, but they did not like it. [30] Cardinal Richelieu, whose domination over the French King was a constant theme of political gossip, had, a few years before, tried and executed an eminent French nobleman at his private residence. Though no contemporary comment draws a comparison between the fate of Marillac and that of Mountnorris, it can hardly have failed to strike informed contemporaries. Considering the Queen's loathing for the great Cardinal, and the King's extreme jealousy lest any of his ministers should try to play the Richelieu to him, the parallel was very unfortunate. Moreover, the King's warrant to Wentworth, though it could be construed to cover a death sentence, had in truth authorized no more than 'censure' on Mountnorris and 'reparation' for his fault.

Wentworth, whose judgment in these matters of political psychology never improved, was angry and defiant when he heard of the talk at Whitehall. He pointed out that Mountnorris had come to no physical harm at all, had indeed been permitted to go to his own home on a plea of ill-health after about a fortnight in the Castle. His ill-health, he implied, was nothing but the result of obstinacy and mortification. The King was ready to grant a pardon as soon as he admitted his fault, but Mountnorris stubbornly refused to admit any fault, and so the pardon was held up. He preferred using other means to get round the Deputy. He sent his wife to petition in heart-rending words that he would lift his 'heavy hand' from off her dear lord, in the name of that saint in heaven, Wentworth's dead wife, who had been her cousin. Wentworth remained adamant: Mountnorris had only to ask pardon, and he would be free. Until then he was to stay in his house, and in April, Wentworth haled him back to the Castle and refused him the use of pen and paper until he would agree to make submission. [31]

All this time a committee was examining the accounts of Mountnorris and accumulating evidence of his previous faults, while he bitterly complained that he had no liberty to defend himself. He had meanwhile been dismissed from his post as Vice-Treasurer, and Wentworth's nominee, Sir Adam Loftus, appointed in his place. [32]

Though Wentworth had gained his point in replacing Mountnorris at the Irish Treasury, the question of the customs farm was still unsettled. All that winter it was being canvassed at Court, while Darcy, regardless of the disgrace of Mountnorris, continually demonstrated with figures the superiority of his scheme to anything offered by Wentworth. The King, who had at first been doubtful of Darcy's good faith, was now beginning to yield to the persistent rumours that Wentworth was far too calculating to be trustworthy in matters of money. The offer made by Mountnorris seemed, in any case, larger: £20,000 rent and half the profits, against £15,500 and five-eighths of the profits. Laud, worried, wrote to Wentworth urging him not to stand in the King's light in this matter of the customs, or at least to make it clear that he was not doing so. [33]

It was, of course, common talk at Whitehall that the persecution of Mountnorris was a ruse to enable Wentworth to get his own way about the customs. Another rumour went round that a large sum of money — £6,000 — had been received by Cottington for some service in connection with the case. This was true; it was the payment for appointment to the lucrative post of Vice-Treasurer, paid over by Wentworth to secure the place for Sir Adam Loftus.

Wentworth admitted this payment and its purpose to Laud in one of his coded letters. [34] But the thing was so widely rumoured that Cottington thought best to make a handsome gesture and pay the sum into the Exchequer. The buying and selling of offices was so ordinary a process that it would not have provoked comment had it not been for the peculiar circumstances by which the dismissal of Mountnorris had been engineered. Much more damaging to Wentworth was the perpetual gossip that Mountnorris had been condemned to death because he had crossed his negotiations about the customs. Writing to Laud, Wentworth professed himself unable to understand why this should be. Mountnorris — he argued — had uttered the treasonous words for which he had been condemned, *before* he had come forward as a rival customs farmer. How could the two things be in any way connected? [35] It was a curious defence, because Wentworth must have been suspicious that Mountnorris would cross his financial plans long before any scheme was actually put forward, and therefore before the slander was uttered. It was also an undeniable fact that he had not prosecuted him until the rivalry over the customs was becoming acute. The ingenuousness of Wentworth's denial — not once but many times — of any link at all between the prosecution and the customs suggests self-deception. He made the denial so often that he came to believe it. There was at least this truth in it: that he would have prosecuted Mountnorris, or any other man, for his provocative indiscretion; it was the kind of contempt for authority that he never let pass. The sinister element in the whole affair was not the prosecution, but its timing. Wentworth seems to have convinced himself of his integrity in this matter: but he did not convince his enemies, and for once, he hardly convinced his friends.

Meanwhile he was urgently desirous to come over to England. Not only did he wish to explain his own plans for the customs in person to the King before Mountnorris could get out of prison, he also wished to justify himself against the criticism from courtiers and others which he believed was undermining him with the King.

Laud had given him friendly warnings: 'Notwithstanding all your great services in Ireland, you want not them which whisper and perhaps speak louder where they think they may, against your proceedings as being over full of personal prosecutions against men of quality.' [36] That was the crux of the matter: if he had directed his assertions of power to the unimportant and the defenceless he would have made less dangerous enemies.

Wentworth's character was as much to blame as his policy for the hostile atmosphere that he had generated. He had an unhappy capacity for giving his public quarrels an appearance of private vindictiveness. Whether he stood to gain by a prosecution, as he evidently did with Mountnorris, or whether he stood to lose as he did over the Youghal case with Lord Cork, he was prone to be, in one way or another, too much personally involved. Furthermore, his natural irritability had been enhanced in Ireland by failing health and a continually growing burden of work. He had never been really well since the spring of 1635; he was intermittently plagued by gout, fearful headaches and sleeplessness, and in May 1636 he had an attack of the stone which he himself admitted was 'above anything I endured since I was a man'. He forced himself relentlessly to the long journeys and the unsparing work in spite of his doctor's advice and Wandesford's anxious protests.

On his first coming to Ireland he had taken great delight in hawking for blackbirds, the best substitute for game that could be found in the neighbourhood of Dublin. As many as two hundred horses would sometimes attend these expeditions in the cold fine winter of 1633; [37] but as the pressure of work increased he had no time for these amusements. Hawking had to be almost altogether abandoned and the most he could do to refresh his aching brain was to walk in the fresh green fields, or occasionally spend a few days at a favourite hunting lodge. On these brief holidays business still pursued him, and even on Sundays he kept his secretaries as busy, after the morning's devotions were over, as on ordinary working days.

At the same time he was responsible for a household of nearly three hundred people, into which he received the sons of many of his friends as pages or gentlemen-in-waiting; young Ingram and young Windebanke entangled themselves with unsuitable girls in Dublin and had to be sent home with a solid portion of fatherly advice. Another young gentleman named Skipwith seems to have aimed too high and made advances to a lady of Wentworth's own family, thereby incurring displeasure and being sent away in disgrace. Wentworth arranged the marriages of his sister Elizabeth, of his brother George, and of Lord and Lady Dungarvan; he was expected to keep a fatherly eye on young Irish noblemen, and once he was called in to arbitrate in a quarrel between Lord Cork and his spendthrift son-in-law, George Goring. He was an anxious father and worried more than was necessary about his elder children. The little girls swung by their arms to improve their figures, which seemed a safe pastime until their companion Alice Wandesford fell flat upon her face and nearly broke her jaw. [38] The children of his last marriage were all sickly; two sons, both christened Thomas, were born and died in Ireland, and a nameless little daughter, mentioned only once in her father's letters, survived only a few months.

Death had made other gaps in Wentworth's friends and family. His two favourite sisters, Anne and Mary, died while he was in Ireland; one brother, Michael, had disappeared into the void of the German wars, and two others, Philip and Matthew, died suddenly within a few weeks of each other early in 1636. His old friend, Carlisle, died that same spring, while Calvert was gone two or three years before.

The deaths of so many of his friends increased Wentworth's sense of distance and loneliness; in Dublin he had only Radcliffe and Wandesford in whom to confide and, as he himself said, 'I were the most solitary man without them that ever served a King in such a place.' Depressed, ill and overwrought as he was, it was hardly surprising that he had 'more choler than at all times [he] was able to govern and control'. [39]

In some moods he irritated his old friend Laud by gloomily predicting his own approaching death. The Archbishop pulled him up short for such fancies. He irritated the King too by multiplying his anxious protests against those who he believed were misrepresenting him. 'I must tell you it is a good service to me not to be frightened at false alarms', wrote the King impatiently. [40]

The alarms were not all false. During the whole winter of 1635-6 the underground struggle over the appointment of a new Treasurer in England vibrated through the Court. Since Portland's death in the spring of 1635 Cottington had worked quietly, surreptitiously, almost frivolously in his own interests. Wentworth openly repudiated all desire for the place. Laud was anxious to keep Cottington out, but had very little hope of winning the King to his own candidate, the reliable Bishop of London, William Juxon.

Francis Cottington has become, by the processes of time and tradition, a shadowy figure in English history. The personal rule of Charles I is associated always with Wentworth and Laud, yet Cottington, for the whole eleven years, was as influential as either of these, and in his own opinion and that of many contemporaries, perhaps the most influential man in England. He had been Wentworth's friend, but he had never been friendly with Laud, and as Wentworth and the Archbishop drew together, Cottington drew away, though under his habitual mask of amiability. In the winter of 1635-6 a further shift of alliance occurred. Secretary of State Windebanke, who had been helpful to Laud in the past, quietly moved over into Cottington's party. This was the loss of a key position which perturbed the Archbishop greatly. [41] Secretary of State Coke was Wentworth's man, but he was much older than Windebanke, less valued by the King, and not valued at all by the Queen.

These alignments were personal as much as, or more than, political. Cottington, apart from a devotion to the Spanish alliance of which he had been the architect, had a wholly opportunist attitude to politics. He wanted to have control of money, for himself, for his friends at Court, and for the Crown in so far as his own position depended on the Crown's solvency. In so far as he had any religion, he was sympathetic to the Roman Catholic faith in which he was ultimately to die — at Valladolid in Spain in 1652. At this time he was officially an Anglican, as he had to be to hold his ministerial place, but he seconded the Queen's insistent pressure on her husband to grant favours to Roman Catholics: a policy which was bitterly deplored by the Archbishop, who was anxious that the ritualism in which he believed should not be taken for Roman.

But in spite of — or because of — the lack of seriousness in his political views Cottington was a threat to the 'thorough' policy of Wentworth and Laud. To have him as Treasurer would be, for them, politically disastrous. Portland had been crusty, critical, personally grasping, and given to delay. Cottington was all things to all men, and would probably grant all things to all men, or at least to all men who he thought would be useful to him. Cottington at the Treasury would mean high summer for the Queen's friends, forays into the Irish revenue, multiplication of monopolies, favours, bribes; brilliant day-to-day juggling with the revenue, and no long-term planning.

The Archbishop's gloom over this probable appointment and its consequences made him hope for Wentworth's return, but he advised him to think of some private excuse for coming over to England, not to give the impression that he thought it politically necessary, which might annoy the King and make Wentworth's enemies rejoice that they had given him cause to fear. [42] Laud was troubled at the intrigues and corruption at the Court, which fill many of his letters, and was insistent that Wentworth should burn his communications because he did not trust the numerous secretaries and clerks who might otherwise have access to them, nor for that matter the hands through which they passed on their way from Lambeth to Dublin. [43]

In early March, to Laud's relief and surprise, the King passed over Cottington and made Juxon Treasurer. Cottington took his disappointment gaily, and let it be known that this arrangement suited him almost better than carrying the onerous task himself. At least it was presumably from hints dropped by Cottington that Windebanke's secretary and Windebanke's son got the gossip which, after a couple of drinks, they were heard retailing in a tavern: Juxon was a hollow man, Cottington would manage all through him, and what the Archbishop thought or did was 'no matter'. [44]

Irritated and depressed by this new turn of events, Laud was therefore as anxious to consult with Wentworth as before Juxon's appointment. By this time Wentworth had thought out his excuse and got leave to come over from Dublin. His old steward Marris had died, drowned in crossing a stream when drunk: the weakness against which Wentworth had so often warned him had been the end of him at last. Wentworth feared that there might be some confusion owing to the poor man's mismanagement during the last months, and there would be his own estate and affairs to settle up — debts to be paid, including one to an old nurse who must not be kept waiting. [45] It made a sufficient reason to ask the King for leave to visit his home in Yorkshire, taking London and the Court on the way.

On June 3rd, 1636, having appointed Wandesford to act in his stead in Ireland, he embarked at Dublin, leaving his wife and children behind, but taking Radcliffe, Mainwaring and a considerable staff for his journey. [46]

NOTES

[1] Kearney, pp. 130-7.

[2] Strafford MSS, III, Wentworth to Cottington, 28th August 1637.

[3] Ibid., IX, folio 28, Wentworth to Coke, 19th May 1635.

[4] Kearney, pp. 131, 134; O'Brien, pp. 41, 49, 66-7.

[5] Knowler, I, p. 106.

[6] Ibid., pp. 107, 396-7.

[7] Ibid., II, p. 34; C.S.P.I., 1633-47, p. 134.

[8] Knowler, II, p. 19.

[9] Ibid., I, p. 152; C.S.P.I., 1633-47, p. 35.

[10] Knowler, I, p. 152; C.S.P.I., 1633-47, pp. 32, 50.

[11] C.S.P.I., 1633-47, p. 41.

[12] Ibid., pp. 82-5, 114-16; Knowler, I, p. 404; II, p. 93.

[13] C.S.P.I., 1633-47, p. 86.

[14] Kearney, p. 139.

[15] For the salt monopoly see O'Brien, p. 244; Knowler, I, 192-3; C.S.P.D., 1635-6, p. 44; for coal see Gilbert, *Calendar of Corporation of Dublin*, III, pp. 305, 306-8.

[16] Knowler, II, p. 23; Carte, I, p. 169; O'Brien, pp. 63-4.

[17] Ibid., II, p. 89.

[18] O'Grady, p. 328.

[19] Kearney, pp. 137-53; O'Grady, p. 348; Knowler, I, p. 202.

[20] Knowler, I, p. 202.

[21] Kearney, pp. 154-9; O'Brien, pp. 76 ff; Knowler, I, p. 473; II, p. 19; Rushworth, *Trial*, p. 425.

[22] O'Brien, p. 68; Strafford MSS, XI, folio 23; XXII, No. 19; XXVII, Nos. 33, 37; G. Boate, *Ireland's Natural History*, London, 1652, p. 62.

[23] C.S.P.I., 1625-60, pp. 237 ff; Rushworth, *Trial*, pp. 242 ff; O'Brien, p. 64; Kearney, pp. 163 ff. See also Upton, *Sir Arthur Ingram*, pp. 218 ff.

[24] On the eve of his trial Wentworth wrote to the Vice-Treasurer Adam Loftus his thanks for 'your discreet concealing from persons very ill-affected to me how the account stood betwixt you and me' (Knowler, II, p. 414). This significant phrase taken with the other aspects of Wentworth's behaviour and the common practice of the time indicates how much he needed to have a trusted friend at the Treasury. See also in Aylmer, pp. 166-7, a comparison between Wentworth's own practice and the conduct he condemned in Mountnorris. But it must be remembered in Wentworth's favour that, inconsistent as his conduct was, the Crown did on the whole profit greatly from his operations. The same could not be said of the conduct of Mountnorris.

[25] C.S.P.I., 1633-47, pp. 107-8.

[26] Knowler gives the authority to inquire into the conduct of Mountnorris as Vice-Treasurer (I, p. 448). The authority to try him by Court Martial is in Strafford MSS, XV, No. 175. It is dated on the same day.

[27] Laud, *Works*, VII, p. 142; *Clarendon State Papers*, I, pp. 440-6.

[28] *Clarendon State Papers*, I, p. 361.

[29] Knowler, I, pp. 497-8; Strafford MSS, IX, folios 130-6, Wentworth to Coke, 3rd January 1636; Rushworth, *Trial*, pp. 189 ff, 217 ff.

[30] Knowler, I, pp. 508-10; Laud, *Works*, VII, p. 217.

[31] *Clarendon State Papers*, I, pp. 449, 554.

[32] Knowler, I, pp. 512-13.

[33] Laud, *Works*, VII, p. 217.

[34] Strafford MSS, VI, folio 298, Wentworth to Laud, 3rd January 1636.

[35] Knowler, I, p. 519.

[36] H.M.C. *Various*, XII, p. 411.

[37] Knowler, I, p. 162.

[38] Alice Thornton, *Autobiography*, pp. 10 ff.

[39] Knowler, I, p. 194; II, p. 18.

[40] Ibid., I, p. 513.

[41] Laud, *Works*, VII, pp. 217, 223; a very long coded letter from Wentworth to Laud, 2nd November 1635, in Strafford MSS, VI, folios 67-8, indicates that Wentworth would have liked to be Treasurer but did not think his chances good enough to admit this openly.

[42] Ibid., loc. cit.

[43] Ibid., pp. 233-4, 237; Strafford MSS, VII, folio 123.

[44] Laud, *Works*, VII, p. 252.

[45] Knowler, I, p. 487.

[46] *Lismore Papers*, Series 2, IV, p. 190.

CHAPTER SEVEN

THE LORD DEPUTY IN ENGLAND

I have ever governed myself as little by opinion as any other man, yet it is not amiss sometimes to understand how the market goes, and good use to be made of it.

Wentworth to Sir John Coke, 1633

ON reaching London, Wentworth took up his residence in one of the magnificent houses in Henrietta Street, Covent Garden, the new residential quarter planned by Inigo Jones. On June 12th he kissed the King's hand at Hampton Court. 'Since his coming his addresses were wholly to the Archbishop, his apparel very plain, his fashion humble enough (yet with the same natural roughness he carried over with him), his train great and of persons of good quality', reported an observer at Court. [1]

Wentworth was graciously received by all, the King had a set of apartments placed at his disposal at Hampton Court, and suitors of every kind flocked about him so that he had his hands full of business. [2] 'Let Will, Nan and Arabella excuse me,' he wrote to his wife, 'for in good faith I am so infinitely pestered with company that I have not time to write unto them, but God Almighty bless them.' 'His Majesty', he informed her a fortnight later, 'is pleased to use me passing graciously, so as in that relation which is the principal, I stand in as good a condition as I can desire myself.' [3]

The King listened attentively to his lengthy report of Irish affairs and then declared his intention of calling a Council for the express purpose of informing them clearly of all that had been done in Ireland. He had found the Deputy's statement so interesting that he would preside in person — a comparatively rare event — and hear once again the whole detailed account. Wentworth therefore repeated it in full Council, concluding with the request that no money for England be asked for out of Ireland, at least until a reserve of £20,000 was in the Irish Treasury; he reiterated his former points concerning appeals to England and the confirmation of the Deputy's power and excused himself for his alleged severity:

' ... where I found a crown, a Church and a people spoiled,
I could not imagine to redeem them from under the pressure
with gracious smiles and gentle looks, it would cost warmer
water than so.'

He had acted throughout with the King's best interests at heart.
Charles here interrupted. 'There was no severity, my lord,' he
said. Deeply moved, Wentworth closed his oration with a personal
apology to the King and Council 'for what might unadvisedly have
slipped from me. Hitherto I thanked God it had done nobody
hurt but myself.' Charles congratulated him with unusual warmth
and Wentworth, falling on his knees, devoutly kissed his hand
while the Council seconded the King's approbation with discreet
applause. [4]

Wentworth was triumphant. 'This discourse was not kept
within doors, but filled all the Town, much spoken thereon to my
advantage, and leaving my ill-willers no words or face to speak
against it', he reported to Wandesford. The King had been
moved and interested; he was sensitive to personal contact and his
minister's genuine enthusiasm had won him. The catalogue of
personal achievements which he sometimes found irritating in
Wentworth's letters had a different effect when uttered defer-
entially in Council and yoked with his own name. Others followed
the King's lead; the Duke of Lennox, the Marquis of Hamilton
and the Earl of Pembroke were friendly, while Laud was frankly
delighted at having his old friend back again. Lady Carlisle, to
whose beauty Wentworth was not indifferent, was very gracious
and the Queen received him well. Even Lord Holland, a constant
advocate of policies opposed to Wentworth's, made overtures of
friendship. It was difficult not to be carried away by this reception
and, in his letter to Wandesford, Wentworth tried to assess the
situation fairly. 'Such hath been his Majesty's usage of me', he
wrote, 'as I am believed to be of more credit, and far more consideration than I take myself to be; yet do I not endeavour much
to undeceive them, in regard that the nourishing this opinion
makes well for my present purpose and future quiet; for as long as
men judge me to be in this condition, they will be less apt to undertake or trouble me, and to say truth, howbeit, I do not take myself
to be in that degree of favour, yet I do believe it to be such, as will

bring me a great deal of peace in my future employment on that side.' [5]

Before the end of July the customs business was settled to Wentworth's satisfaction. The other customs farmers were bought out, leaving only Wentworth and Radcliffe to share the profits with the King. He continued to pay the same rent as before — £15,500, compared to £20,000 offered by Mountnorris — but the King was to have five-eighths of the additional profits instead of half as under the old system, and Wentworth convinced him that these would increase steadily under his management. The previous career of Mountnorris certainly did not suggest that he would be as efficient a customs farmer as Wentworth had already shown himself, and the King did not, in the next years, regret his bargain. The profit of the customs rose from £38,000 in 1634-5 to the startling figure of over £57,000 in the year 1637-8. [6]

The six weeks at Court and in London were perhaps the most triumphant and unclouded of all his public life. It was true that Mountnorris and his friends were still active, and that Lady Mountnorris even pursued him to England and caused some stir by tearfully falling on her knees before him in his house at Covent Garden. He persuaded her to get up and armed her gallantly to her coach, but he would do nothing to release her husband until he confessed his guilt. [7] Apart from this incident, he passed his time in the sunshine of royal favour and enjoyed some of the pleasures of an easy and civilized life.

It was presumably at this time that scandal first got busy because of his attentions to Lady Carlisle. She was a lively, intelligent woman, whose portly charms were much admired by contemporaries. Wentworth, who had been the close friend of her husband, and was still the friend of her brother, the Earl of Northumberland, enjoyed her company and admired her beauty and her wit. She, for her part, had a taste for political intrigue and liked masterful men, especially if they held high positions in the world. After so long an interval of time it is impossible to say anything with certainty about their relationship, but Wentworth made no secret of his admiration for her. They exchanged their pictures — not miniatures for private amorous contemplation, but full-size portraits by Van Dyck, which they could hardly hang anywhere but in the public view. This frankness suggests that they were simply practising the form of flirtation mixed with mutual admiration which was dignified by the name of Platonic love and which was very much the mode in the circle of Queen Henrietta Maria. [8]

Lady Carlisle was not the only recipient of Wentworth's portrait. He seems to have had two portraits done by Sir Anthony Van Dyck in the course of the summer, and ordered a number of copies from these, some full-size and some half-length. Hoskins was also commissioned to copy the face twice over in miniature. In both portraits he was painted in armour, and in one of them, that which he ordered himself, to hang in the gallery at Woodhouse, he rests his hand on the head of a fine Irish wolfhound. The pose with the dog was adapted by Van Dyck from the splendid portrait by Titian of the Emperor Charles V, now in the Prado but then in the collection of King Charles.

London, by the end of July, was emptying fast. It was a bad plague year; the theatres were closed and the nobility and gentry kept away from the city. This enabled Wentworth, always sensible about getting his money's worth, to order the copies of his portraits at a most reasonable price — £50 for the full-length figures, £30 when the portraits were reduced to half-length. The studio of Van Dyck, as he noticed, would have 'had small store of work without them'. [9]

He now realized that he would be staying in England, to see to his own estates and to consolidate his position, at least until the autumn; in consequence he sent for his children. They too were painted by Sir Anthony, Will and Nan stealing the picture in their grandest clothes, little Arabella timidly inserted between them. Their stepmother remained in Dublin, Wentworth having doubts about the wisdom of a journey in her apparently delicate state of health. 'I am still of opinion that these scrambling journeys are in no way suited to a woman', [10] he told her, and with that she had to rest content.

Young Will Wentworth, ten years old, with the assurance of his father and grace of his mother, already fulfilled his social duties admirably. To prepare the way for his father he was sent to York, where he was received with great approbation. 'The young lord is a sweet-natured and handsome youth, full of noble parts, and of a rare understanding for his years', wrote Lord Clifford

213

to Gervase Clifton. 'To tell you the truth, I am in love with him so much, as I would wish him my son before any of his age and rank.' (11)

In August, Wentworth followed his son and arrived at York on the 10th to be 'almost feasted to death'. A week later he was at his house at Gawthorp among his old friends and servants. 'Lord!' he wrote in a letter to the Archbishop,

> with what quietness in myself could I live here in comparison of that noise and labour I meet with elsewhere; ... but we'll let that pass for I am not like to enjoy that blessed condition upon earth. (12)

A week later he moved to Woodhouse to find his orchard heavy with fruit and his park abounding in deer; even the discovery that he had not got with him the papers he most wanted failed to ruffle his humour. 'Like a wise man,' he wrote to his wife,

> I have left all my books of account in one of the trunks within your closet or else in a trunk in my little room within the chamber where I dress myself. I pray you seek for them. (13)

It could not last: no sooner had he left Court than his enemies again gathered strength. The Earl of Arundel wrote to him offensively, Lord Clanricarde continued his pleading for his lands in Galway, the outcry of the friends of Mountnorris and Cork began again, and Lord Wilmot's agent was still whispering that Wentworth was doing far too well for himself out of the customs. Wentworth was determined to use the King's favour while he had it: accordingly he wrote at once complaining of this ill-usage, asking leave to justify himself once more personally to the King and suggesting that Charles should set upon him 'such a mark of your favour as will silence these spirits, and set me right again as well in the opinion of others, as for your own service'. At the same time he asked Laud for his good offices; with disarming frankness he admitted his disappointment at being granted hitherto no reward for all he had done. Other men had been rewarded who had deserved no better than he; he rather indiscreetly instanced three of them. Whether or not the King gave him the earldom he wanted, he wrote to Laud,

I will serve his Majesty by the help of God, with the same diligence, labour, and faith as formerly; yet to confess a plain truth to your grace, with whom I neither must nor can ever dissemble ... with less cheerfulness in myself hereafter.

His reasons were sound enough; he admitted to Laud that he feared Lord Holland and 'some others on the Queen's side' and felt certain they would do him less mischief if he had an open and undeniable mark of the King's support to sustain him when he went back to Ireland. [14] Charles was, however, still determined to give Wentworth his reward in his own time and at no other. He wrote an unsympathetic reply:

Certainly I should be much to blame not to admit so good a servant as you are to speak with me ... yet I must freely tell you, that the cause of this desire of yours, if it be known, will rather hearten than discourage your enemies for if they can once find that you apprehend the dark setting of a storm when I say 'No', they will make you leave to care for anything in a short while but your fears. And believe it, the marks of my favour that stop malicious tongues are neither places nor titles, but the little welcome I give to accusers, and the willing ear I give to my servants: this is, not to disparage those favours, (for Envy flies most at the fairest mark,) but to shew their use; to wit, not to quell Envy, but to reward service; it being truly so, when the master without the servant's importunity does it, otherwise men judge it more to proceed from the servant's wit than the master's favour. I will end with a rule that may serve for a stateman, a courtier, or a lover, never make a defence or apology before you be accused. And so I rest your assured friend Charles R.' [15]

The King might have put it better: he was justified in refusing the title on political grounds but his casual references to Wentworth's deserts, coming not two months after the emotional reception of his speech in Council, cut very deep. He might have refused without that deliberate lash of sarcasm.

Wentworth was hurt and he showed it. Writing to the King, he bowed before the royal decision, but could not forbear to point out that the Earl of Holland, no doubt in conjunction with Clanricarde, was spreading a rumour of unrest in Connaught, and that he wished something could be done to silence him. The King in answer bade Wentworth come to see him before he left for Ireland. Instantly his spirits bounded: 'but to you in your ear', he wrote mysteriously to his wife, 'I am commanded by the King to wait upon him at Newmarket.' Whatever his hopes, they were soon dashed. Laud entreated him not to mention the earldom, and Wentworth obeyed. Charles received and dismissed him graciously but without any suggestion or promise of reward and he left England depressed and heavy-hearted, realizing that his momentary triumph had been of less permanent value than he had allowed himself to hope. [16]

He was by no means happy about the state of affairs in England. Above all, he was anxious that European entanglements should be avoided and he had been apprehensive for the past year about the possibility of war with Spain. The confused struggle which was being fought in Germany had entered upon a new phase during the last two years. The forces of the Roman Catholic Emperor, supported by those of Spain, had inflicted a crushing defeat on the Swedes and their German Protestant allies at Nördlingen in the autumn of 1634. This had been followed in the spring of 1635 by the Peace of Prague, by which many of the German Protestant princes made their peace with the Emperor.

The Swedes and the irreconcilable German Protestants now depended more than ever on the support of France, and Cardinal Richelieu, to prevent the domination of all Western Europe by the Habsburg dynasty, decided at last to put men as well as money into the war. In May 1635 France declared war on Spain.

France, as champion of the German Protestants, was also, logically, champion of King Charles's widowed sister Elizabeth and her son the dispossessed Elector Palatine, whose father's rash acceptance of the Bohemian throne had precipitated the European war sixteen years earlier. There was, inevitably, a strong party in England who wanted the King also to come into the open, and give help to the Protestant Cause and to his own nephew. Wentworth was strongly opposed to this idea of active intervention and war on Spain: it would be expensive in itself, and it would be disastrous to Irish trade and thus to the revenues that he was so carefully building up for the Crown.

His fears were exaggerated. The King, well aware of the financial benefits which he gained from his existing alliance with Spain, was in no hurry to forgo them. France, in any case, seemed less attractive as an ally because in the first year of the war the imperial and Spanish forces were still carrying all, or nearly all, before them. The summer that Wentworth spent in London was famous in France as 'l'année de Corbie' — the year that Corbie was taken by invading armies, and the redoubtable Jan von Werth and his Bavarian troops all but entered Paris. Even if King Charles had felt more inclination towards a French alliance than he did, such lamentable disasters would have deterred him from it.

The danger to Irish trade and English revenue was thus averted by the continuance of the Spanish alliance, but the King's policy, at home and abroad, was too erratic and inconsistent to satisfy Wentworth or to inspire confidence. He had revived the tax of Ship-money on the ports and built himself a very creditable fleet with which, in May 1636, the Lord Admiral so terrified the Dutch herring boats that the States of Holland agreed to pay thirty thousand pounds yearly for permission to fish unmolested. (17) This was certainly a help to the revenues, but Ship-money itself was extremely unpopular. 'I had rather give and pay ten subsidies in Parliament, than ten shillings this new-old way', one of Wentworth's correspondents had cheerfully informed him. (18)

Already Puritan libellers were clamouring. William Prynne had been pilloried and imprisoned for an attack on the stage with an oblique reference to the Queen. He was a bencher of Lincoln's Inn, and to wipe out the stain on their profession the young law students of the Temple presented their Majesties with a masque costing twenty thousand pounds. (19) Straws in the wind eddied now one way, now another.

In 1636 a papal agent came to Court; so also did the two eldest sons of the King's sister, Elizabeth of Bohemia, handsome young men and unimpeachable Protestants, but the papal agent made more rumours in London. The public mind is not subtle; Archbishop Laud's incense and candles and bowing meant Popery, and meant it none the less because he was on bad terms with the Queen. Puritanism was far too deeply rooted in the country and even in the Church to be easily eradicated. When the King published a list of lawful games for Sundays, one clergyman after reading it from the pulpit, gave out the fourth commandment and concluded with, 'Dearly beloved, ye have heard now the commandments of God and man. Obey which you please.' [20] When Bishop Williams was involved in perjury and sent to the Tower it was widely believed that Laud had done it in spite because Williams notoriously favoured cautious handling of the Puritans.

The King's Church policy was as unpopular and his appointments as indiscreet as they had always been. One of the royal chaplains, John Cosin, had been bitterly criticized by the Puritans, which was not surprising, as the fiery little man had knocked down one of the vergers for interfering with the candles on the high altar and violently handled three gentlewomen whose behaviour in church did not conform to his standards. [21] Lulled into repose by a superficial calm, the King did not realize that his government was becoming dangerously unpopular.

He was too loftily convinced of his divine sanction to recognize the need for popularity. He appears to have been indifferent to the fact that none of his ideas for better government — or for any government at all — could be put into effect without the co-operation of the gentry who, as Justices of the Peace, were responsible for carrying out the proclamations he issued. He tried to impress on them the duties they ought to perform in the countryside by forbidding their resort to London, but this was a negative and unpopular form of coercion, while his persecution of the Puritans, his favours to Roman Catholics, his repeated exploitation of ways of raising money without Parliament, induced in a great number of them a sullen distrust of all he did.

Foreign envoys, coming fresh to the situation, were often startled by it. The Venetian resident believed the whole country to be riddled with the disaffection of Puritanism, and Peter Paul Rubens as early as 1630 had thought the mercantile connections of the Puritans, and their close relations with the Dutch, represented a real threat of rebellion, to which the King was strangely indifferent. [22]

Wentworth's answer would never have been conciliation. A government that is not popular must be strong, and he saw that the King's government lacked not only popularity but strength. He had shown very clearly in the North and in Ireland that he put his faith in strength. The first essential was to exact obedience.

That a government should be just and benevolent was desirable: Wentworth thought it very desirable indeed. But before it could be just and benevolent it had to be strong and solvent.

To these ends his policy of 'thorough' was directed. Ireland was a pattern of the conduct he thought wise: keep those who had offended the King in awe, suppress all attempts at resistance, increase the revenue by every possible means, and consolidate the position not by seeking for ephemeral popularity but by offering to the subject the blessings of security and justice. The weakness of this policy, as Wentworth's enemies and the King himself were quick to see, was that everything depended on the government being not merely strong enough at one particular moment to over-throw a single opponent, but strong enough at all times and in all eventualities to stand against a concerted attack from all its opponents. Wentworth's critics were in the right when they said he made too many powerful enemies.

But at least his practice was consistent and might with the support of a King as strong, as ruthless, and even half as able as himself, have been successful. The King, in England, was neither strong, nor ruthless, nor in any way gifted for government, and he had no consistent practice at all. He made no effective displays of strength. His persecution of the Puritans annoyed but did not silence them. He was more cautious than Wentworth in not making powerful enemies, but he made no powerful friends either at home or abroad. He allowed too many of his most influential nobility to drift into an inactive, sulky antagonism to the Court. The King had no use for those who had opposed him; the Earls of Essex, Bedford, Warwick and Bristol kissed his hand perfunctorily on occasion and on occasion moved stiffly among the crowds at Whitehall, but they were exiled from practical politics. It was in their houses and not in the houses of the King's ministers that the young politicians collected; they walked in Warwick's gardens at Holborn, talking of foreign policy, colonization and sea-power; they rode over to Great Tew and paced up and down Lord Falkland's bowling green deep in academic theories, they dis-cussed Socinianism, they threshed out political ideas and legal theories, they reviewed Magna Carta, they deplored Ship-money. They were serious-minded, responsible, a little disillusioned; above all they were estranged from the King and his ministers.

Among these people, opposition was latent and would be immediately dangerous if a crisis were to shake the government. It was from them, much more than from the 'Queen's side' or from hostile, irresponsible courtiers, that the real danger was to come. This Wentworth did not realize although he must have been aware of the complex ramifications that bound the different groups and interests together. Lord Holland, in high favour with the Queen, and a zealous friend to most of Wentworth's Irish enemies, was half-brother to the Earl of Warwick. Lord Clanricarde was half-brother to the Earl of Essex. There was a link, half commercial and half political, that bound together Warwick, Lord Saye and some of Wentworth's old associates in the Commons, John Pym and John Hampden; they had shares in a private colonial venture in the Caribbean on which the King did not smile as it might cause trouble with Spain. Interests in commerce linked such men as these to Lord Cork and to some of the Ulster settlers. It was a connection which was potentially dangerous to Wentworth.

In politics Wentworth prized the influence of the Archbishop above all else. 'I do light my candle to no other saint', he wrote at the close of his English visit, but he knew the limitations of Laud's influence on the King, and in spite of the apparent calm that reigned in England he returned to Dublin without any settled hope for the future. He did not foresee how or in what way the breakdown would come, but he knew it to be possible, and he could see that a breakdown in any one place might spread with alarming rapidity through a network of related interests to the whole of the King's dominions. Neither he nor Archbishop Laud shared the King's serene confidence that all was well.

NOTES

[1] H.M.C., IV, p. 291; *C.S.P.D.*, 1635-6, p. 554.

[2] H.M.C. *Various*, VII, p. 413.

[3] *Strafford's Letters to his third wife*, pp. 11, 16.

[4] Knowler, II, pp. 16 ff.

[5] Ibid., II, pp. 16, 21.

[6] Ibid., II, p. 21; Cooper, p. 244; Kearney, pp. 164 ff. Knowler II, 21. See also Chapter VIII of this book. In spite of the agreement, Wentworth was still nervous enough of Mountnorris to instruct Wandesford not on any account to let him have leave to come to England. Knowler II, p. 15.

[7] Rushworth, *Trial*, p. 217.

8 Some passages in the Strafford MSS seem to throw indirect light on Wentworth's attitude to Lady Carlisle. These are, in vol. XXXIV, three disconnected fragments all in Radcliffe's handwriting. One is the detailed account of Wentworth's early life and marriage negotiations, including the charming description of Arabella already quoted. Another is an elaborate analysis of the origins of the Scots revolt. The third is a lengthy dissertation on the theory of Platonic love. I have little doubt that all three form part of a life of Wentworth which was never finished. If this is so, the fragment on Platonic love must have been meant to absolve Wentworth from the accusation of immorality; it is a conjecture that Radcliffe embodied in it the substance of arguments he had had with his friend. He himself evidently disapproved of this form of friendship between the sexes because of the scandalous rumours to which, however innocent, it always gave rise.

9 Strafford MSS, XXI, Nos. 151, 162, 167.

10 *Strafford's Letters to his third wife*, p. 12.

11 H.M.C. *Various*, VII, p. 430.

12 Knowler, II, p. 26.

13 *Strafford's Letters to his third wife*, p. 17.

14 Knowler, II, p. 28; the letter is abbreviated in Knowler. It is in Strafford MSS, VI, folio 348. The most significant of the omitted passages was published by Lord Birkenhead in his *Strafford*, p. 185.

15 Knowler, II, p. 32.

16 Ibid., pp. 33 ff, 54 ff; *Strafford's Letters to his third wife*, p. 10.

17 Rushworth, Pt II, I, p. 322.

18 Knowler, I, p. 358.

19 Ibid., p. 177; Sanderson, p. 196.

20 Knowler, I, p. 166.

21 Rushworth, III, I, pp. 208 ff.

22 Barozzi and Berchet, *Relazioni dagli Ambasciatori Veneti*, Series IV, pp. 328-34; Rubens, *Codex*, V, p. 212.

CHAPTER EIGHT

TRIUMPH AND FOREBODING

I cannot dissemble so far as not to profess I wish extreme much prosperity to this people, and I should lay it up in my opinion as a mighty honour and happiness to become in some degree an instrument of it.
Wentworth to Laud, 1637

BY the end of November 1636, Wentworth was back in Dublin. Though he did not feel as secure of the King as he could have wished, he had on the whole gained his approbation, and for the next three years he continued to rule by the methods he had laid down, enjoying the fruits of victory over his opponents and critics. How far he himself thought the situation would last, it is hard to gauge. He was always acutely aware of criticism and deeply resentful of it; he knew that neither Clanricarde, nor Cork, nor Wilmot, nor Mountnorris nor their clients and supporters accepted their various defeats or were willing to abide by the consequences. But he seems always to have regarded their opposition as that of self-interested individuals, and not to have sensed that it represented something very much deeper — the hostility of the most influential groups in Ireland, the planters on the one hand and the 'old English' on the other. It was his fundamental weakness as a statesman that he failed to see, beyond the personal hostility which he provoked, the broader and deeper bearing of his actions.

For the time being, however, there was fair weather in Ireland and an unusual degree of prosperity and good order for which he rightly took some credit. No doubt he took rather too much to himself, not sufficiently making allowance for the natural forces of recovery that had come into operation and which made the time of his government easier than that of his immediate predecessors. But his insistence on respect for his own authority, his curbing of the oppressions of the 'great ones', and his genuine and by no means unsuccessful attempts to raise the standards of justice and administration, were certainly factors in the situation.

One indication of Wentworth's growing faith in the future of Ireland can be found in his own extensive acquisition of land during these years. He had, when he first came over, set his mind against buying estates in the country. But he very soon came to the conclusion that the advantages of possessing Irish land were much greater than the risks. For one thing, he had been accustomed as Lord President of the North to deal with local magnates as one of them himself, and by no means the least. In Ireland, as a landless man — simply an officer of the Crown, however high his office — he may have felt at a disadvantage. A dispassionate Deputy with no personal stake in the country at all might in theory have a greater moral strength; but actual wealth and power and a personal stake in the government were of more immediate value. This had been one motive for his relentless determination to take over the customs. Somewhat the same ideas were probably at work in his acquisition of Irish land in the last years of his rule. His were not small acquisitions. He gained by royal grant two manors in Wicklow, and two more by purchase, together with another in Kildare; in all nearly 59,000 acres. Of this rather more than a third was poor or waste ground, but the rents from his Irish estates amounted to over £5,000 a year. This was a long way from his original statement to the Earl of Arundel: 'landless I came hither and landless I shall go hence.' It was also by no means in accordance with his often reiterated resolve not to allow any single settler to take up more than 15,000 acres. His defence would no doubt have been that he was not as other settlers were; that any estate he owned would be a model of good management.

He had his first personal experience of the way in which land could be acquired in Ireland very shortly after his arrival, when a prominent member of the Council, Sir William Parsons, offered to do a singularly dishonest deal with him. It was typical of Wentworth that he entered into it, double-crossed Parsons, and ended up with profits for himself and the King. The land in question was a fertile stretch in Wicklow, called 'Byrnes Country' and at the time inhabited by the O'Byrnes. The details of the transaction have been recently worked out by Mr Terence Ranger and are worth summarizing.

The King had granted the land to Wentworth's old friend Carlisle but the grant could only take effect when the royal title to the land was found. When grants of this kind were made by the King it was the common practice of those responsible for finding the King's title in Ireland to cause delays until the possessor of the grant, losing patience, sold out his right for a small sum to the very officials who were holding up the proceedings. Having acquired the grant, they then went ahead with finding the King's title and took over the land themselves.

Carlisle had been subjected to this process by Sir William Parsons, in association with the Earl of Cork and his son-in-law, Ranelagh. By the time Wentworth reached Ireland, Carlisle was on the point of selling out for £5,000. But Wentworth was known to be a friend of Carlisle and therefore likely to look into the matter. Parsons accordingly tried to win him over by jettisoning his other partners and making Wentworth a party to the business. He suggested that Wentworth should advise Carlisle to accept £10,000, which was to be represented to him as the sum that the O'Byrnes would pay to buy out the grant, though in fact Wentworth was himself to provide this sum. With Carlisle out of the way, Parsons would find the royal title and Wentworth could then quietly grant the land to himself. For an outlay of £10,000 he would thus become possessed of land valued at three thousand a year. In return for his co-operation in the deal, Parsons would naturally expect the Deputy to stand his friend thereafter.

Wentworth reported the matter to the King, with the astonishing suggestion that he should, with the royal consent, enter into the plot. He salved his conscience about Carlisle by pushing up the purchase money to fifteen thousand pounds. This was still represented to Carlisle as the sum for which the O'Byrnes were buying out his grant. In fact Wentworth borrowed the money from the Irish exchequer with the royal connivance. Sir William Parsons, unaware of these higher machinations, now found the royal title to the land. This being successfully achieved, Wentworth reported the return of the land to the King and received from him a grant of two manors worth a thousand a year, while the rest of the land and the major part of the income remained with the Crown. Sir William Parsons was left to digest as best he could the knowledge that the outrageous Deputy had, at one and the same time, taken advantage of his offer and informed on him to the King. [1]

'He was stiff and arrogant in society and showed a rather Puritan
contempt for fashion.'

He described his appointment to the governorship of Ireland as 'the knottiest piece that ever fell into debate with me.' It was to prove his downfall.

Wentworth's children Nan, Arabella and Will by Arabella Hollis, his second wife, who died in tragic circumstances.

Mainwaring was to prove a trustworthy and loyal assistant to Wentworth, while advancing his own interests at the same time.

Pale and stooping
after two long winter
months in the damp
of the Tower of
London.

Queen Henrietta Maria actively disliked Wentworth because he refused to
advance the prospects of her Court favourites.

Archbishop Laud, Wenworth's constant friend and adviser, with whom he had a
temperamental affinity.

THE TRVE MANER OF THE SITTING OF THE LORDS & COMMONS OF BOTH HOW
les of Parliament, upon the tryal of Thomas Earle of Stratford, Lord Lieutenant of Ireland, 1641.

The Kings Maiestie.
His seate of State.
the Queenes Maiestie
the Prince his highnes.
Thomas Earle of Arundell
Lord high Steward of England

F the Lord Keeper.
G the Lord Marques of Winchester
H the Lord high Chamberlaine
of England
I the Lord Chamberlaine of
his Maiestie houshold.

K the Lord cheefe Iustice of
the Kings bench,
L a Pryui Councellors,
M the Maisters of the rolls.
N the Iudges and Barons of the
Exchequer.
J the eldest Sonnes of some of the Nobility.

O the Maisters of the Chancery.
P the Earles,
Q the Vicecounts,
R the Barons.
S the Knights, Citizens & bur-
gesses of the howse of Commons.

T the Clarkes
V the Earle of Stratford
W the Lieutenant of the Tower.
X the Plaintives.
Y the Deputis counsell & officers
Z the Countes of Arundell.

When Wentworth was informed that the king had consented to his execution he cried out 'put not your trust in princes.'

The true maner of the execution of Thomas Earle of Strafford, Lord Lieutenant of Ireland vpon Tower-hill the 12th of May 1641.

A Doctor Vsher, Lord Primate of Ireland.
B the sherifes of London.
C the Earle of Strafford.
D his kindred and Friends

After his execution, Laud said of Wentworth 'he is dead with more honour than any of them will gain which hunted after him in his life.'

If this establishment of a personal and landed interest in Ireland was out of key with Wentworth's original purpose when he came there, it was in accordance with ideas for improvement of Irish agriculture and the 'civilization' of Ireland that he had developed in the last few years, through his observation of the country. It also denoted his growing sense of attachment to Ireland which he no longer regarded — as he had done in 1633 — as a land of exile and essentially a stepping-stone to higher preferment. Whatever profits he was intent on making out of his Irish estates, the tone of pleasure and affection with which he now wrote of the country was in strong contrast to the gloom and contempt of his earlier letters.

One of his estates, the manor of Cosha in Wicklow, which he rechristened Fairwood, gave him real delight. Here he built a small hunting lodge and here he would withdraw from time to time for a holiday, 'playing the Tartar' and living in tents until his house was built. Writing to his old friend and tutor Charles Greenwood he became almost poetic in his praises of the place; it was set among hills, a good dry soil, unlike so much of Ireland, yet 'the daintiliest and plentifullyest watered country I ever saw', and with excellent timber. In September the copses abounded in nuts, and he believed there were at least fifteen hundred deer in the park. Of an evening he had seen as many as five hundred feeding near his little hunting lodge. [2] But even here he had evidence of the need of his strong hand. The dispossessed Byrnes preyed on the country in the guise of 'hooded men', and he had to think seriously of making his lodge into a small fortress and hunting these broken men as well as the deer.

In the flat country near Naas in Kildare he planned something finer than a hunting lodge. Here, with workmen brought from England, he began to build a palatial country residence, spacious enough to lodge the King, should he ever come to Ireland, and to serve otherwise as the official country residence of future Deputies. With a frontage of more than a hundred yards, this magnificent house would be considerably larger than Hatfield House, and more ambitious than anything Wentworth had built yet. In his other great houses he had extended what he found — as at the King's Manor at York, or in the huge additions planned for his house at Ledstone, or the improvements to Dublin Castle. But at Naas he was building from the ground up. The vast pile, which went by the name of Jigginstown, was never completed, and fell into ruin during the wars of the next decade. The huge, vaulted cellars, half buried, are still to be seen today, and above them the gaunt skeleton of a long wall pierced by majestic windows. The building is of red brick, but was to have had a marble pavement to a great entrance hall, adorned with columns of black Irish marble. [3]

Irish marble was quarried near Kilkenny and also in Ulster. Wentworth's letters show an interest in the varieties and quality available: the black was better than the streaked or spotted. In these years an atmosphere of richness begins to pervade Wentworth's Court. It was well-known for correctness, dignity, and good order, but polished marble columns and orders for Venetian brocades suggest a more easy and plenteous life than had hitherto been known at Dublin Castle. [4]

All this buying and building showed Wentworth's mounting confidence in his future and in that of Ireland. He thought also of the beauty and prestige of the Irish capital, and the encouragement of the arts at least so far as he understood them. He had plans for the rebuilding of Christ Church Cathedral at a cost of £30,000 to be voted — in due course — by an Irish Parliament. [5] Sir William Brereton, visiting the country two years after Wentworth's first coming, noticed in Dublin 'much additions of buildings lately, and some of these very fair stately and complete'. Wentworth was also in favour of bringing into Ireland the manufacture of civilized luxuries, not only the manufacture of glass, but a tapestry factory, imitated from that which the King was encouraging at Mortlake in England; workmen and looms were hopefully brought over for the purpose. [6] He regarded a theatre as a suitable place of entertainment in a civilized city. Private theatricals were offered as an entertainment at the Castle during the revels of Wentworth's first Christmas in Ireland. Soon after, he was encouraging John Ogilby, a gentleman of his household, to found Dublin's first theatre in St Werbergh Street. During his absence in England, Archbishop Ussher had closed it down; the reason he gave was his disapproval of the theatre in general and a belief that plague might fall on Ireland if such wickedness were permitted. Wentworth reopened it immediately on his return, and for the next four years, in spite of Ussher's disapproval, stage-plays were a feature of Dublin life as they were of London.

The town was not large enough and the theatre-going habit not so natural to the Irish gentry as to ensure any great success for this earliest of Dublin theatres, but it was not without distinction in stage history. James Shirley, the fashionable English playwright, came over in 1636 and stayed in Ireland working for it for nearly four years, though he complained of inadequate public support and empty seats. One of his plays at least, *Saint Patrick for Ireland*, was written with the special interests of the Irish audience in mind, and more than one appears to have been produced not only at the theatre but also before the Lord Deputy in Dublin Castle. An Anglo-Irish dramatist, the forerunner of a prolific breed, appeared in Henry Burnell, who wrote two plays for the new theatre, one of which was later printed in Dublin. This poetic drama about a Nordic Amazon named Landgartha has little merit, but the size of the cast and the nature of the action suggest that the Dublin theatre had a large company and an impressive wardrobe. Both in this play and in Shirley's *Saint Patrick* some elaborate stage effects were called for. Plays by Ben Jonson, Fletcher and Middleton are also known to have been given during these years. If it can hardly be argued that the later development of the Irish stage owes much to this beginning, it is at least to Wentworth's credit that the long history of the Dublin theatre began under his official protection and with his evidently enthusiastic encouragement. [7]

In August 1637 the Deputy set out on a progress through the country. His intention was to extend the area of plantation to Clare and Limerick where it was unlikely, after the way things had gone in Galway, that he would meet with opposition. Laud, on hearing that the King's title had been successfully 'found' so that the work of plantation could begin, congratulated his friend with a touch of cynicism. He was glad, he said, that the people had 'showed themselves so discreet and so cheerful in their submission to that which, though they had struggled, they could not have refused'. [8]

Wentworth for his part was full of confident plans for Ireland's improvement: believed that Munster could with better husbandry support seven times its present population in happier conditions than those known heretofore; was sure that Limerick would be one of the finest ports in the British Isles if only a little energy and good-will were applied to developing it; and in general looked forward to a time when most of the country would be 'enclosed and husbanded, beautified with towns and buildings and stored with industrious and well-conditioned subjects'. (9) The population, rising to the occasion of a state visit, gave him no impression of being either cowed or resentful. 'Unless my almanack fail me,' he wrote to Laud, 'there is personally fair weather towards me from them.' He was greeted everywhere with speeches of praise which, as he modestly put it, 'rather taught me what I should be than told me what I am'. He was amused and gratified by civic receptions. 'Architecture and invention were not asleep,' he wrote, 'as appeared in their arch triumphals, with their ornaments and inscriptions, the ingenious accommodations of their Cupids, their Apollo, their ancient Genii, their laureate poets and such like.' Among other entertainments was a tableau of the seven planets, whence the sun, instead of rays, 'did benignly squirt of his sweet waters upon us forth of a syringe, my hopes, being all the whilst the instrument was new and had not been used before'. Away from the harassing society of his opponents he contrived, better than at Dublin, to combine dignity with civility in his manner towards the people and his own equals. The multitude found him impressive and gracious, and he pleased his companions by his evident enjoyment of the entertainment they provided for him, whether it were a formal banquet or merely a taste of the *specialité du pays*, in Kilkenny, as it happened, a sort of sour junket. Once the unsuspecting Lord Dillon was lured into a wager over the pushing of a loaded wheelbarrow so soon after dinner that he all but made himself ill, while the Deputy and the rest of the party stood round laughing at his green face with the heartlessness of schoolboys.

All this time he wrote home to his wife such news as he thought would amuse her. 'My lady of Ormonde', he told her, 'is not so inclined to be fat as we thought she was at Dublin. My lady MacCarthy, to my eye, improves not in her beauty. My lady, sister to Castlehaven, if she be not the handsomest in the company, her ladyship is much mistaken; yet be it spoken to you in private without profanation nevertheless to her beauty, my lord of

Ormonde's younger sister seems to me much the handsomer; only if I were of her counsel, I would desire her to beware lest she grew fat too soon.' [10]

One night about two months after his return to Dublin some of George Radcliffe's servants who were working late saw a tongue of flame leap from one of the windows in the new wing of Dublin Castle. The fire came from the Chapel, only a few feet below the rooms in which Lady Wentworth and her two stepdaughters were sleeping. The servants hastened to give the alarm; the inhabitants of the castle snatched up what they could and fled for safety into the courtyard, Lady Wentworth and the children being carried out wrapped up in their blankets. The efforts of the Deputy's servants kept the fire from spreading, but before morning little but a blackened shell was left of the new building. [11]

The seventeenth-century mind was not slow to read a moral lesson into this event, by which the proud labour of years had been destroyed by a careless maidservant who had left a basket of hot ashes in a corner under a wooden staircase. Yet such symbols were hardly needed to remind Wentworth of the instability of his achievements. 'I am', he once wrote, 'but as a dead instrument in the hand of a ready and great master'; [12] but whatever his early hopes may have been, he cannot at this stage of his career have felt at all certain that King Charles, in any moment of threat or crisis, would prove either ready or great.

Apart from the attempt to enhance the authority of the Deputy, Wentworth had done nothing in Ireland to ensure the permanency of his work. The Court of Castle Chamber held its powers only by virtue of a special dispensation granted to him alone: there was no guarantee that any other Deputy would have such powers. The revised penal code, it was true, had the sanction of Parliament, so also had the regulation of the wool trade; but the improvements in administration and the collection of revenues depended largely on Wentworth's personal initiative and supervision.

'Something begins to appear amongst us,' he had written to Sir Harry Vane,

> as if this nation might in time become a strength, a safety and without charge to that Crown … their trade, their rents, their civility increase daily.

But he could not conceal his doubts lest some untoward turn of the King's policy might 'plaguily nip our Spring in the bud'. (13)

He was quick to fear and alert to combat interference from England. He stubbornly blocked the attempt of the English Privy Council to raise the rates of the Irish customs and he continued to resent the grants of land to courtiers and dependents, especially to Scots, which were made or promised by the King. But, concentrating on the danger of outside interference, he failed to see that the seeds of destruction were in his own policy.

He had set out, in the manner of any other energetic Anglo-Saxon settler, to make Ireland civilized and profitable by taking the land away from those who did not know how to exploit it in the modern manner and conveying it to those who did. The benefits of English justice, of increasing agricultural prosperity, and more efficient tax-collecting (which is rarely felt as a benefit by the taxed) could in the nature of things mean little to a people who saw in Wentworth chiefly a redoubtable agent of English expansion. The 'hooded men' who raided Wentworth's property in Wicklow were no ordinary brigands, but the active representatives of Irish indignation and Irish wrongs, and the forerunners of those who, in a few years' time, would set Ireland aflame from end to end.

Wentworth was no different from other Englishmen of his time in failing to understand the strength and bitterness of Irish feeling. He attributed the underground discontent of which he was not wholly ignorant exclusively to the difference of religion; 'the Romish Clergy' he thought were capable of stirring up a general storm 'in an instant' if occasion should offer, and it was here — in the dangers inherent in religious fervour and international entanglements, not in the bitterness of the dispossessed — that he saw the only serious cause for anxiety. It was, in truth, one of the causes, because the progress of the Counter-Reformation in Europe was linked to the power of Spain, and a section of the Irish priesthood were in touch with this movement. But it was not the only or the chief cause of unrest. (14)

He thought too much in terms of his native Yorkshire. There it had been feasible for sovereigns, through the Council of the North, to repress brigandage and to gain support for their government as a protection against anarchy. But in Yorkshire there was no dispossessed race — the disorder and the violence was of Englishmen against Englishmen, and the basic division was between those who had suffered by remaining faithful to the old religion and those who had profited by adopting the new. If a rich and skilful magnate extended his lands at the expense of another it was done within the framework of a law they both accepted, though one knew better how to exploit it than the other. This was an entirely different situation from that of Ireland, where the land was in dispute between natives and planters, with the advantage and the law always on the side of the latter. In such circumstances, the dispossessed would take no great comfort in a settled government, would indeed infinitely prefer anarchy and a chance to regain their own.

Wentworth, like most of his contemporaries, was blind to this reality. Where he differed was in setting the claims of justice and right, and the things due to the Church and the State, far above the immediate necessities of the situation. Other Deputies had seen that they must have support from at least one powerful group in Ireland. It would have been logical for Wentworth to have built his policy on an alliance with the planters, the 'new English', with whose colonizing ambitions he was in sympathy. But his higher faith in justice and his sense of what was due to the Crown and to the Church had caused him to make enemies of them, while in his land policy he also made enemies of the Irish and of the 'old English'.

The stability of his government in Ireland depended, therefore, almost wholly on himself. He had his own nominees and supporters in some key positions: Radcliffe and Wandesford, Lord Chief Justice Lowther, and the two 'old English' peers whose friendship he had won, Ormonde and Dillon. But for the rest, his powerful enemies, Irish, 'old English' and 'new English', were only waiting for the least weakening in his authority to mount a joint attack on him.

He seems to have been only dimly aware of this, and to have underestimated their power, their cunning, and above all — since they were all egotistic and quarrelsome men — the possibility of their alliance against him. But he did realize that his strength and influence as Deputy was dependent on his strength and influence as a man, and he continued to accumulate in his hands every source of power and of income that would contribute to it. Thus, in the next two years, he not only became a substantial Irish landowner, but bought in the minor customs rights that were still in other hands. A few ports had been excluded from the farm, their affairs being managed separately, but by the autumn of 1638 all these had been amalgamated. He involved himself also in a complex speculation over the import and sale of tobacco, taking it over as a monopoly and planning to make considerable profits for the government and for himself by reselling at a high price. The initial moves in building up this scheme were expensive, and involved heavy borrowing by Wentworth from the Exchequer, for which he had the King's private warrant. But both he and the King were confident that the ultimate returns would be valuable.

Another enterprise in which Wentworth was deeply involved was the farm of the alum mines in his native Yorkshire. For the past twenty-five years the Crown had farmed these mines to a series of contractors who had never done so well out of them as had been hoped, in spite of the attempt to establish a monopoly by prohibiting the import of foreign alum. Wentworth's old associate, the unscrupulous Sir Arthur Ingram, had been deeply and rather discreditably involved but seems to have given Wentworth the idea that they might be very profitable. Wentworth's enemy Sir David Foulis had also once been a contractor. Wentworth in 1638 finally took over the farm himself through agents in Yorkshire. The undertaking seems to have been worth rather more than £2,000 a year to him, and he had engaged in long and complex machinations to secure the prize. Ingram had helped him in the early stages of the deal, but Wentworth had been spoiling for a quarrel with him on another business matter (the collection of the recusancy fines for Yorkshire), and as soon as Sir Arthur had served his purpose in the alum business he broke with him. It was not a friendship that had ever done him any credit, but that hardly justified the calculating way in which he postponed a final quarrel until a convenient moment. The alum farm, as Mr J. P. Cooper expressively puts it in his exploration of Wentworth's business affairs, 'led into the murky and devious by-ways where courtiers, great officers of state and business men jostled and exchanged tips'. (15)

With so many complicated speculations on his hands, it is not surprising that Wentworth gained the reputation, among the projectors and monopolists at Whitehall, of being the most astute and ruthless operator of them all. He was 'monstrous rich' they claimed, and though Wentworth was annoyed at the suggestion and inclined to pretend that his responsibilities as Deputy cost him far more than he made, he was by any standards 'monstrous rich'. The figure at which his enemies estimated his income — about £23,000 a year — was a fairly accurate guess. He had of course heavy liabilities and some large debts. The tobacco monopoly was not at first a success, and his linen venture had failed. But if all went well his swelling fortune would be fully consolidated within a few years.

Though he was evasive about the extent of his fortune, and certainly underestimated it when he wrote to Archbishop Laud on the matter, he saw no reason for being ashamed of being rich. His wealth, he argued, had been more honestly come by than that of many other men. 'Have I in the least falsified or neglected the trusts of my most gracious master? Have I corruptly or oppressively taken from his people? Have I been a burden to his coffers? ... Well then thus I am become rich.... Was I not in some measure so before I had the honour to serve his Majesty? ... Can it be other than pleasing to any gracious, noble or generous master, that his honest and faithful servant grows rich under him? I confess I am so great a lover myself to have my servants thrive, as I believe all others like minded.' [16]

That men were jealous of him, he took for granted; he even seems to have taken a certain pleasure in the knowledge of their envy. It was also true that he was generous to his servants. From the more distinguished instruments of his policy like Radcliffe, Wandesford, Mainwaring and his brother George, down to the lesser members of his secretarial and household staff — he saw to it that opportunities for enrichment were not denied them. But he kept these things within bounds. His people enjoyed the advantages of priority and inside information common to those in the inner circle of government; they took the fees and guerdons normally associated with their services. He had given it as his opinion, as far back as 1630, that officials were responsible for, and therefore must prevent, extortionate charges by their subordinates.

Extortion and bribery he did not permit and he seems always to have been very clear in his own mind as to what was permissible and what was impermissible gain.

If riches mattered to Wentworth as a proof of success and an instrument of power, his mind was no less steadily fixed upon his duties to the King and the ideal of prosperous government with which his material interest and his loftier ambitions were alike bound up. 'I acknowledge from my very soul', he wrote to Laud, 'to have received more of His Majesty than I shall ever be able to deserve.' [17]

The summer of 1637, which marked the height of Wentworth's conscious success in Ireland, was shadowed by his recurrent anxiety about the King's foreign policy. For the first few years, since the signing of the advantageous Cottington treaty with Spain, Wentworth had had no anxieties about the preservation of peace. But the anxieties that he had begun to feel on this score had been only temporarily allayed by his visit to England, and soon after his return he grew again very uneasy about the continued presence at Charles's Court of his eldest nephew, the Elector Palatine. The Elector was now twenty years old and becoming actively concerned for the recovery of the hereditary lands in Germany which his father had lost. There was a party in England which supported the young man's evident hope that his uncle would enter into alliance with France against Spain for the purpose of restoring him to his own. In 1635 France, guided by Cardinal Richelieu, had declared war on Spain. The purpose of this war was not, of course, to help the Elector Palatine, but to break the power of the Habsburg dynasty alike in Spain, Germany and the Netherlands. For this purpose Richelieu organized the French war on the Rhine, the Pyrenees and the Netherlands frontier, and subsidized the armies of his allies, Swedish and German, in the heart of the Empire. After the initial disasters which France had sustained in the first year of war, things were now going more smoothly, and the Elector Palatine showed a clear judgment — in his own interests at any rate — in wanting his uncle to give full support to the French as well as subsidizing troops to fight, alongside France's other allies, for the return of his lands.

Since France, under Cardinal Richelieu, had thus assumed the unexpected role of Protestant champion in Europe against the

Emperor and the King of Spain, the French party in England was a somewhat confused body consisting of men like Lord Holland at Court, and the Puritan nobility, led by Holland's half-brother Warwick, outside the Court. The Queen herself was incalculable; her politics were an emotional family matter. When her mother and younger brother rebelled against the Cardinal, she was wholeheartedly on their side and opposed to any alliance that would assist the European designs of Richelieu. At other times she was not greatly interested, though it was natural for Wentworth to fear that her influence might be cast on the French side.

For him, the possibility of war with Spain was a nightmare. Spain was, after England, Ireland's principal customer. The Spanish war of 1624-9 had come near to ruining Irish trade. Another such blow, after a brief time of recovery, would be an even worse disaster. The royal income from the customs, and his own, would be grievously reduced and all his predictions of increasing prosperity would be brought to nothing. Besides, he feared the possibility of a religious revolt, or at least of religious opposition to such a war. Spain's first move, if the King of England declared war, would be to stimulate rebellion in Ireland in the name of Holy Church. While a large part of the Irish priesthood were quiescent or loyal to the English Crown, there was an influential party among them, especially among the secular priesthood, who were linked to Spain as the champion of the Counter-Reformation and the Council of Trent. There were certainly some among these who actively hoped for foreign help to start a rebellion. The Archbishop of Cashel, a particularly subtle and ingenious agent of this party, was believed to receive a salary of a thousand ducats a year from Spain. There were many Irish soldiers in Spanish service who could be shipped over and let loose in Ireland. To embark on war with Spain when such a party existed among the clergy, and without sufficient sea-power to prevent landings in Ireland, was to court disaster. [18]

Wentworth's arguments, in a sober exhaustive memorandum to the King, and in more agitated outpourings to Laud, indicated not only his fear of war but his deep distrust of the competence of the government in England. The King had not the money, had not the sea-power (in spite of an ambitious naval programme), had not the men or the organization, for such an undertaking. Another war, like those dismal attempts with which the reign had started, would make an end not only of Irish prosperity but of those improvements in government for which Wentworth had striven, and would thus almost certainly put the power of the Crown again in jeopardy.

In his letters to Laud he spoke of 'this Brig o' Dread', meaning the peril of a Spanish war, and prayed that they would soon have got safely over it. His fears, once more, turned out to be groundless. The King toyed for a little with the idea of a war conducted wholly on the sea, to show off the fleet on which he had spent so much care and money. But his memories of his last wars in Europe were recent and humiliating. He found his nephew, the Elector Palatine, unsympathetic, and he distrusted a policy which involved close alliance with the Dutch and the loss of the Spanish bullion to the Mint.

Wentworth's anxiety at this time over the danger of war was accompanied by other fears. The long letters he received from the Archbishop made him uneasily aware that the King's government was still very insecurely rooted in the affection and respect of his people. Signs of disrespect, rather than of discontent, multiplied throughout the year 1637. William Prynne, imprisoned already for his attack on the Queen's predilection for amateur theatricals, now published a pamphlet attacking the King's foreign policy and the bishops. Two other Puritan publicists joined in the cry, and all three were duly brought before the Star Chamber and sentenced. All three were pilloried, lost their ears, suffered huge fines, and were sent to prison for life. Wentworth was wholly in agreement with this severity. These people, these 'trash' as he called them to Laud, might do irreparable injury to sovereignty, and sovereignty was for Wentworth the ultimate guarantee of good government. 'Blood may be forborne,' he wrote with conscious restraint, 'yet to be shut up and dark kept all their lives is punishment mild enough for such savages.... It is not prelacy they would end with.... They begin to let forth the very life-blood of monarchy itself. It is not only good then, but necessary this growing evil were looked to early, also in good faith, I forebode very sad events towards the evening.' [19]

The Deputy's forebodings were increased when he received from his correspondents in London an account of the execution of the three culprits. The people had greeted them in the pillory with acclamation; Bastwick's wife carefully received her husband's ears in a clean handkerchief, laughing and joking with him the while, and when the executioner had done with him, climbed upon a stool, put her arms about his neck as he stood in the pillory and kissed him on both cheeks, the people loudly applauding. When the prisoners left London the streets were lined with sympathetic onlookers who showered gifts and good wishes upon them, and at Chester the Mayor and Corporation welcomed Prynne with a civic dinner and a gift of hangings for his lodgings in prison.

Wentworth realized the gravity of what was happening. 'Mr Prynne's case', he wrote to Laud,

> is not the first wherein I have resented the humour of the time to cry up and magnify such as the honour and justice of the King and state have marked out and adjudged mutinous to government. *A Prince that loseth the force and example of his punishments, loseth the greatest part of his dominion*; yet still me-thinks we are not got through the disease, nay I fear do not sufficiently apprehend the malignity of it.

If the King could not make his government popular, he must show himself strong. The 'grievous and over-spreading leprosy' must be stopped; 'less than thorough', exhorted Wentworth, 'will not overcome it, there is a cancerous malignity in it which must be cut forth.' Returning to the subject, 'This evil grows from an universal distemper of the age,' he protested to the King,

> where the subjection nestles itself too near the sovereignty, where we are more apt wantonly to dispute the powers which are over us than in former times: such a spreading evil indeed, as, to my seeming, it hath already left God and your Majesty only capable to correct and stay the madness of it. [20]

The King's next attempt to stay the madness of those who set themselves up against his power was even more disastrous. In November 1637 John Hampden was prosecuted for refusing to pay Ship-money. He was one of many who had resisted this tax, which he held to be illegal, hoping for a prosecution which would give him and his friends a public platform for a legal argument with the sovereign. The King might have been wise to avoid giving his critics this opportunity to advertise their views, but it was not easy for him to do so. He was in a dangerous dilemma. If he prosecuted the refusers of Ship-money, he stirred up a very delicate constitutional question. But if he did not prosecute, he seemed tacitly to admit that he was too weak to do so. Wentworth, who had been doubtful of the wisdom of raising Ship-money in the first place, was sure that — since things had gone so far — the King must prosecute. Unless examples were made of the refusers, he argued, those who had done their duty and obeyed the King would find themselves despised by their neighbours and become 'extremely disheartened and out of liking with themselves'. [21] Something like this was indeed more than possible, for if men could defy the King with impunity it was clear there would be no merit or advantage in obeying.

Wentworth had been a colleague of Hampden in the 1628 Parliament, and liked nothing that he knew of him. There was no natural sympathy and some natural rivalry between him and Hampden, for both were rich, both men of strong character, local influence, good wits and fluent speech, but Hampden all charm, sweetness and diplomacy, Wentworth angular and masterful. From Ireland, Wentworth now directed a blast of wrath towards Hampden. He was, he declared, one of those whose nature 'leads them always to oppose all that authority ordains for them; but in good faith, were they right served, they should be whipt home into their right wits, and much beholden they should be to any that would thoroughly take pains with them in that kind.' [22]

Six months had gone by before all the King's judges had finally pronounced on the Hampden case, and to Wentworth's irritation and dismay, only seven of the twelve gave an uncompromising verdict for the Crown. One of the strongest statements on Hampden's side was made by Richard Hutton, a very upright judge, and an old friend and neighbour of Wentworth, who had matched a sister with his eldest son. These personal considerations as well as his reverence for a judge's position were partly responsible for the respectful tone in which Wentworth, some months later, ventured to disagree with him about Ship-money:

Considering it is agreed by common consent, that in time of public danger and necessity such a levy may be made, and

238

that the King is therein sole judge, how or in what manner or proportion it is to be gathered; I conceive it was out of humour opposed by Hampden beyond the modesty of a subject, and that reverence wherein we ought to have so gracious a Sovereign, it being ever to be understood, the prospects of Kings into mysteries of state are so far exceeding those of ordinary common persons, as they be able to discern and prevent dangers to the public afar off, which others shall not so much as dream of till they feel the unavoidable stripes and smart of them upon their naked shoulders: besides, the mischief which threatens states and people are not always those which becomes the object of every vulgar eye; but then commonly of most danger, when least discovered; nay, very often, if unseasonably, over early published, albeit privately known to the King long before, might rather inflame than remedy the evil; ... it is a safe rule for us all in the fear of God to remit these supreme watches to the regal power, whose peculiar indeed it is; submit ourselves in these high considerations to his ordinance, as being no other than the ordinance of God itself; and rather attend upon his will, with confidence in his justice, belief in his wisdom, assurance in his parental affections to his subjects and kingdoms, than feed ourselves with curious questions, with the vain flatteries of imaginary liberty, which, had we even our silly wishes and conceits, were we to frame a new Commonwealth even to our own fancy, might in conclusion leave ourselves less free, less happy, than now, thanks be to God and his Majesty, we are, nay ought justly to be reputed by every moderate-minded Christian. [23]

During the whole of the year 1637 Wentworth had been preparing for the last trial of strength with one of the 'great ones' of Ireland. He had from his first assumption of office known that Lord Chancellor Loftus was a dangerous man; he also knew that he was dishonest and had frequently abused his position to gain advantage for himself and his family. Since the better administration of justice was an important point of Wentworth's policy, he had always been aware that he would have to challenge Loftus, but even he had been unwilling to begin on so perilous a struggle until he had settled with his other enemies. In the first years of his Deputyship he had taken on, simultaneously, Cork, Wilmot, Mountnorris and Clanricarde, but he had exercised an elementary caution in leaving the Lord Chancellor alone. He had even seemed, both to Loftus himself and to outside spectators, to be friendly to him and his methods. He had shown little interest in complaints made against him; on one occasion he had pressed for the payment of £3,000 to him, out of England, as a reward for his co-operation on the Commission for Defective Titles; and he had agreed with him that his salary of £300 a year was too low and ought to be increased. This latter opinion was in strict accordance with Wentworth's practical belief that if high officers of state were better paid there would be less temptation to them to exploit their position for the purpose of making money. (24) But Loftus for his part was more likely to interpret it as an indication of Wentworth's personal desire to be helpful to him.

The chief offences of which Loftus was guilty were — as usual with the 'great ones' in Ireland — connected with the betterment of his estates and the seizure of land. He made a habit of hearing cases at his private house, a practice which could be reasonably justified on grounds of convenience and economy, but which evidently facilitated intimidation and made it easy for him to obscure the records. It was notorious that justice was not to be had from him except by bribery, offered directly or to one of his officials, and sometimes not even then. One plaintiff who had given rich presents to secure 'justice' was told that it could only be had in return for a signed statement that no bribe had been given — an additional dishonesty which was more than the briber had bargained for. This document being denied, no 'justice' was forthcoming. (25)

In Lord Falkland's time, the accusations against Loftus had been so serious and so persistent that the Lord Deputy had attempted to deprive him of his office. But Loftus had known how to combine with Mountnorris in such a way as to bring Falkland down. His own ingenious answers to charges brought against him had been accepted by the King's Council in England and he had returned home in triumph to be entrusted, in conjunction with Lord Cork, with the government of Ireland during the interim before Wentworth's arrival. (26)

Mountnorris, whose combination with Loftus had proved fatal to Falkland, was now out of office and in disgrace. Wentworth, on his return from England, felt strong enough to act. The first signs of his opposition to the Chancellor may have been noticeable as early as the summer of 1636. When he had appointed Wandesford to act for him in his absence in England, he had advised him to treat Loftus correctly but to consult him as little as possible. [27]

The next sign of the Lord Deputy's estrangement from the Chancellor appeared in the reopening of the case of one Metcalf. Some time before Wentworth came to Ireland, Loftus had ingeniously contrived by a barefaced perversion of justice to get the administration of Metcalf's estate for his second and favourite son Sir Edward Loftus. At the first whiff of inquiry into this matter in the Deputy's Court of Castle Chamber, Sir Edward slipped across into England where, unless Wentworth was prepared to take drastic action and insist on an order for his return to Ireland, he could hold up the course of justice indefinitely by not answering the charge. The drastic action was taken in 1637. Sir Edward Loftus was, with the royal consent, brought over to Ireland in custody, forced to make submission in the Castle Chamber and kept a prisoner for some weeks longer as a punishment for his attempt to evade justice. [28]

The misappropriation of the Metcalf estate was hardly enough in itself to bring down Lord Loftus. It was in any case his son, Sir Edward, who had had to answer for it. Wentworth now took up in the Castle Chamber a much more delicate business. This was not a matter in which the justice of Loftus was questioned, but in which his honesty as a man was impugned by a petition of Sir John Gifford to the Deputy and the Court of Castle Chamber. Gifford's petition was to be the test case, for if Wentworth could first make the Lord Chancellor answer to it in the Court of Castle Chamber, and then compel him to bow to the judgment of that body, he would have won a significant victory. He would have established the authority of the King (through his Deputy) as higher than that of the Chancellor; making the King the ultimate fount of all justice. Knowing the character of Loftus he did not imagine that this would be an easy task, and he had taken the precaution of arming himself for all eventualities by securing from the King authority to deprive the Chancellor of his office if a crisis should arise in which this became necessary. [29]

With so much at stake, the affair itself was domestic and even trivial. Sir John Gifford had a half-sister married to the Chancellor's elder and least favoured son, Sir Robert Loftus. The lady had been something of an heiress and at the time of the marriage Lord Loftus had, according to Gifford, undertaken to settle a house and estate on the young couple. This had never been done, and Sir John Gifford, as the only male relation left to protect his half-sister's rights, forwarded a petition to the Court of Castle Chamber against the Chancellor.

Loftus had not expected that Wentworth, on whose friendship he had come to rely, would proceed with the case. He was openly indignant when he realized that the matter was to be taken up, and at once showed his displeasure by becoming awkward, disobliging and hostile in every way possible to him. [30] Wentworth had expected this and was not surprised. There was however one element in the situation that he had disregarded, and continued to disregard. This was his own connection with the family of Sir Robert Loftus's wife. Eleanor Loftus was the elder sister of Anne Ruish, whose marriage to his youngest brother George, Wentworth had recently arranged. He was thus closely acquainted with the petitioner, Sir John Gifford, and his two half-sisters. He might even be thought to have, through his brother, a financial interest in the case. Moreover his admiration for Eleanor Loftus was no secret in Ireland. He valued her beauty and her intellect, and he enjoyed her company. Whether he regarded the relationship simply as a friendship or as a Platonic attachment there is now no means of knowing, but it is most improbable that she was his mistress. On the other hand Lord Loftus, whatever he thought of his daughter-in-law's virtue, had not the slightest doubt that Wentworth was proceeding with the case on her account and because of his private concern with the financial affairs of a family linked to his own. What Lord Loftus suspected might easily be suspected by others; this was an aspect of the matter to which Wentworth was persistently blind.

Loftus continued, by an expert process of delay, to hold up the case for nearly a year. He sent unsatisfactory answers, made excuses for not appearing, on one occasion said he was ill though in fact he was at the races, and tried from February until November 1637 to wear the Council out by postponements. [31] It was not until February 1638, a year after proceedings had begun, that the Council was at length in a position to give judgment. They were satisfied that Loftus had contracted to settle a house and estate on his son and that he had not done so; they now commanded him to carry out his promise. [32]

Loftus continued to make difficulties while privately sending messages to England asking that the case be removed from the Lord Deputy's biased jurisdiction. All this while he was still performing his duties as Lord Chancellor in his customary idiosyncratic fashion. At harvest time in 1637 he had performed a peculiarly callous act of injustice to a farmer named Fitzgerald. He had given a case against him without hearing witnesses and had then sent him to prison because, he averred, Fitzgerald had been concealing his goods to evade his liabilities. Fitzgerald had in fact done nothing worse than put his corn into barns because, as he very reasonably pointed out, it could not be left in stook in the open fields indefinitely. Fitzgerald, from prison, petitioned the Deputy and his Court of Castle Chamber. 'Sirrah,' bellowed Loftus, 'do you think to come off with petitioning the Lord Deputy?' and he saw to it that the petition was intercepted. Ultimately, however, a petition from Fitzgerald slipped through, and Loftus was requested by the Council to order his release pending further inquiry. This order he simply ignored. At last, on April 20th, 1638, he was questioned by the Council for having disregarded their judgment in the case of Gifford and for having disobeyed their order in the case of Fitzgerald. Loftus, incensed, tried to shout and bluster his way out, and after a noisy and undignified scene — in which Wentworth rather mistakenly requested him to kneel in token of submission to his sovereign — the explosive old gentleman, with knees still unbent, was suspended from his office, and ordered to hand over the Great Seal. [33]

The Chancellor, still defiant, now refused either to hand over the Great Seal or to say where it was, and for this offence he was committed prisoner to the Castle. In his blind anger he had given Wentworth an advantage over him. For months Loftus had been working through friends at Court, especially the Earl of Holland, the elegant leader of the Queen's party, to have his cause removed from Wentworth's jurisdiction to the King's. At the very moment of his committal, the royal order arrived for Loftus to repair to England. But he was commanded to leave the Great Seal in Ireland with the Council. His refusal to do so enabled Wentworth to prevent his leaving the country while he, for his part, represented to the King the necessity of upholding at Whitehall the decision of the Council in Ireland. [34]

The King, who had other troubles on his mind, was not best pleased with his Deputy for precipitating yet another quarrel in Ireland. He was also, as Laud observed, quite unwilling to believe the account of the business which Wentworth sent to him. In this, the committal of Loftus was represented as the unanimous and unprompted act of the Irish Council without any intervention from the Deputy himself. This picture of a mild and silent Wentworth seemed equally unconvincing to Laud, who wrote imploring him to revise his account of the affair as the King did not like to be treated so disingenuously. All the Archbishop got in return was an injured protest from Wentworth assuring him that, though he could if he wanted 'lead the Council as much as another Deputy', on this occasion he truly had not done so. [35] With this assertion the King and the Archbishop had to rest content.

Wentworth had not consciously influenced the vote against Loftus. But he had created a position in which those who might, out of their various interests, have supported Loftus undoubtedly saw that it would be most unwise to do so. For the rest, and in justice to Wentworth and his Councillors, the behaviour of the Chancellor and the conduct which had now been brought to light, was of a kind to make any fair-minded man vote him unfit to continue in office.

The ferocious obstinacy of Lord Loftus prolonged the case for another eighteen months. Sent for at intervals by the Council because of his refusal to hand over the seals or to take any action whatever to implement the judgment against him in the Gifford case, the old gentleman grew only more obstinate and more furious; on one occasion he roundly accused the Deputy of partiality, and of having set on discontented litigants to petition against him. Meanwhile his friends in England, led by Holland, continued to plead with the King — Sir Edward Loftus attempted to slip over and join them but was stopped — and Wentworth was in some anxiety lest Charles should weaken. Charles did not do so; he recognized that the authority of the Crown was at stake and gave orders that the Chancellor was on no account to be released or permitted to come to England until he had complied with the judgment made against him. In the early spring of 1639 Loftus was still obstinate, and Wentworth, with the King's authority, brought to an end the privileges he had enjoyed for most of the preceding year as a 'prisoner' only in name and had him brought to the Castle and shut up in close confinement. Even so it was another six months before he finally capitulated. [36]

The defeat of Lord Loftus was marked by the appointment in Ireland of Sir Richard Bolton as his successor. He was an able, rather colourless man, nearly seventy years old. As Chief Baron of the Exchequer he had shown the qualities of honesty and reliability which Wentworth required in high judicial office, and he had recently performed a tedious but useful service in compiling a manual for the use of Justices of the Peace in Ireland. Of late years, he wrote in his preface to this book published in 1637, the orderliness of Ireland had so much increased that the Justices, who used to be little regarded, could now perform their duties regularly and without fear. [37]

Wentworth's conduct was, in theory, consonant with the King's wishes and tended to promote the authority of the Crown. But Charles disliked the way in which his Deputy's logic and vigour, by committing him to personal attacks that he might not himself have embarked on, embarrassed him in his private relations and sometimes crossed his more immediate lines of policy. Thus, he was anxious during the next months that Wentworth should contrive to heal the breach with the Earl of Cork, from whom he hoped to borrow money. [38]

Charles was also concerned to conciliate the Earl of Clanricarde. This nobleman, who was Earl of St Albans in the English peerage, was younger half-brother to the Earl of Essex and was related through his mother and his wife to a substantial number of the more influential English nobility. There had been a considerable stir against Wentworth in these circles when he had forced through the King's right to the land in Galway regardless of the attempts of the then Earl of Clanricarde to stop him. The wrongs of the father were inherited by the son, who naturally enough sought to re-establish himself in his lands by securing a new grant from the King. Charles was very willing to do this, partly because the increasing threat to his government made him anxious to reduce the number of the discontented, and partly because he judged Clanricarde a reliable subject. In this latter supposition he came nearer to the truth than Wentworth, who always found it difficult to trust a Roman Catholic. Clanricarde was, in the next decade, to show outstanding loyalty to the King in the most desperate conditions, besides a serenity and judgment which rarely forsook him. Wentworth had been seriously mistaken in trying to weaken his power and influence in the west of Ireland; still more perhaps in failing to make a friend of him, as he had done of Ormonde.

The King was therefore justified when, in response to Clanricarde's urgent pleading, he agreed to grant back to him all that his father had held. Wentworth was outraged: this, he pointed out, was to reward Lord Clanricarde for his father's contumacy. What service could the King expect from his subjects if he favoured those who had defied him, while honest and faithful men were by no means always rewarded? In any case, he truthfully asserted, the survey of Galway for resettlement was yet incomplete, so that no grant could be drawn for Clanricarde. [39] If this was not a direct refusal, it was an unwelcome delay and obstruction to the King's wish. It was also an obstruction to Clanricarde's hopes, which he could not but advertise at Court and among his friends to the inevitable disfavour of the Deputy.

Wentworth's capacity for making enemies had increased with the years. As if it were not enough to have the friends and relations of Loftus massed against him, and to have given annoyance to Clanricarde, he courted further trouble by an ill-advised action for libel in the Star Chamber. He had been annoyed intermittently for the last three years by Sir Piers Crosby, the conceited, voluble mischief-maker whom he had sequestrated from the Council in 1634. Crosby had been concerned with Mountnorris in the scramble for the customs, and the overthrow of Mountnorris naturally sharpened his hatred for the Deputy. He and others put it about that Wentworth, for all his parade of giving justice to the poor, had so belaboured a prisoner in the Castle, one Esmond, that he died of it.

The violence of Wentworth's temper was notorious and there seems to have been no doubt that he had shouted and shaken his cane at Esmond. There seems also to be little doubt that Esmond died of natural causes some time after his release, and that his wife was bribed by Crosby and others to put about this slander on the Deputy. (Esmond's offence, incidentally, was an evasion of the customs.)

It would probably have been wiser to let the matter lie. But Wentworth who, like many bad-tempered men, believed himself to be a lamb at heart, felt the need of vindication. Politically too the slander wounded his government at a vital place; knocking prisoners about was not a practice that he encouraged or approved. So, while Lord Chancellor Loftus still sulked in prison and his friends at Court plagued the King with protests, Wentworth stirred up new trouble for himself by bringing an action for libel against Sir Piers Crosby in the Star Chamber. Crosby was also, as it happened, a friend and protégé of the Queen's favourite, the Earl of Holland. In Wentworth's contemptuous view they were rivals in elegance, in vapid good looks and in their exploits with the ladies. Crosby, 'that tawny ribbon' — he sneered — had often boasted of having 'better legs and better feet, cleaner boots and neater shoes, purer shape and better face' than his friend and patron, Holland, whose mistresses he had frequently stolen away. (40)

Whatever rivalries Holland and Crosby had, they were at one in hating Wentworth. Holland had listened to, and passed on, Crosby's scandalous stories; he was often in these months seen whispering with him in corners, and great was his rage when he found that he was to be cited as a witness in the case. He refused, pleading his privilege as a privy councillor. Wentworth, unwisely, pressed the matter. Thereupon Holland went about Court saying, with chapter and verse, that the Deputy was mad, had been under restraint as a lunatic for several months in his youth, and that as for giving evidence for him, he would give it — if at all — for his gallant friend Sir Piers Crosby. (41)

Since Holland was in high favour with the Queen, was irresponsible, influential, and at the heart of affairs, none of this did any good to Wentworth. It was doubly unfortunate at a time when the King needed, to help him in his mounting troubles, unity, co-operation and good-will among his councillors. Since the autumn of 1637 it had been clear that serious trouble was coming from Scotland, where his misconceived attempt to bring the religious worship of the people into line with that of England had met with formidable opposition. The King's authority, as well as his religious faith, were now at stake; he was not willing to compromise on either question, and when in February 1638 the dissident Scots, led by a strong group of their nobles, banded themselves together by signing the National Covenant, it was clear that war could hardly be avoided. The King's urgent need then, until the Scots problem was settled, would be for ready money and for friends.

In the circumstances, Wentworth's capacity for quarrelling and for making difficulties was both inconvenient and irritating. He had alienated the wealthy Earl of Cork entirely; he had exasperated Clanricarde and at least two of the Scots nobility — Mar and Ancram — by obstructing grants of land in Ireland. [42] He repeatedly annoyed the Duke of Lennox (fortunately a man of unshakeable loyalty) by refusing favour to his friends. In the next two years he gave continual evidence of hostility and suspicion towards the Marquis of Hamilton, the principal architect and executant of the King's current policy in Scotland.

The under-cover source of his hostility to Hamilton was the reallocation of the land in Ulster which the Corporation of London had forfeited. First there was trouble over the customs which Wentworth had bought in, but over which Hamilton was trying to assert a claim through the intervention of a dubious agent named Barr. Barr was at length summoned before the Castle Chamber for persistent and sometimes violent interference with the collection of the customs. Wentworth knew that Barr was protected by Hamilton and that the trouble over the customs was linked to a project by which a syndicate of Scots, chief among them Hamilton, were offering to take over the lands in Ulster which had been forfeited by the Corporation of London.

These plots and plans troubled Wentworth exceedingly. He was anxious that the King should do well out of the Londonderry estates, but he was also concerned that the tenants on the lands in question should not suffer by the change of landlord. Among the offers made to the King, he himself preferred that made by a group headed by Sir John Clotworthy, a Devon man by origin, who was already one of the principal English landowners in Ulster. The King was ultimately to reject all offers and Wentworth was to be blamed with equal vehemence by all the disappointed parties, of whom Clotworthy was not the least influential. In the meantime he disliked the Scottish offer most of all because he distrusted all Scots, including Hamilton. [43]

This distrust was partly an ingrained northern prejudice. To the English of the northern counties, the Scots were the hereditary foes whose raids and invasions were a matter of tradition. But Wentworth had other and more practical reasons for his doubts. There was strong and active sympathy for the Covenanters in Ulster, where his Church policy had met with much resistance. Presbyterian ministers, excluded from their parishes in northern Ireland by his own insistence on conformity to the Prayer Book and the Canons of the Irish Church passed in 1635, had often crossed over to Scotland and been well received there. Communication and mutual help between Scots in Ireland and Scots in their own country was a common rule. And a large number of the Ulster planters were clansmen of Hamilton.

If Wentworth was right both in fearing the infiltration of the Covenanters into Ireland and in suspecting Hamilton of double-crossing the King, then his resistance to the increase of Hamilton's influence in Ulster was more than justified. But the King, who persistently underestimated the extent of the Covenanters' influence, and would hear nothing against Hamilton, could only see that his cares were aggravated by the unwillingness of the Deputy to co-operate with one who was, at the moment, his favourite and most influential councillor.

Wentworth was, of course, obedient to royal commands in everything except the disposal of land. He enlarged the Irish army and kept it well drilled and equipped, and he sent over to the Low Countries for supplies of arms. [44] He was ready to serve the King to the utmost of his ability and his power. But the advice that he offered — to the King, to the Archbishop, to the Secretary of State, to the Earl of Northumberland and to his other friends at Court — can have made one impression only. He trusted no one to deal with the coming crisis except himself.

Charles, leaning on Hamilton but harried by Wentworth, probably saw in the Lord Deputy's irritable interference an expression of his personal jealousy of Hamilton. The Deputy was able enough, but too self-willed and too ambitious. He would never be satisfied until he was first in the councils of the realm.

Wentworth's advice was at first confident and straightforward. He was very sure that the rebellion of the Scots against the royal authority must be put down. 'This is such insolency as is not to be borne by any rule of monarchy', he wrote, but he was equally sure that the King must avoid fighting until he was strong enough to win. The most fatal error he could make would be to wage an unsuccessful war, and he was not, when the challenge of the Covenanters was first cast before him, well enough provided to ensure success. Wentworth therefore advised a delaying action.

> I must disadvise a rash and sudden declaring of a war, and yet I would not fearfully sacrifice my will and honour to their mutiny.... The answer, as I humbly conceive becoming His Majesty were to let them know, it was not the custom of the best and mildest of Kings to be threatened into Parliaments, or to be circumscribed with days and hours by their subjects.... Require them to rest satisfied with so much as by his gracious proclamation is declared....I am confident this will not presently provoke them to an offensive war upon England.... The first resolution I should pitch upon should not be to fight with them hastily, unless upon all advantage possible, both because I would give them time to come to their wits again before they should make themselves over-unreconcilable, and that much is to be lost by the King, little unto them upon the mischance of one day.

In the meantime the King should garrison Berwick and Carlisle, threaten to blockade the Scottish ports if the Covenanters continued defiant, muster the Irish army on the Ulster coast one day's shipping from Galloway, and make ready to seize Leith in the spring. Above all he should cultivate a party for himself among the Scots nobles, welcome all overtures of peace, and on no account use violence towards such of the rebels as fell into his hands 'in regard nothing would more sharpen the humour than their execution'. (45)

This advice to show mercy arose purely from policy, not from any respect for the character of the 'gallant gospellers', whom he disliked and despised as much as he did the English Puritans. In his view religion was a pretext for ambitious rebellion by jealous men who wished to see the King's sacred power 'circumscribed and brought under the government of their narrow and shrivelled up hearts'. Later he was even more emphatic: 'This is not a war of piety, for Christ's sake, but a war of liberty for their own un- bridled, inordinate lusts and ambitions, such as threw Lucifer forth of heaven.' [46]

By the summer of 1638 he was offering to Lucy Carlisle's brother, the Earl of Northumberland, Lord Admiral of England, a blue-print for naval and military action and for the future of Scotland. Leith must be occupied, he wrote, also Dumbarton and the Isle of Arran; it would then be possible to blockade and isolate Scotland, and so the more easily bring it under control. When the rebellious country had been reduced, it must be brought 'under the government of at least an English Deputy if not an English law, who may be a curb upon the unruly notions of that people against the Crown, by early foreseeing and timely pre- venting of them in their beginnings, by settling the revenue of that Crown, and turning it into the right veins'.

After this broad hint that he could achieve in Scotland what he had already done in Ireland he went on to explain that Scottish revenues, which were 'drunk and supped up to private ends' ought to flow into the royal exchequer. The Scottish customs, too, should be taken over by someone who could gather them properly. Until these reforms were effected, the King must keep garrisons at Leith and Dumbarton, naturally at the expense of the conquered Scots. Then, and only then, Wentworth triumphantly concluded, 'the King were King of Great Britain indeed and that nation a strength which is become now an offence'. [47]

These views were, of course, confidential but Wentworth never concealed his dislike of the Scots, and it must have been apparent to all that he looked forward to something more than the mere checking of their revolt. The Covenanters early recognized that they had in him their most dangerous opponent and he was not surprised to hear that he had been denounced as an enemy of the Lord at the great Assembly of the Scottish Church in Glasgow. [48]

It was in character that Wentworth should be for strong methods; in character also that he should at once see in the revolt

251

an opportunity for reorganizing the finances of Scotland, and possibly the legal system, so as to enrich and strengthen the Crown. What is strange about this letter is Wentworth's failure to make allowances for the point of view of his sovereign. He had been at Court, on and off, seeking favours, climbing slowly to high office, since the middle years of King James's reign, yet he had apparently forgotten that his King and master was a Scot, and that his native pride, his sympathies, friendships, ties of kindred and affection would have to be reckoned with; that whatever King Charles did, he would never make an Englishman his Deputy-Governor of Scotland.

In the late summer of 1638 Wentworth took another of his hunting holidays at Cosha, his 'park of parks', where the building of his hunting lodge went on apace. He was planning to start 'a breed of horses' there, as well as a small ironworks. As for the Scots, he did 'not take the lion to be so fierce as he is painted'. In Ireland, at any rate, 'the King's affairs, God be praised, go on stilly and prosperously and are like so to continue'. (49) It was not until the winter that the gravity of the situation became, gradually, apparent to him.

The news from Yorkshire was perturbing. Rumours of trouble from Scotland had not united the Yorkshire gentry against the hereditary foe. On the contrary, the embarrassment of the government seemed to have inspired a spirit of contradiction. Since the previous autumn Wentworth had been receiving news which showed that his Vice-President in the North, Sir Edward Osborne, was having difficulty in securing any willing co-operation with the King's plans for war from many of the 'great ones' of Yorkshire who had in the past been recalcitrant to Wentworth's government. Soon after, trouble came from Wentworth's own nephew, Sir William Savile, who showed his independence by refusing to bring a troop of horse to York when commanded and intriguing to get his uncle removed from the office of Lord Lieutenant for the county. 'It was the part of a very young man', commented Wentworth drily. (50) But young Savile's discontent was symptomatic, and Wentworth as Lord President of the North was soon receiving perplexed and anxious letters from his Vice-President, Sir Edward Osborne. There was trouble about re-cruiting for the defence of the country against possible Scottish invasion, there was trouble about the collection of Ship-money, there was among some of the most influential gentry open sympathy with the Covenanters. Sir Matthew Boynten, after making a good deal of trouble, suddenly departed with his whole family for Calvinist Holland. [51] To all these difficulties, Wentworth's personal distrust of the gentry with whom he had had skirmishes six or seven years before added a further complication. Sir Edward Osborne, already baffled and battered on all sides, would be suddenly told from Ireland not to employ Langdale or to trust the Bellasis family. [52] There is no doubt that Wentworth's obstinate determination to keep authority in his own hands, not only as Lord President but also as Lord Lieutenant of the county, was at this time inconvenient as well as unpopular. The gentry who muttered that he had 'grown a stranger to them' and yet would not relinquish his rights over them had a good deal of justification.

In November 1638 a fortuitous disaster occurred: Osborne's eldest son was killed by the fall of a chimney in a room through which he was passing. The younger boy was saved only because he had pursued a kitten under a table, and was found safe and sound in the wreckage with his pet in his arms. Poor Osborne, a most loving father, was prostrated by the loss and Wentworth had to combat a misguided attempt to remove him from his post or at least much reduce his powers. [53]

With the winter months Wentworth's anxieties increased. There were lesser irritants, like the gnat-stings of Sir Piers Crosby, who was trying to hamper recruiting for the Irish army, and the exasperating behaviour of the French, who chose this moment to flood Ireland with recruiting agents of their own, offering better prospects in the French armies than Wentworth could offer in the King's service. [54] This French recruiting drive in Ireland may have been fortuitous, but it may have been a sidelong effort of Richelieu to embarrass King Charles and thus prevent his constant underhand assistance to Spain. Whatever the cause, it was a great annoyance to Wentworth.

Much more serious was the trouble in northern Ireland. The Scots settlers were almost all Calvinists and in sympathy with the Covenanters. As early as Easter 1638 the Bishop of Down lamented that he had lost at least a thousand communicants. [55] Some months later a Scottish minister was reported to be offering the

253

famous Covenant for signature all over Ulster. Wentworth declared that he would 'crush that cockatrice in the egg', but he was not successful; the minister escaped him though his wife was captured and held as a hostage. [56] Meanwhile the episcopal clergy found themselves threatened in Ulster, and one of Wentworth's chaplains was mobbed and plundered because he was wearing a cassock and sash; he later told Wentworth that he did not think he would have escaped alive had the people known he was one of my Lord Deputy's chaplains. [57]

The native Irish population of Ulster gave Wentworth almost as much anxiety. At the first whiff of trouble in the Kingdom there were disorders, raids, abortive risings in Donegal, Antrim and Down. Wentworth, from Dublin, was denouncing alternately the rebellious Scots of Ulster and the uncontrollable 'Os and Macs' of the region, whose excesses he had long deplored. [58] A further complication was shortly added by the King's rash intervention in a clash of Celtic interests.

The Earl of Antrim, chief of clan Macdonnell, had married Buckingham's widow and had long exercised his voluble charm to great effect at Court. Besides being a chief in Ulster, he had of course links — if not rights — among all the Macdonalds of the Isles and the Western Highlands. His principal rival and enemy was therefore M'Callum More, in other words the Earl of Argyll, chief of the Campbells. Argyll was an able and a pious man who controlled much of the Scottish coast looking across towards Ireland, and who was moreover a principal member of the King's Privy Council in Scotland. In view of Argyll's prominence in Scottish affairs and his position of trust on the Council, it is hard to understand what arguments can have prevailed with the King to grant (secretly of course) to Antrim the right to seize from Argyll the lands of the Macdonalds in Kintire. [59]

Since Antrim was a great talker, the grant did not long remain secret. Knowledge of it was certainly not the chief cause of Argyll's subsequent conduct, but it must surely have played its part in causing Argyll to feel little trust in a monarch who could cheat a distinguished subject and one of his own Privy Council in so extraordinary a way. Whatever the reasons behind his conduct, the Earl of Argyll joined his fortunes to those of the Covenanters in the autumn of 1638.

Wentworth now faced a dangerous and delicate situation. Argyll's well-trained, well-controlled clansmen made a formidable fighting force overhanging northern Ireland. Argyll's small but efficient boats infested the Irish Sea, which the navy, largely occupied on the further side of the British Isles in trying to prevent the Scots from communicating with the sympathetic Dutch, was no longer efficiently patrolling. Left to himself, Wentworth would have reckoned to garrison Ulster against attack, and to hold down the Scottish settlers by imposing on them an oath of loyalty to the King against the Covenant. (It was called 'the Black Oath', and though it was widely taken at the time, was indignantly repudiated soon after.) His plans were, however, hampered by the arrival of the Earl of Antrim with permission from the King to wage what was, in effect, a private war on Argyll — a war in which, by royal command, the Deputy was to do all he could to help.

Wentworth viewed the whole business with suspicion. He trusted Antrim's clansmen as little as he did the Scots. Give them control of the strong places, forts and arsenals of Ulster? The purpose of these forts was to hold them in check; if they once became possessed of them, they would terrorize the settlers and reduce Ulster to barbarism. Even if the whole plan had not been contrary to all his Protestant and Anglo-Saxon prejudices, Wentworth would still have judged (rightly as it happened) that Antrim was not the man to lead an invasion of Scotland. [60] He had said in London that, as a powerful chief, he could undertake war at no cost to the government, but Wentworth was not impressed. 'We hear now and then', he wrote of Antrim and his friends, 'that they intend to beat, to bang, to conquer; but the way how, the means wherewith they should make themselves as good as their word, as yet appear not to the ministers of this state.' The means Antrim intended to use became clear when he turned to the Deputy to supply arms, money and transport both for his army (not yet raised) and the ten thousand live cows they proposed to drive with them. Later, bills were presented for ship building and other expenses. 'His lordship', said the Deputy coldly,

shuffles the pack dexterously enough, if pretending to make a war at his own cost, he can thus presently and totally shift off the charge upon the King; deal himself a generalship at sea and land; a command of the King's armies, his ordnance, his arms, his stores, his shipping, make all his own officers, new levies as likes him best, and procure a horse troop for his brother. [61]

Procuring the command of a horse troop in the Irish army for his brother was a natural enough piece of string-pulling. Antrim was not the only one. The Queen and her friends were exceptionally tiresome, as Wentworth told Lucy Carlisle in a frank letter. [62] In another, to Secretary Windebanke, he was dangerously outspoken: 'My life shall be as freely laid down for my gracious master as any that lives, yet I am not weary of it neither, should be very unwilling to die like a fool, or, to deal clearly, desirous to fight but in the company of such as understood their profession.' [63]

He felt very sure that he understood the military profession himself and his letters, all that year, were full of praises of his army. 'We see nothing in the street but cap and feather,' he had gaily told Laud, 'and I trust to have them all in such order by the month's end as our neighbours of Scotland shall not encourage themselves the more in their disobedience by anything they can observe amongst us.' [64] His discipline was fierce; efforts were made in vain — by appealing through Lady Wentworth — to get him to reprieve a fellow sentenced to hanging for desertion and stealing a piece of beef. [65]

But his confidence in his own preparations was not accompanied by any parallel confidence in those of the King. He had so little faith in the King's supply of arms as to continue to buy those for Ireland independently in the Netherlands. When he sent over a garrison of five hundred to hold Carlisle for the King, exception was instantly taken to the officer he had appointed to command them, and very soon after, Wentworth's brother-in-law, Lord Clifford, one of the best known landowners in the North, was removed from the governorship of Carlisle to make way for a son of the Earl of Arundel. [66] This kind of action made it plain to Wentworth that the more frivolous and self-interested courtiers were still quite unaware of the gravity of the situation. Laud had bitterly complained of the extravagance of the Queen and her great friend the Duchesse de Chevreuse who had arrived on an ill-timed visit. (The Earl of Holland instantly began a stormy and very public love affair with her.) Early in 1639 — the year planned for the defeat of the rebel Scots — Northumberland gloomily reported 'the discontents at home do rather increase than lessen.... The King's coffers were never emptier than at this time.' [67] The climax was reached when the King appointed — of all people — the inexperienced, empty-headed dandy Holland as general of his cavalry. The commander-in-chief had to be for political reasons the equally inexperienced but rather more ponderous Arundel.

Wentworth believed Holland's appointment to be the doing of Hamilton. [68] The King's faith in his least competent servants seemed impossible to shake, and Wentworth himself felt threatened when the Earl of Antrim, finding that it was not so easy to lead his clansmen into Scotland as he had hoped, wrote to Court to explain that the fault for his failure lay not with him but with the obstructive Deputy. [69]

The worst of Wentworth's anxiety was caused by the lack of information as to what was going on. He asked to come to England for consultation, was granted leave to do so, and then immediately afterwards was told to stay at his post in Ireland. 'He must be a fortunate servant indeed as well as wise,' he complained, 'that untaught, unguided by his master's word and directions can be able to serve according to the mind and liking of his superiors.' [70] In the early spring of 1639, while the King was still collecting his forces, the Covenanters seized Dumbarton, one of the key places which Wentworth had urged the King to secure. Why had he not been allowed to garrison it with his Irish troops under a loyal officer — Wentworth angrily asked. The alleged Scots loyalist in command had let it go to the Covenanters without a struggle. The King gave no information to his servants, kept them in ignorance, 'disabled either to counsel or to execute anything towards the general and total service of His Majesty or the public'. Meanwhile, leakages to the King's enemies occurred all the time so that they were often better informed than his friends. [71]

Given the fatal loss of Dumbarton and the evident weakness and lack of preparation on the King's side, Wentworth now urged his master to postpone an attack on Scotland for at least a year. Let the undertaking of the present summer be simply a defensive action, a cautious reconnoitring on the Border to prevent invasion; the attack must be put off until the King could launch it with assurance of victory. [72] There was also the moral aspect to be considered; this was, after all, a war 'with your Majesty's own natural howbeit rebellious subjects', and this made it 'a tender point to draw blood first.... I would not have them with the least colour impute it to your Majesty to have put all to extremity, till their own more than words enforce you to it.' [73] Keep the Scots in play with treaties, he advised, and meanwhile neglect no opportunity for gaining strength.

In Ireland, he was troubled by the recrudescence of piracy and the decline of trade, and by fears of treachery in Ulster. Lord Claneboye — a kinsman of Hamilton's — expressed open sympathy with the Covenanters. [74] A conspiracy to betray the port of Carrickfergus to the Scots was discovered in the nick of time, and the traitor, an Englishman unsuitably called Truman, was hanged and quartered. [75]

In England, whence the Deputy received sparse information, the King's affairs went badly. He had failed lamentably to raise the necessary funds for waging effective war; his subjects refused to pay Ship-money whenever they could; the local levies were raised unwillingly and the money for their equipment and transport was sluggishly put forward; the City of London, when the King appealed for help, made the smallest offer that was consonant with an appearance of loyalty — £5,000. [76] The King journeyed northwards to join his army through a country of whose hostility even he must have been aware. His two commanders, by sea and land, deceived even his by now tenuous hopes: Hamilton cruised uselessly off the estuary of the Forth, and Holland, after advancing with great confidence some miles over the Border, wheeled about and fled at his first sight of the Scots. For ten days thereafter the two armies faced each other across the Tweed at Berwick. Then the King offered to treat, and before the end of June the so-called Pacification of Berwick was concluded.

Wentworth, seeing that those about the King took little pains to inform him, sent over a trusted emissary to gather and send him news, and, if he could, to advise the King. John Lesley, Bishop of Raphoe, joined the King's camp outside Berwick at about the time of the Earl of Holland's grotesque performance as a general in the field. He was a Scot himself, well acquainted with the character of his countrymen, and he gave it as his view to those who consulted him that to attempt anything further that summer would be to go upon certain disaster. [77] What he said to the King is unknown, but presumably he elaborated from his own knowledge, and from Wentworth's advice to him, the same story: lose no more reputation, make an armistice, postpone the attack on the Scots until there could be a certainty of defeating them.

This advice chimed marvellously well with the King's own views. He had made every mistake possible in preparing for this war; he had appointed the wrong commanders, he had under-estimated the strength of the enemy, he had counted on support from the English that had not been forthcoming. He could see that now. There was never any thought in his mind of abandoning what he believed to be a just cause. But he was willing to deceive the Scots with an appearance of friendship and an offer to treat. The Pacification of Berwick was signed to gain time.

The King was at last aware of a desperate situation needing a desperate remedy. Only in this extremity was he prepared to consign himself and his fortunes to the relentless, the overwhelming Wentworth. In extremity he turned away from Hamilton, Holland and their like and looked, at long last, towards the most devoted and the most able of his servants. He wrote privately, with his own hand, consulting no one; he wrote little, but trusted to the Bishop of Raphoe to carry in his head what could not be put on paper.

On August 5th, 1639, nine days after leaving the camp by Berwick, the Bishop of Raphoe reached the little town of Naas in Wicklow, where Wentworth was supervising the building of his great palace. Here he put into his hands the King's letter. 'Come when you will,' the brief message ended, 'ye shall be welcome to your assured friend, Charles R.' [78]

NOTES

1 Kearney, pp. 172-80; Cooper, pp. 242-3; Ranger, 'Strafford in Ireland', pp. 37-8, where the relevant manuscript sources are cited.

2 Strafford MSS, X, folios 194-6, Wentworth to Greenwood, 14th September 1638; XI, Wentworth to Coke, 29th August 1638.

3 Knowler, II, p. 105; Kearney, pp. 172-3. Wentworth seems to have had a taste for building in brick. Yorkshire brick-makers are said to have worked at Jigginstown. The stable that he built at Dublin Castle for sixty horses was floored with hard brick specially brought from Holland. (Brereton, p. 141.)

[4] Strafford MSS, XI, Windebanke to Wentworth, 11th November 1637.

[5] Ibid., VII, Wentworth to Laud, 18th October 1637, postscript.

[6] Brereton, p. 144; Strafford MSS, XVII, No. 69.

[7] A full account of Ogilby's theatre with the relevant references will be found in W. S. Clark, *The Early Irish Stage*, Oxford, 1955. Mr Clark suggests late 1637 as the date of opening of the St Werbergh Street Theatre, but there must have been a theatre before this because of the incident of its closing by Ussher mentioned in Strafford MSS, VII, Wentworth to Laud, 10th July 1637. Shirley, *Works*, ed. Dyce, VI, pp. 400-6; Burnell, *Landgartha*, Dublin, 1640.

[8] Laud, *Works*, VII, p. 373.

[9] Strafford MSS, III, Wentworth to Cottington, 28th August 1637; VII, Wentworth to Laud, 16th August, 1637.

[10] Ibid., loc. cit; X, Wentworth to Conway, 21st August 1637; *C.S.P.I.*, 1633-47, p. 169; *Strafford's Letters to his third wife*, p. 21.

[11] Alice Thornton, *Autobiography*, pp. 11 ff.

[12] Knowler, II, p. 112.

[13] Ibid, p. 80.

[14] Ibid., p. 63; Kearney, 'The Counter-Reformation in Ireland', *Journal of Ecclesiastical History*, October 1960.

[15] Strafford MSS, XI, folios 28-9, Wentworth and Council to Coke, 31st May 1638; Rushworth, *Trial*, pp. 121, 402 ff; Turton, *The Alum Farm*, pp. 161 ff; Cooper, pp. 236-40, where the relevant references to the Strafford MSS will be found; see also Upton, *Sir Arthur Ingram*, Chap. V and pp. 226-7.

[16] Knowler, II, pp. 105-7; Cooper, pp. 245 ff.

[17] Ibid, p. 107; see also Aylmer, pp. 129, 166-7.

[18] Ibid, pp. 60-4; Strafford MSS, XI, folios 322-3, Windebanke to Wentworth, 20th September 1637; see also H. F. Kearney, 'The Counter-Reformation in Ireland'.

[19] Strafford MSS, VII, Wentworth to Laud, 10th July 1637.

[20] Knowler, II, pp. 114, 119, 136, 161.

[21] Ibid., p. 67; Strafford MSS, VII, Wentworth to Laud, 18th October 1637.

[22] Knowler, II, p. 138.

[23] Ibid., pp. 388 ff.

[24] Strafford MSS, IX, folio 151, Wentworth to Coke, 9th March 1636; *C.S.P.I.*, 1633-47, pp. 71-2; Knowler, I, pp. 304 ff.

[25] *C.S.P.I.*, 1633-47, p. 225.

[26] Ibid., 1625-32, pp. 358-63.

[27] Knowler, II, p. 14.

[28] Ibid., p. 90.

[29] Ibid., p. 69.

[30] H.M.C., *Cowper MSS*, II, p. 155.

[31] H.M.C. *Various*, III, pp. 159-64; *Ormonde MSS*, New Series, I, 39.

[32] H.M.C., IX, p. 303.

[33] H.M.C. *Various*, III, pp. 164-9; Strafford MSS, XI, folios 56-66.

[34] Knowler, II, p. 160.

[35] Ibid., pp. 160-2; Laud, *Works*, VII, pp. 431-2, 454.

[36] Knowler, II, pp. 179, 257, 260-1, 299; H.M.C. *Various*, III, pp. 175-6, 185-9; H.M.C., IX, p. 296; Strafford MSS, XI, folios 162-78.

[37] Bolton, *A Justice of Peace for Ireland*, Dublin, 1637; the copy in the British Museum contains the autograph of Philip Mainwaring and a note of the price — 9s. — which seems rather high for the average Irish Justice of the Peace.

[38] Laud, *Works*, VII, p. 520.

[39] Strafford MSS, XI, Wentworth to Windebanke, 15th April 1639.

[40] Ibid., X, Wentworth to Conway, 10th December 1638.

[41] Ibid., X, Wentworth to Bankes, 24th December 1638; Wentworth to Holland, 3rd December 1638; XI, Wentworth to Windebanke, 30th November 1638 and 15th April 1639; Knowler, II, pp. 230, 252, 307; Rushworth, II, pp. 888 ff. See also Aylmer, pp. 349-50, for a valuable hint that Holland had an interest in undermining Wentworth.

[42] Strafford MSS, X, Wentworth to Mar, 1st May 1637; Ancram to Wentworth, 11th September 1637; Wentworth to Ancram, 7th December 1637.

[43] Ibid., III, Wentworth to the King, 27th February 1638; XI, Wentworth to Coke, 30th October 1638; XI, folios 148-9; Moody, p. 395; Knowler, II, pp. 222-5.

[44] Strafford MSS, XI, Wentworth to Sir William Boswell, 26th October 1638; Wentworth to Windebanke, 29th December 1638.

[45] Knowler, II, pp. 190-2.

[46] Strafford MSS, X, Wentworth to Charles Price, 8th December 1638; Wentworth to Vane senior, 21st May 1639, folio 90.

[47] Ibid., Wentworth to Northumberland, 28th August 1638.

[48] Ibid., Wentworth to Antrim, 5th January 1639.

[49] Ibid., folios 192-3, Wentworth to Sir Peter Middleton.

[50] Ibid., XVII, No. 909, Osborne to Wentworth, 11th November 1637; X, Wentworth to Savile, 20th September 1638; Knowler, II, pp. 308, 311.

[51] Strafford MSS, X, Osborne to Wentworth, undated, approx. December 1638; Knowler, II, 288.

[52] Strafford MSS, X, Wentworth to Osborne, March 1639; Wentworth to Coventry, 27th June 1637.

[53] Knowler, II, 232; Carte, V, pp. 240–1.

[54] Strafford MSS, X, St Leger to Wentworth, 22nd and 23rd May 1639; Barrymore to Wentworth, 26th May 1639.

[55] Ibid., VII, Wentworth to Laud, 26th April 1638.

[56] Ibid., the same to the same, 17th September and 30th October 1638; the same to the same, 11th February 1639.

[57] Ibid., Wentworth to Laud, 27th July 1638.

[58] Ibid., the same to the same, 3rd November 1638, X, Wentworth to Vane senior, 30th May 1639.

[59] Ibid., X, Wentworth to Northumberland, 19th April 1639.

[60] Ibid., VII, Wentworth to Laud, 7th August 1638, postscript; 3rd November 1638; 10th April 1639.

[61] Knowler, II, p. 304; Strafford MSS, X, Wentworth to Vane senior, 16th May and 7th July 1639.

[62] Ibid., X, Wentworth to Lady Carlisle, 13th May 1639.

[63] Knowler, II, p. 295.

[64] Strafford MSS, VII, Wentworth to Laud, 3rd July 1638.

[65] Rushworth, *Trial*, pp. 196, 201.

[66] Strafford MSS, XI, folios 133-5, for the supply of arms; Knowler, II, p. 364; *C.S.P.D.*, 1639, p. 37.

[67] Knowler, II, p. 267.

[68] Strafford MSS, X, Wentworth to Northumberland, 28th February 1639.

[69] Ibid., X, Wentworth to Antrim, 3rd June 1639.

[70] *Camden Miscellany*, IX, pp. 8-10.

[71] Strafford MSS, X, Wentworth to Northumberland, 15th April 1639.

[72] Ibid., Wentworth to Vane senior, 21st May 1639, folios 88-9.

[73] Knowler, II, p. 314.

[74] Strafford MSS, X, Wentworth to Vane senior, 14th May 1639; VII, Wentworth to Laud, 11th February 1639; XI, Wentworth to Coke, 20th June 1639.

[75] Ibid., XI, Wentworth to Coke, 20th June 1639.

[76] Ibid., VII, Wentworth to Laud, 10th April 1639.

[77] *C.S.P.D.*, 1639, p. 273.

[78] Knowler, II, p. 374.

PART THREE

AUGUST 1639–MAY 1641

Let the tempest be never so great, I will much rather put forth to sea, work forth the storm, or at least be found dead with the rudder in my hands.

Wentworth to Carlisle, 1632

CHAPTER ONE

EARL OF STRAFFORD

It is a very ill time to dispute when Hannibal is ad portas.
Wentworth to Sir John Hotham, March 1639

FAR into the night of August 5th Wentworth sat talking with the King's emissary. Even at this eleventh hour Charles would not openly admit that he had recalled him to take command in a desperate situation, but asked him to find some personal excuse for coming. [1] Nevertheless from the brief letter, still more from the verbal messages of the King, Wentworth realized that Charles was putting himself almost without reserve into his hands. The long years of waiting had been crowned at last. Henceforward he would be his King's principal adviser.

That night he slept little and early in the morning he wrote to the King. Difficult as he knew the task before him to be, he was exhilarated by the prospect of power. Yet he could not answer the King's call as quickly as he wished, for his body had once again betrayed him; he was painfully crippled by an attack of gout and could hardly stand. 'I trust in God', he wrote, 'that He hath not given your Majesty so just a cause, nor me so good a heart, to take my legs from me in such a conjuncture of your affairs as this is.' [2]

During the enforced delay he made all ready in Ireland for his absence. A series of prosecutions begun in the Castle Chamber against those Scots in Ulster who had refused the 'Black Oath' must be continued in his absence. Wandesford and Dillon were to be regents of the country, while Radcliffe supervised commerce and the land policy. Radcliffe, too, was to look after Wentworth's private affairs, a task of great complexity since the sources of his private income were closely bound up with so many different public interests, and his speculations and borrowings were by now intimately linked with Irish revenues and commerce.

He could at least leave Ireland with confidence. Most of the key-positions were now held by men he could trust: Sir Adam

Loftus at the Treasury instead of the conspiring Mountnorris, the admirable Ormonde in command of the Army, Chancellor Loftus in disgrace and soon to be removed. A year or two earlier he could not have quitted his post with half so easy a mind.

He had to make arrangements for his family too. He had suffered brief heart-wringing anxiety about his only son, Will, earlier that year. Thrown from his horse, Will had lain for two days unconscious. Not long after, he was ill with smallpox. On his recovery and return to his lessons at Trinity College he had been welcomed by all his fellow students with Latin odes of congratulation. Wentworth was still anxious about him, did not want him to travel, and knowing their separation was at hand, had him work at his side in his study as he made his preparations to leave. [3]

Lady Wentworth had just given birth to a daughter, the only one of her children who was to survive. She therefore with her new-born child and her stepson was to stay for the time being in Dublin. But the Deputy had other plans for the little girls. They were now ten and twelve years old and he thought that they should come to England to visit their grandmother; they had pretty manners, danced well, and could speak French, though the younger had picked up a Guernsey accent from her maid. He felt that Dublin was not the best school for elegant graces. Besides, old Lady Clare, now a widow, had expressed a desire to see her daughter's children, though not her daughter's husband. So to Lady Clare's house in England the Ladies Anne and Arabella Wentworth, with their maids, nurses, pages and attendants were accordingly sent. 'I must confess', Wentworth wrote to the old lady,

> it is not without difficulty before I could persuade myself thus to be deprived the looking upon them ... but I have been brought up in afflictions of this kind, so as I still fear to have that taken first, that is dearest to me.... Whatever your Ladyship's opinion may be of me, I desire and have given it them in charge to honour and observe your Ladyship above all the women in the world. [4]

Meanwhile he received a foretaste of the welcome awaiting him. The King actually abandoned his own candidate for the bishopric of Elphin, recently vacant, in favour of Wentworth's nominee, and the Queen suddenly gave way over a favour she had been trying to secure for one of her friends in the most gracious letter she had ever yet written the Deputy. For once she may have been sincere when she subscribed herself Wentworth's 'très bonne amie, Henriette Marie R.' [5]

On the evening of September 12th, 1639, he sailed from Dublin, and crossed the bar of Chester thirteen hours later. On the 21st he was at his house in Covent Garden. [6] The King and Court received him with so much enthusiasm that the French ambassador could not conceal his trepidation; [7] Wentworth was to him not so much the King's ablest minister as merely the most notorious supporter of a Spanish alliance in the royal councils.

The enthusiasm of the Court revealed to Wentworth more clearly than the events themselves the gravity of the situation. Yet he was not sanguine of help from his colleagues. Hamilton barely concealed his equivocal attitude to the Covenanters, and Holland's greeting was tempered with the malicious and almost undisguised hope that the Deputy of Ireland would save the faces of the Queen's friends by failing as signally as they had done. 'The nearer I come to it,' wrote Wentworth to Radcliffe, 'the more my heart fails me; nor can I promise myself any good by this journey. God's will be done.' [8]

Such moments of doubt had beset him throughout his career, but they did not last and in the coming months the general tenor of his statements and actions suggests confidence rather than gloom. In the same way when he first came to Ireland, his letters had reflected alternately a depressing estimate of the problems and the men with whom he had to deal and an assurance that he would surmount all difficulties. So now, entering the last phase of his career, he did not lack confidence to meet the challenge.

He was not himself responsible for the situation that faced him. He had not been an advocate of Ship-money which had started so much trouble in England. He had not been consulted on the Church policy which had precipitated rebellion in Scotland. But that rigid conviction of his, that the first essential for a government was to exact obedience, made him the King's most resolute supporter in forcing home these policies now that they had been started. Even so, the major decision to continue the war had been taken before he was sent for. The King was not, in any circumstances, prepared to yield to the rebellion of the Covenanters, and in so far as he now adopted the course which Wentworth had outlined in his letters — that of making a temporary treaty while preparing for a second war — he did so because he had already come to the same decision himself. He sent for Wentworth because, possibly for the first time in their long association, he found himself in absolute agreement not only with his point of view but with the method he suggested for carrying it out. [9]

The King's government was now entering upon its fatal phase and the degree of Wentworth's responsibility must be considered. Without Wentworth the collapse of the King's power, under pressure from the Covenanters and from the dissident English gentry, would no doubt have come sooner and in a manner less dramatic, but — given the King's convictions — the descent into disaster could hardly by this time have been avoided. The intervention of Wentworth postponed but also intensified the crisis in which the authoritarian rule of King Charles ended, and held up — because the removal of Wentworth had to be the first objective — the direct onslaught on the King for about a year. In the longer perspective of seventeenth-century history, the last phase of Wentworth's career can be seen as a delaying action in an inevitable process.

This consideration takes nothing away from the personal tragedy and public drama of these closing months of his career. He was called in to deal with a crisis that he had not himself created but which he was bound by his deepest beliefs, by his own personal interests, and the logic of his own career, to surmount if he could. He was called in because the King now felt he needed him for the very reasons which had, until then, caused him to hold him back from the greatest place in the state: his challenging ruthlessness, his arrogant assurance, his formidable will. He wanted now, at this late hour, to use all Wentworth's force to drive on and go 'thorough' all opposition.

Such capacities, used at an earlier time, before opposition had had time to gather head, might have succeeded. It was now too late. What was needed to save the royal government (if anything could have saved it) was a man of acute and patient subtlety, a man expert in handling his fellows, in perceiving the vulnerable points of individuals, the elements of division in groups and parties; a man who could split the Covenanters by concession and argument, who could have stimulated the fears, provoked the jealousies, flattered the varying interests of nobility, gentry, merchants and lawyers in England. It was a situation that called for the inspired insinuation of a Richelieu, or the cautious and lucid diplomacy of an Oxenstjerna, not for the sledge-hammer blows of a Wentworth.

This then was to be the monstrous irony of Wentworth's career. When his great moment came, it gave him no scope to exercise his genius for administration and finance, but called instead for abilities he did not possess, so that he threw away his future, his fortune and his life in a struggle that he could never have won.

The problem seemed to him much simpler than it was: merely a matter of civil rebellion against authority. He did not understand the religious issue as such. To him ceremonies were 'things purely and simply indifferent'. [10] He used those prescribed by Archbishop Laud because it was the royal desire that he should, not because he believed in them for themselves. If he, with his anti-Popish fervour and his Calvinist upbringing, was not offended by them, why should lesser men presume to raise their voices? He could see only one reason for this disobedience. He had said of Prynne and his fellows, they 'do but begin with the Church that they might have free access to the State'. [11] In Scotland, this humour was apparent in their treasonous Covenant, which was nothing in his eyes but a manifesto of rebellion. He had no understanding for the spiritual fervour that could move men in these matters. As he looked upon a situation in which personal motives and material gain were indeed closely involved with matters of high principle, he could see only the former and made no allowance for the strength and danger of the latter.

This blindness would have been more comprehensible had he been himself a man solely bent on personal advancement and material gain. But he was not. He held his duties to the State and the King as sacred; he gave more than lip-service to his religion, and set time apart daily for quiet meditation and private prayer which was serious, humble and sincere. But he was one of those men (and in this he strangely resembled the King his master) who are devoid of the imaginative power that would enable them to compare themselves to others. Thus in matters of material profit he could perform with an untroubled conscience actions which he fiercely condemned in others; in him they were different and permissible. In a higher sphere, he was able as easily to think that his own religion was sincere while that of the Covenanters and the Puritans, of the Earl of Argyll or Mr Prynne, for instance, was a hollow pretence.

This failure to understand the religious motive caused him to make a major miscalculation. He remained convinced for the next critical months, and in spite of all evidence to the contrary, that the ancient animosity of the English towards the Scots would be stronger when it came to war than the Puritan dislike of ceremonies or the widespread resentment of the King's arbitrary government which was binding them together. He believed that a threatened invasion from Scotland would unite the English behind their King to resist the hereditary foe.

Before Wentworth's arrival, the King had already ordered the public burning of the official Scottish account of what had occurred at the negotiations of Berwick. By the time Wentworth reached Court the Assembly of the Church called in Scotland had declared that Episcopacy was contrary to the law of God, and the Scottish Parliament in session at Edinburgh was about to confirm this resolution. (If the King was intransigent, so were his opponents, and Wentworth could see that there was going to be no great difficulty in making them appear the aggressors.)

A certain stiffening in the King's messages to the Scots Parliament was noticed after Wentworth's arrival and was at once attributed to him. He was also thought to be responsible when the King utterly refused to receive two Covenanting peers who came to London to argue their point of view. They were commanded to leave within six hours. A later meeting with Commissioners from Scotland was in the circumstances an ill-mannered comedy. The King and his councillors, Wentworth among them, scoffingly interrupted the Commissioners and made no pretence even of seeking an agreement. (12)

The King's inner council, that fluctuating circle of his servants in whom alone he confided the highest secrets of policy, now consisted of the Archbishop, the Marquis of Hamilton, the Earl of Northumberland, and Wentworth. (13) It was the first time that he had ever been in this coveted and privileged position. He was, of course, entirely at one with Laud. His relations with Hamilton were cool and suspicious, although openly correct. The position with Northumberland was uneasy. Wentworth admired his ability as an organizer and valued his honesty highly in contrast to his more self-seeking colleagues. He had exerted all his influence to have him appointed Admiral and had applauded his attempts to reform the management of the Navy. [14] Yet at this time there seems to have been intermittent tension between them, probably because Northumberland had so deep-rooted a distrust of the King's present policy that he could not bring himself willingly to work for it. He voiced instead prophecies of gloom and defeat. Yet he was indispensable to the King, and so to Wentworth, because of his abilities and — possibly more — because of his territorial influence. As Admiral, it lay with him to organize the intended blockade of Scotland, and to keep the seas clear for English (and Irish) trade. Furthermore, as the greatest landowner on the Border and one of the most influential men in the North, he would have a vital part to play in the war on the Scots.

In the intervals of state affairs, Wentworth was seeing much of Lady Carlisle, and this, if it was pleasant, was also wise. She was Northumberland's sister, she was the Queen's friend, she was the confidante of innumerable secrets from innumerable sources, and at this time she was ready to use her charm and talents in Wentworth's interests. [15]

In gaining valuable support for the King, Wentworth seemed at first successful. The Spanish alliance could, he thought, be strengthened to produce more money. Things were going very badly with Spain: in September a large part of their fleet had been attacked by the Dutch and destroyed in English territorial waters. A few weeks earlier they had lost the key fortress of Breisach at the head of the Rhine to the French, thus blocking one of their principal lines of communication to Flanders. These two disasters meant that they would be glad to pay heavily for increased English help in getting troops and bullion from Spain to the Low Countries by sea. The upshot was a negotiation which, in a few months, was to lead the Spaniards into making the stupendous offer of four million ducats in return for a guard of English ships for their transports. [16]

The increasing rapprochement with Spain, though it was welcome neither to the Puritans nor to the whole of the business community, had some influential support in the City, both among those whose commerce was with Spain, or depended on Spanish friendship, and among others who merely wanted the maintenance of the peaceful status quo and were therefore not anxious for the King to become involved in the European wars. Alderman Garraway became Lord Mayor in November; he was a man of great character and courage and — even more important — of great wealth. His wide-ranging business interests made him anxious for the continuance of stable and peaceful government, and therefore for the maintenance of the King's authority. It was hoped that, with Garraway as Lord Mayor, the City might be brought to offer a loan of £100,000 for putting down the Scots.

Wentworth himself seemed to be increasing in influence and reputation at Court with every week that passed. He had been fully vindicated against Viscount Loftus, who had been heard by the Council, had injured his case by angry blustering, and had been unanimously condemned. [17] At the New Year of 1640 the King at last gratified Wentworth's personal ambitions. He was raised from the rank of Deputy to that of Lord Lieutenant of Ireland, with the right to choose his own deputy. He was also, at last, given the earldom he had so long coveted. He chose to call himself Strafford, after the hundred in which Wentworth Wood-house is situated. By that name which he carried for little more than a year he is known to history. There is poetic justice in it; for eleven months as Earl of Strafford he dominated the King's policy, and for a shorter and more dreadful space as Earl of Strafford he fought against the power of Parliament and the hatred of the people, to vindicate his own honour and his master's government. What he did and said as Earl of Strafford made the immortal glory, or infamy, of Thomas Wentworth.

Even at this high point of his career he made a small, dangerous and typical error. He had always wanted his son to have some visible part in his fortunes, but the barony of Wentworth did not now seem to him a fine enough name to hand on by courtesy to his much-loved Will; Lord Cleveland's heir also carried the title of Lord Wentworth, and Strafford was resolved that his own child should bear a more distinctive name. Using the King's sudden favour he persuaded him to create, as well as the earldom, a new barony, which he might pass to his son during his own lifetime. It was a natural and not an extravagant request, but unhappily he had set his heart on the barony of Raby. The title had been forfeited by attainder in the reign of Queen Elizabeth, and the estates had passed later into the possession of Sir Harry Vane, who had recently hinted that a barony, the barony of Raby, for instance, would not come amiss. An obscure family connection with the original holder of the title was Strafford's only excuse for thus thrusting himself between Sir Harry and his cherished wish. Vane, a power at Court and wholly in the Queen's interest, was so deeply incensed by this trespassing that he could barely be civil; but Strafford, wrestling with the graver problems of the state, did not pause to consider his contemptible hostility. [18]

It was essential now to unite England against the Scots, and with this in view he urged the King to call a Parliament. He guaranteed that it should give him money for his war. Did any doubt him? He could point to the Irish Parliament of 1634. So the plan was laid; Parliaments were to be called in Dublin before Easter and in London after, and by hasty journeys Strafford would contrive to manage both. [19] The Scots would inevitably resume the offensive and the King, with the power and the votes of the Irish and English Commons behind him, would march to destroy them.

It would be well, none the less, to have some money in hand before Parliament met, to buy arms and make preparations. Strafford, with an eye on those other councillors who had made money from their positions, put down £20,000 as a loan to the Crown. [20] It was a handsome offer, in fact it represented almost the whole of a year's income. Admittedly the continuance of his fortune and his power depended on the continuance and stability of the royal government. There was forethought and calculation in what he did, but there was also generosity. Few of the King's other councillors lent so freely, and none risked so much.

Meanwhile the offence that Strafford had given to Sir Harry Vane, which might have mattered relatively little, assumed greater significance when, early in February 1640, Vane was appointed Secretary of State. There had been considerable pressure from the Queen's party during the last four months to remove Sir John Coke. His loyal friendship had made him a useful ally to Strafford, but he was seventy-six years old. Northumberland referred to him slightingly as 'old Noddie' and there was some justice in the complaint that he was not equal to the strenuous work which devolved on him. More seriously, the tension and rivalry between his staff and that of Secretary Windebank increasingly hampered the never very efficient management of the King's affairs. Coke failed to take hints that he should resign, and so to his great distress was finally told to do so. Several weeks of busy intrigue and disagreement followed, in which — exceptionally — Laud and Strafford were briefly at variance: Strafford hoped that the Earl of Leicester would get the place, while Laud backed Sir Thomas Roe. Ultimately the Queen and her friends obtained the place for Sir Harry Vane, who himself admitted that he had not the necessary quickness of ear and hand to take adequate notes at Council meetings. [21]

Two other changes may also have caused Strafford some anxiety. Hamilton's docile and by no means very intelligent younger brother, the Earl of Lanark, was made Secretary of State for Scotland. The experienced Lord Coventry, for many years Lord Keeper, had died; this moderate man, much respected throughout the legal profession, had been a faithful friend to Strafford. The King could fix upon no one better to replace him than John Finch, Chief Justice of the Common Pleas, a man who was generally despised as a time-server and would be chiefly remembered by members of Parliament, when the time came for them to meet, as the Speaker who had been ignominiously held down in his chair on the last day of the last Parliament. None of these appointments can have given Strafford much confidence.

Northumberland had been promoted to what was probably the most vital position of all — that of president of the Council of War and general of the English forces. This was a good appointment in itself, especially in view of Northumberland's influence on the Border. Who but the head of the great house of Percy should lead the English in war against the Scots? [22] But, quite apart from Northumberland's lack of confidence in the King's policy, there were other drawbacks. He retained his post as Admiral, so that his responsiblities and attentions were too far stretched for him to do justice to either task. Furthermore the King, who kept for himself the ultimate command alike in war and peace, was also relying on Hamilton to conduct the war in Scotland by land and sea. Co-operation was possible between these two, but as so often in this epoch of confused authorities, it was never quite clear where the responsibility of one ended and the other began, or indeed which of them was answerable to the other.

Strafford himself had got his way over the most important of the subordinate military appointments, and had had Lord Conway made general of the cavalry, with his headquarters at New-castle. [23] Conway was an experienced soldier, and Strafford believed him also to be a good and devoted one. Here, unfortunately, he was later to find he had been mistaken.

The two Parliaments had by now been summoned, that of Ireland for mid-March, that of England for early April. An ill-timed attack of gout kept Strafford longer in London than he had intended, but on March 5th, 1640, he left very early in the morning in the Queen's own coach drawn by six horses. [24] She had lent it to him to ease his journey, and this act of kindness, showing her renewed favour, greatly raised his spirits. Nevertheless it took him thirteen painful days to reach the coast. On the 16th he was at Beaumaris ready to sail; hence he wrote reassuringly that whatever befell him he would be back for the English Parliament:

> I will make strange shift and put myself to all the pain I shall be able to endure, before I be anywhere awanting to my master or his affairs in this conjecture; and therefore sound or lame you shall have me with you before the beginning of the Parliament; I should not fail though Sir John Eliot were living.

The present crisis once surmounted, he looked forward to a lasting security. 'This work now before us ... carried through advisedly and gallantly shall by God's blessing set us in safety and peace for our lives ... nay, in probability, the generations that are to succeed us.' In this confidence his spirits were high, and he ended his letter: 'Fi à faute de courage, je n'en aye que trop. What might I be with my legs that am so brave without the use of them? Well, halt, blind, or lame, I will be found true to the person of my gracious master.' [25] On March 18th he landed in Dublin.

Two days before he came, Wandesford, now Lord Deputy since Strafford had become Lord Lieutenant, had opened Parliament. Cork, Loftus, Mountnorris were in England; Strafford's friends, Dillon, Ormonde, Radcliffe, Bolton controlled the Irish Council. They also, by well-placed supporters, controlled the House of Commons. As soon as he had recovered from the fatigues of the journey, on March 20th, he came down in state to the House of Lords with the high officials of the Kingdom grouped about him and his son assisted by two other young noblemen bearing his train. Seated in the chair of State, he heard from the Speaker of the Commons an address of glowing praise. 'Welcome, most worthy Lord,' said the Speaker, 'this is the voice of the House of Commons, and I am sure it is the voice of the whole assembly; it is besides Vox Populi abroad, and I make no doubt it is Vox Dei.... I see your Lordship like another Solon or Lycurgus, studying the good of this your country; *your* country let me now call it, and I beseech your Lordship to account it so.' He went on to praise in every particular the justice, order, prosperity and happiness which a grateful Ireland owed to the best of governors. [26] The words of the Speaker were echoed in the actions of the Commons. Three days later they voted four subsidies of £45,000 each without a single negative, and clamourously insisted on adding a preamble to the bill setting forth their gratitude to the King who had sent Strafford to govern them. He found his administration of the laws, of justice, of the revenue, even of land, set forth in words of the highest praise. 'For this your tender care over us,' the Irish Commons declared to their King, 'showed by the deputing and supporting of so good a governor, we your faithful subjects acknowledge ourselves more bound than we can with tongue or pen express.' [27]

At the passing of the measure they threw up their hats, cheered, shouted, and 'declared that their hearts contained mines of subsidies for his Majesty, that twenty subsidies, if their abilities were equal to their desires, were too little to be given to so sacred a Majesty'. 'Your Majesty', wrote Strafford, 'may have with their free good wills as much as this people can possibly raise.' He added in his report the request that his master would publish in England all that the Irish Commons had said of his government, in order that insidious rumours about his tyranny might be contradicted.

He no doubt also thought that a little propaganda about the blessings of life as enjoyed by obedient subjects under a firm and just authority might not come amiss. (28) In this excellent humour he prorogued Parliament until the first week in June, intending in the intervening time to deal with the English Commons and thereafter to return to Ireland to collect the subsidies and see to the shipping of the army for the war against the Scots.

The Irish Parliament had agreed to the provision of a force of eight thousand foot and a thousand horse. It remained for Strafford to put the raising of this into good hands. The Earl of Ormonde and the Lord President of Munster, the honest old soldier Sir William St Leger, undertook the principal burden of this. The troops were to be ready for transport to Scotland by the middle of May. Strafford, who had a low opinion of the Ordnance office in England, was organizing through his invaluable agent in London, William Railton, the purchase of equipment for them in the Low Countries. Meanwhile he counted on some of the loan raised among the Privy Councillors in England to meet current expenses, and in letters to Whitehall urged on the authorities the importance of sending enough ships to guard the Irish sea both for the transport of troops and the maintenance of Irish trade. (29)

His fortnight in Ireland marked the highest point of his apparent success. The clergy followed the example of Parliament by voting subsidies to the King with equal enthusiasm and adding words of praise and gratitude to him that equalled those of the laity. (30) These fluent testimonials were the work of his friends, no doubt prompted from above by Wandesford. With his knowledge of the mechanism of government and parliaments, Strafford can hardly have accepted them as a wholly spontaneous expression of gratitude. But, however well-prompted and well prepared it had been, a tribute of this kind from Parliament could hardly have been steered through the Commons with no objections and among scenes of such joyful enthusiasm unless a considerable number of those present had been, at the time at least, partly in agreement with it, or had been made to feel that they were. This was undoubtedly in the spring of 1640 a subservient Parliament; the subservience of lesser men to greater was a natural feature of the politics of the time, but it was at least sometimes associated with the more respectable sentiments of trust and gratitude.

277

Stripped of its hyperbolic language, the words of the Irish Commons meant very simple things: that they were in awe of Strafford, certainly, but also that they had confidence in him. He liked to take it as a tribute to his wisdom and justice; but he must have known very well that it was above all a tribute to his strength. When his strength faltered, as it was to do in a few months' time, the Commons of Ireland would speak in another tone.

Before leaving the country he had his brother George sworn of the Council: [31] the young man was to have a strenuous summer, for he had been elected as a member of the English Parliament and was expected, after he had played his part in that assembly, to hasten back to Ireland and assist Ormonde to the best of his ability in military matters, possibly to serve himself in the invasion of Scotland, or — if it suited his brother's interests better — to take his seat on the Council in Dublin.

During his brief and busy time in Ireland, Strafford's health, so far from improving as he had hoped, had taken another turn for the worse. He was now tormented by the 'bloody flux' — their realistic term for dysentery — and his doctors were very much against his travelling. At the same time the spring gales were sweeping the Irish Sea and the captain of his ship was unwilling to sail. Strafford overruled physicians and seamen. 'This is not a time for bemoaning of myself,' he wrote to the King, 'for I shall cheerfully venture this crazed vessel of mine, and either by God's help wait upon your Majesty before that Parliament begin, or else deposit this infirm humanity of mine in the dust.' [32]

On the evening of Good Friday, April 3rd, he took leave of his wife and his friend, Wandesford, not knowing that it was for the last time, and supported by his son went painfully on board ship and put to sea in despite of the weather. For the whole of 'a marvellous foul and dangerous night' and all the next day, the pinnace *Confidence* battled through the storm, thrown this way and that by cross-seas, till at six on the evening of April 4th, as the wind dropped, she crossed the bar of Chester. 'This churlish sea hath shaken this distempered body of mine most extremely', he wrote in a letter to Windebanke, [33] and after dictating a jubilant report of his success in Ireland he collapsed and lay feverish in bed for the next twenty-four hours. On April 6th he managed to write to the King promising to set out for London on the following day, but when the time came the spirit could not master the flesh and for three more days he lay sick at Chester. On April 9th he was busy with letters again, sending a long report to the Earl of Northumberland about the arrangements for the Irish army and adding a question about the best way of getting shipments of supplies through to Dumbarton, which had again been occupied for the King. Some vessels were ready to sail from Chester, but the seas were unsafe and the Earl of Argyll was alleged to have a ship of eighteen guns patrolling the mouth of the Clyde. [34]

On April 10th Strafford got up but was too weak to walk round his room. He dictated more letters, this time to Windebanke. 'Of all things I love not to put off my clothes and go to bed in a storm', he wrote. [35] The news that reached him daily at Chester showed him that the storm he had braved in the Irish Sea was but a foretaste of the storms now awaiting him on land.

The easy submission of the Irish to the King's — or rather Strafford's — will had no parallel in England. Windebanke's reports, which greeted him at Chester, were of discontent everywhere. Ship-money was being refused. The Lords Lieutenant were proving incompetent or unwilling to raise the county levies. False musters were made, far more often no doubt than they were discovered; one that came to Strafford's notice stirred his wrath. The offender, he wrote, 'cannot be too severely punished; if you purpose to overcome that evil, you must fall upon the first transgressors like lightning.' He warmed to his subject as he dictated, issuing commands rather than advice to the vacillating Secretary in London. The King was on no account to trust either Lord Roche or Lord Clanricarde with any important business: the Covenanting lords still in London, Lord Loudoun in particular, should be put under restraint. As for the deputy-lieutenants of Yorkshire, who had refused to levy two hundred men for the Berwick garrison unless coat and conduct money were guaranteed by the government, 'upon my coming to town', wrote Strafford grimly, 'I will give my gentlemen something to remember it by hereafter.' [36]

On the following day he left Chester in a litter and reached Nantwich by the evening. Here he was sumptuously entertained by the local magante, Sir Thomas Wilbraham, and he must have been grateful in his weakened condition for a son old enough to help him in his social duties. Young Lord Raby was nearly fourteen, tall for his age, and with the easy charm, auburn hair and blue eyes of the Holleses. He reached Stone on the 12th; on the 13th he was at Lichfield, where a messenger from the King met him bearing a letter from his master entreating him to spare himself, for they could not afford to lose him at such a time. He travelled on by Coventry, Daventry, Stony Stratford and St Albans, sending off letters of advice and instruction all the way, and on the evening of April 18th arrived in London and was set down at Lord Leicester's house. (37) It was nearer to Whitehall than his own in Covent Garden.

On April 15th the King had already opened Parliament, and Lord Keeper Finch, in a not very well phrased speech, had urged the Commons to show their gratitude to their incomparable sovereign by voting subsidies to fight the rebellious Scots. An attempt to arouse English indignation by producing evidence that the Scots had approached France for help had fallen curiously flat. The outlook was not at all hopeful.

Both the King's supporters and his opponents had worked hard to have their friends elected. The two Secretaries of State, Vane and Windebanke, had of course been provided with seats, though some other Court candidates had been rejected. Strafford had used all his influence in the North; he had arranged to have his brother and a cousin returned for Pomfret, and his Secretary of State for Ireland, Philip Mainwaring, for Morpeth, presumably on the influence of the Earl of Northumberland. A number of other supporters had been successfully placed in other northern boroughs. But the opposing party had worked equally hard, and Yorkshire in particular, Strafford's own county, was bitterly divided between the two groups. The King's critics and opponents were, in general, well represented: John Pym, John Hampden, Denzil Holles, William Strode, Benjamin Valentine and several other members notorious for the difficulties they had caused in 1628 were once more on the benches, together with newcomers who might give trouble like Nathaniel Fiennes, the son of the notoriously Puritan Lord Saye and Sele, one of the most active leaders of the opposition peers.

The Speaker, Sir John Glanvill, was a lawyer of distinction, but he had in the past opposed the Crown on several issues and it was very uncertain how far he could be relied on to further the King's requests if the Commons proved difficult. John Pym, on the second day of the session, took command of the House, more quietly than Eliot had done in 1626, as effectively as Strafford had done in 1628. His opening speech on grievances made it very clear that a majority in the Commons disliked the King's religious policy and resented his extra-Parliamentary exactions even more bitterly than they had done eleven years before.

Strafford, still crippled by sickness, could not attend the House until five days after his arrival. At last, on April 23rd, he took his seat in the Lords. Supported by his kinsman the Earl of Cleveland and his now half-reconciled brother-in-law the Earl of Clare, he assumed his place in his new order of precedence. [38]

While he was received into the House of Lords, Secretary Windebanke was addressing the Commons. His vehement appeal for an immediate vote of moneys had probably been timed to coincide with Strafford's return. On the preceding day the clergy in Convocation had voted six subsidies. But this was more likely to stimulate the Commons to resistance than to inspire them to emulation. Windebanke, though he drew attention to the happy omen that it was St George's Day, got very little response from the Commons. John Pym, with an impressive mixture of firmness and common sense, persuaded the House to ask for a conference with the Lords, because — it was argued — until grievances were settled they could not judge if they had money to vote or no. 'Mr Pym gets the reputation to be as wise as Solomon', wrote an admiring spectator of his astute Parliamentary tactics. [39]

At the unwelcome news of the proposed conference, the King that evening summoned his advisers. Strafford was still confident that Parliament could be managed, although some of his colleagues were by this time extremely critical of him for having persuaded the King to involve himself with yet another recalcitrant assembly. He advised Charles to outmanoeuvre Pym by appealing to the Lords before the Commons did so. [40] On the morning of April 24th, therefore, the King spoke to the Lords, promising that grievances would be redressed in a second session if supplies were granted now. The royal offer, elaborated in a persuasive speech from Strafford, weighed with the majority of the Lords. When the Commons asked for their support in putting redress of grievances before supply, they were rejected by a substantial majority. (41) At this the House of Commons grew resentful and accused the Lords of a breach of privilege in discussing supply at all. Strafford, remembering those fatal quarrels between Lords and Commons which in his earlier days had so often hampered Parliamentary action, was hopeful that a breach between the Houses would weaken the Commons and enable the King's friends there to wrest the initiative from Pym. But John Pym was too experienced a Parliament man to let this happen. With the help of his friends in the upper House, a very vocal minority, he managed, at a joint conference, to talk out the difference of opinion. Meanwhile news came that the war had already begun; the King's garrison in Edinburgh Castle and the Covenanters in the town had fired upon each other; reports from different sources named the King's men or the Covenanters as the aggressors, according to taste. On Saturday, May 2nd, the King once more sent to the House urging the folly of delay in the present state of the nation's affairs, and Strafford, speaking in the House of Lords, called attention to the example that had been set by the Irish Parliament in voting supplies, and threatened that any further delay would be punished by dissolution. (42)

On the intervening Sunday, while members of Parliament prepared for a critical week, the King called the Council once more. The debate seems to have turned on two questions: the first was the withdrawal of Ship-money, and the second the number of the subsidies to be asked for. The King was now prepared to yield on the question of Ship-money, but hoped, on the advice of Vane, to get twelve subsidies — or about £840,000 — in return. Strafford was convinced that this was to strain the Commons too high. (He was well aware of the extreme discontent in Yorkshire because of the incidental cost of the war, in raising and transporting troops: the gentry could not be expected to vote as many as twelve subsidies on top of these other demands.) After long argument he persuaded the King to agree to eight subsidies; he himself would have preferred six, and as he resumed his seat was heard to say so. But he could not so far reduce the King's demand. (43)

Next day, Monday, May 4th, Sir Harry Vane, who may perhaps have had authority from the vacillating King, asked for twelve subsidies against the withdrawal of Ship-money. Just as Strafford had feared, this provoked indignation from some of the members, especially the northern gentry, who complained that the concession on Ship-money would scarcely help their purses at all. The expense of the last attack on Scotland, and the present one, was weighing them down. To demand twelve subsidies from men in this frame of mind was utterly impolitic. Moreover, the King's offer to yield over Ship-money could only be interpreted as weakness. Speaker Glanvill was known to regard Ship-money as illegal, and therefore did not help the King; the Commons broke up, suspicious, resentful and quite unimpressed by Vane's reiterated insistence on twelve subsidies in return for the removal of only one grievance. (44)

It seems unlikely that Strafford could, by any exercise of skill or bribery, have now brought this intractable Parliament under control. He had, however, no time to do so. Credible information had reached the Court that the leaders of the Commons were about to bring up the religious grievances of Scotland along with their own; (45) if this or anything like it happened, the Parliament called to support war on the Covenanters would have virtually declared itself their ally. There had already been some talk in the Commons of voting subsidies only on condition that they were not used for a war on the Scots. (46) If the sympathy between Puritan England and Covenanting Scotland was, so to speak, officially endorsed in Parliament it would be virtually impossible for the King to go on with his war.

A Council meeting was called for six in the morning on Tuesday, May 5th. Strafford, hampered by a renewed attack of illness, arrived late, and Archbishop Laud, who would have supported him in the discussion, had been misinformed of the time of the meeting and came only when the debate was nearly at an end. In view of the danger that the Commons might openly support the Covenanters, it seemed to almost all present that the dissolution must be immediate. Strafford at first resisted this conclusion. This Parliament had been his idea; he had built much on the hope of its success and was therefore more acutely aware than any of his colleagues of the damage that would be wrought by its failure.

He may still have hoped that by ingenious handling he could divide the Commons, and he almost certainly underestimated (as his colleagues did not) the Scottish danger. He may have thought even that risk worth taking, in the belief that the Commons would split if Pym and his group went so far as to suggest making common cause with the Scots.

We have but fragmentary knowledge of what went on at that matutinal Council meeting, and we know nothing of what went on in Strafford's mind. All that can be said for certain is that he gave in, after an hour's discussion, and voted with the majority for the dissolution. [47] It was he who had asked that a Parliament be called. Not his part in its calling would now be remembered, but his part in its dismissal. Before noon the King went down to the House of Lords, sent for the Commons, and coldly imparted his decision. Strafford, conspicuous among his councillors, stood beside him on the steps of the throne.

NOTES

[1] Knowler, II, p. 372.

[2] Ibid., pp. 373 ff.

[3] Ibid., p. 379; Strafford MSS, X, Wentworth to Vane, 25th April and 21st May 1639. The manuscript book of Latin poems by Will Wentworth's fellow-students is vol. XXXVIII of the Strafford MSS. His father's tender and indulgent attitude to him is well illustrated in his surviving letters. Some very touching examples in the Strafford MSS are given at length by Lady Burghclere (II, pp. 147-8) and Lord Birkenhead (p. 318).

[4] Knowler, II, pp. 379 ff. Further correspondence in the Strafford MSS seems to show that the little girls did not enjoy themselves so much with their strong-minded grandmother as with their mild stepmother in Dublin. They were soon moved to Wentworth-Woodhouse where, no doubt, they had it all their own way again.

[5] Knowler, II, pp. 378 ff.

[6] Ibid., p. 431; *Camden Miscellany*, IX, IV, p. 11.

[7] *C.S.P.Ven.*, 1639, p. 578; 1640, p. 12.

[8] *Radcliffe Letters*, pp. 177 ff.

[9] The King's attitude is discussed in *The King's Peace*, pp. 274-6, 291. The evidence of his intransigence and resolution to go on with the war is overwhelming. Mr Kearney suggests that Wentworth's advice counted for much in directing his fatal course, but a perusal of the King's letters and statements chronologically shows that he never really deviated from his intention to force his will on the Scots at whatever cost.

[10] Knowler, II, p. 210.

[11] Ibid., p. 101.

[12] Burnet, p. 160; Baillie, I, p. 247.

[13] *Sydney Papers*, II, p. 626.

[14] Knowler, II, p. 67.

[15] *Sydney Papers*, II, pp. 626-7.

[16] *C.S.P.Ven.*, 1640-2, pp. 44-5.

17 *Radcliffe Letters*, p. 196, *Sydney Papers*, II, pp. 617-18.

18 *C.S.P.D.*, 1639-40, p. 436; also 1639-40, January, *passim*.

19 *Radcliffe Letters*, p. 187; Laud, *Works*, III, p. 233.

20 *C.S.P.D.*, 1639-40, pp. 149, 158; Laud, Works, III, p. 233.

21 Aylmer, pp. 154-5; Dorothea Coke, *The Last Elizabethan*, pp. 269-71; Sydney Papers, II, p. 631; Clarendon, VI, p. 411. For the division between Strafford and Laud see H. R. Trevor-Roper, *Archbishop Laud*, pp. 375-6.

22 *Sydney Papers*, II, p. 629.

23 Ibid., p. 626.

24 *Lismore Papers*, Series 1, V, p. 129.

25 Knowler, II, pp. 393 ff.

26 *Commons Journals, Ireland*, I, p. 134.

27 Ibid., p. 141; *C.S.P.D.*, 1639-40, p. 608.

28 Knowler, II, pp. 396-9, 402.

29 Ibid., pp. 399-400, 401, 403.

30 Ibid., pp. 402-3.

31 Ibid., p. 395.

32 Ibid., p. 403.

33 Loc. cit.

34 Ibid., pp. 404-6; *Camden Miscellany*, IX, IV, p. 12.

35 Ibid., p. 406.

36 Ibid., pp. 409-11.

37 Nichols, III, p. 411; Knowler, II, p. 413; *Camden Miscellany*, IX, IV, p. 12.

38 *C.S.P.D.*, 1640, p. 59; H.M.C., XI, VII, p. 98; *Lords Journals*, IV, p. 65.

39 Harleian MSS, 4931, folio 47.

40 Gardiner, IX, p. 108.

41 *Lords Journals*, IV, p. 67; *C.S.P.D.*, 1640, pp. 39, 66; Rushworth, II, ii, p. 1164.

42 Harleian MSS, 4931, folio 49.

43 *Radcliffe Letters*, p. 234.

44 *C.S.P.D.*, 1640, pp. 40, 115, 153-5.

45 Ibid., pp. 144-5.

46 Harleian MSS, 4931, folio 48.

47 Laud, *Works*, III, 284.

CHAPTER TWO

'ONE SUMMER WELL EMPLOYED'

'An arbitrary government bounded by no law but what my lord
Strafford pleaseth.'
John Maynard, at the trial of Strafford, March 1641

PARLIAMENT was dissolved on the morning of May 5th, 1640.
In the afternoon the King called a meeting of those of his
councillors who formed the Committee for Scottish affairs.
Strafford and Laud were present, Northumberland as the King's
lieutenant general of the army, Cottington to give financial and
diplomatic advice, and Sir Harry Vane, the secretary. It was a
gloomy occasion. The Scots had an army in the field and, by all
accounts, already on the march. The King's coffers were empty
and there was now no hope of a subsidy vote. Northumberland,
president of the Council of War and general of the forces, was
frankly in favour of abandoning the conflict.

Strafford spoke next. Since the Scots were in arms, he said, they
had no choice but to 'go vigorously on'. It was impossible with
honour to avoid fighting; the only way was to prosecute the war
effectively. Even the dissolution of Parliament could be turned to
account. '*They* refused; *you* are acquitted towards God and man,'
he said, urging the King to use the prerogative in this crisis to
raise money and men. Parliament had failed to defend the people
in their hour of need with the rebel Scots at the gate. The King
could, all the more, stand forth as their natural leader and pro-
tector against the invaders. That was the gist of his argument. He
spoke rapidly, and Vane's unskilful pen stumbled in his wake.
'You have an army in Ireland you may employ here to reduce this
Kingdom.... Confident as anything under heaven, Scotland
shall not hold out five months.... One summer well employed will
do it.... I would carry it or lose all', Vane jotted down inco-
herently into his notes.

The Archbishop supported Strafford; Cottington was more
cautious, he feared the intervention of foreign powers and did

not believe the English would support the war. They were 'weary both of King and Church', he said frankly. Strafford would have none of these doubts. He rose truculently: 'If any of the Lords can show you a better way, let them do it,' he challenged. If a minority in the House of Peers murmured at the dissolution of Parliament, they should smart for it; Ship-money — not yet formally withdrawn — must be levied at once, commissions of array be set on foot in the counties and all the levies possible marched to the border to prevent invasion. (1) He carried them with him; commissions went out to all the counties, and the King prepared to enforce where he could not persuade.

Money was the principal need, and Strafford spent what was left of that day with the representatives of the King of Spain. Two envoys from King Philip IV and one from the Spanish Netherlands were closeted with him at his house for several hours. The upshot was the dazzling offer of four million ducats for a guard of thirty-five English warships to convoy Spanish transports up the Channel. (2) If this treaty could be signed in time, the King's troubles were at an end. As a wealthy pensioner of Spain, he would be able to show his own subjects who was master.

Meanwhile in the City, tumults broke out. Seamen and apprentices stormed the Archbishop's palace and he had to escape by the river; placards were posted on gates and doorposts denouncing Strafford and Laud, the provokers of the war. Songs ridiculing the government were shouted outside Whitehall. Strafford scorned these demonstrations; if the Londoners did not like the war they could learn to hold their tongues. 'Black Tom', wrote an enemy, between hatred and admiration, will not 'suffer a guard to attend him, knowing he hath terror enough in his bended brows to amaze the prentices'. (3)

Several members of Parliament, from both the Upper and the Lower House, were arrested and their papers searched for signs of transactions with the Covenanters. The Lord Mayor meanwhile had trouble with the City whence the King was demanding a loan. Aldermen were supposed to submit lists of those who could afford to subscribe, and some refused to do so. The Council, on May 10th, committed the refusers to prison. (4)

Archbishop Laud, taking his cue from his friend, acted with challenging boldness. The Clergy in Convocation promulgated a series of Canons which consolidated those very reforms and ideas most disliked by the Puritans. At the same time they recommended a searching oath of loyalty to the established Church which was to be enforced on all clergy and professional men throughout the country.

Alongside the imposition of this oath there would be, of course, throughout the summer reiterant demands for money and services, exacted from the population by the royal power alone: Ship-money, loans, cash and kind for the support of troops, and the whole troublesome business of selecting and sending forth the men. One aspect of this was constantly in Strafford's mind. The King must make it clear that he had been forced to act without Parliament because Parliament, and not the King, had failed in its duty. In time of crisis, the sovereign must put the safety of his people first. He must use the prerogative to protect them from the danger of invasion. The use of the prerogative was essential, and it was not a violation of the laws, but a true defence of them for the preservation of the state. It might be necessary to abrogate the Petition of Right in order to provide for the levies which would shortly be needed on the border. Such an abrogation was but a temporary expedient, the bitter necessity of the times [5] forced on the King by the captious ill-behaviour of Parliament and his own fatherly care for his subjects, and not to be taken as a precedent in normal times.

Strafford's control might have given steadiness and coherence to the efforts of the Council. For eight days after the dissolution he fought against his wasting illness, but on May 13th, exhausted by continuous dysentery and the blood-letting of his physicians, he had not strength to stand; a week later an attack of pleurisy prostrated him. With an unexpectedly gracious gesture the King visited him in person. Strafford, disregarding his attendants, came down to receive him. Directly after, he had a relapse from which it seemed unlikely that he would recover. George Wentworth and George Radcliffe were sent for. But Strafford could not slip out of his master's service so easily. Early in June he was transacting business from his bed, receiving visits from ministers and keeping his secretaries busy; by the middle of the month he was on his feet again and on July 5th he was back at the Council Board. [6] The royalist poet Shirley, the principal writer for his theatre in

Dublin, hailed his return in joyful verse: 'There's fire at breathing of your name', he wrote. Fire was certainly needed to inspirit the King's party. [7]

Seven weeks had cumulatively aggravated the dangers and the Council was hampered by fear. Even Laud, hounded and roared at by the apprentices, had relapsed into trembling inaction. Vane was sulky, Windebanke was frightened, and Hamilton secretive and obstinate. Northumberland, once Strafford's friend, resented a policy which he thought doomed to disaster, and Holland was mysteriously often at his Puritan brother Warwick's house with a suspicious group of politicians. It was even said that the meetings transferred themselves sometimes to his own spacious mansion at Kensington. [8] Cottington alone had recovered his natural high spirits and was as cheerful as ever. He was full of ideas for raising money, impounded for the King a cargo of pepper belonging to the East India Company, and was probably behind the King's decision when he suddenly seized the bullion which wealthy City merchants were in the habit of depositing in the Tower. There was also talk of debasing the copper coinage. The City suspected not Cottington but the terrible Strafford of having planned these damaging assaults upon them, and a deputation of merchants waited on him. They found him with Cottington and it did not effectively appear from their interview that he knew much about these manoeuvres. They got nothing out of him, beyond the dry and menacing statement that the remedy lay in their own hands: and that the King of France had recently sent troops to gather money from recalcitrant citizens. If they would give the King the loan he had asked for, none of these other expedients would be necessary. [9]

Strafford's hopes of the Spanish treaty had meanwhile been dashed. During his illness both the French and the Dutch envoys had worked against him, undermining the potential friends of Spain at Court and in the City. It was the Dutch envoy, Heenvliet, who destroyed the project finally by indicating that if the King undertook to convoy Spanish transports this would be regarded by the Dutch as a breach of neutrality. It was evident that, even for four million ducats, King Charles could not in his present state risk a war with Holland. [10] An attempt to negotiate a loan from Venice met with no success, [11] and Strafford, by the middle of

July, must have accepted his failure to raise money abroad. The King had now nothing to rely on but the loyalty and the purses of his own subjects.

The Covenanters were by this time almost ready to march. In the interim since Parliament had been dissolved, the hostile mood of the English had not altered. Petitions had been signed against the oath of loyalty to the Church; there were on all sides complaints of the expense and trouble caused by levying troops; among the men themselves there was riot and disorder — officers were murdered at Faringdon and in Somerset; park fences were torn up, game injured, and — repeatedly — churches were broken into and communion rails torn out and burnt in demonstrations of Protestant fervour.

The signs were clear enough, although Strafford still refused to read them. He allowed himself to be cheered by absurdly optimistic reports from Lord Conway, at Newcastle, who believed that the strength of the Scots was greatly exaggerated. He may also have been deceived, as men in power can easily be, by the obsequiousness of his own supporters and the confidence which the King now so evidently felt in him. History records the major demonstrations of the Londoners against him and the lampoons scattered in the streets. It says nothing of those little knots of impressed onlookers who always gather to gape at famous men; it says nothing of the beggars who waited patiently for alms and called out 'God bless you' outside every great house in London, and Strafford's as much as another. It is possible that he did not realize, and could not altogether believe, how deep and wide was the hatred which now encompassed him. He could measure against the lampoons, which he probably did not read, the adulatory ode addressed to him by James Shirley, and the devotion of other literary protégés, like Richard Brathwaite, who christened his son, born this year, 'Strafford'. [12]

The news from Ireland was in some respects more perturbing than the news from England. In March the Council, Parliament and the whole country had seemed perfectly under control. By June there were already signs of trouble. That impressive vote of confidence that Strafford had received depended on the certainty of his continuance in power. As soon as he (and his King) failed to dominate the English Parliament, as soon as his position in

England began to look unsafe, his hold on Ireland was bound to weaken. The Irish Commons had not voted great sums of money and an army of nine thousand to help a King who could get nothing whatever from the English Commons. They had voted money to a governor whom they had learnt that it was dangerous to disobey, not to one whose power, with that of the King his master, was likely to disintegrate in the next few months. This was the doubt which was moving among the gentry of Ireland, 'old English', 'new English' and Irish alike. They had evidence already of the King's weakness. Strafford's urgent request that the Irish seas be guarded had been neglected for lack of ships.

Confidence had ebbed very far by the time that Christopher Wandesford, now Lord Deputy, opened the second session of Parliament in June. [13] There were other causes of uncertainty and speculation. Ormonde was at Kilkenny, where his wife was ill, and could therefore do little to help. It was probably also known that the Earl of Cork was now in high favour at Court, where the King hoped to borrow money from him. Given the uncertain state of English affairs to which Strafford was so deeply committed, this might mean that the Earl of Cork would yet turn the tables on the Lord Lieutenant. Such a reversal of fortunes, with all that it entailed for the internal politics of Ireland, was not out of the question. Over and above these causes for political fear and doubt, it was also known that Strafford was seriously ill. Strafford overthrown or Strafford dead would be equally useless to those in the Irish Commons who were thinking of their own incomes and careers.

The Irish Commons who, three months before, had ransacked their vocabulary for words of praise for Strafford, were now easily swayed against him. All groups — Irish, 'old English' and 'new English' — had grievances and could be brought, once the leadership fell into the control of his opponents, to voice those grievances. Wandesford lacked the strength and the skill to prevent this disastrous turn of events. He yielded to the demand that boroughs, disfranchised by Strafford, be permitted again to elect members, and he could not prevent long, wrangling protests about the subsidies — so vociferously voted three months before. The Commons were resolved first to reorganize the basis of assessment and undo the work done by Strafford five years before. After an unprofitable fortnight, Wandesford prorogued Parliament until

October. [14] The Irish army, in the meantime, could not sail for Scotland because no ships had come to transport it.

Strafford would have liked to cross over into Ireland, hearten his friends, put the fear of God into his enemies, and bring the Irish army over himself. But at this crisis the Earl of Northumberland, general of the English army, fell ill. At the same time Lord Conway, suddenly changing his cheerful tune, wrote from Newcastle that the Scots were upon him with twenty thousand men, he could not hold the town a week, and intended to evacuate, burn the suburbs and sink the fleet. He was a man in whom Strafford had greatly trusted; and now he sent this counsel of despair. 'For love of Christ', implored Strafford, 'think not so early of quitting the town, burning of suburbs and sinking of ships'; the Scots could not have twenty thousand men, it must be a rumour — and the English army in full force would be ready to relieve him before the Scots drew near. [15]

The day after the news came, August 16th, saw the Privy Council assembled once again. The King suddenly took the initiative; he would go north himself to hearten the army. Then they would see if the mutinous levies would not follow him. The Council were astonished: Hamilton said drily that there was no need to leave London, Holland remarked that the soldiers wanted pay and even the King's presence would not help them to it, Lord Keeper Finch quavered that the Londoners would not like to be left. Strafford even, delighted as he was to find his master at last prepared to take a decisive step, feared for his person if Conway's rumours should be true. He therefore swept aside the doubts of Hamilton and Holland, congratulated the King on his intention, but persuaded him to wait five or six days till the border was secured by the levies now on their way thither. After a little argument Charles gave in. [16]

The only problem left was still the most serious. Who was to replace Northumberland? There was only one man who would not shirk responsibility for the war, and that was Strafford himself. He pleaded that he was not a soldier but in the end he gave in; it meant abandoning Ireland to Wandesford's indecisive hands but there was no other man on whom the King could fully rely and he was after all responsible for the Irish army which was to supply a large part of the King's forces. 'God hath his work', he wrote to

Conway announcing his appointment, 'and I trust will dispose all to the best.' [17] On August 20th the King left London, and on August 24th Strafford followed. [18]

He reached Huntingdon the first night and sat up till the small hours writing letters; he could not have slept, for his dysentery had come on again and it hurt him to breathe so that his doctor wanted to let blood. The Scots were now reported over the border and he wrote reassuringly to Cottington that this aggression had already caused the English to rally to the King's cause. Newcastle was to be relieved at once, and he himself, if his body would but equal his spirit, would be in the North before it came to serious action. He did not promise idly; two days later, travelling light, with only two servants, he joined the King at York. [19]

On the morning of August 27th, the next after his arrival, he called together such of the local gentry as were assembled at York, intending to make a last bid for support in his own county. The outlook was not hopeful; two of the members of Parliament arrested in May had been Yorkshiremen, and all through the summer protests against the expense of raising and supporting the army had poured into London, protests which significantly enough were addressed directly to the King — a calculated insult to Strafford, who was Lord Lieutenant of the shire. The reason they gave was that, through his long absences, he had 'grown a stranger to his country'. [20] In an address at once businesslike and firm he now urged them to do all in their power to assist the King. He emphasized what he himself believed — that the Scots took religion for a cover to disguise political ends. 'It is now no time of disputation', he told them, 'but of preparation and action'; at such a moment, it was little short of treason to refuse the King's service. 'I say it again, we are bound unto it by the Common Law of England, by the law of nature, and by the law of reason, and you are no better than beasts if you refuse in this case to attend the King, his Majesty offering in person to lead you on.' After the threat he descended to a more persuasive tone and ended with the promise in the King's name that if they gave their support now they should in future be eased of a great part of the military services to which they had been subject since the Armada. [21]

This meeting over, Strafford was for marching towards Newcastle. The Scots were nearly upon the town and Lord Conway with his army was making ready to contest the passage of the Tyne. He had urged Conway to hold the river at all costs, for if once the Scots crossed it panic might spread among the ill-trained English levies. If only he could join Conway himself he was sure that he could put the necessary valour into the men, but he was again very ill, and the King, fearing for his life, commanded him to stay in York for at least another two days. 'Dear my lord,' Strafford wrote to the vacillating general, 'take the advice of the best men and do something worthy yourself.' This letter dispatched, late on August 27th, he took to his bed and impatiently awaited news. [22]

The messenger rode to Conway's camp near Newburn and delivered his letter at a consultation of the general and his officers, but they shook their heads over it, for they had no heart to the war and their men as little. While the messenger awaited their decision outside the tent a soldier hurried in with news; suddenly all was in confusion and Colonel Goring, coming out of the tent in a crowd of officers, was heard loudly jibing that Strafford need have sent no orders to fight. The Scots had taken the matter into their own hands. [23]

It was true; they were crossing the Tyne. Independent of Conway's orders some of the English engaged them and got the worst of it. Conway ordered a retreat and when some of the cavalry tried to charge, the Scots turned it into a rout. The commissary-general, Lord Wilmot's son, was taken with many other officers, while fleeing stragglers streamed across the county of Durham spreading universal panic. [24]

All through the night of the 28th sweating horsemen galloped into York with news of the rout. Not until the following morning did Sir Arthur Aston ride in with an official message from Conway. In the Manor House at York he found the ante-chamber full of anxious courtiers, who drew back as he strode through; he heard indignant murmurs against his commander which showed him which way the wind blew. In the next room Strafford was in bed, propped up on pillows, haggard and sleepless. He hardly waited to greet Aston. Why had not Conway fortified Newcastle, he demanded; why had he not faced the enemy before they crossed the Tyne? Tired and angry, Aston suspected Strafford of making Conway into a scapegoat, and Conway was his friend. There had been no money to fortify Newcastle, he said shortly, and a battle in any circumstances must have been disastrous. At that moment Hamilton interrupted and Aston resentfully withdrew; he was convinced that Conway was to be victimized, and when Strafford sent for him again his humour was worse than before. Could Conway still hold the Tyne? Strafford fired at him. Very hardly, said Aston. Why not? demanded Strafford — could he not rally his men? Aston pointed out that since the Scots had crossed at Newburn there would not be time to make fortifications or bring up cannon to defend the right bank. Aston's agitation, by this, had convinced Strafford that the news was not merely a scare. He asked him one more question: did Aston advise bringing up the reinforcements to stiffen Conway's army or should they meet the Scots separately? After a little thought Aston advised the former. At once Strafford rose and called for his horse. [25]

By evening he reached Darlington, where he waited for the levies that were still to come in. On the following evening there were 11,000 foot and 1,500 horse in or about the town and more were expected; on August 31st he fell back with his troops to Northallerton and was there joined by Conway's retreating forces, all together a little short of seventeen thousand. Strafford gave orders that they were to hold the Yorkshire border against the Scots and in the meantime every Justice of the Peace in Durham was ordered to see the cattle driven off southwards and have the millstones broken or hidden against the coming of the enemy. [26] Two days were spent putting the army in order; the levies were dismayed by the rumours they heard and scared by the advent of the beaten troops, many of the officers discontented, rebellious and incompetent, and the Scots steadily advancing through an undefended country.

Strafford issued trenchant, decisive orders, harangued the men, and exhorted the officers to support him; discipline and training were all lacking. Meanwhile Hamilton, on whom he depended for the ships to bring over the Irish army, had made no move and Strafford waited in vain for the landing of his Irish troops in Scotland to make the planned, and now desperately needed, diversion in the rear. On the evening of the second long, hopeless day, alone in his room, his courage gave way; taking his pen he wrote upon a scrap of paper to Radcliffe. 'Cousin Radcliffe,' he scribbled:

> Pity me, for never came any man to so mightily lost a business. The army altogether unexercised and unprovided of all necessaries. That part which I bring now with me from Durham the worst I ever saw. Our horse all cowardly, the country from Berwick to York in the power of the Scots, an universal affright in all men, a general disaffection to the King's service, none sensible of his dishonour. In one word, here alone to fight with all these evils, without anyone to help. God of his goodness deliver me out of this, the greatest evil of my life. Fare you well. [27]

A violent attack of stone now hideously increased his troubles; tortured by pain and irritation, crossed every way by the sloth, unwillingness, or mere stupidity, of his officers, baffled by Hamilton, and distracted by the mismanagement and intrigues of courtiers and officials in York and at Whitehall, he strove furiously to assert his military authority and stiffen the army. Recalcitrant officers were arrested, plunderers hanged. He ordered the Earl of Newport to erect a gallows before each regiment's quarters as a salutary reminder to the men. Newport was an experienced soldier; as the son of the most famous of all Queen Elizabeth's generals in Ireland, the great Mountjoy, he probably found the pretensions of Strafford to military knowledge especially galling. He complained to the King. [28] But though Strafford gave offence and multiplied his enemies, under this hectoring treatment the beaten army does seem to have regained some appearance of order and discipline. In fairly good condition it fell back to York, where the trained bands of the county were now assembling to stiffen it. The King, reviewing his troops there on September 10th, was able to feel a renewed hope at the sight of them. [29] An untoward accident had, meanwhile, held up the advance of the Scots when the Earl of Haddington and a number of officers had been killed or injured in the explosion of a powder magazine at Dunglass. [30]

But the Council in London, who had the impossible task of raising money to keep this army in being, wrote ever more despondently. They put forward the idea that the King should revive yet another ancient custom and call, not a Parliament, but a Council of Peers. As Charles considered this at York, he received a petition from twelve English peers asking for a Parliament. 'Your whole Kingdom', they wrote, 'is become full of fear and discontent.' [31] Even he by this time was aware of this. The petitioners were, of course, chiefly the usual leaders of opposition in the Lords — Warwick, Essex, Saye and the rest — but they were also men of large possessions and far-reaching influence, who, alienated and angry as they now were, could easily shake his government. He had also had warning that the City of London intended to petition for a new Parliament. He decided therefore to summon a Council of Peers to York for September 24th, with hints — which soon crystallized into promises — of a Parliament in November.

This was not yet an act of despair. Both the King and Strafford had hopes. The calling of the Council and the promise of Parliament might stimulate the flow of contributions to the royal coffers and encourage the northern gentry to more energetic efforts in the war. Such a mood, coupled with the bitter plaints now coming from the plundered and occupied counties of Durham and Northumberland, might at last provoke a fighting spirit against the Scots. [32] A victory, even at this late season, might rally support to the government on the eve of the meeting of Parliament. This was the idea which enlivened the spirits of Strafford and his royal master in the early autumn of 1640, but they were both of them still most lamentably miscalculating on the religious issue. They could not accept the — admittedly unprecedented — truth that the majority of their countrymen did not want a victory against the Scots.

The Yorkshire gentry, faced with a demand for a month's more money for their troops, petitioned the King with an offer to pay only on condition that Parliament was called. Strafford, haranguing two hundred of them at York, refused to hand on the petition unless the Parliamentary clause was removed: the King was calling Parliament, he told them, and it did not behove them to demand it in this fashion. His attempt to ingratiate himself once more with them personally did not make, on all, the effect he hoped. He was 'for the most part extolling himself in terms of comparison before any other', wrote Sir Henry Slingsby. But he hinted at great reliefs to be offered them by the King, and when all but a very small vocal minority had agreed to drop the request for Parliament, he led them into the presence where Charles not only agreed in future to halve the military burdens of Yorkshire but made the even more welcome concession that, in the event of the death of any of them in the war, the Crown would renounce the wardship of their children. As this right of the Crown to grant the wardship of minors was a great source of revenue to the King and an even greater source of irritation and suffering to the landed gentry, the offer was gratefully received. To all appearances the gentry of Yorkshire were now the King's dutiful servants, prepared to meet the necessary charges for the next critical weeks. (33)

It might be that the tide was on the turn. The King, while Strafford used his persuasions on the Yorkshire gentry, called a Chapter of the Knights of the Garter and had Strafford elected. This was a very signal mark of his favour, done deliberately to show his faith in him, in spite of the ill-fortunes of the summer and Strafford's all too evident personal unpopularity. Strafford was led forward to receive the blue ribbon from the King by the Earl of Holland and the Marquis of Hamilton, men whom he greatly distrusted, but with whom he was now on terms of barbed and courtier-like friendship. (34) Little by little, in the anxieties and despairs of these last months, he had achieved the peak of his worldly ambitions — had become an Earl and Lord Lieutenant, and now a Knight of the Garter. Did he — could he — possibly deceive himself, if only for a few hours, that the clouds were lifting? It was a false hope: each of the four men who, that September day, played the chief parts in the ceremony — Holland, Hamilton, Strafford and the King himself — were to die within the next decade by the same Parliament and in the same manner.

A few days later a young professional soldier trained in the Spanish service, Captain John Smith, surprised and ignominiously defeated an over-confident party of Scottish raiders, bringing the commanding officer and a handful of prisoners to York. It was 'the only action redounding to his Majesty's honour and the credit of our nation, perform'd in all that service', (35) and for a few days after it a more hopeful spirit reigned in the King's army at York. But when the Council of Peers met on September 24th the dominant men in it were for a treaty with the Scots. Lord Bristol made himself so busy with messages to and from the Covenanters that Strafford sneeringly called him 'their Mercury'. [36] The first days of the Council were chiefly spent in arranging an armistice, choosing commissioners to negotiate a treaty, and selecting the place for the discussions.

There was a minor misunderstanding created by Lord Savile, son of Sir John Savile, the enemy of Strafford's youth. His zeal for peace and alliance with the Covenanters had impelled him to send them a letter suggesting a settlement to which he had appended the forged signatures of a number of English peers. These noblemen, though most of them in sympathy with the contents of the letter when they came to know it, were at first slightly taken aback by the evident assumption of the Covenanting leaders that they had undertaken to help them. The singular confusion was soon smoothed out, [37] and Commissioners were chosen on the English side, almost all of whom were personally hostile to Strafford as well as opposed to the King's policy of the last ten years.

The Covenanters refused to accept York as a suitable place for meeting the English Commissioners. This, all things considered, was reasonable. The King's army was in strength at York, and Strafford — known to be their bitter and reckless enemy — was the King's principal adviser there. It was possible that he might simply seize on them and hold them prisoners; he was known to have advised the arrest of their Commissioners in London earlier that summer. Furthermore, he had prosecuted their sympathizers in Ireland for treason. [38] For these reasons, the place ultimately chosen for the talks was the small cathedral town of Ripon; for this reason too it was evident that some kind of security against Strafford, which could only mean his removal from the King's councils, would inevitably be one of their demands.

The hesitations and suspicions of the Covenanters were however so prolonged as to make some of the English peers wonder if they were in earnest about the treaty. Strafford backed the doubters unobtrusively, but on September 28th Lord Bristol saw his drift and suddenly questioned him directly. If the Scots refused to come to York, would my lord of Strafford advise breaking off negotiations? Strafford hesitated. Bristol pressed him. If the armistice came to an end could the army fight? Strafford was for a moment at a loss and the King intervened, but in a minute he had regained his composure and took up Lord Bristol's questions. He was not for breaking off negotiations, but the King must stand upon honour and justice. As to the army's prospects he was caustic. 'I [have] the honour to be of his Majesty's Privy Council,' he said, 'yet I [am] not of the Almighty's Privy Council, to undertake to bespeak the event of war beforehand.' [39] He went on to give an account of the numbers and condition of the army, throwing the burden of decision back again upon the Peers. 'He explains all,' icily commented Lord Bristol, and Strafford resumed his seat in silence. [40] He had convinced no one that the war could be successfully prolonged.

But his hopes were not dead. The King had announced the date of the forthcoming Parliament for November 2nd, timing the announcement to coincide with the assembly of the Council of Peers, and with a further appeal to London for a loan. On October 6th a favourable answer from London reached York. With the two hundred thousand pounds that the City was now prepared to advance, Strafford argued, something could be done to repel the Scots. The arrogance of their demands, the large cash indemnity they were seeking, the victorious airs that they had assumed as they took possession of the counties of Durham and Northumberland, and the self-righteous tone of the official statements which they issued, had created a certain feeling against them in the Council. [41]

For a few days in this second week of October, Strafford seems seriously to have believed that the war could be resumed. He opened to George Radcliffe in Ireland a sinister scheme for the mass expulsion of all the Scots in Ulster in order to guard against any stab in the back from the Covenanters in that region. The plan, at once ferocious, confused, and exceptionally difficult to put into action, reads like a paranoiac fantasy. [42] Radcliffe when he got the letter refused to agree to the scheme, but by that time the war with the Covenanters had come to an end.

While Strafford feverishly planned impossible schemes, some of the peers in the Council also seemed inclined to oppose the Scots. Lord Herbert of Cherbury urged the King to fortify York, call off the treaty, and attack at once. There were a few others to whom these bolder actions seemed more pleasing than the idea of tamely accepting defeat at the hands of a traditional enemy. But the lack of reality in their advice was soon made evident by Lord Bristol and the King's level-headed opponents. The money promised by London had not been promised for the continuation of the war, but in hopes of peace and a Parliament. It would not be forthcoming on any other terms. The treaty negotiations continued, and after a preliminary agreement had been reached at Ripon, in the last week of October, the Scots were asked to send Commissioners to London to ratify the terms with Parliament. Meanwhile their army would continue in occupation of the northern counties at the expense of the English. [43]

For the closing days of the Council of Peers the King seemed to have abandoned Strafford. Six weeks before he had made him a Knight of the Garter; a fortnight before, even, he had seemed to command exceptional consideration from the King, while hostile courtiers complained of his dominating ways and were amazed at the King's forbearance. [44] In the last week of October, Charles appeared to change his tactics. He sent for Lord Clanricarde and listened for two hours to a wearisome argument between him and Strafford about the lands in Galway; at the end of it, he confirmed his grant to Clanricarde, and Strafford had to accept this final overruling of his own plans. [45]

The King's decision was wise in relation to Ireland, where Lord Clanricarde was to serve him faithfully in the darkening years to come. But it is possible that his reason for yielding to him at this moment had more to do with England than with Ireland. Clanricarde was half-brother on his mother's side to one of the most prominent of the opposition peers, the Earl of Essex. The King in his stumbling, obvious way was doing his best either to win his enemies or to quiet their suspicions.

At the Council of Peers, during its final sessions, Strafford was savagely baited, and the King did little or nothing to protect him. Lord Bristol openly accused him of having been the author of the war, with his empty promises of an Irish army which would defeat the Scots. And where was this vaunted army? Strafford wrathfully defended himself, saying that the army was waiting and ready, but no ships had been sent to transport it. His direction of the blame on to Hamilton, who had promised shipping, was not well taken by the King, who intervened in Hamilton's defence, and only the arrival of deputations from Cumberland and Lancashire, come unwillingly to pay the money demanded by the Scots, ended the acrimonious interchange. [46]

On the last day of all he came in for a double attack, being accused at one moment as an incendiary and at the next — with less justice — as a defeatist who was more responsible than any of the Commissioners who had negotiated with the Scots for the humiliating terms which had had to be accepted. He was now everybody's scapegoat — the evil councillor who had forced the King into his ill-advised war, and the incompetent general who had been responsible for the defeat. This time he did not lose his temper, but made a dignified and resigned speech in his own defence, and was able, when he described the scene to Radcliffe a few days later, to treat it almost with humour. [47]

These last days in York were painful to him for other reasons. As Lord President of the North, the office which he had held since 1630, and which he still held, he believed himself to have established an authority which was generally respected. But the events of the summer had shown him that the local gentry were as apt to oppose him as they had ever been and that his personal unpopularity had increased rather than abated in his absence. As the King's government weakened, latent opposition became active and silent critics grew vocal. When the writs went out for Parliament, Strafford made it clear which candidates he wanted returned both for the county and the city of York. All four were defeated, and this in spite of the presence of the King's soldiers, allegedly there to keep order. In the other Yorkshire boroughs the opponents of Strafford were in a considerable majority, though he managed — as he had done in his youth — to treat Pontefract as a family pocket-borough, and put in his brother George, and a cousin confusingly also called George Wentworth. His friends were successful at Richmond, which returned his staunch supporter Sir William Pennyman and another of his own kindred. But the defeats for the county and the city were cruelly indicative of the way in which his credit and reputation had sunk. Few had ever loved him, and now it seemed that they no longer feared him. It was said by some in York that his candidates failed not in spite of, but because of, his support. [48]

When the Council of Peers broke up, and the King was preparing to go south to open Parliament, it had at first been assumed that Strafford would stay in York in command of the army, proceeding to Ireland as soon as peace terms allowed him to do so. [49]

But as so often with King Charles he made a last minute change of plan. On the confused evidence that has survived it is impossible to say with certainty what went on in his quarters at York in the last forty-eight hours before he left. It had become clear during the Council of Peers that Strafford was the target of the general hatred. The Scots regarded him — as much as or even more than Archbishop Laud — as the incendiary who must be removed from the King's Council. In England he had become, popularly, a bogey figure — 'Black Tom '; and among the politically active and conscious — peers, gentry, merchants, lawyers — he had been singled out as the man responsible for a wicked and unnecessary war on the Scots which had ended in shame and defeat. From Ireland there were now rumours of a concerted attack on him.

Whether or not he had been responsible for the policy which led to the war (and in fact he had not), he was unquestionably the councillor responsible for the events of the summer, for the persistence in war after the Short Parliament failed, and thus, logically, for the disaster of the defeat. The King's opponents blamed him for the policy itself, and the King's friends were glad enough to blame him for its failure, loading on to his overburdened shoulders the results of their own omissions and errors. But some of them, among them Hamilton, had the grace to recognize the injustice by which they would be enabled to escape the consequences of their own mistakes. Hamilton sought him out and earnestly advised him to flee the country; later he said that Strafford had been 'too great-hearted' to act on such advice. The estimate was true, but it was only a part of the truth which lay behind Strafford's decision at this critical time.

After Hamilton had urged him to flee, and perhaps knowing that the suggestion had been made and had been rejected, the King sent for Strafford. He no longer wished him to stay with the army in the North; he wished him to come to Westminster and face the hostile Parliament. Whether the King and his minister had any clear or concerted plan of action is matter for conjecture. King Charles was never at any time given to long-term planning; he had, almost to the scaffold foot, a Micawber-like faith that something would turn up. It seems improbable that he had much more than this now.

But in the last year he had come to lean on Strafford, and although, in bald and dreadful truth, Strafford had given him the wrong advice and had failed to produce that glorious victory against the Scots which could alone have saved the royal government, he still trusted him, he still had confidence in him. Charles was slow to form his opinions, slower still to form his attachments; it had taken him a long time — far too long — to give his confidence to Strafford, and he still withheld the personal friendship that he had for other, lesser men. But there did undoubtedly now exist between the two men a bond of complete confidence. The King could not go to face the most critical Parliament of his career without Strafford to uphold and guide him.

It must also be attributed to Charles as a quality — if hardly a useful one in politics — that he was apt to favour his friends and servants most when fortune was against them. Buckingham he had loved from boyhood, but never more than when the whole country had turned on him. He was most confident of Hamilton when the evidences of his failure were most apparent. So later, in the Civil War, he would elevate his nephew Rupert to the highest command *after*, and not before, his catastrophic defeat at Marston Moor. So now with Strafford, it was as though his failure had made him indispensable in a way that his success had never done.

Later it was said that the plan cogitated between the King and Strafford was for turning the tables on Parliament by impeaching those members of Lords and Commons who could be shown to have corresponded with the Scots. But even the King, even Strafford, deaf as they were to public reactions, must have come to understand by the autumn of 1640 that corresponding with the Scots was a virtue in almost all eyes but their own. They can hardly have contemplated such an action as an opening move. It might conceivably be possible in some weeks' time if public opinion veered away from the Scots when their demands came to be discussed; but to attempt it in the present climate of opinion would have been such folly as even Charles could hardly commit. In the spring of that year, the King had made an attempt with the Short Parliament to blacken his opponents as friends of the

Scots, just as he had also tried to blacken the Scots for seeking allies abroad. These manoeuvres had failed to turn the strong current of public sympathy for the Covenanters. What hope could there be of turning it now that it had been running with increasing strength for so many months longer? (50)

It seems more probable that what the King and Strafford foresaw and planned was the logical continuation of what they had done at the Council of Peers. There, Strafford had drawn to himself all the odium for the King's policy and its failure. He would in all probability be impeached by Parliament and would thus again to a great extent draw off criticism from other men and other aspects of the royal policy. He had complete confidence in the rectitude of all he had done; he also had confidence in his ability to demonstrate this — given an open platform and freedom to argue his cause. Four years earlier the opponents of Ship-money had secured such a platform and freedom to argue their case when the King prosecuted Hampden. Hampden had not even won the case, but he and his lawyers had made the issues involved in Ship-money so well known that in the length and breadth of the country his example in refusing to pay had been widely applauded and widely followed.

Was this what Strafford had in mind? By answering the charges brought against him, clearly, openly, before all the world, with the logic and eloquence which he knew he could wield, would he in effect vindicate himself and the King's policy, to all those who made up the public opinion of England: the nobility and gentry, the lawyers in that urban warren between Holborn and the river, the merchants of London and the great sea-ports, the foolish mobs and the chimney-corner statesmen, the yeomen farmers, and the sea-captains, the schoolmasters, clergy, university scholars, the artisans and master-craftsmen, and all the rest who had seriousness enough to listen to a sermon or read a pamphlet, or wit enough to argue on matters of national importance with a neighbour over a pot of ale? Could he sway opinion back into the King's favour, as it had been so successfully swung away?

It was his abiding illusion that he could do this, and it was not perhaps wholly an illusion. He had swayed the Parliament of 1628; he had on occasion — if not always — impressed the gentry of Yorkshire and evoked the plaudits of the people of Ireland.

If he knew himself now to be the worst hated man in England — and he seems to have recognized the painful truth at last — he could not wipe out of recollection the events of the last ten years, the gratitude of the citizens of York in that fearful plague summer, the cheering multitudes who not so long ago had greeted his progress through Ireland. There must be some who thought of him with gratitude, or who could be won over by a frank account of his stewardship as he saw it, not as his enemies represented it.

This would seem to have been his likeliest course of action when the King asked him to come to London: to come prepared for an impeachment and ready to face and defeat it, in the King's name and his own.

The King was fully aware of the dangers to which this course exposed his faithful servant and he expressed his gratitude in terms which touched the vulnerable heart of Strafford. The Queen too, it seems, had added messages of the most flattering kind. [51] Of one thing Charles seems to have felt able most strongly to assure the minister — that he need not fear either for his life or his fortune. The blows that he would have to bear would, if they struck home, at worst damage his reputation and perhaps necessitate his withdrawal from power. In the ultimate resort the King would not let him perish.

Strafford cannot wholly have trusted the King's word. He had seen enough of his vacillations, even in better times, to build relatively little on such a promise. But did he really know, when he agreed to come to London, that he was gambling with his life? He may have done so. Certainly his last request to the King, that he might have two or three days' leave to set his affairs in order at Woodhouse, [52] suggests that he knew his journey to London might be his last.

Late at night on November 2nd he came to his home. [53] Far away from his public responsibilities and his friends, he could be at peace for three days, drinking in the still autumn air, seeing once again the woods and streams and pastures, the hills over which he had ridden in his early manhood, passing for the last time among men and women who had known him and his father and grandfather before him as masters of this land, tenants, dependants and servants of the family, who had taken an intimate and local pride to see him cleave his way through to rule the nation.

In those days he had much to think of. His political and his personal fortunes were inextricably bound up with each other. All through the summer he had been using his personal credit — £4,000 borrowed here on the strength of his interest in the alum mines, £6,000 on the tobacco farm; he had also used whatever cash he had in hand, to meet the needs of the King's army. At one time he was writing to Radcliffe to send or bring money from his coffers in Ireland to make good what he had currently borrowed in Yorkshire out of the recusants' fines; [54] and for one such transaction of which we have evidence there must have been many more of which no evidence remains. The confusion in his private and public accounts must by now have been dizzying even to so clear a head as his. But looked at from the financial point of view alone, what he had done in the last year was to stake his private fortune on the success of the King's policy. If, by taking this final risk, he could redeem the King's position, he would also consolidate his own now desperately threatened fortune. He took this final risk — the risk certainly of reputation, and possibly of life — out of loyalty to his sovereign; but also in some degree for his own and his children's sake. Others of the King's supporters were then and later to flee abroad taking what could be saved of their gains, which was by no means always negligible. But for Strafford, who had laboriously and proudly built a fortune, who had counted much on the rich dowries he would give his daughters and the glorious position that his only son would inherit, such a flight would have seemed disastrous, an abdication not only from power but from all that power had brought to him and his, a renunciation not only of his own position, but of the position he had built for his children. It was not in his obstinate and tenacious character to abandon the King, or the policy in which he had believed, or the fortune he had first accumulated in the King's service and then risked to maintain the King's power. Questions of principle and of profit were equally involved in this last perilous decision. The gesture he now made in going towards this last and worst trial had something of classical grandeur and noble sacrifice; but it was also a calculated risk, like the last gamble of some master-financier, staking much to save all. 'I would carry it or lose all,' he had said at the Council table in May. It was still his mood, and in every sense, if he did not now carry it, he would lose all.

307

On the evening of November 5th he wrote to George Radcliffe. He told him all that had passed at York, and that he must now go south to join the King.

I am tomorrow to London, with more danger beset, I believe, than ever man went with out of Yorkshire; yet my heart is good and I find nothing cold within me.... (55)

What he hoped, Strafford hardly knew himself, but this was certain: he feared nothing, as, early on a November morning, he rode away from Woodhouse on the road for London.

NOTES

[1] *C.S.P.D.*, 1640, pp. 112-13.

[2] *C.S.P.Ven.*, 1640-2, pp. 44-5.

[3] Ibid., p. 47; H.M.C., VII, ii, p. 56; Rushworth, II, ii, p. 1177.

[4] Rushworth, II, ii, p. 1182.

[5] Ibid., p. 569; see also the King's declaration on the dissolution of Parliament, Rushworth, II, ii, pp. 1160-7.

[6] *C.S.P.D.*, 1640, pp. 215, 306; *Radcliffe Letters*, p. 199; Carte, I, p. 100; Rushworth, II, ii, p. 1203.

[7] Shirley, *Works, ad*: Dyce, VI, pp. 428-9.

[8] *C.S.P.D.*, 1640, p. 278; Rushworth, II, ii, p. 991.

[9] Rushworth, II, ii, p. 1216; Rushworth, *Trial*, pp. 590 ff.

[10] *C.S.P.Ven.*, 1640-2, pp. 50, 53.

[11] H.M.C., III, p. 82; XIII, p. 3; *C.S.P.Ven.*, 1640-2, p. 45.

[12] Brathwaite, *Barnabae Itinerarium*, ed. Haslewood, London, 1820, I, p. xxxvi.

[13] *Commons Journals, Ireland*, I, p. 248.

[14] *Commons Journals, Ireland*, I, pp. 248-55; Whitaker, pp. 249-51; Kearney, pp. 189-91.

[15] *C.S.P.D.*, 1640, p. 588.

[16] Ibid., p. 591.

[17] Ibid., p. 601.

[18] *Camden Miscellany*, IX, IV, p. 13.

[19] *Radcliffe Letters*, p. 203; *C.S.P.D.*, 1640, p. 627.

[20] Reid, p. 433; Slingsby, p. 57.

[21] Rushworth, II, ii, p. 1235.

[22] *C.S.P.D.*, 1640, p. 642; Knowler, II, p. 413.

[23] Rushworth, II, ii, p. 1236.

[24] Ibid., pp. 1237-8.

[25] *C.S.P.D.*, 1640, pp. 646 ff.

[26] Ibid., p. 649; Rushworth II, ii, p. 1240.

[27] The usual version of this letter is in *Radcliffe Letters*, pp. 203-4; Lord Birkenhead found Strafford's original at Belvoir Castle and published it in his *Strafford*, p. 257. I have used this version.

[28] *Lismore Papers*, Series II, IV, p. 146.

[29] *C.S.P.D.*, 1640-1, p. 47.

[30] Ibid., p. 5.

[31] Rushworth, II, ii, pp. 1260-2.

[32] Ibid., pp. 1271-2.

[33] Rushworth, *Trial*, pp. 614 ff; Slingsby, pp. 57-8; *C.S.P.D.*, 1640-1, pp. 56-7.

[34] *C.S.P.D.*, 1640-1; pp. 48, 57.

[35] Walsingham, *Britannicae Virtutis Imago*, Oxford, 1644, pp. 7-8.

[36] *Radcliffe Letters*, p. 214.

[37] Rushworth, II, ii, pp. 1261 ff, 1276 ff.

[38] Ibid., p. 1293.

[39] *Radcliffe Letters*, p. 214.

[40] *Hardwicke State Papers*, II, pp. 230 ff.

[41] Ibid., pp. 241, 248.

[42] *Radcliffe Letters*, pp. 206 ff.

[43] *Hardwicke State Papers*, pp. 246-8, 256; Rushworth, II, ii, p. 1306.

[44] *Lismore Papers*, Series II, IV, p. 146.

[45] *C.S.P.D.*, 1640-1, p. 197; *Radcliffe Letters*, pp. 205-6.

[46] *Hardwicke State Papers*, II, pp. 280 ff; H.M.C. Report, X, pt VI, p. 137.

[47] *Hardwicke State Papers*, II, pp. 293 ff; Rushworth, II, ii, p. 1309; *Radcliffe Letters*, p. 217.

[48] Keeler, *The Long Parliament*, pp. 74, 75-6; *C.S.P.D.*, 1640-1, p. 158.

[49] *Radcliffe Letters*, pp. 215-16.

[50] Rushworth and others make it clear that there were rumours in London of some plan to arrest the King's opponents, but the only evidence that such a thing was contemplated by the King and Strafford are the memoirs of the Earl of Manchester (British Museum, Additional MSS, 15, 567) and the *History* of Archbishop Laud. Manchester's memoirs were written apparently after 1649, and those of Laud in the Tower two or three years after the events he is describing. Manchester's account is so vague about dates and even about events that I cannot find his evidence convincing. He no doubt heard the rumour that an arrest was planned, and so crystallized it into a fact. He would not have been in a position, in November 1640, to know the inner secrets of the Court. Laud's comment is even stranger, for he *would* have been in a position to know, yet he records the plan to arrest the King's opponents in a way that shows that he also knew nothing at first hand. The matter may have been, probably was, discussed between the King and Strafford. I find it very hard to believe that any such *coup* was agreed upon or in readiness for execution. It was naturally to the interest of the King's opponents to stimulate and give substance to any rumours of a *coup* in order to enhance the atmosphere of suspicion surrounding Strafford. See a discussion of this question between Mr J. P. Cooper and the present writer in *History To-Day*, V, pp. 307, 485.

[51] *Radcliffe Letters*, pp. 218-19.

[52] H.M.C., *Ormonde MSS*, II, p. 2.

[53] *Camden Miscellany*, IX, IV, p. 13.

[54] *C.S.P.I.*, 1633-47, p. 245; *Radcliffe Letters*, p. 206.

[55] *Radcliffe Letters*, p. 214.

CHAPTER THREE

THE IMPEACHMENT

Yet all shall be laid on my shoulders, the matter is not great, they were made to bear and I to suffer.

Wentworth to Laud, August 1638

IT seemed later that Strafford had walked with open eyes to his death, and contemporaries looking back on past events called him saintlike or foolhardy as their politics dictated. he Troyalist Hamon Lestrange declared that 'his repair to London was in effect a rendering up of himself captive to the will of his deadliest enemies' but 'he was opinionated of his own innocence, and innocence usually makes men bold and daring.' Clarendon, who was an active member of the House of Commons during the whole drama of Strafford's arrest, impeachment and trial, thought that he had acted out of sheer contempt of the people's anger or the machinations of his enemies. One sympathetic observer at the time said that he was 'under the same necessity that was enjoined upon our Saviour: somebody must be sacrificed to appease the people and he is thought the fittest.' [1]

Strafford had time to consider his policy as he rode to London. In the darker time of year and the still painful state of his health he travelled more slowly than he had done in August. On Sunday night, November 8th, at Huntingdon news reached him of the doings in Parliament, which had been sitting for the past week. He seems to have been neither surprised nor perturbed to hear that his enemies in Ireland had already begun the attack. Complaints brought before the Commons had caused them to go into a committee of the whole House on Irish affairs. There had been some opposition to this and the House had divided, those who wanted to discuss Irish affairs getting their way by 165 votes to 152. [2] If Strafford knew these figures that Sunday night at Huntingdon, they would give him some confidence that there was at least a substantial neutral minority in the House. He also found the character of the complaints from Ireland more reassuring than otherwise. There was nothing that he could not answer, and his whole Parliamentary strategy now was to challenge, and then refute, accusation. In this way he could steadily rebuild his own reputation and that of the King's government, while undermining the confidence and destroying the supports of the opposition.

He had kept open the letter he had written to Radcliffe three nights before at Woodhouse, and now added an almost buoyant postscript:

> To the best of my judgment we gain much rather than lose. I trust God will preserve us; and as all other passions I am free of fear, the articles that are coming I apprehend not. The Irish business is past, and better than I expected, their proofs being very scant. God's hand is with us, for what is not we might expect to have been sworn from thence? ... All will be well and every hour gives more hope than other. God Almighty protect and guide us. [3]

When he reached London on the evening of November 10th, Parliament had been sitting for a little over a week and the leadership of the Commons, as in the previous April, had been assumed by John Pym, one of the members for the Devonshire borough of Tavistock. Before Parliament met, Pym had talked seriously to Edward Hyde, the member for Saltash. 'They must be of another temper than they were the last Parliament,' he had said, 'they must not only sweep the house clean below, but must pull down all the cobwebs which hung in the tops and corners, that they might not breed dust and so make a foul house hereafter.' Pym had sat in every Parliament since 1614, when he and Wentworth had both been newcomers. He had seen Eliot involve two Parliaments in catastrophe, and had seen Wentworth come within an inch of leading one to success. He had learnt from both of them much about how to manage or mismanage the Commons, and as his words to Hyde most clearly showed, he knew this time that speed and ruthlessness would pay.

The anger of the Commons at the May dissolution had smouldered ever since, now to burst forth in flames. The difficulties experienced by the King and his supporters in getting their candidates returned were an indication — if more was needed — of the weakness and unpopularity of the government. Strafford had seen it at close quarters in Yorkshire, where his nominees had been defeated.[4] There had been other Court defeats. Sir Edward Nicholas, secretary to the Council of War, and another of the royal clerical staff — Windebanke's nephew and right-hand man — had failed to secure seats, thus robbing the government of informed and useful support. Worst of all, the royalist candidates for the City of London had been defeated, among them Thomas Gardiner, the Recorder, whom Charles had hoped to have elected for Speaker. Certain other courtiers and royalists who had obtained seats would, within the first few weeks, be excluded on technical or other grounds by a Committee of Privileges dominated by Pym and his supporters. Among these would be two more of Strafford's nominees — Sir Edward Osborne and his nephew Sir William Savile, who, after being rejected in Yorkshire, had been accommodated with seats elsewhere.

Very noticeable were the number of members with connections in Ireland. Lord Cork's eldest son and two sons-in-law; Lord Wilmot's son; Sir William Jephson, a Munster landowner; and Sir John Clotworthy, an Ulster landowner of strongly Presbyterian sympathies who had several times crossed Strafford's will in the past. This dour and heartless man was evidently an important link — and had probably been so for some time — between the English opposition to the King and the opponents of Strafford in Ireland. His election had been contrived, by the influence of the Earl of Warwick, in two separate boroughs.[5]

With Parliament so well filled with Strafford's enemies, the country at large vented its rage equally on the Archbishop and the clergy. When Laud, entering his study at Lambeth, found his portrait had fallen from the wall during the night, it was small wonder that he took it for an omen.[6] As graciously as he could in these distracting circumstances, the King had opened Parliament on November 3rd. Lord Keeper Finch had the difficult task of explaining to the assembly why it had been called. In the face of open hostility the poor little man, who well remembered how the Commons had used him in 1629 when he was their Speaker, bleated inconsequently of the virtues of the royal family, of the Scots war and the King's necessities. They must remember, he told them, that not one man but the whole body of the wise Privy Council had voted for the war. Nervous for his own life and fortune, because his subservience to the Crown had given him a deplorable reputation, Finch thus injudiciously attempted to spread the blame for the King's policy. It was an error, for, given the present temper of the Commons and the Londoners, no member of the Privy Council now felt immune from insult. In their timorous anxiety they longed for Strafford's audacious firmness to shield them all. [7]

The Commons wasted little time. Inspired petitions poured in from the counties complaining of the war; petitions came in, too, from the emboldened victims of the King's government, and the Commons at once set up committees to inquire into their cases. A few days later an order was passed for the exclusion of all monopolists from the House; it meant the removal of twelve of the King's supporters. [8]

Meanwhile Pym, without yet naming Strafford, was preparing the ground for the attack. When the Irish complaints began to come in, Pym asserted that 'all the subjects of Ireland have power to come here' — a welcome dictum to every 'great one' who had been under Strafford's jurisdiction in Dublin and had failed to get a judgment against him reversed by the King. [9] Mountnorris was before the Committee for Irish affairs with the tale of his wrongs on the very first day that it met. [10] Wilmot and Loftus would soon follow.

Pym had made himself leader and spokesman of the Commons in an admirable oration on the morning of November 7th. In this speech he had picked up the complaints made in a number of petitions that had come in from different parts of the country against the clergy, the Commission Court, the unnecessary war on Scotland and all the disorders it had brought. He spoke briefly of Ireland, which he said had been governed in 'a fiery and violent form which might in turn be a pattern to England'; [11] he indicated that the army, raised by this fiery and violent government, might have been intended to quell the English. Next day, in the Committee on Ireland, Sir John Clotworthy made his first contribution to the coming attack. He spoke with great and bitter conviction of the persecution of the true Protestants in Ulster for opposing the bishops and sympathizing with the Scots. The Irish Papists were left alone, he said; only true Protestants were persecuted. As for the new Irish army, it was wholly composed of Papists; moreover it was cherished and regularly paid while the original standing army, largely Protestant, was neglected and slighted. No one challenged these facts. [12]

The Commons had now been given a fearful if rather vague picture of an armed, Popish tyranny in Ireland. It remained to link this menace with the idea of Popish plots and threats of military violence nearer home.

On the morning of November 10th the Yorkshire gentry presented a petition complaining of the Laudian forms of worship and of the expenses of the recent war. One of Strafford's few supporters, Sir William Strickland, objected to it but was instantly silenced by the Puritan, Philip Stapleton. [13] This might have been the signal for an open attack on Strafford, but Pym seems to have been unwilling yet to name him. He waited until the following day, and by then Strafford himself was in London.

John Pym was a master of timing. This is apparent repeatedly in the three years during which he dominated the Parliament which reshaped the government of England. To take the right decision was important: to act on it at the right moment was equally important. The decision to impeach Strafford must have been taken by Pym and his ring of supporters in Lords and Commons as soon as they knew that Parliament was to be called. It was evident from their conduct that they had already a very clear idea of the evidence they wanted to use. But at what moment should the attack be launched? They cannot have been altogether sure that Strafford would come to London. If he did not, and was impeached in his absence, much of the force of the procedure would be lost, and he would have no difficulty in escaping abroad where he might live to be avenged. It was therefore in all probability welcome news to Pym that he was on his way southward. But once he reached London, the attack would have to be swift and effective. Strafford's presence would hearten the King's supporters in both Houses; whether or not Pym believed in the possiblity of a military *coup*, he knew that Strafford's energy and courage were to be feared: and that nothing and no one else in the King's party was to be feared.

Strafford reached London late on the evening of November 10th. On the 11th one of the London members opened the day's proceedings in the Commons by reading out an account of the number of guns and troops in the Tower of London, together with a hearsay story that Strafford had spoken of shortly subduing the City. One of the Court members vainly tried to quiet the stir made by this announcement by saying that the guns and soldiers were merely in readiness for a review by the King prior to their disbandment. Pym, who wanted the stir increased rather than quieted, added to the atmosphere of suspicion and fear by reminding the House of a wild rumour of a Popish plot, started by a woman named Anne Hussey a few weeks back; Secretary Windebanke, he implied had been extremely negligent about the investigation of this business.

Fear of armed force and of popery being thus established, Sir John Clotworthy rose to make the astonishing revelation that Sir George Radcliffe in the previous May had said that the King, with the help of the Irish army, could 'have what he pleaseth in England'. From an accusation of Sir George Radcliffe, the known friend, the 'creature', of Strafford, it was but a step to the archenemy himself. Clotworthy's speech was the overture to the open attack on Strafford, an attack which, time and again, came round to Popish plots, to the guns and men at the Tower, to the alleged threat of bringing an Irish army into England; an attack which was punctuated by further comments on the ill-behaviour of Secretary Windebanke in trying to hush up a Popish plot, and made more secret and sinister by a decision to lock the doors of the House against interruption. [14]

Strafford had taken his seat in the Lords that morning, but he had not spoken or otherwise signalized his dominating presence. The matter under discussion, in the calmer atmosphere of the Upper House, was the treaty with the Scots. At some point in the morning, messengers were sent to the Commons to require a joint conference in the afternoon. It was believed by some in the Commons that this message was a subterfuge to find out what was going on behind their locked doors. [15] Whether it was or not, at about this time Strafford seems to have realized that the attack on him had begun. He left his seat and drove to Whitehall.

The Commons under Pym's guidance had by this time resolved to accuse him to the Lords of High Treason and to demand his immediate restraint and sequestration from the House. Only Lord Falkland made a momentary stand, protesting that it would be wiser to examine the evidence before proceeding to so grave a step. In the general atmosphere of plot and panic, it was easy for Pym to overrule this objection. The evidence would all be examined in time: the first essential was to remove Strafford from the King's right hand. The Committee elected to draw up the preliminary charges made short work, and by the afternoon were ready to go up to the Lords.

Strafford was at Whitehall closeted with the King. Pym sent a message to the Lords informing them that the Commons wished to wait on them with an important communication. One of the loyal peers left his seat and hurried across the gardens of Westminster to the palace; he found Strafford still with the King. What he had suggested or what had been agreed during their last interview is unknown. It was said that when the messenger arrived with news of the impeachment, there was general consternation among the King's friends. Strafford alone, 'with a composed confidence', said simply: 'I will go and look mine accusers in the face.' He hoped to reach the Lords before Pym, and to be in his place to answer when he was accused. He hastened from the palace and drove with all speed to Westminster, but Pym had already left the House of Commons with his supporters at his heels and Strafford's coach drew in at the outer gateway as he entered the House of Lords.

Pym declared that the Commons of England accused Thomas Wentworth, Earl of Strafford, Lord Lieutenant of Ireland, of High Treason. The Lords had expected no less and agreed to consider the charge while Pym withdrew. Now came Strafford hastening through the group of waiting Commons before the doorway. As he advanced to his place a cry rose along the benches, 'Withdraw! Withdraw!' With 'a proud, glooming countenance' he moved on while the cry grew louder and some of the peers rose to their feet to stop him. Then he stood still, asking for an explanation. Pym's message was read to him and the Lord Keeper told him he must withdraw pending the Lords' decision. Slowly he turned and retraced his steps.

Outside in the lobby the Commons were waiting; busybodies stared and whispered, pointing, passing to and fro in front of him unbowing, their hats on their heads. It lasted perhaps ten minutes, then the peers called him back. He was brought to the bar and told to kneel. He obeyed in silence and the Earl of Manchester read him the formal intimation of the Commons' charge. He learnt that he was to be sequestered from the House and placed in confinement until the hearing of the cause. Rising he protested against the unprecedented severity of this measure and asked leave to speak; Manchester informed him that he could reach the ear of the Lords only by petition. Slowly he moved away, bareheaded and stooping, between the long lines of his peers, seeing no one, saluting no one; while Lord Cork, his hat pulled firmly upon his brows, stared at him in unconcealed triumph.

Outside the House of Lords, the loiterers were still waiting. Maxwell, the Gentleman Usher of the Black Rod, stepped forward and demanded his sword. Strafford ungirded it without a word and Maxwell before the crowd of onlookers shouted to his servant to take it. 'What is the matter?' some of the gaping multitude mocked the prisoner. 'A small matter, I warrant you,' he answered, and passed on, while closing in on his heels they jeered, 'Yes, indeed! High treason is a small business.' He passed through them as best he could to the outer door but his coach was not at hand, and he must turn back once again 'through a world of gazing people' to another door. He had stepped down towards his coach when Maxwell once more intervened. 'Your lordship,' he said, 'is my prisoner and must go in my coach.' And in Maxwell's coach, at last, he left Westminster, driving slowly through the gathering crowds, 'all gazing, no man capping to him, before whom that morning the greatest of England would have stood discovered'. (16)

That night from his temporary prison in Maxwell's house he wrote to his wife in Ireland.

Sweetheart,

You have heard before this what hath befallen me in this place, but be you confident that if fortune is to be blamed, yet I will not by God's help be ashamed. Your carriage upon this misfortune, I should advise to be calm, not neglective of my trouble, and yet so as there may appear no dejection in you. Continue on the family as formerly, and make much of your children. Tell Will, Nan and Arabella I will write to them by the next. In the meantime I shall pray for them to God that he may bless them, and for their sakes deliver me out of the furious malice of my enemies, which yet, I trust through the goodness of God shall do me no hurt.

God have us all in his blessed keeping. Your very loving husband, Strafford. (17)

Pym was working with all his energy. That it would come to a duel of wits between him and Strafford was clear to him; Strafford's calm after his arrest showed that he was confident the Commons would trip up on the impeachment. A failure to substantiate the charges would be a setback for Pym and his followers from which they would not easily recover. Such a failure had caused the breakdown of the Parliament led by Sir John Eliot in 1626. This precedent must have been often in the minds of both Pym and Strafford.

Pym was taking a very considerable risk, because the chances of failure were large. But he had to take the risk, because Strafford was the only minister the King had whose ability was really dangerous. His management of the Irish Parliament in 1634, his attempts to play off the House of Lords against the House of Commons in the spring of 1640, his tactics at the Council of Peers — these and many other things, besides his original leadership of the Commons in 1628, bore witness to his skill in political management if he were given the least advantage. His ruthlessness and vigour had also to be reckoned with. As long as he remained alive, he was a potential danger. This could not now be said of any of the King's other councillors, not even of the Archbishop, who was old and had lost all hope and energy.

If Pym and his associates were to bring the King's policy under their control, and this was the purpose of their actions, they must eliminate Strafford. Only by doing this could they be sure not only that Parliament would gain the initiative in the direction of policy, but that it would also maintain it. It is not really to be doubted that John Pym thought himself morally as well as politically right in marking out Strafford for destruction. But he was also well aware that the means he would have to use were questionable. It was in the first place extremely difficult to work out charges against him which, in law, amounted to High Treason. This being the case, it was essential to create an atmosphere of tension, so that men could be constantly reminded of the extreme wickedness of

318

Strafford and of the danger of letting him live. Idiotic statements like that from one scared Member of Parliament that Strafford was a notorious tool of the Jesuits [18] were wholly welcome to Pym. He could also rely on the members for London to stir the City from time to time into a ferment. Moreover, in less than a week from Strafford's impeachment, Pym was already taking steps to insure against any failure to prove him legally guilty of High Treason. He was investigating the ancient and terrible form of procedure known as Attainder. [19] An act of Attainder was simply a method of condemning a man to death by act of Parliament, regardless of how his case might stand in law: the atrocious practice had been developed in England during the Wars of the Roses, and had fallen into disuse in the past century.

On November 12th Denzil Holles resigned from the committee for drawing the charge. He had realized that Pym was out for Strafford's life; deeply as he abhorred Strafford's politics, the judicial murder of his sister's husband was more than he could stomach. Sir Walter Erle and John Hampden were co-opted in his place.

On November 13th George Radcliffe was impeached and a warrant sent to Ireland for his arrest. He would have been Strafford's chief witness, and this was the simplest way to silence him. Orders went out that all letters, records, petitions and papers connected with Strafford were to be laid open to the committee. On the 18th, members of Parliament were forbidden to visit him without licence or to tell him what went forward in the House. On the 19th, a request for bail was refused, and on the 20th, Pym approached the House of Lords with the demand that Privy Councillors might be examined to substantiate the charges. [20] His purpose was to get evidence of what had happened at the meeting immediately after the dissolution in May. The position for him and his colleagues was delicate. Young Vane had found and privily communicated to them his father's rather incoherent notes of that meeting. From these it looked as though Strafford had talked of bringing over the Irish army. But it would be difficult to use the notes as evidence without indicating that they had been more or less stolen. What Pym hoped to do was to get damaging admissions from Privy Councillors, and especially from Sir Harry Vane, by asking them leading questions about that critical session. [21]

This demand to examine Privy Councillors should have given the King an opportunity to work up resistance in the House of Lords. It was, truly, an outrageous demand since it meant that things said in the highest council of the Kingdom, on the most private and vital affairs, were no longer privileged. Considering the large number of Privy Councillors in the Lords, it could have been made into an issue. But here Strafford's personal character did him and his cause an ill-service. During his months of supreme power he had lost friends, not made them. Northumberland and Newcastle were now alienated; Leicester was no longer friendly; Clanricarde (Earl of St Albans, in the English house) hated him; so did the Earls of Newport and Holland, the Earl of Arundel, and of course all the opposition peers. Those who pleaded privilege and the secrecy of the King's Councils were easily outvoted, and Pym gained a first and notable advantage against his adversary. (22)

On November 21st Audley Mervyn, a member of the Irish Parliament, appeared with a remonstrance from Dublin. That House of Commons which in March had cheered him to the echo and voted him a second Solon and the best governor Ireland had ever known, had now voted a series of charges against him which accused him of every kind of tyranny, oppression and injustice, and stated that Ireland, once a smiling prosperous land, was now — thanks to him — in such 'extreme and universal poverty' as never before in her history. Strange things had indeed been happening in Dublin. Poor Christopher Wandesford, as Lord Deputy, exerted no control at all; he had managed to prorogue the House, but not until *after* the Remonstrance had been voted. It was the work of the strong Protestant settler party, but with some support (and more neutrality) among the Catholics. It was inspired no doubt by knowledge of the expected impeachment in England and organized by that group whose chief representative in the English Commons was Sir John Clotworthy. The Speaker and all the government spokesmen in the Commons had been taken entirely by surprise when it was brought forward. George Radcliffe had tried to raise questions on it, but among tumultuous cries from its supporters, it was rushed through without a debate. (23)

The Remonstrance, duly sent by the English Parliament to the King, was sent by him to Strafford for an answer. The group of Councillors who brought it was headed by Archbishop Laud, but

Lord Cork was of their number. Strafford answered the charge lucidly and without anger, suggesting that some investigation should be made before these statements were accepted as true. The reaction of the Irish House of Commons to this was the rather astonishing statement that they had a right to be believed, and that it would be illegal to make any investigation of the truth of their Remonstrance. A little later, possibly realizing that this assertion could be double-edged, they solemnly protested that the famous words in which they had once praised Strafford had been surreptitiously inserted into the preamble of the subsidy bill last March, without the knowledge of any of them. [24]

Thirteen days after Strafford's arrest, and three after the arrival of the Irish Remonstrance, on November 24th, 1640, Pym placed the articles of Strafford's impeachment before the House. He may have been nervous. Symonds d'Ewes reports: 'He spake low and I heard him not.' [25] Much of the day was spent in voting on these articles. By the following morning they had been submitted to the Lords and that same afternoon Strafford was brought to hear them. He listened attentively, asking at the end that he might have time to consider his answer, and leave to consult counsel and call witnesses, and if he might know the names of those the Commons intended to produce against him. Such questions, he was informed, could only be decided on petition. [26] When he left the House of Lords he was taken in a closed coach through derisive crowds to the Tower of London. [27]

The Earl of Strafford entered the Tower in outward form like any other fallen minister. He was sequestered from his seat in Parliament, from all his offices and from the Privy Council. But, like no other minister, while in the Tower awaiting his trial for High Treason he was still the power behind the Crown. Browbeaten by the recalcitrant Lords, bullied by the Commons, broken by the Scots, the King still relied on Strafford. It was an extraordinary situation: the King, under whose government the prosecution acted, still looked for help and advice to the minister he could not save from the Tower.

On the very day of Strafford's commitment the Lord Keeper had gained permission to carry messages between him and the King, [28] and such messages official or unofficial passed ceaselessly. Visitors from the Houses of Lords and Commons had to get permission to see the prisoner and to promise to reveal nothing, but permission was always given and the promise, to judge by results, usually broken. The Lords, to counteract the influence of these go-betweens, at length forbade any visitors to see the prisoner after dark. [29] With the winter coming on this was a serious check on the actions of Strafford's friends.

Parliament raced ahead in its onslaught on the defeated government. 'Reformation goes on ... as hot as toast', wrote an observer. 'I pray God the violent turning of the tide do not make an inundation.... The Parliament men would not receive the communion at St Margaret's, Westminster ... before the rails were pulled down and the communion table was removed into the middle of the chancel.' [30] This did but indicate the temper of the country. The Scots had shown the English the way by declaring war on the unpopular bishops, and the Puritans of both countries now joined hands to make good their victory. At Ipswich, Sudbury and Great Marlow the altar railings were pulled down, while the Londoners received Prynne, Burton and Bastwick with jubilant rejoicings and a few days later presented a monster petition for the abolition of episcopacy, root and branch. On December 18th Laud himself was accused, sequestered from the Upper House, and confined as Strafford had been by the Usher of the Black Rod. 'God is making here a new world', wrote the Covenanter Baillie, [31] his heart overflowing with gratitude.

All this while, hardly a voice was raised in the Commons to defend the King, his ministers, or his bishops. The fierceness with which any dissident member was quelled by the dominating party was one reason for this. But Pym had also pushed through the excited Commons in the first flush of their indignation a series of measures that effectively curbed the King's party. While petitions against exactions and levies were daily coming in, Pym moved and passed a resolution to deal with every sheriff and Justice of the Peace who had taken part in these exactions. Only afterwards did the more moderate Commons realize that this affected half the House itself, and all the King's friends. Already monopolists had been expelled. For fear of like treatment no man who had been a sheriff or justice dared lift up his voice against the extremists lest the threatened inquiry should be enforced. On December 7th the illegality of Ship-money was warmly agreed on by a House where many members had officially exacted the tax three years before. [32]

Meanwhile a wit had scrawled over the door of St Stephen's an exhortation to 'remember the judges'. They were not forgotten; all those who had supported the royal government were placed under arrest, one of them was even seized while trying a case in Westminster Hall. On December 21st Lord Keeper Finch was impeached; he fled the country that night.

Rumours of an international Popish plot still hung in the air, and when a crazy Jesuit stabbed a Justice of the Peace in Westminster Hall every member of the Queen's party went in terror of his life. Secretary Windebanke fled with the King's permission on the night of December 5th. When he reached the coast there was a thick fog and no ship would sail for him; he put out in an open boat and had himself rowed across the Channel.

By the New Year the general excitement showed signs of narrowing on to the immediate issue of Strafford's trial, and the news he himself obtained must have encouraged him. The Commons and the Lords were already galling each other slightly. The examination of the witnesses caused the first crack in the alliance: the Commons insisted that they must have their representatives present when the Lords examined witnesses, but the Lords stiffly remembered that the accused was a peer of the realm, and there was talk of privilege. But in the end they gave in. [33]

Strafford had petitioned to be allowed counsel; on this point the Lords did not finally decide though they settled upon seven lawyers who might help him in drawing up his answer if they wished to. [34] It was a test of courage, for every apprentice in London knew that the lawyers were under no obligation, and therefore, if they went to Strafford's help, it was because they believed in his cause. Not one of them failed.

Apart from these graces the Lords had little mercy on their prisoner and, except where they scented an attack on privilege, not only gave the Commons their way but even encouraged them. Early in December they ordered Sir William Balfour, the Lieutenant of the Tower, to have the Earl of Strafford confined to three rooms only, to keep two soldiers constantly in the outer of these, to lock his door at night and to allow him to take exercise only under escort. Strafford bore it with equanimity; indeed his behaviour in the Tower caused grave misgivings to the prosecution. He was steadfastly cheerful and good-humoured, attended the chapel daily, choosing to sit in Prynne's old seat where he could see the altar, took exercise under the guard of Balfour, talking amicably the while, ordered fresh liveries for his servants, and inspected the new silver-handled heading axe with detached, half-humorous interest. [35]

His chief anxiety was for his friends in Ireland. His last message to Wandesford before his arrest had been an entreaty to '*tenir roide*', as he put, against the factionaries. Wandesford had failed miserably and knew it. He was now a sick man and the news of Strafford's impeachment seemed to break his resistance; he lingered feverishly for some days, murmuring broken legal phrases, promising justice to the poor. On the night of December 3rd he died, saying softly, 'Lord Jesus receive my spirit.' And for the first time in history the Irish keened for an English governor. [36]

Strafford heard of it a few days before Christmas; he was profoundly moved for he had lost not only a loving and beloved friend, but one of his best supporters in Ireland. Characteristically his first action was to write to his wife bidding her keep up her courage and reassuring her that he would soon be free to cheer her defenceless loneliness in Dublin. Charles appointed Lord Dillon to take Wandesford's place, but he was unacceptable to Parliament because his son was married to Strafford's sister. Ormonde, as a friend to Strafford, was equally ineligible. [37]

Petitions from malcontents across the Channel flowed in to the Commons, and the Irish deputies who had presented the Remonstrance were co-opted on to the committee for drawing up the charge. Urged on by Lord Cork's group the Commons raised no doubts; any petition complaining of injustice was unquestioningly welcomed and 'reparations' or rather rewards were offered to those presenting them. The judgments given against Loftus and Mountnorris were reversed, [38] and Strafford was not surprised to learn from his friends that the very heart of the charge was to be his Irish administration.

This was on the whole reassuring, for, as he wrote to one of his supporters, they might prove what they would, he had never done anything he was ashamed of. 'To suffer, so it be not for our own ill-doing, is the condition of our frail humanity, and to a constant mind it must not sure be very hard to undergo.' [39]

Meanwhile the Scots Commissioners had come forward with charges of their own accusing him of sowing dissension between the two countries and of inflaming the King against them. [40] His old enemy of Yorkshire days, Sir David Foulis, next petitioned for release and by Christmas the mass of evidence had swelled to such proportions that witnesses had to be examined even during the recess. Some of them gave trouble: Sir Harry Vane's memory played remarkable tricks, growing suddenly very precise and exact when he found out the particular damning evidence that was needed of him. Cork was obliging from the outset: 'Old Richard', reported Strafford, 'hath sworn against me gallantly.' [41]

The King's party and the waverers in the Commons, afraid either to oppose or to support so violent an attack on the royal government, even though disguised as the impeachment of a minister, absented themselves in great numbers, so that on January 15th, 1641, it was resolved that forty members should constitute a quorum. A week later Pym checked the miscellaneous attack on every unpopular feature of the royal government, reorganized the Committees and outlined a programme for dispatching all the impeachments, Strafford's in particular, and returning thereafter to examine the Justices of the Peace and sheriffs. [42] That secured him until Strafford had been destroyed; the threatened members would for the most part buy subsequent immunity by present acquiescence.

On January 16th the House of Lords finished questioning the peers whom the Commons had asked for as witnesses and handed over their depositions to the Committee. At this juncture Strafford petitioned to be allowed to answer separately anything alleged against him by these witnesses before their evidence was engrossed into general articles, but he was refused and the Committee spent the next twelve days embodying their new material in the charges. Not until the afternoon of January 30th was the prisoner at last brought in before his peers to hear in detail the charge against him. [43]

William Railton, Strafford's most trusted personal adviser and agent, coming out of the Tower the day before, was shocked by the menacing crowds gathered about the gateway and asked the

Lords for safety's sake to have the prisoner brought to Westminster secretly by night and lodged near by until the morning. The request was disregarded and Strafford came by the river in broad daylight. He landed at Westminster stairs and made his way under a strong guard of soldiers towards the Parliament buildings; there were isolated shouts and curses from the crowd but no attempt at violence. (44)

When he came into the House of Lords, pale and stooping after two long winter months in the cheerless damp of the Tower, there was even there a stir of pity for him, and one of his friends moved that he might be allowed to sit during the reading of the charge. It was a privilege that in common humanity no one could deny him.

The clerk of the House then read out the charge. Without betraying any emotion Strafford listened attentively to the nine general and twenty-eight specific accusations, and when the reading was over his leading counsel, Richard Lane, asked on his behalf for a few days in which to prepare an answer. The Commons had taken more than two months to evolve their charge, yet very grudgingly did the Lords allow the prisoner a fortnight in which to make his reply. This grace obtained, Strafford was taken back to the Tower. (45)

Once more in his room in the Tower, Strafford broke out into unrestrained jubilation, writing that very night to Ormonde and another of his supporters to assure them that he was now almost certain of an acquittal. To his wife, he was even more hopeful. 'Sweetheart', he wrote,

> The charge is now come in, and I am now able, I praise God, to tell you that I conceive there is nothing capital; and for the rest, I know at the worst, his Majesty will pardon all, without hurting my fortune and then we shall be happy by God's grace. Therefore comfort yourself, for I trust these clouds will away and that we shall have fair weather afterwards. (46)

Strafford's relief was not without cause, for the charge, taken piece by piece, was not as formidable as it looked. The chief informers about Ireland had been Loftus, Mountnorris and Clotworthy, (47) and the accusations they had brought were not of a kind to perturb the prisoner, convinced as he was of his own rectitude in his dealings with them.

The nine preliminary charges declared in general terms that Thomas Wentworth, Earl of Strafford, had traitorously attempted by assuming regal power to subvert the fundamental laws of the Kingdom, that he had misappropriated the revenue, encouraged papists, fomented war with Scotland, betrayed the army, and prevented the calling of Parliament. This was merely the opening flourish, drawn up with the intention of predisposing the listeners in Strafford's disfavour. There followed twenty-eight particular accusations, and here Strafford's keen eye at once picked out the vulnerable places. Two, and two only, dealt with the northern administration. Although the House of Commons was shortly to abolish the Court of the North, declaring that 'it hath overwhelmed that country under a sea of arbitrary power, and involved the people in a labyrinth of distemper, oppression and poverty', they could not find one serious act of oppression with which to charge Strafford. They had to confine themselves to a constitutional attack: the first article accused him of exerting undue influence to acquire from the King extraordinary powers of jurisdiction; the second article declared that he had openly stated that 'the little finger of the King was heavier than the loins of the law', a curious metaphor which at first struck no chord in Strafford's memory. (18)

The next sixteen articles dealt with the Irish administration and here Strafford was confident that he could refute the accusations. Articles three and four formed a somewhat unstable foundation for those which followed; the third alleged that he had called the Irish a 'conquered nation' and denied the validity of their charters, and the fourth that he had threatened to make Acts of State equal to Acts of Parliament. In article five he was accused of illegally using martial law to avenge himself on Mountnorris. The next three were an attack on his land policy. The ninth article accused him of increasing the arbitrary powers of the Church. The following five charged him with increasing the customs duties, tampering with exports for personal profit, exploiting the tobacco monopoly, interfering with the linen manufacture, and arbitrarily limiting freedom of shipping.

The charges were intended to build up a convincing picture of his iron-handed tyranny and his use of the royal prerogative or even of force to override the common law and invade the property of the King's subjects. In Ireland the army had sometimes been used to collect the taxes; this, in the fifteenth article, became a 'levying of war' on the King's subjects. In the sixteenth he was accused of prohibiting appeals to England with a view to increasing his personal power. Articles seventeen and eighteen marched together; in the one he was charged with saying that the Irish army should be a pattern for England, and in the other of having fostered the papists and even conscripted them into the said army. The nineteenth and twentieth were designed to show his implacable enmity to the Scots; he had tyrannously subjected all Scots in Ireland to an illegal oath, he had urged the King to declare war, he had called the gallant Covenanters 'rebels and traitors', and he had seized Scottish ships on the seas. Then came the events of the last eleven months and the charges based on them. In article twenty-one he was accused of calling a Parliament only to make it hateful to the people so that the King might act independently of it; twenty-two enlarged the preceding with the charge that he had compelled the Irish Parliament to support him and raised thereby a huge army with which to enforce the King's Prerogative in England against the people's will; twenty-three elaborated twenty-one with the statement that he had wantonly dissolved the English Parliament before subsidies could be granted and offered to bring over the Irish army to subdue England, while twenty-four added that he had openly accused the Commons of forsaking the King. The next three made out that he had threatened the Londoners to make them give money, advised the King to seize the bullion in the Mint, debase the coinage and enforce his will with arms if he were resisted, and that he had compelled the Yorkshire gentry by threats of distraint to contribute to the charge of the army. Though these accusations might be hard to prove they could not fail of an immediate effect on all who heard or read them. The twenty-eighth article was frankly incredible; in it he was accused of deliberately betraying the English to the Scots at Newburn. [49]

There were two separate elements in the charge; Pym, Hampden and most of their English colleagues were deeply concerned for what they believed to be the traditional liberties of Englishmen. They saw Strafford as a public enemy, and the King's policies, which he had advised, supported or executed, as morally wrong and politically dangerous. But the witnesses from Ireland on whom they had relied for so much of the evidence were looking at the matter from a different and much less exalted point of view. Sir John Clotworthy was, possibly, an exception: the consistent inhumanity which this repellent man was to show throughout his later career has the stamp of a genuine religious fanaticism. It is probably therefore just to infer that he was inspired in his attacks on Strafford by sincere hatred of him for his persecution of the Presbyterians of Ulster. Cork, Mountnorris, Loftus, Piers Crosby and others who came in to 'swear gallantly' against him — as Strafford put it — were mainly concerned to get rid of a governor of Ireland whose authority had caused them a great deal of personal loss and annoyance. Such machinations and combinations to undermine a Deputy who had crossed their interests had been frequent in the last twenty-five years. Grandison and Chichester had had troubles of this kind. Strafford's predecessor Falkland had been recalled through the cabals and libels of Loftus and Mountnorris. The impeachment of Strafford which was thus in English politics a matter of the deepest significance, to the King, to Parliament and to the future government of England, was in the politics of Ireland (or more truly of the 'new English' in Ireland) simply a rather more spectacular way than usual of getting rid of an unpopular Lord Lieutenant.

This was by no means clear to the English managers of the prosecution, who were chiefly concerned to show that Strafford's operations in Ireland were the logical application of that same royal policy which they feared in England and which Strafford had implemented in Ireland: namely the persistent use of regal or vice-regal power to override the common law and to invade the liberties and possessions of the subject.[50]

Strafford, who knew the facts of his Irish administration, was well aware (as the prosecution were not) that many of the Irish charges could not fail to reveal, when brought to the light of day, the elements of personal spite and personal interest that lay behind them. This was a real weakness, which Pym was only to realize at the trial when the prisoner successfully turned several of the charges inside out to the discredit of his accusers.

Strafford also noted with relief that neither the venom of his enemies nor the zeal of Pym had conjured forth any really convincing charges of High Treason. The last group concerning his actions in the summer of 1640 came the nearest, but it seemed unlikely that they would be able to bring adequate proof of these.

Even so, Strafford spent more than his allotted time drawing up his answer. It was not easy to go over in detail the whole of his administration when all his more important papers were kept from him by the prosecution. At times his memory must give out. Besides, he was not only working day after day, sometimes for as much as fourteen hours, at his own defence; he was also advising the King.

Charles was pursuing a policy of studied moderation in the hope of winning over some of his critics and thus dividing the opposition, at least in the Lords, if not in the Commons. Without resistance, he passed a bill binding himself in future to triennial Parliaments. Later, he set himself to gain the support of that group of peers who had forced him into calling Parliament, by elevating some of them to the Privy Council; at the same time three of his less unpopular supporters were raised to the House of Lords. Meanwhile he had opened negotiations with the Prince of Orange, Stadtholder of Holland, hoping that by the marriage of his eldest daughter to that Prince's eldest son, he could gain the financial support of one of the richest families in Europe.

On February 17th Strafford appealed in person to the peers for an extension of time for his answer and after an acrimonious debate he was granted only another week. [51] The general feeling of the House was still against him. Pym's fear was that the bishops' vote would save his enemy from destruction: twenty-four voices for Strafford might be difficult to vote down in the House of Lords. As early as the previous November, Pym's colleague St John had dropped hints in the House of Commons that bishops ought not to take part in a *causa sanguinis*, a trial involving the death sentence. Sly Bishop Williams, a friend to the King's critics and bitter enemy of Laud, took the matter up, and after proving with a great display of learning that bishops could not be legally prevented from taking part in a *causa sanguinis*, concluded that they ought none the less to withdraw from this one. They did so, and twenty-four votes on the King's side and Strafford's were thus cut off. [52]

At nine in the morning of February 24th Strafford came at last to the House of Lords to answer the charge. Almost at the same moment the King arrived. To the general astonishment he had Strafford brought to him privately before the proceedings began and they spent the best part of an hour closeted together; when Charles at length took his seat on the throne and the prisoner was brought to the bar, he saluted him with the greatest expression of tenderness and anxiety before the whole House. [53]

Strafford's counsel read his answer singly to each charge; it took three hours. In Strafford's name the Commons impeached not a single man but by implication the King's government. He had answered the challenge: his replies formed at the same a political argument, a personal defence, and an oblique attack on his accusers. He argued that some of the charges amounted to no more than that he carried out the law in a defensible and salutary manner; far from denying these accusations, he prided himself on them. In the second place he rebutted all charges against his personal integrity, pleading misinterpretation, misreport, or sheer libel. Thirdly he denied altogether many of the minor and more insidious charges. He pointed out that the vaunted death sentence on Mountnorris had amounted in the end to a few days' restraint and he utterly denied any knowledge of the illegal and oppressive methods said to be used by him in Ireland; he justified those actions he did not deny by precedents in Irish and English law and only in the case of the last group of charges pleaded the emergency of a country at war. As to the accusations that he had used threats to force the Yorkshire gentry to contribute to the upkeep of the army, this contribution had been imposed not by him but by consent of the Council of Peers. Here and there he admitted to a natural uncertainty of memory which strengthened rather than weakened his cause. [54]

When it was over he asked permission to call his own witnesses and to cross-examine those produced by the Commons in support of their accusations. The Lords refused to answer till they had consulted the Lower House, a signal that the alliance between them was still stronger than he could have wished. [55]

Nothing now prevented the matter from coming at once to open trial, nothing but the rival dignities of the two Houses. The respect shown for the Commons by the Lords when Strafford petitioned them was not altogether reflected in their relations; his remarks about the part played by the Council of Peers in imposing the final contribution on the Yorkshire gentry had borne fruit. The Commons were full of suspicion and the Lords of indignant denials.

Many wrangling conferences took place before an amicable arrangement about the trial was achieved. The Peers wished Strafford to have the benefit of counsel, the Commons did not; they compromised by allowing him counsel for matter of law, but not for matter of fact. Next came the question of witnesses; here again a compromise was reached and Strafford was permitted to call his own witnesses and cross-examine the witnesses for the prosecution but not on oath. He was even allowed to call members of Parliament, but the Commons added a rider that no such members were under obligation to appear. Strafford himself was only informed of this permission three days before his trial, so that it was impossible for him to bring witnesses from Ireland. The Irish Commons had in any case taken the precaution of impeaching Lord Chancellor Bolton, Lord Chief Justice Lowther and the Bishop of Derry so as to make it impossible for them to be called as witnesses. [56]

Another knotty point was the prosecution. The Commons insisted on managing it themselves through a Committee. Moreover they wished to be present during the hearing, consequently the trial had to be held in Westminster Hall as the House of Lords was not large enough, and a further argument ensued as to whether they should wear their hats or no; it was beneath the dignity of the House of Commons to sit bare, but the Peers would not hear of them sitting covered in their presence. In the end they agreed to come not as the House of Commons, but as a mere Committee, in which case they could be hatless without forgoing their dignity. At the same time Strafford's enemy, the Earl of Arundel, significantly announced that he would perform his duties as Lord Steward in person at the trial, and insisted that his place should be on a raised dais directly opposite the prisoner so that he might have an uninterrupted view of him throughout. In these circumstances the opening date was fixed for Monday, March 22nd, 1641, and Sir William Balfour was commanded to bring his prisoner to Westminster Hall between eight and nine o'clock in the morning. [57]

Popular excitement, waning during February, was sedulously aroused throughout March. On the 1st the unhappy Laud was brought in a closed coach through angry crowds to the Tower. On the same day the Commons, without the Lords' consent, published the articles of accusation; [58] they were distributed with incredible speed all over England. The answers were not issued. The force of the printed word was colossal; the accusations were accepted as proven facts, read and discussed everywhere, while few criticized their logic or inquired into their origin. The Irish and Scots Remonstrances were also circulated. Strafford became a monster; he had betrayed King and country, encouraged papists, levied war on loyal subjects, forced and browbeaten a defenceless people in Yorkshire and Ireland, used threats in courts of justice, perverted the law to his own ends, whipped, pilloried and hanged the naked Irish, besides, as article thirteen graphically alleged, driving thousands of poor children in Ulster to starve in the fields.

Strafford's personal troubles daily increased. He was short of money, worried about his debts, and anxious about his defenceless family in Dublin. He was selling timber off his Irish estates and bringing over some of his plate from Dublin to raise money on it. [59] In the intervals of working out his defence he was seeing his brothers-in-law, the Earl of Clare and the Earl of Cumberland, and the dowager Lady Clare; for fear of the worst he wished to have his family affairs settled and the future of his wife and infant daughter, and his three elder children, secured: no easy matter in the confused state of his public and private revenues. His creditors, all this time, were petitioning the Lords that they might not suffer if the Wentworth estates were confiscated, and the Londoners displayed their Christian charity by demanding that the arch-enemy should be more rigorously confined than he was at present. [60]

One consolation he had in these last months. The family of his second wife, so long unreconciled, were suddenly and generously prepared to forget the past. The old Countess could not do too much to assure him of her affection and care for his children, while his brother-in-law Lord Clare intervened persistently in his favour in the House of Lords, and Denzil Holles tried to form a party in the Commons who would forgo the impeachment in return for concessions on the King's Church policy. [61]

Strafford, meanwhile, planned the strategy of his defence; Lane his leading counsel assisted him with his legal knowledge, but he admitted afterwards that the defence was not only the most brilliant he had ever heard, but was almost exclusively thought out by Strafford himself. (62) He acted on the general principles that had dictated his first anwers; he could prove legal justification for many of his alleged crimes, and could establish his innocence of many others or else discredit the accusers. Thus he would awaken political, legal and moral doubts in many minds, break up the solid front of public opinion that Pym and his colleagues (and his own past indiscretion) had marshalled against him, bring the House of Lords into collision with the House of Commons, and in all probability, if there was any justice to be had from his peers, secure an acquittal.

He was fighting for his reputation, his fortune and his life. But he was fighting also for something greater. He was fighting to defend the methods of government he had employed and in which he believed. He was fighting to justify and to preserve the sovereign power of his master. If he won, if his peers acquitted him, it would be a mortal blow to the hopes and the policy of the King's opponents.

He had an absolute faith in his cause and, in the last resort, unshaken confidence in his own rectitude.

NOTES

[1] Lestrange, 201; Clarendon, III, 205, H.M.C., *Egmont*, I, p. 129.

[2] Rushworth, *Trial*, p. 1.

[3] *Radcliffe Letters*, pp. 222-3.

[4] Clarendon, III, 3.

[5] On the elections and on individual members see Keeler, *The Long Parliament*, and Brunton and Pennington, *The Long Parliament*. On Clotworthy, see also Kearney, pp. 201-2.

[6] Laud, *Works*, III, pp. 237-8.

[7] Rushworth, III, i, pp. 12-16; *Radcliffe Letters*, p. 220.

[8] *Commons Journals*, II, p. 24.

[9] Rushworth, III, i, pp. 21-4.

[10] D'Ewes, p. 12.

[11] Ibid., p. 10 n.

[12] Ibid., p. 13.

[13] Ibid., p. 19; H.M.C. *Various*, VIII, p. 54.

[14] D'Ewes, pp. 24-6. Clarendon states (III, 3, 115) that Pym referred to Strafford's 'amours' in the debate about the impeachment, and that letters to Eleanor Loftus were made public during the trial. This is supported by no other evidence. He is probably confusing things said and revealed privately with what was said and done in public.

[15] D'Ewes, p. 27 n.

[16] *Lords Journals*, IV, pp. 88-9; *C.S.P.D.*, 1640, p. 255; Brit. Museum, Additional MSS, 15, 567, folio 32; Baillie, I, pp. 272-3; *Lismore Papers*, Series 1, V, p. 164.

[17] *Biographia Britannica*, VI, p. 4182.

[18] D'Ewes, p. 51 n.

[19] Ibid., p. 45.

[20] *Commons Journals*, II, pp. 27, 28, 30, 31; d'Ewes, p. 32.

[21] Laud, III, p. 296.

[22] *Lords Journals*, IV, p. 95.

[23] Rushworth, *Trial*, pp. 11-14; *C.S.P.I.*, 1633-47, pp. 247, 252.

[24] *C.S.P.I.*, 1633-47, pp. 258, 265-6.

[25] D'Ewes, pp. 60-4.

[26] *Commons Journals*, II, pp. 35-6; *Lords Journals*, IV, 97-8.

[27] H.M.C., XII, II, p. 262.

[28] *Lords Journals*, IV, p. 90.

[29] Ibid., p. 106. Writing some years later, Abraham Wright, a protégé of Laud and Juxon, suggested that some of those who visited Strafford in the Tower were *agents provocateurs* set on by the Commons to induce him to indiscreet utterances and to spy on him. Wright's account of Strafford's death, *Novissima Straffordii*, was published in *Historical Papers*, ed. P. Bliss and B. Bandinel, Roxburghe Club, 1846. My attention was drawn to it by Miss Dorothy Mason at the Folger Shakespeare Library, Washington, D.C., where the manuscript now is. Otherwise I should have missed this little-known item of Straffordiana.

[30] H.M.C. *Various*, II, pp. 259 ff.

[31] Baillie, I, p. 283.

[32] *Commons Journals*, II, pp. 46, 50; Clarendon, III, 14.

[33] *Commons Journals*, II, pp. 38-42.

[34] *Lords Journals*, IV, p. 100.

[35] Ibid., IV, p. 106; H.M.C., XII, ii, p. 267.

[36] *Radcliffe Letters*, p. 221; Alice Thornton, *Autobiography*, pp. 19, 26.

[37] Knowler, II, p. 415; Rushworth, III, p. 222; Carte, V, p. 245.

[38] *Commons Journals*, II, pp. 61, 64, 71.

[39] Knowler, II, pp. 414 ff.

[40] Nalson, I, 686-8; Rushworth, *Trial*, pp. 769-72.

[41] H.M.C., IV, pp. 60 ff.

[42] *Commons Journals*, II, pp. 63, 66.

[43] Ibid., pp. 68 ff, 76; *Lords Journals*, IV, pp. 133, 149.

[44] H.M.C., IV, p. 45; Baillie, I, p. 297.

[45] *Lords Journals*, IV, p. 149.

[46] *Biographia Britannica*, VI, p. 4183.

[47] Baillie, I, 273.

[48] See Reid, pp. 438 ff.

[49] Rushworth, *Trial*, pp. 61 ff.

[50] Ranger, p. 31.

[51] *Lords Journals*, IV, p. 165.

[52] The exact part played by Williams has often been disputed. Hacket gives his speech in favour of bishops being allowed to vote in capital cases at some length, and a fragmentary and apparently unique pamphlet of it is in the possession of the London Library. The anonymous diary of the proceedings in the House of Lords in the British Museum (Harleian 6424) is however absolutely explicit in saying that Williams spoke in favour of the bishops' right to vote, but then advised abstention in this particular case.

[53] *C.S.P.Ven.*, 1641, p. 128.

[54] *Lords Journals*, IV, p. 105; Rushworth, *Trial*, pp. 22 ff; H.M.C., *Cowper MSS*, II, p. 275.

[55] *Lords Journals*, IV, p. 171.

[56] *C.S.P.I.*, 1633-47, pp. 258-9.

[57] Ibid., IV, pp. 177-93; *Commons Journals*, II, p. 109; Clarendon, III, 95.

[58] *Lords Journals*, IV, p. 174.

[59] *Lords Journals*, IV, p. 206; *C.S.P.I.*, 1633-47, p. 250.

[60] H.M.C., IV, p. 58; *C.S.P.D.*, 1641, p. 524.

[61] Knowler, II, p. 417; Clarendon, III, 35.

[62] H.M.C., *Cowper MSS*, II, p. 279.

CHAPTER FOUR

THE TRIAL

My actions from the highest to the lowest shall all be cast into the balance and tried whether heavy or light. Content in the name of God! Let them take me up and cast me down. If I do not fall square in every point of duty to my master; nay, if I do not fully comply with that public and common protection which good Kings afford their good people, let me perish and let no man pity me.

Wentworth to Carlisle, 1632

AT seven o'clock on the morning of March 22nd, 1641, Strafford came down to the Traitor's Gate with Sir William Balfour and took his place in the barge that was to convey him to Westminster. Five other barges with twenty soldiers in each surrounded him on all sides, and when he landed at Westminster stairs he walked between a double row of two hundred picked men of the London Trained Bands to the doors of Westminster Hall. Only the hideous formality of carrying a naked axe before the prisoner was omitted by the King's express command.

In the midst of Westminster Hall a long raised platform made an island among the crowding spectators, and here Strafford was to take his place; behind him in ascending rows sat the Commons, the Scots Commissioners, the privileged few who had secured reserved seats, and the pushing many who had somehow fought their way in; in front of him in two parallel lines sat his peers in their robes. The highest place among them on the steps of the throne would be taken almost daily, though usually only for a part of the time, by the ten-year-old Prince of Wales. The Judges sat in front of the peers, and the Earl of Arundel, his staff of office in his hand, was serene on a raised platform in their midst, with the clerks of the House at a long table before him. In front of them a narrow bar divided them from the rest of the Hall. [1]

Below this bar Strafford was to stand, just behind him there was a place railed off for his staff whence they could hand him from time to time the notes he might need. His most devoted and helpful assistant throughout the trial was Guildford Slingsby, a young man who had entered his service seven years before and had become a trusted friend as well as a highly efficient secretary. To the left, against the wall, was a bench for the defending counsel Richard Lane and his colleagues. To the left also and in front of the prisoner sat the Committee for the Prosecution, [2] their backs to the door of a little ante-room into which they could retire for refreshment, and which, significantly enough, was also a waiting-room for their witnesses.

Accompanied by Balfour, Strafford came slowly forward and knelt at the bar until Arundel, with a gesture, gave him leave to rise. He was dressed in black, wearing for sole ornament the insignia of the Garter. [3] Standing at the bar he waited for about half an hour, until at nine o'clock a movement in a curtained alcove above the seats of the peers indicated that the King and Queen had come to their places in the private box reserved for them, and the proceedings could begin.

The Earl of Arundel then called upon the prisoner by name, telling him he was to answer before his peers to a charge of High Treason. Next the clerk of the Parliament read the charge; he had not gone far before there was a slight movement among the peers and someone brought a chair for the prisoner. The clerk proceeded heedless of the interruption and when he had done, Strafford's answer was read in the same manner. As it was now two o'clock the Court adjourned and the prisoner was taken back to the Tower. The people of Westminster, whose politics differed on principle from those of the Londoners, received him as he left the Hall with expressions of sympathy and respect which he answered with unruffled civility.

On the following morning the trial began in earnest. The managers of the prosecution were well chosen: John Pym was the leading spirit and he was well supported by John Glyn, John Maynard and Geoffrey Palmer, three of the most prominent young barristers in the House, while the curt interjections of George Digby, the son of Lord Bristol, now and again sharpened the edge of the attack. The whole committee was under the chairmanship of Bulstrode Whitelocke, a less effective speaker, but a man of great learning and judgment.

Pym opened the attack by immediately assaulting Strafford's first line of defence, his emphasis on the legality of his actions. 'He hath taken as much care, hath used as much cunning to set a face and countenance of honesty and justice upon his actions, as he hath been negligent to observe the rules of honesty in the performance,' he asserted. 'My Lords, it is the greatest baseness of wickedness that it dares not look in his own colours.' He had warned the Lords against what he knew to be the greatest danger, the legal correctness of the prisoner's acts; he now declared that he would unmask all Strafford's 'intentions in their natural blackness and deformity'. Gathering force he generally and specifically derided the written defence, citing examples of his tyranny, corruption and violence, and ending with the flourish that Strafford might well plead his acts were permissible for 'the habit of cruelty in himself is more perfect than any Act of Cruelty he hath committed'.

When he had finished he asked leave to call witnesses on several points hitherto omitted from the articles, notably, breach of Parliamentary privilege, misappropriation of revenue and illegal billeting of soldiers. Permission was given and the first witness called. Sir Piers Crosby stepped forward. Strafford instantly protested. Crosby had so recently lost a notorious libel case against him that the peers backed the objection and the managers after a little hesitation produced Sir John Clotworthy instead; he was followed by the Lords Mountnorris, Ranelagh and others, all offering evidence on the intimidation of members of Parliament. Much of their evidence consisted of things said and done not by Strafford but by George Radcliffe, and on one occasion when Strafford was not even in Ireland. This was not very impressive, and to mend matters John Glyn now asked leave to read the Remonstrance of the Irish Parliament. Strafford protested that it was not in the charge; the Commons insisted that it had bearing on it.

'Your lordships may observe,' exclaimed Strafford passionately, 'that this is fallen out *since* my impeachment of High Treason here. It is a strong conspiracy against me.' The fearful word hissed into the silence. Pym started up. 'My Lords,' he protested, 'these words are not to be suffered; charging the House of Commons with conspiracy, we desire your lordships' justice in this.' Falling on his knees Strafford asked the Lords to pardon his sudden outbreak. [4] Nothing had been further from his mind than to accuse the honourable House of Commons; he meant only certain factionaries outside Parliament. The laugh was against the prosecution now for appropriating an accusation before it had been made, and though the Remonstrance was read the edge of it was blunted and the Commons proceeded hastily to the question of misappropriating revenue. Here again their witnesses failed to prove anything conclusive and when Strafford tried to ask the Vice-Treasurer of Ireland how great the deficit had been before he became Deputy, Pym objected to 'interlocutory discourses' between the accused and a witness and the question was overruled.

Since none of the accusations brought so far had been included in the original charge the prisoner asked for a little time to collect himself before answering. The Commons denied him, but he appealed to the Lords, who mercifully spent half an hour discussing his privileges as a peer before they finally confirmed the Commons in demanding an immediate answer.

Strafford had not wasted his half-hour; he had spent most of it hurriedly writing notes, as Symonds d'Ewes observed. [5] He now defended himself lucidly and in detail, pointing out that as Irish law differed from English he had naturally guided his actions by the customs of the country he was governing. He had, he admitted, borrowed from the Exchequer, but with the King's consent, and the money had been repaid. He urged the Lords to look into his papers and accounts, to examine the state of Ireland before they believed the evidence of witnesses who made statements but offered little proof of what they asserted.

Above all he urged the Lords to look more narrowly at the Remonstrance; less than a year before, the Irish Commons had acclaimed and approved his policy by a general vote of gratitude, and now in the very hour of his impeachment they reversed their views. There was more in this than met the eye; as to a conspiracy, he concluded, 'I meant what I said.' Some of his hearers must by this time have known very well what he meant: the machinations of Cork, Loftus, Mountnorris and the rest.

Pym rose again but he did no more than give the lie direct to Strafford's assertions and promise that the separate articles should prove all. The Court adjourned. The day had passed in a rally of assertion, denial and counter-denial between Strafford and the prosecution. But the weakness of the charges was already becoming apparent — the reliance on second-hand evidence and the personal animosity of so many of the witnesses from Ireland.

On the following day Maynard opened the proceedings with a speech that did much to sway the balance in favour of the Commons. He answered Strafford's reiterated protest that no single charge could be called treason by the powerful argument that, though singly they were little, all together they were unanswerable. 'It is a habit, a trade, a mystery of treason exercised by this great lord,' he asserted. Appealing more particularly to the Lords he drew attention to Strafford's frequent prosecutions of noble gentlemen and peers. 'His will and violence must out,' he said pointing to the prisoner, 'though he burst a Kingdom in pieces for it.' Maynard had a biting tongue and knew how to sharpen the articles to a point with a sudden insinuation: 'My Lords, it is no wonder he would make the King's little finger so heavy, that could make his own toe heavy enough to tread the life of a peer under his feet.' While this sidelong reference to the Mountnorris affair was fermenting in the minds of his hearers he hurried to the first article and called his witnesses.

Dexterous as Maynard was he could not force home a charge as ill-conceived as the attack on Strafford's northern policy. The two articles he had to handle were a patchwork of contradictions. It was an awkward fact that Strafford had never been acting President of the North since the time when he persuaded the King to grant increased powers to that Court. Thus the Commons had tried to substantiate their charge of personal ambition by elaborately re-dating some of Strafford's actions and the King's commission. The accused had only to call two witnesses to correct these chronological errors to dispatch the first article.

The second article accused Strafford of saying that 'the little finger of the King was heavier than the loins of the law.' When much depended on the spoken word, the Commons were unfortunate in having a deaf man as one of their witnesses. As Strafford bitingly remarked, he 'appears to have such an infirmity of hearing that he must now be whoopt to at the bar, before he can hear'. A little later Sir William Pennyman rose to give evidence that Strafford had used the phrase in the reverse order, declaring that the little finger of the law was heavier than the loins of the King.

Pennyman was a member of the House of Commons. He had hardly done speaking when Maynard said unpleasantly that Sir William should have communicated his knowledge to the House of Commons before coming out with it like this in open court. Strafford interposed; if his witnesses were to be threatened, he declared, he would call no more. 'I would put myself on God's mercy and goodness and not make use of any member of either House rather than acquit myself by their prejudice.' Maynard unwisely persisted in his threatening tone. Strafford appealed to the Lords. 'This gentleman is my noble friend and I would give him my life on any occasion.' The situation was becoming embarrassing, but Arundel intervened and the Commons withdrew their menace.

The second article was by this time almost as much weakened as the first, and Maynard asked leave to produce another witness, Sir David Foulis. Strafford's exception to him as prejudiced was overruled by Arundel, and Foulis confirmed the Commons' evidence word for word. In the confusion of cross-statements it could not fairly be said that either side had proved anything conclusive.

The first two days set the pattern for what followed. The Commons made their anxiety for Strafford's death too clear, and created thereby an increasing sympathy for him. 'They have so banged and worried him as it begets pity in many of the auditors', wrote one observer. [6] On at least one occasion, Arundel, although it was growing late in the afternoon, refused to accept Strafford's plea of illness as a reason for adjournment. [7] The managers of the prosecution — especially Maynard and Glyn — harried him very close; but their threatening was not confined to him personally. They tried to discredit his witnesses: they were his friends, his dependants, his servants — naturally enough as he had not been allowed time enough to send for any independent witnesses out of Ireland. They became irritable when he excepted against their witnesses; after the Crosby incident, there came one after another Cork, Mountnorris, Lord Esmond and others with evident personal scores to pay off. Once a petty official who had been dismissed for extortion was called. Strafford's objections were overruled (even Piers Crosby was allowed to give evidence later in the trial), but the effect of them was not wholly lost. Some of the audience began to suspect that behind these grand accusations about subversion of the laws there lay too much 'private practice for private men to work out their own ends and preferments thereupon'. [8]

342

Among the Commons, on the other hand, there was muttering that all his complaints and objections were simply to gain time, and that he had friends among the peers who helped him in these delaying tactics by constantly asking for adjournments to discuss the points he raised. They objected also to the length of his answers and the general arguments which he used. Could he not somehow be compelled to answer briefly without enlarging on every issue? [9]

Strafford's method showed 'great subtlety and judgment', as even Symonds d'Ewes, a most determined enemy, admitted. [10] He argued that he had acted within the law and cited statutes and precedents to justify his conduct. He persistently pointed out that, even if he had committed the actions of which he was accused — as sometimes undoubtedly he had — they were not treasonous. 'Almost every article,' he said, in a voice between mockery and scorn, 'sets forth a new treason that I never heard of before.' With wearisome reiteration Pym and Maynard asked the peers to take no notice of the prisoner's views on single articles, but to look upon the charge as a whole as one of 'constructive treason'.

When it came to the detailed oppressions and tyrannies charged against him, he denied some, defended others, and from time to time neatly turned the tables on his accusers. When Lord Ranelagh gave evidence that Strafford had tried Common Law cases on paper petitions in the Castle Chamber, he asked him if he had not frequently done the same in his office as President of Connaught. The managers of the prosecution instantly objected to the question, the Court adjourned, and next day Ranelagh was excused from answering. [11]

The sixth article on examination proved so discreditable to Mountnorris that the Committee had to insist that 'the merit of the case was immaterial' so long as Strafford's procedure was proved illegal. This particular oppression consisted of the power he had brought to bear on Mountnorris to make him give up an estate he had taken by a mean subterfuge from a poor man. Such embarrassments taught the Committee to examine their charges a little more carefully, an inquiry which led to their staying four articles entirely and two in part. At the same time they pressed the Lords to forbid the prisoner making 'impertinent excursions' and under this heading prevented him from producing his

343

accounts as evidence against the financial statements of their witnesses.

All these too obvious injustices played into Strafford's hands. While the prosecution grew daily more nervous, the prisoner retained his confidence and calm. Two or three times he raised a laugh against his accusers; he congratulated Lord Cork on remembering word for word a statement made seven years before and reciting it without a slip exactly as it appeared in the charge; he expressed no astonishment that Sir Piers Crosby, already shown to be perjured in the Star Chamber, should give a verbatim account of a conversation with him — also seven years ago — when he had never had 'such a discourse as is mentioned in all my life'; he found it hard to believe that one Salmon had heard him use threats in Ulster when he was, curiously enough, in Yorkshire at the time. When the charge of seizing Irish flax had been thrashed out he expressed incredulity that the seizure of one cartload in *Connaught* which had alone been proved would have caused the death of 'thousands of poor children' in *Ulster*. It appeared that his accusers in the House of Commons could believe this, but he could not.

He plied his eloquence with masterly skill, breaking from sarcasm or practical exposition to sudden impassioned words. He gave too an impression from time to time of honest uncertainty, in effective contrast to the assured attitude of the prosecution. Faced by categorical statements of what he had said six or seven years before he pleaded that it was not in human power accurately to remember these things, but that he thought he had not spoken so, or had not intended so. 'I thank God I never spoke such unmannerly language all the days of my life,' he protested once; on the other hand he confessed to hasty speech and an outspoken manner. 'My tongue hath been too free. My heart perhaps hath lain too near my tongue; but God forbid every word should rise up in judgment against me.'

Accused of making undue profits on the customs he admitted that they had increased under his management, but, he protested, 'nothing can be imputed to me unless that the Kingdom of Ireland is an increased and growing Kingdom, and the trade enlarged to such a proportion as makes the customs of far more value.' Certainly, he had done very well out of his share in the proceeds, but 'I never knew the making of a good bargain turned on a man as treason.' The tobacco monopoly was cited as an example of his rapacity, but, as he caustically remarked, 'that there should be near £100,000 profit a year, is a wonderful estimate and admirable to him'; and suddenly carrying the attack on to the Commons' own ground, he protested against the seizure of his tobacco warehouses and the ill-usage of his servants; 'if you will speak of a tyrannical and arbitrary way of government...' he broke off expressively. Another time Maynard unwisely stressed the noble birth of one of his victims and Strafford appealed with candour to his peers to know if noble birth placed a man beyond the reach of justice.

Once or twice the prosecution used words spoken by the indiscreet Radcliffe as proof against Strafford, and when he protested Pym blandly remarked, 'The spirit of my lord of Strafford could move in Sir George Radcliffe.' Once a witness cited words that he alleged George Wentworth had used; but George Wentworth was later debarred from giving evidence as to what had been said on that occasion as — it was alleged — he would only speak in his own justification, which was not permissible.

In these circumstances even article fifteen, the famous charge of 'levying war' on the King's subjects by billeting soldiers on the Irish to bring in the taxes, failed of its intended effect. The Commons, presumably following a prearranged plan, 'stood up and maintained the said article to be High Treason' and called on the Lords to take an immediate vote on the guilt of the accused. But the peers were not impressed and refused to reach a premature decision.[12] By April 3rd, the thirteenth day's sitting, the prosecution had reached the nineteenth article without conclusively proving anything that could be called treason.

April 4th was a Sunday and gave the managers of the prosecution time to collect themselves. The heaviest part of the charge was still in hand, but if Strafford could once mangle and discredit their charges based on his activities in the last year, if he could create the least doubt as to whether he had curtailed the last Parliament, encouraged the war on the Scots and offered to use the Irish army in England, he would elude them altogether.

Among the articles there was one, the twenty-third, which could be counted on — if it were proved — to do him irreparable harm.

345

This was the article which accused him of the intention of bringing over the Irish army. The only evidence that the prosecution felt able to bring was the statement they had got from Sir Harry Vane that Strafford, at the Council table, had advised the King to use the Irish army '*here* to reduce *this* Kingdom' — a single testimony of a spoken word.

On the success of Vane as a witness all depended. It was essential therefore that the moment of his calling should be well chosen and well used. If Strafford had started the day by dissecting in his usual relentless manner the articles leading up to the twenty-third, defeat would be probable. The managers therefore changed their tactics and when Strafford was brought to the bar on April 5th he was told that he was to answer the next five articles not singly but as a whole.

He protested that he had not been warned, but his objection was overruled, John Glyn declaring petulantly that he had never known before of a prisoner who presumed to dictate to the prosecution how they should proceed. Bulstrode Whitelocke then produced some written statements about Council meetings submitted by Lord Morton and the Earl of Northumberland. Strafford again protested: the use of written depositions debarred him from questioning the witnesses, he said, this was to treat him worse than the lowest felon. But John Glyn appealed to the peers not to allow the prisoner's persistent appeals for preferential treatment, and the trial proceeded.

The Commons had built up their case well and moved from one article to another making the charges corroborate and support each other. Lord Traquair cited words showing that Strafford had wanted no peace with the Scots. Bishop Juxon admitted that he had advised war; Sir Harry Vane and Lord Conway said they had heard him assert that the King should take money as he needed it if Parliament failed him. Lord Bristol, Lord Newburgh, and Lord Holland confirmed this emphatically.

Then Sir Harry Vane was called once more. What words, Whitelocke asked him, had he heard the Earl of Strafford use at the Council about the time of the dissolution of the Short Parliament. Vane was garrulous with nerves; he never, he said, 'in the whole course of [his] life loved to tell an untruth'. Besides, Northumberland's written testimony would also bear him out. (Nothing in the part of Northumberland's testimony which had been read out did in fact do so.) Then, it came: 'My Lord of Strafford did say in a discourse' — another parenthesis about his duty to tell the truth here briefly interrupted Vane's flow — ' "Your Majesty having tried all ways, and being refused, and in case of this extreme necessity, and for the safety of the Kingdom, you are acquitted before God and man and you have an army in *Ireland*, which you may employ here to reduce this Kingdom," or some words to this effect.' Vane stumbled and recovered himself, begged to make himself clear. 'It is true, my Lord of Strafford said these words, "You may".' But what he meant by them — Vane was now apologetic, almost martyred — what he meant by them, he could not say, but that these words were spoken, if it was his last hour, he must say, 'It is the truth.'

Lord Clare was now on his feet; so also, surprisingly enough, Lord Savile, Strafford's old enemy. They both wanted to know which Kingdom was meant, England or Scotland?

The Commons handled Vane gingerly, but he did not fail them. He was positive, he said, that Strafford had used the pronoun 'here', not 'there', and had said 'this Kingdom', not 'that Kingdom'. Lord Clare pressed him to explain the sequence of the words, to say how and when they had arisen in the debate, but Whitelocke cut him short. There could be no question, he said, but that England was intended. At this the Earl of Southampton rose to support Clare; Sir Harry Vane, he suggested, might be mistaken in his memory. Vane merely reaffirmed his statement in the same words. Still Clare protested; did Sir Harry Vane really think Lord Strafford had meant England? Had it appeared so at the time? What had anyone else said to the point? What *did* 'this Kingdom' really mean? Arundel intervened: Sir Harry Vane, he said, was called merely as a witness to Lord Strafford's words, not as an interpreter. But Maynard had his own use for Lord Clare's question. 'The question is put,' he said, 'whether "*this* Kingdom" be *this* Kingdom.'

Once or twice in Vane's evidence he had referred to the written deposition of Northumberland as substantiating his charge. Strafford now asked if he might see this, but it was categorically refused. He took the refusal stoically and proceeded with a fine mixture of calmness and passion to dissect the evidence that had been brought. 'Look to what is *proved*,' he entreated his judges, 'not to what is enforced on those proofs from these gentlemen; for words pass and may be easily mistaken.' He went on to show conclusively that words and words alone were proved against him, and they not always certainly. He did more; the Commons when they accused him of urging the King to use his prerogative had opened a constitutional issue, and Strafford accepted the challenge. He did not deny the words, or at least not the opinions; he denied the Commons' interpretation of them. 'It hath been once my opinion,' he said,

> 'which I learnt in the House of Commons; it hath gone along with me in the whole course of my service to the Commonwealth, and by the Grace of God I shall carry it to my grave; that the prerogative of the Crown and liberty of the subject should be equally looked upon, and served *together*, but not *apart*.'

Surely, he argued, no lawyer had ever denied that in times of dire emergency there must be a power in the royal prerogative; it was a necessary safeguard to the state. 'If this be a foolish opinion,' he said, 'I crave your Lordships' pardon; but I think a man should not forfeit his life and honour and posterity for a foolish opinion.'

He had made his plea for the prerogative and went back now to the particular charges. He pointed out that Vane might have been mistaken; that other witnesses — Lord Conway for one — had based their evidence on casual phrases and private conversations:

> 'If words spoken to friends, in familiar discourse, spoken in one's chamber, spoken at one's table, spoken in one's sick-bed ... if these things shall be brought against a man as treason, this, under favour, takes away the comfort of all human society.... If these things be strained to take away life and honour it will be a silent world; a city will become an hermitage; and no man shall dare to impart his solitary thoughts or opinions to his friend and neighbour.'

Vane was but a single witness. Though Strafford was not allowed to see Northumberland's written evidence, the relevant passages about the Irish army were in the end read out: they entirely contradicted Vane's evidence. In turn Strafford called Hamilton, Juxon and Cottington; all three denied having heard him utter any such opinion at any time. Cottington, once he was called, began to enjoy himself and maliciously made sport of the Commons' evidence. If Strafford had said that Parliament had not given the King money, why should he not say so? It was the truth. But Strafford was the last man to have told the King he was 'absolved from all rules of government'; on the contrary he had urged the King to keep well within the law and only in the last extremity, after the Commons had refused the subsidies, had he advised the King to use the prerogative. Moreover he had insisted that such a use of the prerogative, being the result of emergency, should never be drawn into precedent and that any invasion of the property of subjects must afterwards be made good. Cottington's testimony was confirmed by both Hamilton and Goring.

Strafford icily congratulated Sir Harry Vane on remembering his words so perfectly as to be able to give a better account of them 'than the party that spake the words, or any man in the company besides'. As for his opinions, he said, 'if I had forborne to speak what I conceived, for the benefit and advantage of the King and people I had been perjured towards God Almighty and now,' he continued,

> 'it seems by the speaking of them I am in danger to be a traitor. If that necessity be put upon me, I thank God, by his blessing I have learnt not to stand in fear of him that can kill the body; but I must stand in fear of him that can cast the body and soul into eternal pain. And if that be the question, that I must be a traitor to man or perjured to God, I will be faithful to my creator; and whatsoever shall befall me from popular rage or my own weakness, I must leave it to God Almighty, and to your Lordships' honour and justice.'

This was not the last arrow in his quiver; if the private opinion of a minister delivered under his privilege as a Councillor could be thrown in his teeth for treason with never an act to support it, he urged the peers, there would be an end to all government: who, on such terms, would venture to be a counsellor to the King?

Whitelocke and Maynard attempted to redress the balance in favour of the prosecution, Whitelocke by denying Strafford's theory of the prerogative, Maynard, more ingeniously, by insinuating that his plea for the secrecy of private conversation proved a general disaffection to the Commonwealth. Glyn concluded by reasserting the truth of the twenty-third article; true, he admitted, Sir Harry Vane was the only witness to Strafford's words, but the greatest of all witnesses, '*Vox populi*', had always declared it to be Strafford's intention to bring over the Irish army to crush English liberty. He went on to argue that Cottington's evidence of Strafford's care for the restoration of the subject's property only showed that he had had an intention of seizing it in the first place. Here Cottington sharply protested that the evidence he had given bore no such interpretation, but Glyn, heedless of the interruption, swept to his close. Following Maynard's lead he accused Strafford of pleading the privilege of a Councillor simply to cover treason; was this not the utmost height to which treason could reach? Did not such a plea smirch the nobility of England themselves, and every Councillor among them?

As he finished, Strafford stumbled wearily to his feet and asked the Lords to conclude for the day. The Court had sat for ten hours and he was too ill to endure any longer. The Court was adjourned.

He was allowed the next day to rest, and he spent it drawing a petition that Sir Harry Vane's dispatches to Lord Conway might be examined to see if they did not give a clearer account of his policy at the Council Board in the previous May than had yet been produced. The Lords, after some debate, ruled that Vane's dispatches were private papers and might not be tampered with, and Conway, who was afraid that the responsiblity for the defeat at Newburn might be transferred to him if Strafford were acquitted, asserted that he had, in any case, burnt them. [13]

Although Vane's evidence had created a stir on all sides the denials of the other Privy Councillors almost discredited him. It is probable, however, that Vane was not lying in the narrowest sense; his report of Strafford's words may have been true; he had made notes of the meeting and must have heard something like what he had set down there. It was the interpretation that he allowed the Commons to make of the words that was false. Because the interpretation was false the other Councillors did not recollect the words themselves. The fatal phrases had been spoken in the heat of debate and had referred to Scotland, therefore they passed individually unnoticed. Had they meant what the Commons asserted, Strafford's other colleagues could not have forgotten a suggestion so reckless, violent and uncalled for. Strafford and his witnesses denying the words, were nearer to the truth than Vane with his positive assertions.

On April 7th, the twenty-fifth, twenty-sixth and twenty-seventh articles were brought up. The first of these had two parts; it accused Strafford of enforcing Ship-money and threatening to hang the London aldermen. As to the intemperate statement made in the previous May that no good was to be had from the City of London until some of the aldermen were hanged, in the face of very strong evidence that he had indeed said this he could only plead that it was a hasty word, and excusable 'to a free-spoken man as he is'. When it came to Ship-money he boldly cited the Hampden case; seven judges had supported the King, he declared, and Ship-money had only since then been declared illegal. He was therefore on the right side of the law at the time of the action.

The twenty-sixth article concerned the seizure of the bullion at the Mint and the threatened debasement of the coinage. But the Commons brought only witnesses who testified to the un-sympathetic reception they had received from Strafford when, on behalf of the City of London, they went to protest to him. No evidence at all was offered that he had been responsible for seizing the bullion or had known anything about it, and there appeared to be some evidence that he had abandoned the idea of debasing the coinage — which was not his own in the first place — when he realized its dangers.

The twenty-seventh article, in which he was charged with having levied money on the Yorkshire gentry by his own authority to support the Trained Bands of the county, was hotly argued on both sides. Strafford's witnesses, who included his nephew Sir William Savile and his brother-in-law Sir Edward Rhodes, flatly contradicted the assertions of some of their fellow Yorkshiremen about the occasion, only a few months back, when Strafford had persuaded the gentry to offer a month's pay for their own troops. As to the authority by which money had been levied, if Strafford failed to show that the Council of Peers had positively authorized the levy, he successfully demonstrated that they had been aware of the matter, had discussed it, and had done nothing to withdraw the warrants for collection.

At the end of a long and on the whole unsatisfactory day for the managers of the prosecution Glyn rather wearily said that they proposed to hold up the twenty-eighth article for the time being, but desired to bring further evidence of another kind next day, and with that they adjourned.

On the following day, April 8th, they reverted to the question of the Irish army again, and Sir Walter Erle, apparently against the advice of the more cautious Whitelocke, produced what he took to be conclusive evidence of Strafford's guilt. He triumphantly argued that Strafford's general's commission had been made out to permit of his landing his troops not only in Scotland but in any part of England or Wales. To this, Strafford replied, easily enough, that his commission was the same word for word as that made out for the Earl of Northumberland. The phrasing was, in fact, normal. Something particularly confused in Erle's geographical statement enabled him to add that he 'hoped the Gentleman knew that they came not on foot out of Ireland but had ships to waft them'. Poor Erle was so mortified by his failure that George Digby had to 'bring him handsomely off', as one narrator put it, by briskly speaking for him and assuring the peers that they could produce more evidence still, but in such dire plots as those that Strafford had woven, it stood to reason that sometimes there would be not so much a clear proof as 'dark probabilities'. [14]

John Glyn now asked that Strafford should say what he could in his defence without further delay, after which he would sum up for the prosecution and the Lords could be left to decide. Strafford hesitated and appealed to the peers; he had not been warned that he was to make his final defence today, nor did he yet know whether he alone was to plead or whether his counsel, Lane, might also be heard. Would not the prosecution speak first, he would answer in time, and not to lose the benefit of the last word they could speak again in answer to him. The Commons objected, but the Lords compromised and the hearing was postponed until the next day.

That night Strafford was again taken ill and in the morning he sent a messenger to the House of Lords to ask for a postponement. A trick was suspected, and John Glyn took exception to what he called the prisoner's 'wilfulness'. But a deputation of peers who went to the Tower to see him were satisfied that the illness was genuine. He promised to reach Westminster Hall next day though four men had to carry him. (15) In the meantime the Lords confirmed their previous decision that for matter of fact he could have no counsel, but they would hear Lane on matter of law if Strafford insisted.

The spectators in Westminster Hall on the next day, April 10th, were even more tightly packed than they had been on previous occasions. The sustained duel between Strafford and his accusers was by now famous. 'I prithee come to the winding up, which I think will be near Easter,' wrote Sir Thomas Knyvett to a friend, 'tis worth a hundred mile riding to see.... Bring your lady too for she may be placed to see and hear as much as the men, there being everyday a great many.' He was not himself much won over to the prisoner, whom the prosecution had 'laid open to be so foul a man'. But he could not but admire his courage. 'I think there was never any man of so unmovable a temper, for in all this time, although his provocations sometimes have been great, yet he hath not discovered the least passion, but when he speaks he doth it with so much bravery and modest courtship of both the houses and in such language as begets admiration in all the beholders, especially in a business where he can make good clear work for himself.' (16)

It had been, from first to last, for the audience a superb entertainment — with sudden surprises, moments of drama, pathos, sudden laughter, and tense excitement. Strafford himself, who had at the outset been an object of hatred to the majority of those present, had won many over, not only by his arguments. He 'got all the time a great deal of reputation by his patient, yet stout and clear answers, and changed many understanding men's minds concerning him', (17) wrote Archbishop Laud, who all this time, confined in the Tower, waited anxiously for reports from Westminster. But the 'understanding men' were in a minority; more of the spectators were impressed by his indomitable resistance, brought day by day to his stake for the Commons to bait. This was no sullen captive bear, but a proud, wily, dauntless beast whose powerful blows time and again sent the snarling dogs of the prosecution head over heels and sprawling. Compared with such a bear-baiting the sport of Paris Garden was tame.

z

Nobler comparisons and nobler sentiments came into the minds of the cultivated courtiers in the better seats. Sir Richard Fanshawe and Sir John Denham were both to compose verses on the occasion.

> Great Strafford! worthy of that name though all
> Of thee could be forgotten, but thy fall,
> Crusht by Imaginary Treason's weight,
> Which too much merit did accumulate —

In these words Denham began the poem in which he described the calmness of the accused against the excitement and agitation of those about him:

> Such was his force of eloquence, to make
> The hearers more concerned than he that spake;
> Each seemed to act that part he came to see,
> And none was more a looker-on than he.
> So did he move our passion, some were known
> To wish for the defence, the crime their own.
> Now private pity strove with public hate,
> Reason with rage, and eloquence with fate:
> Now they could him, if he could them forgive,
> He's not too guilty, but too wise to live. [18]

Denham, a devoted King's man, touched the heart of the matter here, since none were more aware than the prosecutors that if the accused was acquitted it might well be in his power, within a short time, to reverse the position; they would become the accused and he the accuser.

The crowds who pushed in to Westminster Hall on April 10th to hear Strafford speak in his own defence were to be disappointed. Strafford indeed came, but no sooner was everyone placed than Glyn asked permission to call two new witnesses to articles fifteen and twenty-three. Strafford protested that if the prosecution were allowed to produce new evidence he must be given the same liberty. The Lords adjourned for an hour to consider the point, and gave it in favour of Strafford, but added that the Commons might waive their witnesses if they preferred to leave matters as before.

Strafford followed up the victory. Might he call witnesses on any of the charges, he asked, or only on those the Commons opened again? Once more the Lords withdrew and consulted with the judges, once more they were favourable to Strafford, but with the same reservation.

The Commons had to choose between forgoing their new witnesses or risking a re-trial of many articles best forgotten. After a brief consultation the managers decided to call Strafford's bluff; they did not believe he had any witnesses. Glyn rose to say they would proceed to their evidence on the fifteenth article. Instantly Strafford declared that he had further evidence on the second, fifth, twelfth and fifteenth articles, which must also be heard. Pym's party rose in their places. 'Withdraw! Withdraw!' they advised Glyn with deafening reiteration. 'Adjourn! Adjourn!' shouted the Lords of the same party to Arundel. They did not wait for him to do so. All those who were against Strafford crowded to the doors; the hall was in chaos, everyone shouting and arguing and the managers noisily blaming each other. Across the tumult Strafford turned and looked towards the King. They both laughed. [19]

NOTES

The description of Strafford's trial is from John Rushworth's volume devoted to it, except where otherwise stated.

[1] Baillie, I, pp. 314 ff; Nalson, II, 37; d'Ewes Journal, Harleian MSS, 162, folio 348. D'Ewes several times mentions the presence of the Prince of Wales among the peers and his departure about midday.

[2] Baillie, loc. cit.

[3] Whitelocke, p. 40.

[4] Ibid., loc. cit. Rushworth ascribes the objection to Strafford's suggestion of conspiracy to Glyn. D'Ewes (folio 350) gives it to Pym. I have followed d'Ewes.

[5] D'Ewes, Harleian MSS, 162, folio 350.

[6] H.M.C. *Various*, II, p. 261.

[7] D'Ewes, Harleian MSS, 162, folio 358.

[8] H.M.C., *Cowper MSS*, II, p. 280.

[9] D'Ewes, Harleian MSS, 162, folio 359.

[10] Ibid., folio 362.

[11] Ibid., folio 358.

[12] Brit. Museum, Additional MSS, 471, 45.

[13] *Lords Journals*, IV, p. 209; Brilliana Harley, p. 117.

[14] Rushworth's account of Strafford's trial jumps unaccountably from the conclusion of the twenty-seventh article to his final speech in his own defence. The gap is covered by Whitelocke, *Memorials*, pp. 40-1, *A Brief and Perfect Relation*, London, 1647, and Brit. Museum, Additional MSS, 471, 45.

[15] *Lords Journals*, IV, p. 211; *A Brief and Perfect Relation*, p. 55.

[16] H.M.C. *Various*, II, p. 261.

[17] Laud, *Works*, III, p. 440; the opinion is borne out also by the reports of Rossetti, the agent of the Vatican, Folger Library, Washington, Strozzi Transcripts, vol. 103, March-April 1641.

[18] John Denham, *Poetical Works*, ed. Banks, New Haven, 1928, pp. 153-4; Fanshawe's rather longer poem on the trial is in *Il Pastor Fido ... with an addition of divers other Poems*, London, 1664.

[19] *A Brief and Perfect Relation*, pp. 55-7; *C.S.P.D.*, 1640-1, p. 539; Additional MSS, 471, 45. This British Museum manuscript is an account of the trial combined with a rather fragmentary Parliamentary Diary from 22nd March to 26th April, 1641. I cannot identify the writer, who was evidently a friend or connection of Sir Philip Percival. It contains one or two details that I have found nowhere else, like the description of the attempt to force a vote on article 15.

—◦❧ ❧⟳❧❀❧⟳❧ ❦◦—

CHAPTER FIVE

THE ATTAINDER

*If I miscarry this way, I shall not even then be found either so indulgent
to myself or so narrowly heartened towards my master as to think myself
too good to die for him.*

Wentworth to Carlisle, 1632

AMONG the members of Parliament who crowded out of
Westminster Hall went Sir Arthur Hazelrig, a Leicestershire
squire and close supporter of John Pym. A white scroll was
sticking out of his pocket. It contained the substance of the
charges against Strafford re-drafted as a Bill of Attainder. [1]

Ever since the first days of the impeachment, Pym and his inner
group of supporters had known that they might have to fall back
on this antiquated and terrible machinery for putting Strafford to
death. It was clear, on the morning of April 10th, that they were
failing to prove him guilty by the ordinary rules of evidence and the
usual definitions of treason. It was unlikely that a majority of the
peers would be satisfied of his guilt after what had already
happened, still more unlikely that they would be satisfied if many
of the articles were reopened.

For two reasons, therefore, the method had to be altered. In
support of a Bill of Attainder before Parliament, Pym could produce his promised new evidence on the twenty-third article without
any opportunity being given for Strafford to produce new
evidence at all. Ordinary rules of justice and equity had nothing
to do with what was now to be simply a process of legislation. The
second and more important reason for proceeding against Strafford
by Bill of Attainder was that it would permit the peers, when the Bill
reached them, to vote for Strafford's death if they wished him dead,
without necessarily accepting the case against him as legally
proved. It was an ingenious method for meeting the scruples of
those who, though politically opposed to the accused, had been
troubled by the weakness of the actual charges against him.

As soon as the Commons were safely back in their own house,

Pym rose to his feet to offer the new evidence for article twenty-three. It was not, in fact, new evidence at all. It was simply that piece of paper information on which Pym had based the questions which had elicited from Secretary Vane his damningly detailed account of Strafford's alleged threat to bring over the Irish army. The notes made by him at the fateful Council meeting on May 5th had been found accidentally by his son, young Sir Harry Vane, some months later. After deep soul-searching he had thought it his duty to copy them out and deliver the copy to John Pym. Pym, after copying them in turn, had destroyed young Vane's copy. There was a great deal of copying and confusion in the whole business. But here, on paper for all to see, was — so it was averred — an authentic version of Secretary Vane's original minutes. Under the hieroglyphic abbreviation 'LL^t Ir^n', which could mean nothing but 'Lord Lieutenant of Ireland', occurred the words 'You have an army in Ireland you may employ *here* to reduce *this Kingdom*.'

The revelation of this paper and its origins in the House of Commons was followed by expostulations from old Sir Harry Vane, who declared himself astonished and appalled at his son's betrayal, but allowed himself in the end to be soothed by the advice of the Speaker and the filial expressions of young Harry. It is quite possible that this was play-acting on old Sir Harry's part. One of the Committee for the prosecution, George Digby, Lord Bristol's son, evidently thought so. It was now apparent to him, if not to his more innocent colleagues, that old Sir Harry's evidence had been prompted to him word for word from the paper which his son had betrayed to Pym; it was possible even that at some point before the trial old Sir Harry had been allowed to refresh his memory by consulting the copy of his notes. The actual notes, as he admitted, had been burnt, with the King's agreement, shortly before Parliament met. [2]

Digby seems to have been alone in his disillusion. The constant reiteration that these copied notes were additional evidence against Strafford produced a bewildering but not unconvincing effect on most of Pym's adherents and the atmosphere was now favourable for the introduction of the Bill of Attainder by Sir Arthur Hazelrig. It was read once before the House adjourned. [3] The following day was Sunday, and the Commons dispersed to consult their consciences and seek the guidance of Heaven.

On the Monday they held a conference with the Lords, and Vane's notes were read. Pym had now secured the effect that Strafford had so nearly spoiled for him on the previous Saturday; he had shown his alleged new evidence to the peers without exposing any of the charges to a re-trial or allowing the accused to bring new evidence of his own. The Commons went further; they indicated that there were other Councillors, Cottington in particular, whom Vane's paper incriminated. [4] This was a veiled threat that they doubtless hoped would keep the King's friends in wholesome fear.

In spite of the new moves in the House of Commons the trial was still to be concluded, and the fate of the Bill of Attainder in the House of Lords would be strongly affected one way or the other by Strafford's summing up in his own defence, which had not yet been heard and which Pym had no power to prevent.

Through a crowd of anxious and sympathetic spectators Strafford walked on the morning of April 13th from the river to Westminster Hall to make his last speech. He was a tragic figure, tall, gaunt, with bowed shoulders, his pale face lined with pain and fatigue, but in the midst of the whispering, excited crowd, alone unmoved.

In his speech he addressed himself to the Lords, appealing directly to their logic and justice. He answered Pym's manufactured theory of treason by showing that he had committed no known treason by any existing law, protesting that he had acted throughout with integrity to the King and zeal for the public good, and according to the laws and traditions of his country as he understood them. He spoke lucidly, running over one by one the heads of the arguments on every article of the charge. He was neither emotional nor rhetorical at first, but held his audience throughout by his quiet, incisive logic, and the occasional stroke of irony: 'he admired how himself who was an incendiary in the twenty-third article against the Scots is become their confederate in the twenty-eighth.' [5] For more than two hours he continued, hardly a spectator stirring, all eyes fixed on that solitary, dominating figure, the white face lit with a consuming fire, the beautiful hands moving now and again in the dramatic occasional gestures that he loved.

'I hope I am clear before your lordships,' he concluded at last, half apologetically, 'in good faith I am clear in my own poor judgment.' Now, with the force and passion he had so far held back, he turned from his own defence to the vindication of the monarchy:

'I have ever admired the wisdom of our ancestors, who have so fixed the pillars of this monarchy that each of them keeps due measure and proportion with other, and have so handsomely tied up the nerves and sinews of the State that the straining of one may bring damage and sorrow to the whole economy. The prerogative of the Crown and the propriety of the subject have such mutual relations that this took protection from that, that foundation and nourishment from this; and as on the lute, if anything be too high or too low wound up, you have lost the harmony, so here the excess of a prerogative is oppression, of a pretended liberty in the subject disorder and anarchy. The prerogative must be used as God doth his omnipotency, at extraordinary occasions; the laws ... must have place at all other times, and yet there must be a prerogative if there must be extraordinary occasions. The propriety of the subject is ever to be maintained if it go in equal pace with this; they are fellows and companions that have been and ever must be inseparable in a well-governed Kingdom; and no way so fitting to nourish both as the frequent use of Parliaments. By this a commerce and acquaintance is kept between the King and the subject. This thought has gone along with me these fourteen years of my public employment, and shall, God willing, to my grave. God, his Majesty, and my own conscience, yea all who have been accessory to my most inward thoughts and opinions can bear me witness. I ever did inculcate this: the happiness of a Kingdom consists in the just poise of the King's prerogative and the subject's liberty and that things should never be well till these went hand in hand together.'

This was the climax but not the end of his speech; once more he warned the peers against creating new treasons:

'My Lords, you see what may be alleged for this constructive — rather this *destructive* treason. For my part I have not the judgment to conceive that such a treason is either agreeable to the fundamental grounds of reason or law. Not of reason, for how can that be treason in the whole, which is not in any of the parts? or how can that make a thing treasonable which in itself is nothing so? Nor of law, since neither statute, common law, nor practice hath from the beginning of this government ever mentioned such a thing. And where I pray you, my Lords, hath this fire without the least token of smoke lien hid so many hundreds of years, and now breaks forth in a violent flame to destroy me and my posterity from the earth? My Lords, do we not live by laws, and must we be punishable by them ere they be made? Far better it were to live by no law at all, but be governed by those characters of discretion and virtue stamped in us, than to put this necessity of divination upon a man and to accuse him of the breach of a law ere it be a law at all? ... My Lords, if this crime which they call arbitrary treason had been marked by any discernment of the law, the ignorance of the same should not excuse me; but if it be no law at all, how can it in rigour, in strictness itself, condemn me? Beware you do not awake these sleeping lions by the raking up of some neglected, some motheaten records — they may sometime tear you and your posterity in pieces. It was your ancestors' care to chain them up within the barrier of a statute; be not you ambitious to be more skilful, more curious than your fathers were in the art of killing. My Lords, it is my present misfortune but forever yours.... You, your estates, your posterities lie all at the stake if such learned gentlemen as these, whose lungs are well acquainted with such proceedings, shall be started out against you: if your friends, your counsel were denied access to you, if your professed enemies admitted to witness against you, if every word, intention, circumstance of yours be alleged as treasonable, not because of a statute, but a consequence, a construction of law heaved up in a high rhetorical strain, and a number of supposed probabilities. I leave it to your Lordships' consideration to foresee what may be the issue of so dangerous, so recent precedencies. These gentlemen tell me they speak in defence of the commonweal against my arbitrary laws; give me leave to say that I speak in defence of the commonweal against their arbitrary treason.'

He had made his strongest point, and now lowered his tone again:

'I have now troubled your Lordships a great deal longer than I should have done; were it not for the interest of those pledges, that a saint in heaven left me, I would be loth my Lords ... '

So far he had not faltered, now his voice choked, the tears streamed down his cheeks, and for a few seconds he could not speak. Brokenly at last he concluded:

'What I forfeit for myself is nothing; but I confess, that my indiscretion should forfeit for them, it wounds me very deeply.... Something I should have said; but I see I shall not be able and therefore I will leave it. So my Lords even so with all humility, with all tranquillity of mind, I do submit myself clearly and freely to your judgments; and whether that righteous judgment shall be to Life or Death, Te Deum Laudamus, Te Dominum Confitemur.'

In these last words he transferred his appeal, and his submission, from his peers to God, and ended, not looking at his audience, but with eyes raised to heaven. [6]

Glyn was to answer, but for nearly an hour he conned his notes while the people shuffled and murmured, before at last he rose to measure his eloquence against Strafford's. His biting, close-packed, sometimes derisive words fell far short of what had gone before. When he had done, John Pym rose to conclude the argument for the prosecution. He was a persuasive speaker, in a sharp, pragmatical style, but he had nothing new to say. Wisely, he was brief. Even so, just before the end, his memory failed him, he wavered into silence, lost the thread, and had to pull out his notes and start again after embarrassed shuffling. [7] The strain of that day which had inspired Strafford, racked with sickness and suspense, to give the most powerful speech of all his public career had made Pym nervous and unsure. It was the difference between them: Strafford a natural fighter, exhilarated by challenge, at his best in conflict; Pym a subtle and ingenious manager of men, liking to move from one secured position to the next, taking risks only by necessity and without zest.

Had Strafford saved himself by the great speech in his own defence? There were those that thought so. He may have thought so himself. In the Tower he was heard to sing psalms of thanksgiving as he paced up and down in his room. [8] But the Commons continued to debate their Bill: a useless measure, if the Lords should reject it, as, surely, they would. The King had worked hard to make himself a party in the Upper House. Bedford, the ablest of the moderate lords, was beginning to see himself as the King's chief minister; he had practically undertaken to secure Strafford's life on the understanding that he should never again hold public office, an offer which not only the King but Strafford himself had made during his trial. Lord Bristol, too, had been nearly won in the same way, a dangerous move for the Commons, who had put his son, George Digby, on the Committee for the prosecution.

Pym realized clearly enough the danger of his position. He had staked everything on the removal of Strafford; if he failed, the Commons — or rather his party in the Commons — would be deeply discredited. The King would then be able to make use of the reaction to create support for himself in a divided House of which Pym would no longer be the leader. Already, under the stresses of the trial, the Commons showed signs of breaking from his control. All the more tenaciously did he and his supporters keep the Bill of Attainder before their attention.

On April 14th the Bill of Attainder was read a second time and directly afterwards a conference was demanded with the Lords, to explain the necessity for the new measure. It was tantamount to a declaration that they set no value on any judgment given as the outcome of the trial, and they underlined this decision by passing a resolution that the charge had been, in the opinion of the Lower House, conclusively proved.

It was close fighting now between Strafford and Pym, and immediately after this declaration came a petition from the prisoner in the Tower protesting against attempts to intimidate his counsel. [9] The Commons' resolution rendered Lane open to a charge of breach of privilege if he so much as mentioned the possibility of Strafford's innocence on any of the charges. The prisoner still seemed to be holding his own, for the peers, regardless of the hectoring Commons and their Bill, were resolved to hear Lane plead the legal arguments in Strafford's defence.

Richard Lane was as cool as Strafford, and when they appeared on April 17th in Westminster Hall both of them seemed confident, and Strafford, contrary to his habitual expression, looked 'well and cheerfully'. [10] Lane spoke shortly and with admirable clearness; he cited all known statutes of treason and demonstrated that by no interpretation whatever could Strafford's alleged crimes be brought under any of them. When he had finished, his colleague the Recorder of London, Thomas Gardiner, rose and declared to the Lords that it was impossible for him to add anything to what Lane had said unless he had leave to mention the facts as well as the law. The Lords were already restive, feeling that the Commons had forced them into an untenable position by insisting that Strafford could have counsel only for law and not for fact; they adjourned the Court while the case was considered and Strafford went back to the Tower.

A Sunday again intervened. Strafford's mood seemed calm and buoyant. He wrote to his eldest daughter, reassuring her: 'Your father as you desired hath been heard speak for himself now these three weeks together.' For the rest, it was a letter full of tender reassurance, promising to her and all his family a quiet life and a happy reunion, however reduced their fortunes might in future be. Nan was in her fourteenth year and her father was unlikely to write anything that would needlessly alarm her, but it seems probable that his letter reflected a genuine optimism. He was never good at hiding his feelings, and he hardly anticipated when he wrote to her that the folded paper would survive the centuries with her words across it: 'This was the last letter I had from my Lord.' [11]

It is hard to guess how much Strafford in the Tower really knew of what was going on at Whitehall and Westminster. He may have heard through Lady Carlisle that the Queen was giving way to her fears; he may have been confusedly aware of plots and intrigues stimulated in her circle for re-establishing the King's power and releasing or rescuing him by a military *coup*. [12] He may have darkly believed — as George Wentworth certainly did — in a conspiracy at Whitehall between his enemies and rivals, Hamilton, Arundel and Vane, to get rid of him and share the profits of his customs contracts and other public revenues. [13] He had always been too willing to believe in plots against himself, but there is no conclusive evidence to show that, at this time, he suspected other manoeuvres than those of the Earl of Cork and his Irish enemies, which were patent to anyone with eyes to see. It looks much more as though the King's wiser scheme to divide the peers and build a party for himself had Strafford's approbation, and the wilder plots which were to ruin everything were hardly known to him until too late. But they were known to Pym, who as early as the first week in April had been aware that there was a movement on foot among some of the courtiers with commands in the Army to overawe Parliament by force. [14] He does not appear to have apprehended any immediate action, but he held the information in readiness to use when it suited him.

Meanwhile on April 15th and again more intensively on the 19th the Commons argued over the guilt of Strafford. Had he committed treason? Assuming that the key articles were proved — and this meant especially the fifteenth and the twenty-third, which concerned the use of military force against the King's subjects — assuming that these were proved, was he guilty of treason? Was he guilty, on the charge as a whole, of treason or merely of subverting the laws? Was subverting the laws a kind of treason?

A powerful ally to Pym appeared in Lord Falkland; he was son and heir of that Deputy of Ireland whom Strafford had succeeded and whom he had never treated even with tact, let alone with generosity. Young Falkland was so well known for the nobility of his nature that no one could or would credit him with any but the purest motives. He was genuinely concerned about the justice of the matter, and more especially the meaning of the term 'cumulative' treason. His argument was simple and persuasive; 'how may hairs' breadths make a tall man and how many make a little man no man can well say, yet we know a tall man when we see him from a low man; so 'tis in this, how many illegal acts makes a treason, is not certainly well known but we well know it when we see it.' So Falkland, from his five foot three of honest patriotism slung his deadly bolt at Strafford's six foot of treason. [15]

This was effective and much-needed support, which Falkland pushed further in a second speech in which he argued that 'in equity, Strafford deserved to die' — though all his lawyer listeners must have known that no Court of equity could pronounce a death sentence. Falkland's reputation carried more weight than his matter, and needed to, for the lawyer with the highest reputation in the House came down on the opposite side. John Selden, strong opponent of the Court and supporter of Parliament on almost every legal issue, refused to concede that Strafford had, in law, committed anything that could be called treason. In despite of Selden, the Commons resolved that subversion of the laws was treason. [16]

On the following day, April 20th, the Commons began work by repealing the sentence on William Prynne as a sign that although Strafford occupied most of their time other matters were not forgotten. The rest of the day passed in debate on the Bill, Strafford's friends making a desperate stand, while the more vocal of their opponents insisted, in defiance of much that had been heard in Westminster Hall, that every charge had been fully proved. [17] On April 21st the morning began with the repeal of another Star Chamber sentence, then the House turned again to the Bill. Only 263 members out of nearly five hundred were present and some of them were ready to escape before the voting, being equally afraid of Pym's party and their own consciences. There had been dangerous-looking crowds in the city over the week-end, and a large number of doubtful members or open supporters of the King's party had stayed away. Pym had the doors locked and forbade any man to go out. The additions and amendments were twice read, and the House then adjourned for dinner.

In the afternoon the Bill was read a third time; excitement was now at its height. Pym had the House well in hand, when George Digby rose. His agitation was plain to see. For once in his life he spoke not with his habitual easy wit but with nervous sincerity. All along, he said, he had worked wholeheartedly with the Committee for the prosecution of Strafford; he believed him guilty, but the case was not proved. Secretary Vane's evidence that Strafford had offered to reduce England with an Irish army was not supported by any other witness who had been present at the time. Mr Pym had assured Digby that he had more, and conclusive, evidence that Vane's account was correct. But he had no such evidence. When he had produced it, it was nothing but a second-hand copy of notes taken by Vane himself. It was simply the same evidence in another form, and Vane remained, in effect, the only man among all those present who had heard the alleged offer to bring the Irish army into England.

George Digby was young, impulsive and brave; in the face of a mutter of opposition he went on:

'Let every man lay his hand upon his heart and sadly consider what we are going to do with a breath, either justice or murder.... Let every man purge his heart clear of all passions.... Away with personal animosities, away with all flatteries to the people, away with all fears, away with all such considerations, as that it is not fit for a Parliament, that one accused by it of treason should escape with life. Of all these corruptions of judgment, I do, before God, discharge myself, to the uttermost of my power, and do with a clear conscience wash my hands of this man's blood, by this solemn protestation, that my vote goes not to the taking of the Earl of Strafford's life.' [18]

He ended, and sat down leaving Pym's party to answer the challenge.

Whether his speech helped or hindered Strafford's cause was hard to tell; the member for Windsor supported him with a vigorous assertion that the Commons were about to 'commit murder with the sword of justice', [19] but the waverers were frightened by the ugly looks bent on Strafford's defenders and especially these two. They were not all young and daring with useful connections in the House of Lords and at Court; and they had Pym's examination into the Ship-money levy still hanging over them.

The Bill was put to the vote. When the general movement had subsided, the tellers in a breathless silence gave in the numbers. Two hundred and four had voted for the Bill, fifty-nine had voted against. Amid the wild cheering of his supporters Pym carried the Bill to the Upper House and in a short speech asserted that the Commons would justify their action wherever and whenever the Lords appointed. [20]

As the Commons dispersed, an agitated gentleman clutched at the arm of one of Strafford's friends. The Bill would be thrown out in the Lords, he explained breathlessly; would he please tell my Lord of Strafford, that a great many gentlemen could not help themselves for fear of Mr Pym, but the Bill would get no further.

They would not have voted for it, but they knew it would do no harm. (21)

But Pym had not navigated the Bill through the Lower House to see it cast out by the peers and rejected by the King. The work of intimidation, once begun, had to go on. Rumours of plots and foreign invasions hung in the air; the Londoners were encouraged to show their feelings in noisy petition and tumult. On April 22nd Digby was accused of betraying the confidences of the Committee for the prosecution; (22) he cleared himself, but the member for Windsor, who had supported him in his attack on the twenty-third article, was expelled from the House, (23) and the names of all members who had voted for Strafford were posted up about London and Westminster with the legend 'These are the Straffordians, enemies of justice, betrayers of their country.' (24) It was a breach of privilege, but it served its purpose and the Commons made no protest.

It was still possible that the pusillanimous members who had voted unwillingly for the Attainder on the plea that the Lords, or the King, would stop its passage might be right in their belief. The King had made it very clear from the outset that he did not intend to let his servant die. He had been gracious to him at more than one of his public appearances, and he had significantly forbidden the carrying of the axe — the symbol of death — before him. Yet there were those at Court who feared the King's weakness as the chief danger. (25) Charles himself was still confident that he could and would save Strafford's life. On April 23rd he wrote assuring him that, although he could no longer employ him on state affairs, he should not suffer in life, honour or fortune. (26) It was a generous letter, and one of the few signs of personal regard that the King ever gave to his servant. The sending of the letter seems to have coincided with the development of that policy by which Charles planned to save Strafford through the good offices of Bristol and Bedford in the House of Lords.

On April 24th, by which time he would have received the King's letter, Strafford was writing to Hamilton to ask for his intervention in the House of Lords on this same plea. The letter was presumably intended to be shown at the proper time in the House, where Hamilton sat under his English title as Earl of Cambridge. Strafford wrote:

It is told me that the lords are inclinable to preserve my life and family, for which their generous compassions the great God of mercy will reward them: and surely should I die upon this evidence, I had much rather be the sufferer than the judge.

All that I shall desire from your lordship, is that, divested of all public employment, I may be admitted to go home to my own private fortune, there to attend my own domestic affairs, and education of my children, with as little asperity of words or marks of infamy as possibly the nobleness and justice of my friends can procure for me. [27]

On the same day petitioners from London came to Parliament with a petition against Strafford's life alleged to carry twenty thousand signatures. [28] Intimidated by these demonstrations the peers showed little zest for the Bill one way or the other when it came to its first reading on Monday, April 26th. Nerve-racked with the increasing anxiety of each day, Edward Hyde, one of Pym's most ardent supporters, walked that evening up to the bowling-green in Piccadilly to clear his brain and breathe the fresh spring air. The gardens were crowded with people, here and there some of the peers and Parliament men passed to and fro deep in discussion; Strafford's fate was the only talk, 'the great business' on which all the affairs of the Kingdom waited. Bedford came up to Hyde and asked him his opinion. Bedford himself felt that the opportunity was not to be lost — Strafford's life would buy any concessions from the King, and he would prevent Strafford's death if it cost him his crown. They must therefore use the chance that fate had sent them. A little further on they met Essex and Hertford both arguing the same point. Essex was immovable in his opinions; Strafford disgraced and retired from public service would still contrive to be a power in the state. The King's unwillingness to yield him showed how the King's affections lay. 'Stone dead hath no fellow,' repeated Essex, shaking his wise head. [29]

And now Cottington had suddenly resigned as Chancellor of the Exchequer, and it was said the King had offered this lucrative post to John Pym. The move was part of Bedford's scheme for a new and broad-based government, but Pym knew more than Bedford of the King's secret plans with his army officers; he also knew that no money would be forthcoming from London for the urgent necessities of the state until Strafford was dead. He refused the offer. [30]

On April 27th the Bill was read again in the Lords. Then, suddenly, things began to move. The King attempted to introduce extra troops into the Tower under the command of an officer he trusted. Sir William Balfour, lieutenant of the Tower, loyal to Parliament, would not receive them. Rumours of intended force and intended invasions blazed through London. Questions were asked in Parliament about a ship commissioned by Strafford's faithful secretary Guildford Slingsby, fully manned, ready to sail, that had lain for the past eight weeks at Tilbury. [31] Strafford himself at about this time seems to have sounded Balfour, with an offer of £20,000, to connive at his escape. The move was unwise and out of line with his own plans, which were, at this moment, more akin to Bedford's. But since the King was now ready to make his *coup* it is probable that Strafford acted on an instruction from the Court. [32] But from the moment that Balfour refused to receive the new troops in the Tower, the King should have known that his army plot had failed. He tried to wipe out the evil effects of his false move by making the Earl of Newport, Strafford's enemy and a half-brother of the popular Earl of Warwick, Constable of the Tower, and having the guard on Strafford's prison doubled. [33]

In an atmosphere now thick with rumours, the peers on April 29th heard Oliver St John argue, in the presence of Strafford, the case for ordaining his death by Attainder. He spoke at length and in the viciously vindictive manner that had characterized much of the attack on Strafford. Assuming that the major charges were sufficiently proved, he urged the peers to pass the Bill, despite any scruples they might have about the legal quibbles over proofs on the meaning of treason. 'He that would not have had others to have a law, why should he have any himself?' Noble and honourable game was protected by rules of sportsmanship, but 'it was never accounted either cruelty or foul play to knock foxes and wolves on the head ... because they be beasts of prey.' At the close of this, the most insulting speech yet made about him, Strafford raised his eyes and hands in mute appeal towards heaven. [34]

But Pym's Bill seemed to hang by a thread. Young Vane's famous paper, which had mysteriously vanished, was found again with the key words altered. In the fatal phrase, 'there' had been substituted for 'here'. Even some of the more hostile peers began to doubt the evidence. [35] On Friday, April 30th, the King discussed the situation with Bristol and Bedford and he seems to have got Bedford's approval for another of his personal interventions in Parliament. If he were to speak to both Houses and emphasize the danger inherent in passing a Bill which would create new precedents for treason and perhaps initiate a practice by which the illegal could be made legal, and the laws of the land be stretched or set aside at will by Special Act of Parliament, he might sway the uncertain peers against the Bill. This, presumably, was the argument which the Earl of Bedford advised.

Whether at this point there was, or could be, any communication with Strafford in the Tower is doubtful. He certainly knew the King's intervention to have been disastrous after it had happened. Before, he may have felt (as Bedford did) that the right speech from the King could achieve something.

The King did not make the right speech. The Earl of Bedford was taken dangerously ill in the night, and Charles, without his help and apparently prompted by Lord Saye, declared before the assembled Parliament of England that in his conscience he could on no account agree to the condemnation of Strafford.

'My lords I hope you know what a tender thing conscience is: yet I must declare unto you that to satisfy my people I would do great matters; but this of conscience, no fear or respect whatsoever shall make me go against it.' [36]

Not one straw of opportunity did he give to Bristol and those who would have supported a reasoned objection to the Bill. Instead he opposed the impassable barrier of his private conscience to the will of his Parliament and the desires of his people. The speech, wrote sad old Archbishop Laud in the Tower, 'displeased mightily and I verily think hastened the Earl's death'. [37]

The next day was Sunday, and while Lords and Commons pondered the King's ill-chosen words, Whitehall was decked for festivities and the King's eldest daughter was married to the thirteen-year-old Prince of Orange. The children, with their attendants in cloth of silver, went through the ceremony gravely, and the anxious courtiers passed the evening in games and amusements, only the young Elector Palatine added grotesquely to the King's difficulties by shutting himself up in his room and declaring that the princess had been promised to him from babyhood.

On the Monday the peers met in no favourable mood. Bedford was dying, and the other leader of the moderate group, Bristol, was unable after Charles's speech to draw his supporters together. In the House of Commons, Pym had acted at last, at the right and critical moment, on the information he had about the plot between the Court and the Army. A Committee was appointed to inquire into it, and before this he laid the information he had had concerning the King's projected *coup*. A little after ten o'clock, some members, leaving Westminster, were pestered by the crowds to know what was happening. 'There is hot work and a great fire within,' one of them jested as he hurried through.

From lip to lip the rumour spread. The House of Commons was in flames; the papists, the army, Strafford — it was all one — had blown up Parliament. 'In a clap', as Baillie wrote, 'all the city is in alarum; shops closed; a world of people in arms runs down to Westminster.' It was more than the mob; respectable burgesses forgetting their business and their position fell in with the stream. [38] All that day and all the next they stormed Westminster, crying 'Justice, justice!' They flung themselves upon the carriages of the peers, clamouring to know which way they would vote; they mobbed Lord Bristol's house threatening vengeance on him and his 'false son'. [39] Meanwhile in the besieged Houses the Committee on the Army Plot made shocking revelations, and while the King's incriminated supporters fled the country, Pym called for the closing of the ports, and a new oath or protestation of loyalty to Parliament was enforced upon all members.

In his prison at the Tower, Strafford realized that the end was upon him. After the King's speech in Parliament, after the revelations of the Army Plot, the chances that a majority of the peers would wish — or dare — to reject the Bill were very small. For six months, he had been playing with his life as a stake; now he saw that he was going to lose it. Or could he yet save himself and the King? At Westminster there had been some who shouted that if they did not have Strafford's life, they would have the King's. [40]

In more ways than one, their danger was linked. Between the first
revelations of the Army Plot in the House of Commons on May
3rd, and the explosive full revelations on May 5th, Strafford wrote
to the King one of the most famous letters in history, pleading not
for life but for death. He 'turned 'gainst himself his conquering
eloquence', as Richard Fanshawe was later, in a poem, to write of
him. (41)

May it please your Sacred Majesty ... I understand the
minds of men are more and more incensed against me, notwithstanding your Majesty hath declared, that in your
princely opinion I am not guilty of treason, and that you are not
satisfied in your conscience to pass the Bill.... This bringeth
me in a very great streight, there is before me the ruin of my
children and family, hitherto untouched with any foul crime:
here are before me the many ills, which may befall your
Sacred Person and the whole kingdom should yourself and
Parliament part less satisfied one with the other than is
necessary for the preservation both of King and people;
they are before me the things most valued, most feared by
mortal men, Life or Death.

To say, Sir, that there hath not been a strife in me, were to
make me less man than, God knoweth, my infirmities make
me, and to call a destruction upon myself and my young
children may be believed, will find no easy consent from
flesh and blood, and therefore in few words as I put myself
wholly upon the honour and justice of my peers, so clearly
as to wish your Majesty might please to have spared that
declaration of yours on Saturday last and entirely to have
left me to their lordships; so now to set your Majesty's conscience at liberty, I do most humbly beseech your Majesty for
prevention of evils which may happen by your refusal to
pass this Bill; and by this means to remove I cannot say this
accursed but I confess this unfortunate thing, forth of the way
towards that blessed agreement which God I trust shall ever
establish between you and your subjects.

Sir, my consent shall more acquit you herein to God than
all the world can do besides; to a willing man there is no
injury done, and as by God's grace I forgive all the world,

with calmness and meekness of infinite contentment to my dislodging soul; so Sir, to you, I can give the life of this world with all the cheerfulness imaginable, and only beg that in your goodness you would vouchsafe to cast your gracious regard upon my poor son and his three sisters, less or more, and no otherwise than as their (in present) unfortunate father, may hereafter appear more or less guilty of this death. God long preserve your Majesty. Your Majesty's most faithful and humble subject and servant Strafford. [42]

What was the meaning of this letter, what the thoughts that prompted it? 'To say, Sir, that there hath not been a strife in me were to make me less man than, God knoweth, my infirmities make me.... ' There had indeed been strife and the letter served two purposes. He knew that by releasing the King from his promise he gave up the only protection that he had against the now audible and rising hatred of the people, and the will of the House of Commons. But could he, by doing this, by taking this ultimate risk, yet redeem what had been lost? It was just possible that he could.

Earlier that year, in the lull between his impeachment and his trial, there had been a momentary crisis over the hanging of a priest named Goodman. The King had reprieved him. The Commons had been indignant. There had been demonstrations in London. Goodman from his prison had petitioned the King to let him die rather than that he should cause discord between the King and his people. This petition being made known in the House of Lords had swayed them against the Commons, and the clamour for Goodman's death had been abandoned. [43]

Had Strafford this precedent in mind? If the King would show his letter to the peers it might have a double effect. In the first place it would show him willing to die, however unjustly, to further the agreement of King and people. Such an offer might, as it had done with Goodman, stimulate the peers into showing their independence of the judgment of the Commons.

But the letter contained more than that. The argument was lucid, the purpose clear — as was usual with Strafford's political utterances. He had expressed a respectful criticism of the King's intervention in Parliament, and he had liberated the King from

374

that very scruple of conscience which he had there publicly set up as a barrier against his consent to the Bill. The letter was intended, privately, to release the King from his personal promise given on April 23rd in his message to Strafford; but it could be used publicly to release the King from the promise he had himself made before Parliament on May 1st. So used, it would cast the responsibility for Strafford's life or death back upon his peers, modify the ill effect of what the King had said, and conceivably lead to the rejection of the Bill of Attainder.

It was not so used. Perhaps the King did not receive it in time; perhaps he failed to understand its possibilities. Perhaps it could have done no good. Even as Strafford wrote it the landslide had begun in the House of Lords. The menacing crowds frightened the more moderate peers, and even Strafford's friends began to offer reasons for absence or abstention. The Earl of Bristol, showing less courage than his son had done, announced that since he had been a witness he could not vote on the Bill. The same excuse was seized on eagerly by several others whose loyalty to the Court would otherwise have made them vote in Strafford's favour. The Earl of Hertford and four more on whose support the King had counted, so long as he guaranteed Strafford's removal from public life, now simply absented themselves. All the Roman Catholic peers, with some justification, feared the violence of the mob and would not come. Even the Earl of Cumberland, brother of Strafford's first wife and friend since boyhood, began to waver, suggesting that so close a relationship to the accused disqualified him from voting. Inevitably, suave Bishop Williams reminded the bishops that, as they had taken no part in the trial, they should refrain now from exercising their right to vote. With incredible feebleness the whole bench of bishops followed this crafty, cowardly and mistaken policy. [44]

Lord Chief Justice Bankes bleakly declared that, if they were satisfied of the proofs of the fifteenth and twenty-third articles, then Strafford was guilty of treason. On the following day, May 8th, the Bill was put to the vote. Through the crowd that besieged the doors, the peers pressed in to take their seats. It was a thin House. The Bill of Attainder against the Earl of Strafford was passed by twenty-six votes to nineteen. [45]

Now there was only the King. On Sunday, May 9th, the mob stormed Whitehall; the Queen and her ladies hid in their apartments, shivering and confessing, expecting hourly that the people would rush the gates of the palace. Distractedly Lord Clare and Denzil Holles wandered from room to room, now joined by George Wentworth, now by Slingsby, still cogitating some wild scheme to save Strafford's life. But the Constable of the Tower, Lord Newport, had openly declared that if the King gave no consent he would have his prisoner killed on his own authority. Through the windows of the Gatehouse, Radcliffe looked out on the swaying crowds. 'What am I to do? How can I help you?' he wrote in anguish to Strafford. (46)

Prevented from giving evidence for him, and cited more than once in evidence against him, the hapless Radcliffe longed at least to see and speak to his friend. It was not possible, and Strafford, himself now in great anguish of mind, answered, 'I think it best you stay where you are and let us see the issue of tomorrow.' Those who came to him were now closely watched and sometimes in danger. Messages passed between him and Guildford Slingsby, but since the incident of the ship which Slingsby had chartered he did not think it safe or wise to let this faithful friend and servant be seen with him in person. Some time on that day of strangled, torturing hopes he wrote to him:

> I would not, as the case now stands, for anything you should endanger yourself. Your going to the King is to no purpose. I am lost. My body is theirs but my soul is God's. There is little trust in men. God may yet if it please him deliver me.... The person you were last withal at Court sent to move that business we resolved upon which if rightly handled might perchance do something, but you know my opinion in all and what my belief is in all these things.... ' (47)

A surviving paper without superscription contains what is probably Strafford's last political memorandum to the King. It may be this was the 'business we resolved upon', of which he wrote to Slingsby. The advice is explicit. The King should once again speak to Parliament: he should clearly state from his own personal knowledge that the charge made in the twenty-third article was utterly false, and he should complain of breach of Parliamentary privilege by intimidation. Finally he should offer, instead of the Bill of Attainder, to accept a bill disenabling Strafford from all public employment. He should have Strafford's letter, releasing him from his promise to preserve his life, ready to read out if the occasion offered. [48]

For the last time in his life, King Charles either could not or would not act on Strafford's advice. At Whitehall he prayed and hesitated. He sent for the judges and found their statements on treason unhelpful. He sent for some of the bishops. The most persuasive of the group was, naturally, Bishop Williams; but it is not easy to discover what they said to the King, for the biographer of Williams in justifying his master has done his best to confuse the trail. It looks as though only Bishop Juxon and the inflexible Bishop Ussher urged the King to act as his conscience directed. But the specious argument was put forward that his public and his private duty were different things, and that he could go against his conscience as a man when his conscience as a King required it. [49] The doctrine has an unmistakable tang of Williams about it: the offspring of the same guileful mind which argued that bishops could vote in capital cases, but not in this particular one. The distribution of blame between the bishops hardly matters; their culpable weakness had placed the King in his present quandary. Had they shown more courage and more judgment the Bill could have been stopped in the Lords.

The long afternoon passed and the King could make no decision, while the angry crowds surged shouting in the gates and alleys of Whitehall. Charles had the letter which Strafford had written absolving him from his promise, the letter that could have been used in a different way and would not be so used: the last letter from this mighty subject and faithful minister in the long sequence going back now for eleven years, couched in the familiar, parenthetic style, written in the familiar clear, angular hand, ending as always with the prayer: 'God long preserve your Majesty.'

It was not to preserve himself; that the King said and believed, and it was probably true. At nine o'clock on that May evening when he gave way, with tears in his eyes, it was to preserve his wife and children from the thrusting mob at the gates. He would give his consent to the Bill. Early the next morning the Earl of Manchester and the Earl of Lindsey were to convey his decision to the peers. 'My Lord of Strafford's condition is happier than mine,' he said. [50]

NOTES

[1] *C.S.P.D.*, 1640-1, p. 540.

[2] D'Ewes, *Notes*, Harleian MSS, 164, folio 162; Verney, pp. 37-8, Clarendon, III, 130-6. The scene in the House between the two Vanes is from Clarendon and may therefore be somewhat heightened in effect. George Digby in his speech on April 21st (Rushworth, *Trial*, pp. 50-3) denied that he believed in any collusion between old Vane and his interrogators before the trial, in such a way as to suggest that this was exactly what he *did* believe in. To have said so would have been an infringement of privilege; Digby was quite clever enough to 'plant' the idea with his hearers by explaining and then denying this suspicion. It was certainly the production of Vane's notes that convinced Digby at the eleventh hour that there was after all *no* substantial evidence for treason. The incident may have had the same effect on others who had not the courage to say so, but in general Pym seems to have got away with this rather horrible piece of political sleight of hand by the sheer emphasis that he put on the newness and significance of evidence that was neither new nor significant.

[3] *Commons Journals*, II, p. 118.

[4] Ibid., p. 119.

[5] *C.S.P.D.*, 1640-1, p. 543.

[6] There are variant versions of this speech. I have used chiefly the text given in *C.S.P.D.*, 1640-1, pp. 540 ff, which is fuller than that in Rushworth. Strafford's tears when he spoke of his wife, and Pym's failure of memory, are attested by several independent witnesses (Baillie, Verney, etc.). Strafford's final looking towards heaven is mentioned by the compiler of the vivid *Brief and Perfect Relation*.

[7] Verney, p. 43; Baillie, I, p. 348.

[8] H.M.C., XII, ii, p. 279.

[9] *Lords Journals*, IV, pp. 217 ff; *Commons Journals*, II, p. 122.

[10] H.M.C., loc. cit.

[11] Strafford MSS, XL; the letter is quoted in full both in Lady Burghclere's *Strafford*, II, p. 311, and in Lord Birkenhead's *Strafford*, p. 314.

[12] *Manchester's Memoirs*, Brit. Museum, Additional MSS, 15, 567.

[13] *Radcliffe Letters*, pp. 228 ff.

[14] D'Ewes, Harleian MSS, 163, folio 328.

[15] Verney, p. 15.

[16] Ibid., pp. 53-4; *Brief and Perfect Relation*, p. 68; *Commons Journals*, II, p. 123.

[17] D'Ewes, Harleian MSS, 164, folio 181.

[18] Rushworth, *Trial*, pp. 50-3.

[19] H.M.C., *MSS of Lord Montagu of Beaulieu*, p. 130.

[20] *Commons Journals*, II, pp. 123-5.

[21] Knowler, II, p. 432.

[22] Rushworth, III, i, p. 248.

[23] *Commons Journals*, II, pp. 137, 158–9.

[24] Rushworth, *Trial*, p. 59.

[25] H.M.C., *Cowper MSS*, II, p. 278.

[26] Knowler, II, p. 416.

[27] Burnet, *Lives of the Hamiltons*, pp. 182-3.

[28] Rushworth, III, i, p. 233.

[29] Clarendon, III, 161-4.

[30] *C.S.P.D.*, 1640-1, p. 560; see *The King's Peace*, pp. 420-1; Pearl, pp. 205–6.

[31] D'Ewes, Harleian MSS, 163, folio 110; *Husband's Exact Collections*, p. 233.

[32] Rushworth, III, i, pp. 238, 254; H.M.C., *Portland MSS*, 1, p. 719.

33 *Lords Journals*, IV, p. 236.

34 *Brief and Perfect Relation*, p. 79.

35 *C.S.P.D.*, 1640-1, p. 560.

36 Rushworth, III, i, p. 239.

37 Laud, *Works*, III, p. 441; Rossetti (Strozzi transcripts, 103, 7th-17th May, 1641) and others also report the uproar caused by this speech.

38 Baillic, I, p. 352; *C.S.P.D.*, 1640-1, p. 569.

39 *Brief and Perfect Relation*, p. 85.

40 Harleian MSS, 6424, folios 58, 59.

41 Fanshawe, *Il Pastos Fido*, p. 303.

42 Rushworth, *Trial*, pp. 743 ff.

43 Rushworth, III, i, p. 166; in the House of Commons the objection to Goodman's reprieve was linked to the evident belief that, if the King exercised his prerogative of mercy in this case, he would do the same also for Strafford when the time came. The connection has been made clear by Valerie Pearl, who shows that the attack on the King in this instance came from Alderman Pennington in the name of the citizens. It was very shortly followed by clear indications that no money would be forthcoming from London for the necessities of the state 'till the Earl of Strafford have lost his head'. Pearl, *London and the Outbreak of the Puritan Revolution*, pp. 201, 205–6; d'Ewes, ed. Notestein, p. 383.

44 Harleian MSS, 6424, folios 50, 63-4.

45 *Brief and Perfect Relation*, p. 85; another figure is given in *C.S.P.D.*, 1640-1, p. 571 — fifty-one votes to nine. The whole question is doubtful because after the Restoration the proceedings were expunged from the Journals of the House of Lords.

46 *Radcliffe Letters*, p. 224.

47 Rushworth, *Trial*, p. 774.

48 *Camden Miscellany*, IX, IV, pp. 23-5; the original is in Strafford MSS, XL.

49 Hacket, *Scrinia Reserata*, p. 161; Parr, *Life of James Ussher*, pp. 45-6.

50 Knowler, II, p. 432; Gardiner, IX, pp. 366-7.

CHAPTER SIX

THOMAS WENTWORTH

He is dead with more honour than any of them will gain which hunted after his life.

WILLIAM LAUD, 1644

LORD CLEVELAND was charged to take word to the prisoner in the Tower, but his heart must have failed him for it was one of the royal secretaries, Dudley Carleton, who, late on the evening of May 9th, came alone into his room.

Later that night he visited the Archbishop, consoling the broken old man with the news that his friend had accepted the King's decision with courage and resignation. To others he told a different story; Strafford had been astounded by the news so that Carleton had need to repeat his message before its meaning penetrated, then with a sudden gesture of anguish he had cried out, 'Put not your trust in princes nor in the sons of men for in them there is no salvation.' [1]

Whether indeed the memory of his unwearying service and the recollection of a world which with all its pain and cruelty he had intensely loved wrenched up from the depths of Strafford's soul that outcry against the King, which Carleton in charity hid from Laud, or whether Carleton himself invented the tragic story, no one now can tell.

On the morning of the 10th the Commons were told of the King's consent. They received the news in breathless silence; but as they hurried out to dinner in the dazzling sunshine, Maynard, unable to contain his high spirits any longer, caught hold of the nearest arm he saw, which was that of John Bramston, the son of an impeached judge, and almost shouted, 'Now we have done our work; if we could not have effected this we could have done nothing.' [2]

On the 11th the King sent his son to the House of Lords with one last appeal for his servant's life.

'I did yesterday satisfy the justice of this kingdom', he pleaded, by passing the Bill of Attainder against the Earl of Strafford; but mercy being as inherent and inseparable to a King as Justice, I desire at this time in some measure to show that likewise, by suffering that unfortunate man to fulfil the natural course of his life in a close imprisonment; this if it may be done without the discontentment of my people will be an unspeakable contentment to me ... but if no less than his life can satisfy my people I must say 'Fiat Justitia'. Thus I rest ... your unalterable and affectionate friend, Charles R.

If he must die, it were charity to reprieve him till Saturday. [3]

Even the pitiful postscript was disregarded.

He had been Earl of Strafford, Lord Lieutenant of Ireland, Lord President of the North, Lieutenant-General of the King's forces, Knight of the most noble Order of the Garter; now by Act of Attainder, he was Thomas Wentworth, as naked of honour, riches and titles as when his godparents received him from the hands of the priest at the font of St Dunstan's in the West, and with that submissive reverence to order which never left him, he gave himself no other name in the few last letters he wrote.

The duties of the world still disturbed him. He had his wife and children to think of, his brothers, his friends, his servants; there was Wandesford's eldest boy, left partly in his care by his father's will; there were the Yorkshire gentry whose expenses in victualling the army during the last summer he had guaranteed. He had contracted over a hundred thousand pounds of debt in the last year in the King's service, [4] while some of his goods had already been seized in Ireland and his estates were forfeit. Through the intervention of his brothers-in-law and the will of the King, he knew that this part of the law would not be enforced on his innocent children. But when he petitioned the Lords that he might have a week to set his affairs in order, they would not agree, and the execution was irrevocably fixed for Wednesday, May 12th. [5]

In common decency no one spoke of enforcing the law to its uttermost limit; the Act of Attainder provided that Wentworth should be hanged, drawn and quartered as a traitor, but he was granted the privilege of the axe. [6] He asked the King to let him die at least in the privacy of the Tower, but Charles had not the power to grant even this last mercy; [7] an army of workmen were already erecting the ramshackle stands of boards that were to serve for the spectators now crowding into London, and during those last days the distant sound of hammering can rarely have been out of his ears.

He asked to speak with Laud for spiritual help but Sir William Balfour would not let them meet without the permission of Parliament. 'It is not a time now either for him to plot heresy or me to plot treason,' said Wentworth, 'but I have gotten my dispatch from them and will trouble them no more; I am now petitioning a higher court, where neither partiality can be expected nor error feared.' [8] To Radcliffe he had written two days before the passing of the Bill.

Gentle George, let me have your prayers for the forgiveness of my sins and saving of my soul. Meet I trust we shall in Heaven, but I doubt not on earth. Howbeit of all men living I should be gladdest to spend an hour with you privately, if that might be admitted, that might comfort me.

They could not have their hour. All that Radcliffe could do was to write a last letter of farewell, promising to devote all that remained of his life to the service of his friend's family and asking pardon for any unwitting wrong he had done him. Wentworth could hardly trust himself to answer. Turning over the scrap of paper he wrote on the back:

Dear George, — Many thanks I give you for the comfort you gave me in this letter. All your desires are freely granted; and God deliver you out of this wicked world according to the innocence that is in you.

He added some brief instructions on his affairs and sent it back without signature or farewell. [9]

He had written already before he knew of the King's consent to thank Guildford Slingsby, who had been throughout his trial, faithful, efficient, always at his side. Now he was anxious for his safety.

Keep out of the way till I be forgotten and then your return may be with safety.... Time is precious and mine I expect to be very short.... God direct and prosper you in all your ways; and remember there was a person whom you were content to call master, that did very much value and esteem you, and carried to his death a great stock of his affections for you.... In more equal times my friends, I trust shall not be ashamed to mention the love to my children for their father's sake. (10)

His other friends came to offer what help they could to his children and his family. Sir William Pennyman came, Sir Gervase Clifton, and the Earl of Cleveland with his son; his brothers-in-law the Earls of Clare and Cumberland; Sir Philip Mainwaring, and his nephew Sir William Savile.

Wentworth passed much of his time with Ussher; when Laud was refused him his mind turned at once to the harsh Primate of Ireland and Ussher responded generously, saying later, when he had received the last burden of Wentworth's conscience, that in his knowledge of men 'never such a white soul returned to his maker'. He had expected to find the fallen statesman embittered and distracted, railing against the enemies who had ringed him round and cut him down; but he found Wentworth calm and constant in faith, the dross of his nature purified away, facing death in humble repentance for his sins and with perfect forgiveness towards his enemies. This, later, he was to tell the King, who shed tears in vain and too late. (11)

But he had been to Whitehall before he came to the Tower and had spoken, some said, rigorously. Charles besought him to tell 'my lord of Strafford' that had it not been for personal danger he had never consented to the Bill, that he believed him innocent and would remember his children. All this Ussher told the prisoner and Wentworth in return used the last favour of his master to put forward a plea for his children and his friends. He asked for a year's grace to find the money that his estate might owe to the King on the various branches of the revenue for which he had been responsible. He reminded the King that the Bishop of Derry, John Bramhall, was under a threat of impeachment in Ireland and George Radcliffe in England, and assured him that both were innocent; he recommended to his notice Robert Dillon, as a very able man, he suggested that Ormonde be given the place among the Knights of the Garter that his own attainder vacated, and that either Ormonde or Cottington be made Lord Deputy of Ireland. Lastly he asked the King to remember that he had promised a place at Court to one of the Yorkshire gentlemen who had given evidence for him at his trial. [12]

These worldly matters once decided, he devoted himself to the care of his soul, confessed to Ussher, and gave himself up to the contemplation of eternity. His humility astonished the Primate, for he cast himself with perfect faith on the mercy of God, arrogating to himself in those last hours none of the merits he had so often boasted when he was great.

Wentworth had one more request for Ussher; when he left him he asked him to go to Laud, tell him how little he feared to die, and ask him, for the sake of their past friendship, to stand at his window in the morning and bless him as he passed. Laud thanked Ussher for his good news of Wentworth's courage but shook his head over that last request; he doubted he would have the strength to come, and sent word to Wentworth to forgive him if he failed. His prayers and his blessing went with him always in spirit. [13]

There had been so much to do and think of that Wentworth had little time to make long farewells. He charged his brother George with many messages, to his wife, his children and his friends in Ireland, Ormonde above all others. [14] Ussher was to bid farewell to his supporters in London, to the Earl of Leicester, and to the light-hearted, unreliable Cottington who had been so staunch at the end. He wrote only one letter of farewell, to his son:

My dearest Will, these are the last lines you are to receive from a father that tenderly loves you. I wish there were a greater leisure to impart my mind unto you, but our merciful God will supply all things by His grace, and guide and protect you in all your ways; to whose infinite goodness I bequeath you.

Be sure you give all respect to my wife, that hath ever had a great love unto you. Never be awanting in love and care to your sisters, but let them ever be most dear unto you: and the like regard must you have to your youngest sister; for indeed you owe it her also, both for her father and mother's sake.

The King I trust will deal graciously with you, restore you those honours and that fortune which a distempered time hath deprived you of together with the life of your father. Be sure to avoid as much as you can to inquire after those that have been sharp in their judgments towards me, and I charge you never to suffer thought of revenge to enter your heart.

And God Almighty of His infinite goodness bless you and your children's children; and His same goodness bless your sisters in like manner, perfect you in every good work, and give you right understanding in all things.

You must not fail to behave yourself towards my Lady Clare your grandmother with all duty and observance; for most tenderly doth she love you and hath been passing kind unto me. God reward her charity for it. And once more do I, from my very soul, beseech our gracious God to bless and govern you in all, and join us again in the communion of His blessed saints where is fullness of joy and bliss for evermore. Amen. Amen. Your loving father. (15)

A more joyous Maytide had rarely been welcomed in London. Every inn and every house in the city was crowded with visitors; everyone spoke of the feasts there would be after Black Tom Tyrant's death, and the good times coming for England. Only at Court there was gloom and anxiety; Denzil Holles desperately offered the King to save Strafford's life if they would both agree to forswear the Episcopal Church and let the Archbishop suffer. But Holles had no authority to do this, and Wentworth, when he heard of it, refused the offer. (16)

London was astir early on May 12th. By two in the morning the crowds were already thick on Tower Hill; before dawn there was nothing to be seen but a sea of heads choking the whole open space, blocking every alley and gateway within remote sight of the high scaffold on the hilltop. Some of the richer had brought perspective glasses to train upon the scaffold. A hundred thousand people were said to be there. (17)

Not until eleven o'clock did Sir William Balfour come to escort the prisoner to his death. He found him waiting, dressed in black as was his custom, very calm, his two chaplains with him. The mob were pressing against the Tower gates, impatient for their prey; Balfour was convinced that they would fly upon their victim when he came out and tear him limb from limb. He spoke his fears to Wentworth and advised him to send for his coach; he could not walk up Tower Hill in safety. Wentworth, who had already been waiting for some time, wanted no more delays. He shook his head. 'No, I dare look death in the face,' he said, 'and I hope the people too; I care not how I die, whether by the hand of the executioner or by the madness and fury of the people; if that may give them better content it is all one to me.' [18]

By this time those who had leave to be with him had gathered together. There were his two brothers, William and George, his cousin Cleveland, Archbishop Ussher, and his own chaplains. Wentworth said he was ready and they set out, formally: 'never man looked death more stately in the face.' One of his Gentlemen led the way, he followed between Ussher and Cleveland, his friends about him, then the chaplains, followed by the guard of soldiers and last of all his own servants. He looked up towards Laud's window as he approached and the Archbishop was standing there to greet him. Wentworth knelt down. 'Your prayers and your blessing,' he said. Laud could not answer; he extended trembling hands above his friend's bowed head and fell senseless. 'Farewell, my lord; God protect your innocency,' said Wentworth as he passed slowly on. [19]

The gates were thrown back and a pathway opened narrowly through the people. Silence spread over the great crowd to its utmost edge. He passed through slowly, his hat in his hand; some of them saluted him, he recognized their courtesy with a slight gesture now to the left, now to the right. He walked, they said afterwards, like a general marching to victory, his face grave and steadfast in the spring sunshine.

On the scaffold he made his public declaration first, justifying himself without resentment, asking his listeners to remember him, and one day, when the times changed, to judge him by his actions.

'I come here to submit to the judgment that is passed against me; I do it with a very quiet and contented mind; I do freely forgive all the world. I speak in the presence of Almighty God before whom I stand, that there is not a displeasing thought that ariseth in me against any man; I thank God, I say truly, my conscience bears me witness, that in all the honour I had to serve his Majesty, I had not any intention in my heart, but what did aim at the joint and individual prosperity of the King and his people although it be my ill hap to be misconstrued. I am not the first man that hath suffered in this kind, it is a common portion that befalls men in this life; righteous judgment shall be hereafter; here we are subject to error and misjudging one another.'

He declared that he had never spoken against Parliaments, never professed any faith but that of the English Church, never desired anything but the happiness of the Kingdom.

'I wish that every man would lay his hand on his heart and consider seriously whether the beginnings of the people's happiness should be written in letters of blood. I fear they are in a wrong way; I desire Almighty God, that no one drop of my blood rise up in judgment against them....

'I desire heartily to be forgiven of every man if any rash or unadvised words or deeds have passed from me, and desire all your prayers and so farewell, and farewell all things of this world. God bless this Kingdom and Jesus have mercy on my soul.'

When he had done he took each of his companions in turn by the hand, said farewell, and asked them to join in prayer with him. Slowly his chaplain read the twenty-fifth psalm, and to the isolated few who now stood before the merciless gaze of the crowd watching the last moments of their friend the words rang with a tragic meaning.

'Unto thee O Lord, will I lift up my soul; my God, I have put my trust in thee: O let me not be confounded, neither let mine enemies triumph over me....

'Turn thee unto me, and have mercy upon me: for I am desolate, and in misery....

'Look upon my adversity and misery: and forgive me all my sin.

'Consider mine enemies, how many they are: and they bear a tyrannous hate against me....

'Let perfectness and righteous dealing wait upon me: for my hope hath been in thee.

'Deliver Israel, O God: out of all his troubles.'

When the chaplain's voice ceased, Wentworth knelt and for some time was deep in prayer. Rising, he saw his brother George 'weeping extremely', and drew him towards him. 'Brother, what do you see in me that deserves these tears?' he reasoned gently. 'Doth my fear betray my guiltiness or my too much boldness my atheism? Think now (and this is the third time) that you do accompany me to my marriage bed.' He looked, almost with relief, towards the block. 'That stock must be my pillow; here must I rest, and rest from all my labours; no thoughts of envy, no dreams of treason, jealousies of foes, cares for the King, the state or myself shall interrupt this sleep.... '

Once more he charged his brother to carry his blessing to his wife and children, 'not forgetting my little infant, that knows neither good nor evil and cannot speak for itself; God speak for it and bless it. I have nigh done, one stroke will make my wife husbandless, my dear children fatherless, and my poor servants masterless, and separate me from my dear brother and all my friends; but let God be to you and them all in all.'

Now he made ready for the block. 'I do as cheerfully put off my doublet at this time as ever I did when I went to bed,' he said, and the quick, boyish smile once again lit up his harsh features. Half in jest, he put aside the handkerchief with which the executioner offered to cover his eyes: 'Nay, for I will see it done.' Kneeling before the block, he spoke once more, firmly, for all to hear:

'I am at the door going out, and my next step must be from time to eternity; to clear myself to you all, I do solemnly protest before God I am not guilty of that great crime laid to my charge, nor have ever had the least inclination or intention to damnify or prejudice the King, the state, the laws or religion of this Kingdom, but with my best endeavours to serve all, and to support all.'

Last of all came his chaplain; he took both Wentworth's clasped hands and lifted them in his; they prayed very quietly, no one hearing. Then he drew back among the little knot of strained spectators grouped on the scaffold, and Wentworth laid his head on the block and signed to the executioner to strike. (20)

A deafening shout rose from the multitude as the executioner lifted the bleeding head; from the outer edge of the crowd riders galloped out into the country, shouting to all they passed as they clattered through the villages, 'His head is off! His head is off!' Bonfires flamed on hilltops, blazed in market-places; as soon as it was dusk, windows were lighted with candles, and shattered by the angry crowds if they were left dark. Through the jubilant city the Scottish Commissioners made their way to the King at Whitehall, wondering how they would find him. The long strain relaxed at last, Charles was cheerful and calm. (21) He had little cause to be.

Step by step the King had thrown away every advantage Wentworth had made for him; he had mismanaged the interview with the Lords on May 1st, and had openly revealed the defencelessness of his situation by that piteous letter of May 11th. There could be no effective reaction in favour of a ruler too weak to enforce his will and too obstinate to deny it. Far from appeasing the King's critics, Wentworth's blood whetted their appetite: 'Some took for their theme the judges and courts of justice,' wrote young Bramston, 'others the bishops and ecclesiastical courts; some the ministers of state; no part of the King's government but was inveighed against by one or other, whereby they so inflamed the people against the crown, as they could never allay the heat, and the fire brake forth and many of them were burnt in the flame.' (22)

The Council of the North, the Court of Star Chamber, the Court of High Commission, and the Court of Castle Chamber were abolished; Church and State, foreign and home policy were the province of Parliament; the army was to be in their hands. There the King resisted them, and for that last right, fifteen months after Wentworth's death, civil war broke out. In vain did bewildered men and women protest. 'They promised us all should be well if my lord Strafford's head was off, and since then there is nothing better.' (23)

389

Often, in the years of his misfortune, the King would bitterly, in the presence of others, regret the great sin he had committed when he consented to the death of his faithful servant. He came in the end to accept the worst evils that befell him as divine punishment for this unpardonable act. It was perhaps an indirect and posthumous outcome of Strafford's fall that George Digby, moving as Strafford himself had done, from the ranks of the opposition to those of the Court, became the increasingly influential, trusted (and disastrous) adviser of the King. Digby's courage in breaking with the prosecutors of Strafford, in speaking against the Bill of Attainder and finally voting against it, gave him a special place not only in the favour of the King but also in his heart. It was such a place as Strafford himself had never enjoyed.

Neither the King nor his opponents in England were mistaken as to the magnitude of the defeat on the one side and the victory on the other when Strafford went to the block. He had become a symbol of the power which the King believed to be his right. In delivering him up to death Charles betrayed not only a faithful servant but the monarchy itself.

But England and the English monarchy were not alone concerned. For the first time in the story of the British Isles, all three kingdoms had joined in the attack on a single man; Strafford was truly as the poet Denham wrote: 'Three Kingdoms' wonder and three Kingdoms' fear.' The Covenanting Scots had rightly seen in him the implacable opponent of the kind of Church and the kind of state in which they believed. In essence their quarrel with him, like that of the English, was for the vindication of great things.

The attack from Ireland was different. It was a concerted move of the 'great ones' to rid themselves of a troublesome ruler who had been almost too much for them. After nearly seven years they had brought Strafford down. The Earl of Cork celebrated the occasion in his diary: 'The oppressing Earl of Strafford ... the twelfth of this month was beheaded on the Tower hill of London, as he well deserved.' [24]

Material for the charges brought against the Irish administration had been supplied by Lord Loftus, Lord Cork, Lord Mountnorris, and others of the 'new English' who, as Strafford had once quite truly said, made a practice of undermining the Deputy when it suited them. Those who dominated and shaped the attack from

Ireland were not new to the technique of discrediting and overthrowing their governors. Mountnorris, Loftus and Cork had all
at one time or other informed against Strafford's predecessors.
But this was the first time that so many of them had brought
themselves to sink their private dislikes and act together. More
unusual still, they had gained the active support of the 'old
English' and the native Irish members of the Dublin Parliament.
The Remonstrance which had started the attack had been the
joint work of all groups. This brief and devastating alliance, which
had taken Strafford's few friends by surprise and swept them off
their feet, had revealed the real weakness of his government. In
putting the interests of the Crown first he had made no allies;
he had dominated the politics of Ireland, but he had not won
men over to his way of thinking. There was no single group, and
hardly an important man, whose interests he had not at some time
crossed, or whose susceptibilities he had not offended. There was
no group therefore without a grievance, and very few men in high
position who felt cordially towards him. (Ormonde was the
outstanding exception.) 'New English', 'old English', native Irish
and their respective leaders all alike believed that they had more
to gain than to lose by overthrowing him. Sectional grievances
could not but seem more important than the general benefits to
be derived from a strong government.

This unity was ephemeral. The 'old English' and the Irish came
very soon to see that they were worse off, not better off, for the
destruction of Wentworth. Lord Cork might shed crocodile tears
over the sufferings of the 'mere Irish' at Wentworth's hands. Sir
John Clotworthy might pretend distress at the plight of the
natives of Ulster, but neither of them was in normal times much
concerned about the wrongs of the people. Even before the death
of Strafford, the 'old English' and the Irish had begun to realize
that his fall would leave the 'new English' resoundingly triumphant, with the grateful and predominantly Puritan Parliament in
England ready to support them at need. The 'old English' and
Irish had disliked and feared Strafford's plans for expropriation
and settlement; but the process was likely to be intensified, not
slackened, by his removal. This they recognized too late.

By the end of March whispers of an Irish rising began to be heard.
By June the 'old English' and the Irish were at angry cross-purposes

with the 'new English' in the Dublin Parliament. Meanwhile, Strafford's army, eight thousand strong and largely Irish, was unpaid and growing dangerous. Parliament was slow with the subsidies, and the customs revenues had dwindled since Strafford's efficient management had been withdrawn. To add to the uncertainty and tension in Ireland, the central administration of justice was paralysed by the simultaneous impeachment of Chancellor Bolton and Lord Chief Justice Lowther. [25] The Council in Dublin, short of money and weak in authority, watched helplessly while the situation worsened. In October the Irish rose in Ulster, the rebellion spread with extraordinary speed to the other provinces, and for the next eight years anarchy prevailed.

The rising of 1641 was the consequence of the policy of expropriating the Irish which had been ruthlessly pursued for the last half-century. Strafford had carried out this policy with considerable vigour, and had thus helped to create the conditions of the rebellion. By a trick of fate he had also, almost literally, put arms into the hands of the rebels. His new army, disbanded in the late summer of 1641, was absorbed into the ranks of the Irish insurgents, to whom they brought their arms and the results of their training.

But the ill-timed disbanding of the army and the paralysis of the Dublin Council in the summer of 1641 were not the outcome of Strafford's government; they were the result of his overthrow. His removal precipitated the revolt which, had he continued in power, he might have averted and would certainly have crushed.

When they destroyed him, the 'new English' won a disastrous victory. They removed a strong man from the head of the state at a time when a strong man was most desperately needed. Lord Cork and his generation paid the price of their error, in their estates, their revenues and the lives of their sons.

Twenty years later — after the Civil Wars, after Cromwell, after the Restoration — Strafford's disciple Ormonde would take over the government of his native land in a state of irretrievable political ruin. He would always respect the memory and speak well of the government of Strafford. Though Strafford's policy had been, inevitably, based on the fundamental wrong inherent in the seizure of Irish land, he had believed and had tried to establish a standard of justice other than the right of the strongest, and he had worked hard to create an economy and a society in which life would be better for the native Irish as well as for the English settlers. Not for many years would Ireland again enjoy so great a measure of prosperity and order as it had done under his administration.

———

The years passed on over England and over those whom Strafford had loved. His friends and faithful colleagues for the most part escaped the wrath of his enemies once he was dead. Sir George Radcliffe, released from prison, lived for many years the disconsolate life of frustration and intrigue which was forced on many royalists during the misfortunes and exile of the royal family; remembered and as far as possible rewarded as Strafford's friend, he had a place in the household of the Duke of York. The devoted secretary, Guildford Slingsby, who had been at Strafford's side at his trial until his implication in the Army Plot, took his master's advice and fled abroad. Later, he returned to fight for the King and was killed early in the Civil War. The same fate overtook Sir William Wentworth, Strafford's next brother, who fell at Marston Moor.

Sir George Wentworth, the best loved brother, dutifully fulfilled the tasks that had been assigned to him on the scaffold. Going over into Ireland he took the last messages to the Countess and her stepchildren, settled the affairs of the desolate household in Dublin (with support and help from Ormonde and Sir William St Leger, against the hostility and cold triumph of so many others). Before the Rebellion swept the land, he had brought Strafford's widow and daughters home to Yorkshire. Slowly, with help from Radcliffe, he restored order to the remnant of the mighty fortune that his brother had accumulated. The two girls, Anne and Arabella, were never to have the dowries of £10,000 apiece that their father had planned for them, but they and their stepmother — 'that poor distressed family at Woodhouse' — were the object of chivalrous consideration from the Parliamentary general, Fairfax, during the Civil Wars.

Their brother, Strafford's cherished only son, went to Denmark during the summer after his father's death. This was arranged no doubt in part to shield him from the popular hatred which still pursued his father. There may have been another cause, as the irrepressible Lord Loftus, seeing that his great enemy's estate had not been forfeited, suddenly claimed that his granddaughter was betrothed to the heir, and sent the young lady over to Yorkshire to assert her rights. By the winter of 1641 she seems to have withdrawn and young Wentworth was back in England; he was received at Court and created Earl of Strafford by the King, who thus tried to wipe out a part of the irreparable wrong he had done to his father. At the same time he dismissed Sir Harry Vane finally from his post as Secretary. Young Strafford began his education at Oxford a few months later, but shortly after the outbreak of the Civil War, he had leave to go abroad, where he seems to have remained for the next ten years, chiefly in France.

Returning to England in the Commonwealth, he and his sister Anne were married much about the same time; he to a daughter of the Earl of Derby who, like his own father, had been executed for his services to the King; she to the young Lord Rockingham, who was said a year or two later to 'use her basely'. By this time young Strafford and his sisters were, like other royalists, reconciled uneasily to the existing government. There were debts, difficulties, family disagreements; young Strafford seems to have been indolent, lacking in character, not the man to build up the position the family had once held. But after the Restoration things were easier. The financial position steadily improved. Arabella, still unmarried at thirty-five, was safely disposed of soon after to a son of the Earl of Clancarty, and as Lady Arabella MacCarthy makes a last appearance on the fringe of history as an unsuccessful candidate for a place as Lady of the Bedchamber to Princess Mary on her marriage to William of Orange.

Her brother, emerging briefly but with credit from his more usual obscurity, was the only peer to enter a reasoned protest against the banishment of Clarendon in 1667. Twenty-six years earlier Clarendon had been among the bitter enemies of Strafford, but young Strafford seems to have remembered his father's injunction to bear no malice against those who had compassed his death. It is possible that the cruel desertion of a loyal servant by the King poignantly reminded him of what had happened to his father; here and there the arguments he used seem to echo, faintly, his father's arguments of twenty-six years before. The accusation of Lord Clarendon by the Commons, he said, was in general terms: no specific treason was cited or had been proved.

For the rest he lived an undistinguished and uninteresting life in which a principal interest seems to have been the erection of monuments to the dead. He largely rebuilt the little church at Wentworth. In it he put up a tablet to his father's old steward, Richard Marris. He put up a monument to his first wife, with an unusually touching inscription; but he had her buried with pomp in York Minster and put up another monument to her there. He also put up a monument to his father which he seems later to have thought inadequate. When he died, in his seventieth year, he was found to have left a thousand pounds for the erection of a noble tomb in York Minster; thither he wished his father's bones to be transported, together with those of his three wives, Margaret Clifford, Arabella Holles, and Elizabeth Rodes.

The thousand pounds was perhaps not forthcoming; at any rate no tomb was erected in the Minster. The body of the great Earl of Strafford was left where it had been quietly interred after his death. Legends grew up, that he had been buried secretly to preserve his resting-place from the desecrating hands of enemies. Some said that Elizabeth, his widow, who outlived him forty-seven years, was buried in the same secret grave with him near her dower house in the church at Hooton Roberts. But the story is baseless. There was no mystery about his burial place until later generations began to fabricate it. He lies in the family vault of the little church at Wentworth Woodhouse. On the wall above, he kneels in stone, a figure not without force and dignity though sculpted by a clumsy hand. The inscription is respectful but restrained, as though at the time those who composed it were loath to say too much. 'His soul through the mercy of God lives in eternal bliss, and his memory will never die in these Kingdoms.' [26]

His memory has not died, but it has been the subject of controversy.

> Here lies wise and valiant dust
> Huddled up 'twixt fit and just,
> Strafford who was hurried hence
> 'Twixt treason and convenience.
> He lived and died here in a mist,

A Papist and a Calvinist.
His prince's nearest joy and grief,
He had, yet wanted all relief.
The prop and ruin of the State;
The People's violent love and hate;
One in extremes, loved and abhorr'd.
Riddles lie here, or, in a word
Here lies blood, and let it lie
Speechless still, and never cry.

So ran a broadsheet [27] in the summer after his death, a summer when 'everything sells that comes in print under his name', and supposititious letters, prayers and even poems were offered by hopeful booksellers to a gullible public until the House of Commons threatened prosecution and put a stop to it. [28]

He had indeed died "twixt treason and convenience'. There is no moral justification for the members of the House of Commons who had resolved to compass his death as a political necessity, however weak the evidence against him; there is no moral justification for the King, whatever the ingenious Bishop Williams may or may not have said. But both could alike plead that it was 'convenient': for the Commons to demand his life, for the King to yield it. After his death he became a hero of royalists and later of Tories, while to the Whigs he appeared, as the eighteenth century rolled on, in ever blacker and more sinister guise. Yet neither party wrote much about him, because his career reflected a certain discredit on both; neither the King nor Parliament emerges with honour from the story of his trial and death.

Administrative and financial efficiency are not in themselves passports to favour in England. For that reason his greatest gifts aroused more criticism than praise while he lived, and were obliterated from memory after his death, partly because his work did not survive and partly because the interest of posterity was concentrated on the more startling incidents of his career — his conversion to the Court in 1628 and his dramatic trial and death.

But his tragedy, which was also the tragedy of the King's government, was not confined to the last months of his life. His inordinate ambition and self-confidence as well as his ability fitted him for the highest place in the state, at which, through long years of frustration, he always aimed. But he lacked an essential quality of statesmanship: his judgment of human relationships was always poor, and he had neither the good nor the bad qualities necessary to manipulate his fellow men, or even to make and keep friends in the society and age in which he lived. Had he brought to the human side of politics the skill that he brought to administration and finance, the outcome of his rule might have been very different.

Looking back on him Clarendon said: 'It was his misfortune to be of a time wherein very few wise men were equally employed with him, and scarce any whose faculties and abilities were equal to his'; and Laud wrote him a bitter epitaph: 'He served a mild and gracious Prince, who knew not how to be, or be made great.' [29]

But Wentworth's tragedy was as much of his own making. Charles might have been made great by a minister who knew how to handle him. The lesser men who 'were equally employed' with Wentworth would have hindered less and helped more had his gift been for bringing out the best, and not the worst, in his colleagues. There was nothing easy about this strong, demanding man. He met opposition with obstinacy or force, rarely with persuasion. He could not be indifferent to criticism or patient with stupidity; he could not accept and work with men as he found them. He was for ever railing against those human frailties, errors and follies which have to be accepted because they cannot be changed, and from which he himself was by no means so free as he liked to believe.

From the upheavals of his career, from the reports of his friends and his enemies, from the massive tomes of his correspondence, there emerges the image of a strong and resolute man, of great practical ability, of powerful intellect, of tireless energy; over-confident in his own opinions, over-certain of his own rectitude; not always scrupulous in the pursuit of public power and personal advantage; but a man of generous vision and unswerving loyalty, faithful to his King, just to his servants, true to his friends. Of his essential qualities who, now, can judge? The last word rests with George Radcliffe:

'I lost in his death a treasure which no earthly thing can countervail; such a friend as never man within the compass of my knowledge had; so excellent a friend, and so much mine.'

NOTES

[1] Laud, *Works*, III, pp. 441-2; Sanderson, *Complete History of King Charles*, 1658. If the mysterious letter to Slingsby, written on May 9th *before* he knew of the King's decision, refers to a plan for the King to approach the House of Lords on the following day, Monday, May 10th, Strafford would naturally be taken aback to find that the King had reached his decision on Sunday evening without waiting till Parliament met on Monday. His letter to Radcliffe written on the 9th and referring to 'the issue of tomorrow' implies the same hope. Richard Brathwaite in his *roman à clef*, *Panthalia* (1659), describes Strafford under the name of 'Sophronio', and states that he was reading Seneca 'on the tranquillity of the mind' when told that the King had consented to his death. It is a very probable detail.

[2] Bramston, *Autobiography*, p. 75.

[3] *Lords Journals*, IV, p. 245.

[4] H.M.C., IV, p. 83.

[5] *Lords Journals*, IV, p. 246.

[6] Harleian MSS, 6424, folio 67.

[7] *C.S.P.D.*, 1640-1, p. 540; Laud, *Works*, III, p. 442.

[8] *Brief and Perfect Relation*, p. 98.

[9] Knowler, II, pp. 417 ff; *Radcliffe Letters*, p. 224.

[10] Rushworth, *Trial*, p. 774.

[11] *Brief and Perfect Relation*, p. 97; MSS of R. R. Hastings, II, p. 82.

[12] Clarendon, IV, 42; Carte, I, p. 116; Knowler, II, p. 418; Strafford MSS, LX.

[13] *Brief and Perfect Relation*, p. 98.

[14] Carte, III, p. 32.

[15] Knowler, II, pp. 416 ff.

[16] Laud, III, p. 442; Burnet, *History of his Own Time*, p. 50. Holles assured Burnet that he had a good chance of succeeding, but he was a man who combined a very unreliable memory with an inflated idea of his own influence.

[17] Rushworth, *Trial*, p. 773; H.M.C., X, p. 78; *Brief and Perfect Relation*, p. 97.

[18] *Brief and Perfect Relation*, pp. 99-100; Rushworth, *Trial*, p. 782; Brit. Museum, Add. MSS, 1467, folio 37.

[19] *Brief and Perfect Relation*, p. 97; Rushworth, *Trial*, p. 782; Laud, *Works*, III, 445.

[20] Rushworth, III, i, pp. 267-9; *Brief and Perfect Relation*, pp. 96-7. This version of Wentworth's words to his brother and of his last speech while kneeling at the block are in the *Brief and Perfect Relation*, the extremely vivid anonymous account from which later writers derived a great number of details. It was clearly written by someone very close to Wentworth. A few more details are to be found in Brit. Museum, Add. MSS, 1467, folio 37.

[21] H.M.C., Report X, p. 78.

[22] Bramston, p. 74.

[23] H.M.C., Report VII, p. 439.

[24] *Lismore Papers*, II, V, p. 106.

[25] *C.S.P.I.*, 1633-47, pp. 271, 279, 298-9, 362; Carte, V, 247. On the developments in Ireland immediately after Strafford's death see Kearney, pp. 209-15.

[26] Hunter, *South Yorkshire*, I, p. 400; II, pp. 86, 97-9; G.E.C., *Complete Peerage*, under 'Strafford', first and second creation; H.M.C., *Bath MSS*, II, p. 159.

[27] The earliest version of these lines is that of the broadsheet calendared in *C.S.P.D.*, 1640-1, p. 574. They are generally thought to be the work of John Cleveland and are in the editions of his poems. Among the rather extensive pamphlet and broadsheet material about Strafford, which trickled on for many years, some lines from *Strafforiados: the Lieutenant's Legend* (1652) are interesting because they reveal that there was at least a

recognition in quarters not necessarily friendly to Strafford that he had attempted to govern in the interests of the underprivileged. The work is a doggerel poem supposed to be a soliloquy by Strafford on his fall. Three verses seem worth quoting:

> None were so high but would comply with me and my commands,
> For else were they forc'd to obey, and perish in my hands.
> None durst devour the widow, poor, nor seize another's right,
> But I brought in to scourge his sin, and crush him with my might.
>
> But what's all this? I did amiss, for so the Commons say;
> All this did tend to mine own end and profit every way.
> My Port advanc'd, my State enhanc'd, and my revenues too,
> The common laws I did dispose and wrest them God knows how.
>
> First I did fleece our merchandise and grievous imposts raise,
> For private gain I trucked with Spain, and with injurious lays
> Impair'd men's state t'increase their hate, no pity did I render;
> Thus with all ill I'm twitted still; my good deeds none remember.

[28] Brit. Museum, Add. MSS, 1467, folio 38; H.M.C., *Cowper*, II, p. 283.
[29] Clarendon, II, 205; Laud, *Works*, III, p. 443.

APPENDIX

THE relevance of Wentworth's land policy in Ireland to the constitutional question in England is perhaps best illustrated by the juxtaposition of the following two quotations from his letters. In the first he is illustrating to Secretary Coke the way in which predatory settlers first cheated the King out of his rights and then perpetuated the fraud under cover of the common law. In the second he is frankly emphasizing to Laud his intention of preventing the lawyers from interpreting the common law in a manner harmful to the prerogative and rights of the Crown.

The two together indicate very clearly how the common law could be manipulated by self-interested people, and the way in which Wentworth intended to override it, sometimes in the interests of evident justice but always in the interests of the Crown.

I am indebted to Mr Terence Ranger's article, cited already several times, for leading me to these highly illuminating expressions of Wentworth's opinions.

1. Strafford MSS, V, folio 29, Wentworth to Secretary Coke, 7th December 1633:

In this [i.e. in the undervaluing of an estate] it is confessed that the King was greatly deceived, yet my lord chief Baron would by no means that, the patent being good in law, there could be any relief for the Crown in equity, it [the estate] being by mean conveyance now come into the hands of purchasers not privy to the fraud, and was very positive and absolute in his opinion: whereupon, foreseeing the consequences of it to be very great, I roundly replied that it was true in the case of a common person the Chancery would never bind a purchaser unless there were proof of his privity with the fraud: but that of a King was quite differing, who could be entitled to nothing but by record, whereof, in acceptation of law, no man could be ignorant; that otherways the King's case was the worst of all men, for thus a man coseneth the King today, and tomorrow passeth it away to a stranger and leaves the Crown irremediless. Considering now it was but justice the King desires, it neither could nor should be denied him, and that I would myself sit in Chancery to hear the cause and do my master right . . . .

When he heard me so resolute you would wonder how round he came and presently bethought himself of an expedient, so as I trust we shall recover at least to the Crown the ancient rent . . . .

In this Sir George Radcliffe assisted me very effectually, without whom I were not able to buckle up these Fathers of the Law that use to deal with us *puros laicos* (as they term us) according to their own good pleasure, so great is the advantage of their profession.

2. Strafford MSS, VIII, folios 33-4, Wentworth to Laud, 23rd October 1633:

Tis true my Lord the common lawyers have a great sway in the administration of justice, yet not of that papal plenipotency but they may be contained and brought within the bounds of the sobriety and moderation of ancient times, but then let not the word *Thorough* be left out in any case, for it is the chief ingredient . . . . If we grow faint, our joints double under us at the beginning, how shall we ever attain to the end of our journey, and to faint in the way when so fair a prize is before us as the honour and greatness of the best King upon the whole earth were most shameful . . . .

It grieves me to the soul that your lordship should apprehend any so wretched as to tread still so tenderly as if we were upon the ice. I take our footing to be, God be praised, much more assured, and that the work is feasible enough if we ourselves be not in fault ... for myself I vow to your Grace there shall no such narrow consideration fall into my counsels as my own preservation, till I see my master's power and greatness set out of wardship and above the expositions of Sir Edward Coke and his Year books. I am most assured the same resolution governs in your Lordship. Let us then in the name of God go on cheerfully and boldly. If others do not their parts I am confident the honour shall be ours and the shame theirs. And thus you have my Thorough and Thorough.

BIBLIOGRAPHY

AYLMER, G. E., *The King's Servants: The Civil Service of Charles I, 1625-1642*, London, 1961.

BAILLIE, ROBERT, *Letters and Journals*, ed. D. Laing for the Bannatyne Club, Edinburgh, 1841-2.

Biographia Britannica: or the lives of the most eminent persons who have flourished in Great Britain and Ireland, vol. VI, London, 1763.

BIRCH, THOMAS, *The Court and Times of Charles the First*, 2 vols., London, 1848.

The Court and Times of James the First, 2 vols., London, 1848.

LORD BIRKENHEAD, *Strafford*, London, 1938.

BOATE, G., *Ireland's Natural History*, London, 1652, p. 62.

BONN, MORITZ, *Die Englische Kolonisation in Irland*, Stuttgart and Berlin, 1905.

BRAMSTON, JOHN, *Autobiography*, ed. Lord Braybrooke for the Camden Society, London, 1848.

BRERETON, SIR WILLIAM, *Travels*, ed. E. Hawkins for the Chetham Society, Manchester, 1844.

Brief and Perfect Relation of the Answers ... of the Earl of Strafford, London, 1647.

LADY BURGHCLERE, *Strafford*, London, 1931.

BURNET, GILBERT, *Memoirs of the Lives and Actions of James and William, Dukes of Hamilton*, London, 1677.

Calendar of State Papers: Domestic (*C.S.P.D.*)
Ireland (*C.S.P.I.*)
Venetian (*C.S.P.Ven.*).

Camden Miscellanies, vol. IX, containing 'Papers relating to Thomas Wentworth, first Earl of Strafford', London, 1895.

CARTE, THOMAS, *The Life of James, Duke of Ormonde*, 6 vols., Oxford, 1851.

CARTWRIGHT, J. J., *Chapters in the History of Yorkshire*, Wakefield, 1872.

CLARENDON (Edward Hyde, first Earl of Clarendon), *The History of the Rebellion and Civil Wars in England*, ed. W. D. Macray, 6 vols., Oxford, 1888.

State Papers collected by Edward Earl of Clarendon, ed. R. Scrope and T. Monkhouse, Oxford, 1767.

COLLINS, ARTHUR, ed., *Historical Collections of the Noble Families of Cavendishe, Holles ...* , London, 1752.

Letters and Memorials of State [commonly called *Sydney Papers*], London, 1746.

COOPER, J. P., 'The Fortune of Thomas Wentworth, Earl of Strafford', *Economic History Review*, sec. ser., vol. XI (December 1958), pp. 227-48.

D'EWES, SYMONDS, *Autobiography*, ed. J. C. Halliwell, London, 1845. *Journal: from the beginning of the Long Parliament to the opening of the trial of the Earl of Strafford*, ed. Wallace Notestein, New Haven, Conn., 1923.

DIETZ, F. C., *English Public Finance, 1558-1641*, New York, 1932.

ELIOT, SIR JOHN, *Negotium Posterorum*, ed. A. B. Grosart, London, 1881.

The Fairfax Correspondence, ed. G. W. Johnson, London, 1848.

The Fortescue Papers, ed. S. R. Gardiner for the Camden Society, London, 1871.

GARDINER, S. R., ed., *Debates in the House of Commons in 1625*, Camden Society, London, 1873.
 History of England from the Accession of James I to the Outbreak of the Civil War. 1603-1642, 10 vols., London, 1883-4, vols. VI-IX.

HACKET, JOHN, *Scrinia Reserata*, London, 1693.

Hardwicke State Papers, London, 1778.

LADY BRILLIANA HARLEY, *Letters*, ed. T. T. Lewis for the Camden Society, London, 1854.

HEATON, H., *The History of the Yorkshire Woollen and Worsted Industries*, Oxford, 1920.

HILL, CHRISTOPHER, *Economic Problems of the Church*, Oxford, 1956.

Historical Manuscript Commission (H.M.C.), Reports II, IV, VI (Appendix I), VII (Apendix II), IX, XI (Appendix VII): *Bath MSS; Cowper MSS; Egmont MSS; Montagu of Beaulieu MSS; Ormonde MSS; Portland MSS; Salisbury MSS; MSS from Various Collections*, II, III, VII, VIII, XII.

HOLLES, GERVASE, *Memorials of the Holles Family, 1493-1656*, ed. A. C. Wood, Camden Society, Third Series, vol. LV, London, 1937.

HUGHES, E., *Studies in Administration and Finance*, Manchester, 1934.

HULME, HAROLD, *Sir John Eliot*, London, 1957.

HUNTER, JOSEPH, *South Yorkshire*, London, 1828-30.

JORDAN, W. K., *Philanthropy in England, 1480-1660*, London, 1959.

Journals of the House of Commons, England.

Journals of the House of Commons, Ireland.

Journals of the House of Lords, England.

Journals of the House of Lords, Ireland.

KEARNEY, HUGH F., *Strafford in Ireland*, Manchester, 1959.

KEELER, M. F., *The Long Parliament*, Philadelphia, 1954.

KNOWLER, WILLIAM, ed., *The Earl of Strafford's Letters and Despatches*, 2 vols., London, 1739.

LAUD, WILLIAM, *Works*, ed. W. Scott and J. Bliss, Oxford, 1847-60.

LEONARD, E. M., *The Early History of English Poor Relief*, Cambridge, 1900.

LESTRANGE, HAMON, *The Reign of King Charles*, London, 1655.

The Lismore Papers [the private diaries and papers of the Earl of Cork], ed. A. B. Grosart, London, 1886-8.

MAXWELL, CONSTANTIA, *The History of Trinity College Dublin, 1591-1892*, Dublin, 1946.

MOIR, T. L., *The Addled Parliament of 1614*, Oxford, 1958.

MOODY, T. W., *The Londonderry Plantation, 1609-41*, Belfast, 1939.

MME DE MOTTEVILLE, *Mémoires*, Paris, 1855.

MURPHY, H. L., *A History of Trinity College, Dublin*, Dublin, 1951.

NALSON, JOHN, *Impartial Collection of the Great Affairs of State*, London, 1682.

NICHOLAS, SIR EDWARD, ed., *Proceedings and Debates of the House of Commons in 1620 and 1621*, Oxford, 1766.

NICHOLS, JOHN, *The Progresses, Processions, and magnificent Festivities of King James the First*, 4 vols., London, 1828.

NOTESTEIN, W., and others, ed., *Commons Debates, 1621*, New Haven, Conn., 1935.

O'BRIEN, GEORGE, *Economic History of Ireland in the Seventeenth Century*, London and Dublin, 1919.

O'GRADY, HUGH, *Strafford and Ireland*, Dublin, 1923.

PEARL, VALERIE, *London and the Outbreak of the Puritan Revolution*, Oxford, 1961.

RADCLIFFE, GEORGE, *Letters*, ed. T. D. Whitaker, London, 1810.

RANGER, TERENCE, 'Strafford in Ireland: a Revaluation', *Past and Present*, April 1961.

The Rawdon Papers, consisting of letters on various subjects ... to and from Dr John Bramhall, ed. E. Berwick, London, 1819.

REID, R. R., *The King's Council in the North*, London, 1921.

RERESBY, SIR JOHN, *Memoirs*, ed. A. Browning, Glasgow, 1936.

RUSHWORTH, JOHN, *Historical Collections*, London, 1680.

The Tryal of Thomas Earl of Strafford, London, 1680.

RYMER, T., *Foedera*, vol. XIX, London, 1704.

SLINGSBY, SIR HENRY, *The Diary ... and extracts from family correspondence and papers*, ed. D. Parsons, London, 1836.

Strafford MSS, now in Sheffield Central Library.

Private letters from the Earl of Strafford to his third wife, ed. R. Monckton Milnes for the Philobiblon Society, London, 1854.

TAWNEY, R. H., *Business and Politics under James I*, Cambridge, 1958.

THORNTON, ALICE (*née* Wandesford), *Autobiography*, ed. C. Jackson for the Surtees Society, London, 1875.

TREVOR-ROPER, H. R., *Archbishop Laud*, London, 1940.

TURTON, R. S., *The Alum Farm*, Whitby, 1938.

UPTON, ANTHONY F. *Sir Arthur Ingram: A study of the Origins of an English landed family*, Oxford, 1961.

VERNEY, SIR RALPH, *Notes on the Long Parliament*, ed. J. Bruce for the Camden Society, London, 1845.

WARWICK, SIR PHILIP, *Memoirs*, 3rd edn, London, 1703.

WHITAKER, T. D., *History and Antiquities of Craven*, London, 1878.

INDEX

INDEX